THE A

TEACHING PIANO

The classic guide and reference book for all piano teachers

Edited by Denes Agay

Associate Editor:
Hazel Ghazarian Skaggs

Contributing Authors
Denes Agay
Joseph Banowetz
May L. Etts
Rosetta Goodkind
Stuart Isacoff
Ylda Novick
Sylvia Rabinof
Walter Robert
Hadassah Sahr
Hazel Ghazarian Skaggs
Anita Louise Steele
Judith Lang Zaimont

Yorktown Music Press, Inc.
New York/London/Paris/Sydney/Copenhagen/Berlin/Tokyo/Madrid

Order No. YK 21956
International Standard Book Number: 0.8256.8111.1

Exclusive Distributors:
Music Sales Corporation
257 Park Avenue South, New York, NY 10010 USA
Music Sales Limited
8/9 Frith Street, London W1D 3JB England
Music Sales Pty. Limited
120 Rothschild Street, Rosebery, Sydney, NSW 2018, Australia

Printed in the United States of America by
Vicks Lithograph and Printing Corporation

Contents

Foreword

DENES AGAY

> Music is here so that people may enjoy it. Performers and teachers are called upon to transmit this joy. The pedagogue who forgets this aim, or—worse—lets his student forget it, has failed in the proper exercise of his calling.*
>
> —Margit Varró

Around the end of the nineteenth century, the French composer Jules Massenet remarked that a piano teacher needs to know only four sentences to pursue the profession: (1.) "Bonjour, Mademoiselle"; (2.) "Not so fast" (or "Not so slow"); (3.) "Less pedal, please"; and (4.) "Give my regards to your mother." This cuttingly facetious statement was not only a criticism of nineteenth-century teaching standards, but also of the modest demands that society made on the pedagogic community. Of course, Massenet was not speaking of the many great artist-teachers who guided and inspired subsequent generations of virtuosos, but rather of the multitude of piano instructors whose task was to furnish a thin veneer of musical culture and social poise for the youngsters (especially girls) of the middle and upper classes, for whom a measure of pianistic capability was regarded as well-nigh indispensable. These conditions prevailed not only in Europe but in the United States as well, where the piano in the parlor was the symbol of social respectability and upward mobility. During the last decade of the nineteenth

*From "Der Lebendige Klavierunterricht" by Margit Varró. Copyright 1929 by Associated Music Publishers, Inc. Used by permission.

century there were more pianos than bathtubs in American homes.

In those good old days, piano pedagogy, in today's organized and systematic sense of the term, did not exist, at least not for the overwhelming majority of teachers. This does not mean that there were no good teachers. Even Massenet's comment implies, on closer examination, an irreducible minimal level of competence at which a teacher could operate and get by: a sense of tempo and rhythm, a feeling for the proper sound and clean phrasing, and enough psychological acumen to create a friendly and relaxed atmosphere. Indeed, today we are again hearing authoritative voices which urge a reduction of pedagogic complexities and a return to the simpler and more serene teaching stance of the past.

Alas, this would hardly be possible. The many changes that occurred during the last century—in idioms and repertory, in music's role in education and society, the economic demands of efficiency, and relentless striving for more and more professional competence—would make a reversal to the more easygoing and somewhat naive attitudes of the past anachronistic, to say the least. Today's music and today's society require the teacher to be a thorough professional, with the proper aptitude, education, and motivation. We might say that the requirements can be reduced to the following three broad and intertwined attributes:

- A secure *knowledge* of all relevant musical facts, concepts, and procedures, including the know-how to apply this knowledge within a systematic teaching plan. This category also includes a degree of technical competence and a thorough familiarity with the keyboard literature for all periods.
- Discriminating *taste* and judgment in selecting the right teaching repertory for each student. The teacher should not for a moment forget that he or she is not only instructing the youngster how to play the piano, but is also the student's guide through the world of music, and will inevitably put his or her imprint on the pupil's musical taste and future attitude toward music.
- A warm and inspiring *personality* conducive to easy, natural, and constructive communication with the student. Such a personality trait can be reinforced by familiarity with the pertinent tenets of psychology.

The purpose of this volume is to provide information and guidance on all technical, theoretical, and practical matters of importance to piano teachers. It is meant to define as clearly as possible the basic ingredients and concepts of music, to clear up ambiguities of terminology which so often plague and confuse the teaching process, to outline logical procedures in all phases of the curriculum, and, in general, to furnish a secure platform of data and agenda from which the teacher can operate with authority, confidence, and efficacy.

A perusal of the contents pages will give an idea of the many areas of pedagogy which the book covers. The contributing authors, all of them outstanding, active pedagogues, deal with their subject matters in a scholarly, authoritative, yet down-to-earth manner which makes their articles both eminently informative and easy to read, grasp, and apply.

For obvious reasons, the beginning phases of instruction are accorded special emphasis, as these early stages of study form the foundation upon which all subsequent keyboard skills and musicianship qualities are built. There is also substantial information which applies principally to developing and advanced students. Of special interest to all teachers should be the detailed and abundant information on all aspects of twentieth-century music, including the popular idioms.

To the key attributes of a good piano teacher–knowledge, taste, and personality–may be added something more subtle, elusive, but no less important: a keen, inquisitive musical mind, which finds a soul-satisfying, Epicurean pleasure in discovering and savoring all kinds of good music, from Bach to Bartók, from baroque to jazz. This goes to the heart of the matter: Why does anyone, child or adult, study piano? Why all the expense, the long, hard, continuous effort, the fuss and bother? Just to satisfy some vague cultural need? Certainly not! The purpose of study is to acquire a skill, an understanding, a disposition to be able *to enjoy music* through playing and listening–a precious gift for a lifetime. To instill this ability is, in essence, the teacher's task and goal. It is hoped that this book will prove of valuable assistance in carrying out this objective.

Denes Agay

ONE

ESSENTIALS OF PIANO PERFORMANCE

Elements of Technique

DENES AGAY

The technique of piano playing is a complex and somewhat elusive discpline. It certainly is not an exact science; no rigid and infallible rules can be formulated which could apply to all players and all types of music at all times. The factors which produce a fine tone and technique are too numerous and too variable for permanent and universally valid codification. A brief look at the history of piano playing and piano pedagogy can illustrate this point and, at the same time, put present-day technique in its proper perspective.

AN OVERVIEW: FROM "FINGER ACTION" TO "WEIGHT CONTROL"

The pianoforte, first constructed by Bartolommeo Cristofori of Florence around 1709, began to gain wide popularity in the latter half of the eighteenth century. The first public piano recital, so far as records show, was given by Johann Christian Bach, the youngest son of Johann Sebastian Bach, in 1768. The early piano, like the clavichord and harpsichord, had a very light action, so no special physical strength or muscular effort was needed to produce the tone and to play fluently. Everything was done by finger action only; the fingers stayed close to the keys, which were manipulated with minimal motion and remarkable agility. Mozart is said to have played with this harpsichord touch.

Around the end of the eighteenth century, however, several important changes took place. The piano became sturdier, its mechanism was gradually improved, and thus its dynamic range and expressive capabilities were substantially expanded. This, in turn, inspired a corresponding enrichment of piano literature. The early sonatas of Beethoven are the best examples of this new development. Great performers and pedagogues emerged—Clementi, Czerny, Hummel, and others—whose études and exercises became the backbone of pianistic education for generations to come. The piano literature grew not only in volume but in diversity of forms, emotional content, and richness of color. Beethoven was followed by Schubert, Schumann, Chopin, Mendelssohn, and Liszt, all of whom helped make the sound of the piano one of the most engrossing and eloquent musical languages the world has ever known.

Fingers and finger action alone proved inadequate to release and convey all the poetry and drama inherent in the sound of the modern piano, and an involvement of the larger muscles of the arms and shoulders became necessary. Curiously enough, however, the principles of early piano technique, which regarded the fingers as the sole playing agents, were hard to dislodge. It is not too surprising that Clementi demanded a "fixed hand" from his pupils and often made them practice with a coin on the backs of their hands. Somewhat more puzzling is that Kalkbrenner (1788-1849), who contributed so much to modern piano pedagogy with his method and his études, is completely unyielding in his insistence that "the arms must be kept practically motionless, while the fingers are in action." Even decades later, in the age of Lisztian pyrotechnics, there were still influential pedagogues who tenaciously clung to the "fingers only" theory. Ehrlich (1822-1899) recommended that the student practice with a book pressed between the upper arm and the body to prevent any arm motion.

It was not until the end of the nineteenth and the beginning of the twentieth century that Deppe, Breithaupt, Matthay, and Leschetizky officially formulated the epoch-making theory of piano playing by *weight control.* This method created quite a pedagogic revolution in its day and is, with some of its exaggerated aspects and practices mellowed and modified, still an eminently sound path to the mastery of keyboard technique.

The essence of the weight-control method is quite simple: the hands and fingers are not the main playing agents, but rather extensions of a more powerful, intricate playing apparatus consisting of the arms and shoulders, and indeed the entire body. A completely loose and relaxed muscular system and a judicious control of arm weight—either suspended or pressing down on the keys by degrees—are the prerequisites of good tone production and technique.

The original, orthodox dogma of "weight and relaxation" as propagated by Deppe and Matthay has always had substantial opposition from the adherents of the older, so-called Viennese school, who continued to follow the Hummel-Czerny path of finger dexterity as the only road to superior technique. The exponents of this group swore by Hanon, who maintained that "if the five fingers of each hand were equally well trained they would be able to execute anything that has been written for the instrument." Subsequently a number of very articulate critics pointed out certain pedantic inconsistencies in the weight approach, and listed scientific evidence to prove that some tightening of arm and shoulder muscles is often physically inevitable and that too much emphasis on relaxation can restrict velocity and brilliance.

In our days the vying between the two factions (weight control and finger action) has lost much of its meaning, and aside from occasional ripples it has nearly disappeared. The two systems are not incompatible; indeed, they can complement each other very successfully. A completely relaxed and freely rotating forearm still needs nimble fingers to play, and a fine, singing tone without the proper application of arm weight is inconceivable. In other words, the infinite varieties and complexities of touch, tone, dynamics, and articulation inherent in modern pianism demand the participation of the entire playing apparatus: upper body, arms, hands, and fingers. Each member and joint has to perform the task for which it is anatomically and physiologically best suited, and perform that task without undue strain. The requirements of the music must determine the proper role of each element in the playing apparatus, and no preconceived doctrines can dictate the details of execution.

POSTURE AND HAND POSITION

The study of technique usually begins at the very first lesson, when the student learns how to sit at the piano, correct body posture, and in what position the arms, hands, and fingers are to be held. Because of the complete individuality of each body and each pair of hands there can always be slight deviations and adjustments, but the following general guidelines are suggested:

- Sit facing the middle of the keyboard, with both feet firmly on the floor in front of the pedals (a footstool or box should be used if the child's feet do not reach the floor).
- Adjust the height of the seat so that the elbow is in line with the keyboard, far enough for easy maneuverability, but not so far that the arm is stretched forward.
- Do not lean back in the chair with your full weight. The entire body should be relaxed; the back straight, without stiffness and just a hint of leaning ever so slightly forward.
- Allow the upper arm to hang loosely, with the forearm, wrist, and hand in line with the keyboard. When lifting the arm, the elbow moves away from the body; shoulders are not raised.
- Hands are vaulted with palms down; they assume a shape as if lightly holding a small round object from above.
- Fingers are gently curved, with the fleshy part of the fingertips (not the nails) touching the keys. The thumb and fifth finger have a somewhat special position: the thumb strikes the key with the side of the nail joint and the fifth finger remains almost straight. The position of the fingers greatly influences the quality of tone: firm fingertips produce a brilliant sound; for a mellow, cantabile effect, fingers are held somewhat flattened so that the fleshy parts hit the keys.

It is best to visualize the pianist's entire body, from feet to fingertips, as a unified, finely integrated playing mechanism. In this sturdy, supple, and flexible system of levers, joints, and supports, each individual part has its special, well-defined function and is activated and coordinated with the others by that most remarkable of all computers, the human brain. To make this entire miraculous mechanism work smoothly and efficiently takes time, patience, and intelligence. Or, to put it simply, it takes practice.

PRACTICE

The only road that leads to a reliable piano technique is practice. This requires time, effort, concentration, and discipline. There are no miracles, no shortcuts. Still, the prospect of traveling this road should not be discouraging. While practice is by no means fun or entertainment, it does not have to be a tedious routine or drudgery. With consistently intelligent work habits, practicing can be a stimulating and rewarding endeavor; and it is not only the feeling of accomplishment, the satisfaction of overcoming hurdles and difficulties, that can make it so. There is, or should be, a genuine esthetic pleasure in the ability to play an even, pearly scale or a soaring arpeggio.The driest technical patterns can gain musical significance by proper associations and a little imagination. Is the practicing of broken triads dull? Remember what exquisite diversity of moods Beethoven achieved by various manipulations of such simple sequences in his "Moonlight" Sonata (both the first and last movements).

It should be noted that piano practice is both a physical and a mental activity; brains and brawn are equally important. Hours of mechanical finger gymnastics are a waste of time unless the mind is involved. Schumann expressed this admirably: " . . . there are many persons who imagine all will be accomplished if they keep on spending many hours each day in mere mechanical practice. It is about as if one should busy himself daily with repeating the ABC as fast as possible and always faster and faster. Use your time better." Exactly! Do not start your work without knowing not only what should be practiced, but also why it should be practiced, and how the technical and musical problems should be solved. It is not the amount of time spent at the keyboard that counts, but rather the length of undivided attention.

This does not mean, however, that the mind has to focus on all aspects of playing, at all times, with equal intensity. This would be unnecessary and self-defeating, if not impossible. If attention is focused on too many details simultaneously, the meaning of the whole may be lost. A child sometimes is able to read letters and words very well, but does not comprehend the meaning of the entire sentence. Similarly, the pianist may read well note by note, but if he or she does not hear the entire phrase, the performance becomes a blurred sequence of disjointed notes and figures. This can be prevented. From the very beginning, one main purpose of practice should be that certain aspects and mechanical details of the performance gradually become automatic, not requiring special attention, so that the mind is freed more and more to concentrate on new technical problems and musical nuances.

We know, for instance, that a great portion of the beginner's attention is engaged by reading notes. To a certain extent this is inevitable, but it should not be allowed to persist for too long. Note reading has to become an easy, almost reflexlike activity so that it does not deplete the young player's attention span. Similarly, more and more technical details and play patterns (touch, passing of the thumb, fingering of scales and arpeggios, etc.) should become instinctive and a matter of course. Alertness and the ability to concentrate are precious commodities which are not available in unlimited supply. For this reason they should not be squandered indiscriminately, but rather nurtured, judiciously rationed and regenerated with appropriate periods of rest. In short, practice requires constant mental alertness, applied selectively where it is most needed.

It is important, for both practical and pedagogical reasons, that students adopt sound practice habits from the very beginning of instruction. To that end, the following summary of suggestions will be helpful:

- Establish a definite practice period for each day and try to adhere to it. This period should be scheduled so that it neither interferes with other duties and priorities nor encroaches on the student's reasonable diversionary activities.
- Practice in a physically pleasant surrounding (a well-lit room, with fresh air and comfortable temperature).
- Practice requires mental involvement. Be alert throughout your work session and concentrate on the task at hand. Try to shut out aural and visual distractions (radio, television, loud conversation, etc.).
- Do not practice when fatigued, upset, or preoccupied with other problems and duties.
- Have a plan before you begin. Know in advance what you will work on and what you are aiming for in each piece—for instance, elimination of technical hurdles in one work, fine shadings in another, memorizing part of a third, etc.
- Divide the piece into musically feasible "practice units" and work on them in succession. The size of these units should be determined by the piece's style, texture, and technical difficulties. A polyphonic piece, which usually requires more intense concentration, should be broken up into smaller sections than a piece with simpler textures.
- The practice unit should be large enough to encompass an entire specific technical or musical problem. It can be as short as a motive, phrase, or passage, or it can be longer, extending to a sentence, period, or even a self-contained section of a piece. In general, the elements of musical form should be the guiding factors here,

and not the bar lines. Measure-by-measure practicing should be avoided as too fragmented and, in most cases, unmusical.

- Practice is in essence a constructive repetition of these small sections until the player's goal is attained. The number of repetitions necessary must be decided individually in each instance. As long as some progress is made by each repetition, the process is productive and can be continued, but not to the point of boredom, staleness, or fatigue.
- Special attention should be paid to connecting these practice units to establish a smooth continuity. Once a unit is mastered, it should be repeated together with the preceding section or sections.
- It is a good idea to practice with one hand at a time at first and begin two-handed play when each hand's part is fluent. Exceptions are certain polyphonic and other interwoven textures where voice leadings are divided between the two hands; these should be practiced with both hands from the start.
- It is recommended that the student practice a piece more slowly at first than the prescribed fast tempo. This will enable him or her to survey the music at a comfortable pace, grasp the details, and evaluate the technical and musical problems to be solved. Also, the student can pay more attention to all aspects of performance: correct fingering, tone accuracy, proper articulation, and touch. The prescribed tempo should be attained gradually but steadily so that the pertinent playing disciplines become correctly adapted and firmly embedded.
- Establishing the correct fingering of a piece is one of the first and most important phases of sound practicing. To improvise fingering as you go along, or to employ a poor fingering plan, can only lead to wasted time and disappointment. Printed finger numbers should be observed, unless they seem unsuitable for the individual player, in which case adjustments can and should be made. If numbers are not marked in a score, fingering should be written in with a pencil, section by section.
- There are valid reasons why a piece should first be practiced with even decisiveness on a medium dynamic level (***mf***), even if ***pp*** or ***ff*** are prescribed. This will bring all parts of the piece and the problems involved into a clear focus and will help in unfolding and developing the needed playing habits and skills. As soon as the technical preparation allows, the work should be practiced at the prescribed dynamic levels as well as proper tempo.
- To avoid an early lagging of interest and concentration, it is best to work at each practice session on different kinds of material: études, pieces, some new and some old at various stages of readiness.
- Ideally, the best test for a finished assignment is to be able to play it three times without mistakes. This may not be attained at each practice session, but it should remain the goal.

The above suggestions should be called to the student's attention gradually, consistent with age, grade level, and personality. If parents or other adults are able and willing to supervise the young student's homework at the piano, they also should be made aware of the recommended procedures.

The manner in which new pieces are assigned for home practice requires careful thought and individualized attention on the teacher's part. If properly attended to, this preparatory phase can be of great help in making the student's practice sessions more efficient. In general, the student should get an idea at the time of assignment how the piece should sound, and what its style and mood are. In most cases, especially at the early grade levels, the teacher will "preplay" the piece or certain parts of it to convey its overall character and the desired sound for which to strive. Often he or she may also give the student some prepractice help with certain aspects of the task ahead; for instance, how to analyze the piece, select and connect the practice units, avoid certain pitfalls and common errors, and so on. As the student advances, less and less preplaying should be necessary and the task of assaying and discovering the piece should be left more and more to the student. At these stages the teacher may want to restrict the demonstration to specific aspects of technique, expression, phrasing, or other details of execution as the need arises. It is important to be aware that the purpose of preplaying is not to have the student mechanically imitate the teacher's conception of the piece, but rather to inspire and stimulate the student to achieve the desired effect independently.

TONE AND TOUCH

Touch is the manner in which a key is struck and pressed down to produce a tone. Touch also means the manner in which several successive tones are sounded and connected. In this sense we speak of *legato, non legato,* and *staccato* touch.

Tone production on the piano differs from all other instruments. On a string instrument, the tone is produced directly by the player's two hands; on a wind instrument it is produced by the player's lips and hands. On the piano, however, the tone is produced directly by the hammers and strings and only indirectly by the player's hands. In other words, the pianist has much less control over the ultimate fate of the created tone than a violinist or clarinetist. To understand this more fully, with all its implications, let us take a brief look at the piano mechanism in action.

When a key is pressed down, its extension inside the piano moves up, like the motion of a seesaw. This upward motion raises and activates two units of the mechanism: an ingenious and quite complex set of levers, called the *escapement,* which throws the hammer against the string and also lets the hammer fall back immediately, so that the string can vibrate freely even while the key is pressed down; and another lever which, simultaneously with the downward motion of the key, raises the dampers over the strings for free vibration. When the key returns to its original position, the dampers fall back on the strings and choke the sound.

Visualizing this piano action step by step makes it clear that the pianist does not directly hit the strings, but rather throws the hammer against the strings. The hammer is out of the player's control the instant it leaves the escapement; that is, before it reaches the strings. It is also important to remember that, with the exception of one, all basic physical factors that produce and influence a tone (the size and composition of hammers and strings, the points of impact, etc.) are built into the piano. The one factor controlled by the player is the *speed* at which the hammer is thrown clear of the escapement, which in turn determines the volume (loudness or softness) of the sound.

If this is the case–if volume is all the player controls–then what about tone quality? Who or what determines all the colors and nuances of the piano sound? Are these evoked by the player, or custom made by the piano manufacturer? There have been a number of differing and rather controversial opinions expressed on this subject in the past. Recently, however, a very reasonable and to all parties acceptable consensus seems to have emerged, which can be summarized as follows: it is an undeniable and scientifically proven fact that when producing a single tone, the pianist controls little more than the volume. However, when two or more tones are sounded, either together or in succession, the color possibilities controlled by the player rapidly multiply. This is a physical–acoustical phenomenon, mainly a result of the predominance and blend of certain overtones.

These findings underline the importance of the human element in the process of tone production. In analyzing these elements we find that there are four main player-controlled factors which determine the volume and quality of sound:

- the manner and intensity of striking and pressing down the keys
- the dynamic proportioning of component tones in chords and polyphonic textures
- the dynamic and agogic alterations of tones within melodic sequences
- the effective use of the pedal

It is extremely important to realize that, with the exception of pedaling, all these actions have to take place during that infinitesimal moment between the key's being depressed and the hammer's leaving the escapement. No subsequent hand or body motion can alter the tone one iota. This does not mean, of course, that all preparatory and follow-up gestures are out of place. Not at all. The pianist's entire deportment, indeed every gesture, can and should be both functional and graceful, without being marred by unnecessary histrionics.

A discussion of touch and tone production would not be complete without emphasizing the need for mental preparation. Physical actions alone are not enough, even if executed in a most efficient manner. The mind must be able to "hear" the desired tone color before the fingers act. The human voice and the instruments of the orchestra often provide useful blueprints to follow. This is why one frequently encounters such directions as "with a singing tone," "quasi pizzicato," etc.

PEDALING

Pedaling directly and substantially influences the volume, quality, and color of tone, and is one of the most intricate and delicate of all aspects of piano technique. When should the study of pedaling begin? Opinions differ. Some are for starting at a very early stage in the instruction, while others feel that some degree of musical maturity is needed before beginning. The soundest approach lies somewhere between the two; the student should be able to meet certain physical and musical prerequisites before being confronted with the challenge of pedal use. Allowing exceptions for unusual cases, these criteria should be:

- the right foot's ability to reach the pedal without changing the correct posture of the body
- the ability to read notes quite fluently
- the ability to coordinate hand and foot work
- some familiarity with the basic terms of elementary theory, especially harmony

The first lesson in pedal use should also include an examination of the piano's damper mechanism–what it is and how it works. The dampers, a row of felt pads, rest over the strings across the entire width of the instrument, with the exception of the uppermost register. Two actions can lift the dampers: depressing a key or depressing the pedal. We have already noted that when a key is depressed, the corresponding damper over the string unit is raised, and when the key is released, the damper falls back on the strings. When the pedal is pushed down, the entire row of dampers is lifted. This not only allows the struck strings to ring freely (even after the keys are returned to their original positions), but also makes all other strings with relative overtones available for sympathetic vibrations, thus making the tone richer and fuller.

The correct position of the right foot and its noise-free manipulation are also part of preliminary studies. The heel should rest on the floor, with the ball of the foot (and not only the toes) lightly touching the pedal. The up-and-down motion of the mechanism must be managed silently; there should be no trampling when pressing down and no sudden, violent release.

One of the secrets of effective pedaling lies in correct timing, in the syncopated, after-beat nature of the foot work. Hands and foot do not move simultaneously; the pedal is depressed *after* the keys are struck. This can be well practiced by playing single chords or simple cadences in slow $\frac{4}{4}$ time. The chord is played on the downbeat and the pedal is depressed a beat later; the hands are lifted on the third count and the pedal released on the first beat of the next measure, simultaneously with the playing of the next chord.

In successive exercises the foot can learn to follow the hands somewhat faster, perhaps at a half-beat distance. When a degree of smooth coordination between hands and foot exists, a moderate use of the pedal can be introduced in the performance of appropriate pieces.

It is not necessary, nor indeed advisable, to introduce new aspects of pedaling or to go through special exercises at each consecutive lesson. Pedaling should be studied at a rather comfortable, deliberate pace. Each new step and discipline must be allowed to sink in and become the player's second nature before proceeding to other problems. Pedaling may be carefully planned and practiced, but it must also become almost intuitive to be truly effective.

There are no hard-and-fast rules to cover every aspect of pedaling. The player, and especially the beginner, may be well advised, however, to keep the following suggestions in mind:

- Pedal changes are usually determined by the piece's harmonic structure. Change pedals often; do not let two or more harmonies overlap.
- Even within one harmonic function a pedal change will be necessary if, for instance, the notes of a broken chord or arpeggio form a melodic phrase or theme. Unless the pedal is changed at the proper spot, the notes will blend and lose their individual importance, and the outline of the melody will be lost.
- As a rule, less pedal should be used when playing in the bass than in the treble register.
- In polyphonic works, pedal should be used very sparingly or hardly at all.
- Whenever possible the pedal markings of the composer should be observed. This, however, is not always feasible. Beethoven's and Chopin's pedal marks, for instance, cannot be accepted today in their entirety, since these masters were writing for pedal mechanisms which were different from ours.
- The player should listen carefully to what he or she plays at all times. The most important factor in good pedal technique is a critical ear.

SCALES

Throughout the history of piano playing, there has seldom been a prominent artist or pedagogue who did not stress the importance of scale and arpeggio practice. Yet today some doubt prevails as to the value of practicing isolated studies of scales and arpeggios. Teachers who recommend it believe that such practice is an excellent preparation for the performance of the entire classic and romantic piano literature, for, as Czerny said, "In every piece written today or one hundred years ago, they [scales and arpeggios] are the principal means by which every passage and every melody is formed." The teachers who do not support scale and arpeggio practice are also in agreement with Czerny, but for different reasons. They say that since pieces contain scales and arpeggios, the proper study of such pieces—that is, the breaking down of pertinent parts into technical exercises—is a more practical and enjoyable procedure than that prescribed by finger-exercise enthusiasts.

Through scale practice, which generally precedes the study of arpeggios, two objectives are fulfilled: the student's technique, including mobility, finger strength, control of touch, and evenness, may be developed in all key patterns; and the student derives an awareness of tonality.

Generally, pedagogues are not in accord as to when scale study should be introduced. It is not unheard-of for scale study to be taught at the first lesson. At the other extreme, some teachers avoid teaching scales during the elementary years, either because students are not physically ready or because scale practice might take the joy out of elementary piano practice. Some teachers may, however, introduce students to a study of tonality through the playing of the two tetrachords that form the scale. The first tetrachord, the first four notes of the scale, is played by the left hand, and the second, the last four notes of the scale, by the right hand.

Preparatory Exercises

One way to prepare the student for scale study during the first year is to teach five-finger patterns in all keys. The technical standards for these preparatory exercises must, however, be as exacting as that required for the playing of scales, since in essence they are the first five notes of the scale.

It should be emphasized that the ability to play even and smooth five-finger patterns is not as easy as it might appear. On the contrary, to produce five consecutive tones, equal in volume and quality, with five unequal fingers is quite a task, one requiring considerable practice. The difference in the size and strength of the fingers is not the only reason for the difficulty. The topography of the keyboard, with its black keys in groups of twos and threes, is such that different degrees of finger curvatures are needed in all five-finger positions.

Considering the anatomy of the hand and the design of the keyboard, the most natural and relaxed hand position can be attained by placing the long fingers (2,3, and 4) on the black keys and the thumb and little finger on the white keys. The result will be a key pattern of E–F-sharp–G-sharp–A-sharp–B. This pattern suggests a Lydian mode rather than the tonality of a major or minor scale; and for this reason, while it is an interesting and usable tone sequence, it is not an ideal sound pattern to prepare for scale study. The slight adjustment of A-sharp to A yields the first five notes of the E-major scale, which in effect can qualify as the most natural of all five-finger positions to serve our purpose. This may be followed closely by the first five notes of the A-major and D-major scales. Next, the all-white key groups starting on G, C, D, and A can be explored; the former two are the G-major and C-major scales, respectively, and the latter two should be identified and ultimately recognized by ear as minor-key patterns. The first five notes of the B-major and F-major scales can be added next. It is well to avoid five-finger positions with the thumb on the black keys at this time. They can be and will be useful in other areas but not as scale-preparatory studies, since the thumb on the black key does not appear in any scheme of good scale fingering.

It should be remembered that the purpose of these exercises is a firm and secure finger action, a full, rounded tone, and an even touch in five-finger play. The aim is not speed. The teacher or student can make up these little drills, which should be played at a slow-to-moderate tempo, in all the suggested keys, each hand separately. They should be practiced regularly and frequently all through the first year of study, prior to the introduction of scales. Here are a few of the many possible patterns.

Still another factor, however subtle, which also can influence the evenness of play concerns the locations of the points of impact—the spots where fingers touch the keys. Because of a simple physical law, slightly less weight or energy is required to depress a key on its very edge than further back. This is probably what Czerny had in mind when he insisted that "the white keys must be struck at about half an inch from their end nearest the player." The great teacher indulged here in what seems to be a bit of wishful thinking. His advice is excellent theoretically, but almost impossible to execute in practice. In their natural position over the keyboard, the fingers do not touch the keys along a straight line but rather along a slightly curving arc, such as this:

Strictly speaking, then, in order to produce even tones, each finger will have to expend different amounts of energy to depress the keys, depending on how far from the edge the point of impact is. This difference may be negligible if the fingers are in their prescribed gently curved position, but will definitely become a disturbing factor if the middle fingers are flattened and touch the keys some two inches or more from the edge. The strong second and third fingers may still be able to come forth with the required extra strength, but the weaker fourth finger will usually not be able to keep up and blend with the others. This is one more reason why it is so important to maintain a good well-rounded hand position at all times.

Passing the Thumb and Crossing the Fingers

When the student can play the five-finger exercises evenly and with good control of tempo and dynamics, he or she may then—still using five-finger patterns—pass the thumb under the third (then the fourth) finger and cross the third (then the fourth) finger over the thumb.

In addition to five-finger exercises, some teachers use the playing of clusters as preparation for scales. In the C-major scale, this would be:

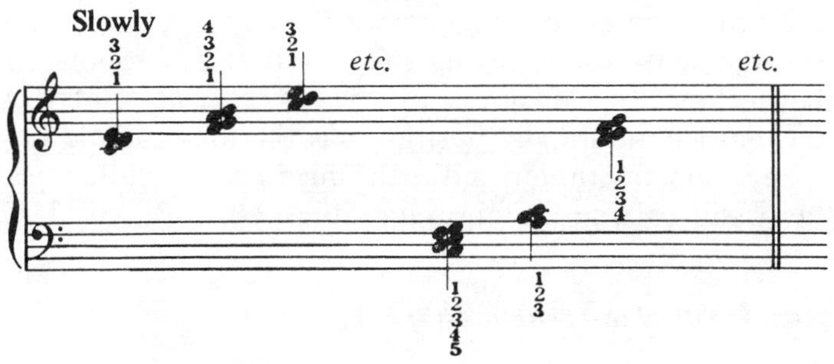

Through cluster practice the student learns the notes and fingering, and also acquires the keyboard feel, to eventually execute the scales.

In playing scales, the single most essential technical requirement is the smooth passing of the thumb under the third and fourth fingers. All pedagogues agree on this. There is no such unanimity, however, when it comes to answering the question of how this smooth passing of the thumb can best be achieved. According to some authoritative voices, the thumb should be on its way after it has struck the key and should move parallel to the other playing fingers. In equally noteworthy sources one may read that the thumb should not be in a hurry and should be held until the finger which it follows has struck its note; then it should move swiftly. With so many individual factors to be taken into account, it is not wise to be too doctrinaire on this point and make a clear-cut decision in favor of one approach or the other. The safest and most satisfactory solution probably lies somewhere between the two. The thumb should not be in a hurry, but neither should it be sluggish and jerked suddenly to be in place for the impact. The commonest faults are raising the wrist when the third or fourth finger plays, and dropping the wrist when the thumb depresses the key. These habits must be scrupulously avoided, for they can produce unwanted accents, make the play uneven, and hinder the attainment of speed. The thumb should pass horizontally without the hand's twisting and without the wrist's raising or dipping. It must also be remembered that only the nail joint touches the key, and not the entire thumb.

No less important, though slightly easier, is the crossing of the third and fourth fingers over the thumb. Here the commonest bad habit is the sudden move, the "kicking up" of the elbow. All unnecessary motions of the wrist and elbow can best be avoided by playing the scales with a "light" arm anchored in the shoulder. The hand should be led by the arm, gliding over the keyboard with the entire playing apparatus, all the muscles and joints strain-free and relaxed. Test this position before playing scales by placing a rounded hand lightly on the keys and leading it by the arm in a silent *glissando* up and down the keyboard. This is, we are told, how Chopin usually warmed up for his scale practice.

At first, scales should be played by each hand separately, slowly, in a one-octave range. When hands begin to play together it is best to start in contrary motion. This way identical fingers will be called on to play simultaneously and identical muscles will be involved in mirror-like motions. Later the hands may begin to play in parallel octaves. Speed should be attained very gradually, and only after the play in octaves has achieved the desired quality and momentum should the other scale patterns (in thirds, sixths, etc.) be introduced.

The study of scales usually begins with the key of C major. There are impressive arguments for changing this habit, with proponents maintaining that technically, C major is not the easiest scale to play. As mentioned, the most natural hand position has the long middle fingers on the black keys and the thumb and fifth finger on the white ones. In addition, the passing of the thumb is smoothest when the third or fourth finger is on the higher plateau of a black key. Also, the crossing of fingers can be managed with minimal motion if the thumb is on a white key and the third and fourth fingers cross over to a black one. There is one scale which meets all of these specifications: the B-major scale.

Why then do we insist on starting with the key of C-major? Why don't we begin with B-major? The reasons are mostly historical and theoretical; they are numerous and deeply rooted. The C-major scale is historically the first diatonic scale; it is a direct descendant of the Ionian mode. All other major scales are transpositions of its pattern of whole steps and half steps. Our entire notation system is a good visual proof of this: the existing lines and spaces can accommodate only the notes of the C-major scale. To notate any other scale, additional signs (sharps and flats) had to be devised and placed on the staff, a somewhat makeshift solution which is still used today.

Another reason why C major seems so natural a beginning is its position as a central orientation point in the spectrum of scales. In the circle of fifths, C is the zero point from which the other scales fan out, sharps to the right and flats to the left. This entire arrangement would lose its logic and its usefulness as a visual aid if C were shifted from its focal point at "twelve o'clock high."

To sum up: while it is true that technically the C-major scale is not by any means the easiest to play, it must also be considered that this scale provides the firmest keystone, the most secure theoretical underpinning for the entire system of diatonic tonality. This does not mean that C major must be the first scale to be learned; it does mean that until a method is devised which can reconcile, adjust, and coordinate all technical and theoretical aspects of scale study, good old C major will be hard to dislodge.

CHORDS AND ARPEGGIOS

The primary requirement in playing chords is that the notes be sounded simultaneously. To achieve this one must anticipate striking the keys by shaping the hand and assuming the necessary finger position before the impact. This should be done without strain or stiffness.

The playing of three or four notes simultaneously needs three or four times more force or energy than the playing of a single note. This requires a rather strong playing apparatus, which can be furnished by uniting the fingers, wrist, and forearm into a forceful yet still flexible tool. The weight of the upper body may also be added to achieve extra volume and bravura.

The playing of *arpeggios* should begin only after a thorough practice of broken triads. As is the case with scales, the key factor in arpeggio playing is the smooth passing of the thumb. Here, however, the task is somewhat more difficult, because the thumb has to bridge an interval of a third or fourth, instead of a second. As a rule, the thumb must span the interval of a fourth when passing under the third finger. This occurs most commonly in two arpeggio patterns in scales starting on white keys, and should be given special attention: ascending arpeggios of the right hand, with the triad in root position; and descending arpeggios of the left hand, with the triad in second inversion. Students with small hands may have to delay the study of these particular configurations until after the arpeggios of the other chord positions have been practiced.

In *legato* play, the finger preceding the thumb has to hold the key depressed until the thumb has struck its note. To facilitate this, especially in the middle range of the keyboard, a lateral, outward motion of the wrist and forearm is recommended. This motion should be gradual and not too pronounced; under no circumstances should it be sudden or vehement. Its purpose is to bring the thumb closer to its destination for a more comfortable, cleaner impact.

At first, arpeggios should be practiced one hand at a time in two-octave range; up and down in the right hand and down and up in the left. Of the following two patterns the second is preferable, as it discourages an accent on the note played by the passing thumb.

It is best to begin two-handed play in contrary motion, for the reasons already mentioned in connection with scale practice.

Technique is only the means and not the end. The real goal of practice is not just finger dexterity, but the ability to convey a musical thought of emotional interest and esthetic validity; in other words, to become musical.

"What is it to be musical?" asked Schumann, and he answered: "You are musical if you have music not in your fingers only, but in your head and heart."

GLOSSARY OF TECHNICAL TERMS

Arpeggio: In piano music the term means the following:

(1) arpeggiated chord: the notes of the chord are not sounded simultaneously but in more or less rapid succession, usually from the bottom up. This is actually a type of embellishment indicated by a vertical wavy line (⌇) or a group of small notes placed in front of the principal note.

(See also "Ornamentation," p.123)

(2) *small arpeggio*: written-out broken chord patterns moving up or down within a one-octave span.

(3) *grand arpeggio*: broken chords moving up or down beyond a one-octave span.

Broken chord: the notes of the chord are not played simultaneously, but successively, in any order or play pattern, as notated.

Cantabile touch: In a singing fashion; bringing out the melody in a smooth, expressive manner. See *Pressure touch.*

Close figures: Melody patterns usually involving all five fingers within a span of less than a fifth. It always entails some chromaticism.

Contrary motion: The two hands playing together, moving in opposite directions, either toward or away from each other. One motion is the mirror image of the other.

Divided chord: A triad divided into two parts, a single note and a double note, which are sounded alternately; also, a four-note chord divided into two double notes sounded alternately.

Double notes: One hand playing two notes simultaneously; identical to "harmonic interval."

Five-finger position: A fixed position of the five fingers on five consecutive keys of a scale.

Forearm rotation: A rolling, rotary motion, clockwise and counterclockwise, of the hand, wrist, and forearm as a unit. It is especially useful for strain-free performance of broken chords and tremolos.

"Heavy" arm: A playing position in which the weight of the arm applies a degree of pressure through the fingers on the keys.

High finger action: Individual fingers are lifted to a position higher than usual before striking the keys. A fine drill to develop a firm touch, as well as the strength and independence of fingers.

Jeu perlé: A very light, even *leggiero* touch usually applied in fast non legato passages.

Lateral motion: Extending the five-finger position by sidewise motion of the wrist and forearm. Also a "light" arm carrying the hand sidewise up and down the keyboard in leggiero passages.

Legato: Smoothly connected, "bound together"; describes execution without any break between successive tones. The depressed key is released the instant the next key is struck and fully depressed. *Legatissimo* is a very smooth legato.

Leggiero (correctly *leggero*): Lightly, without pressure; may apply to both legato and staccato play, usually in rapid, soft passages. Requires a "light" arm. *Leggermente* or *leggeramente* have, for all practical purposes, the same meaning.

"Light" arm: A playing position in which the arm is carried and suspended from the shoulder and its weight is not transferred to the fingers. It is applicable in both legato and staccato play and is a requisite for attaining velocity with a leggiero touch.

Non legato: The successive tones are somewhat detached, with the effect between legato and staccato. The depressed key is released just an instant before the next key is struck.

Parallel motion: The two hands playing together, moving in the same direction at a fixed distance of a certain interval. (Usually in thirds, sixths, or octaves).

Phrase, phrasing: See "The Riddle of the Phrase," p. 55.

Portato: Cantabile playing with a somewhat emphasized non legato touch (♩♩♩). Not to be confused with *portamento*, which means a smooth, almost gliding transition from one tone to the next and which can be executed only by the voice, string instruments, and trombone.

Pressure touch: Certain amount of arm weight applied to the keys.

Shifting hand position: Changing the five-finger position within a piece.

Staccato: Sharply detached manner of playing. The key is depressed with a quick thrust and released immediately, well before the next key is struck. Three main types of staccato are distinguished, depending on which part of the playing apparatus is primarily involved: finger staccato, wrist staccato, and forearm staccato. Staccatissimo is a very sharp staccato; in modern notation it is usually marked by the wedge-shaped sign (▼).

Syncopation: See "What Is Jazz," p.549.

Tenuto: The note is held for its full time value, sometimes even a bit longer (♩).

Tremolo: In piano music, a rapid alternation of two notes which are at an interval greater than a second. The alternation can also take place between a single and a double note, two double notes, and—if performed by both hands—between two chords:

Trill: A more or less rapid alternation of the written note with its upper or lower diatonic neighbor. (The neighboring note can also be altered by an accidental.) See also "Ornamentation," p.123.

Wrist action: Hand and fingers move up and down as a unit, loosely anchored at the wrist. Also, loose and graceful up-and-down motion of the wrist, lifting and lowering the hand; this motion is employed when striking and releasing the keys in connection with the articulation of slurs and phrases.

Tempo

DENES AGAY

Tempo is the rate or speed of movement at which a composition or section is performed. It is usually indicated by a verbal instruction (tempo mark) or a metronome mark.

History shows that composers, teachers, performers, and editors are seldom in agreement on tempo, as it depends to some extent on the interpreter's personal makeup and temperament. For instance, Beethoven's tempo mark over the last movement of his Sonata in A-flat op. 26 is simply *allegro.* In various subsequent editions the editors, all outstanding authorities, attached the following metronome marks to the allegro indication:

Bülow – Lebert	♩ = 116
Casella	♩ = 138
Schnabel	♩ = 160

There is a recorded performance of this movement by Sviatoslav Richter registered at the speed of ♩=176. Furthermore, not only are such wide discrepancies in individual interpretations a matter of course, but there are inconsistencies even in the tempos taken by one performer of a given work at different times. Mozart mentioned in a letter that he liked to perform his works the way he felt at the moment. Brahms did not like to hear his compositions played at the same tempo each time. Pianist José Iturbi, when listening to recordings he has made in the past, is said always to disagree with their tempos.

Varying interpretations of tempo are also caused by changes in prevailing norms and attitudes toward performance. The "Eroica" Symphony took Beethoven one hour to conduct; today it averages forty-six minutes.

Thus, tempo is a rather subjective concept. At the same time it is also one of the most important factors in effective performance. How, then, does one determine the right tempo of a piece, while making due allowance for the term's flexibility? The composer's own tempo mark is the prime criterion. In the absence of such indication, which is overwhelmingly the case in works of the baroque period, the texture, mood, and form of the piece can furnish sufficient clues. Dense chords, frequent harmonic changes, and rich ornaments will generally require slower tempos than clear, thin, transparent textures. The baroque dance forms also carry unmistakable connotations of tempo. We know that a sarabande is usually slow and solemn, a minuet moderately paced and graceful, a gigue fast and merry. Improvisatory fantasias and preludes will be rather free in delivery, while inventions, fugues, and most imitative contrapuntal forms should be delivered at a generally steady tempo. In conjunction with an analysis of the work, reliable editorial suggestions may also be considered.

From the second half of the eighteenth century and especially throughout the nineteenth and twentieth centuries, composers have furnished tempo marks with increasing clarity, sometimes in their native tongues, but more often by the internationally accepted Italian terms. The most frequently used Italian tempo marks, from slowest to fastest are:

Largo: very slow and broad
Adagio: very slow
Lento: slow
Larghetto: not quite as slow as *largo*
Andante: "walking" tempo; implies a slow, steady movement
Andantino: a little livelier than *andante*
Moderato: moderate tempo
Allegretto: not quite as lively as *allegro*
Allegro: quick, fast
Vivace: lively; usually a shade faster than *allegro*
Presto: very fast
Prestissimo: as fast as possible

It should be reemphasized that none of the above terms has an absolute meaning; each is open to various individual interpretations and only when coupled with an authoritative metronome mark can a more exact indication of pace and movement be given. On the other hand, these terms not only indicate tempo, but also carry connotations of the music's mood and type. For this reason they are occasionally used as titles for a piece or a movement (Samuel Barber's *Adagio for Strings*, the *Largo* from Handel's Xerxes, etc.).

The following frequently used terms are predominantly descriptive in nature, but also convey instructions as to a framework of tempo:

Grave: seriously, solemnly; slow or very slow tempo
Maestoso: majestically; usually slow-to-moderate tempo
Tranquillo or *calmo*: calmly
Con moto: with motion; moderate-to-lively tempo
Grazioso: gracefully; usually between *andante* and *allegretto*
Giocoso: happy, playful; usually *allegretto* or faster
Animato: animated
Con brio: brisk, lively
Scherzando, scherzoso: in a jesting, playful manner; usually *allegretto* or faster
Appassionato: in a passionate manner; may refer to any tempo
Agitato: agitated; indicates lively or fast tempo
Con fuoco: with fire; fast or very fast tempo

Modifications of the main tempo are marked by the following terms:

Ritardando (*rit.*): becoming gradually slower
Rallentando (*rall.*): becoming gradually slower
Allargando: getting gradually broader and slower
Ritenuto: held back; it is used interchangeably with *ritardando* and *rallentando*, but, in strict interpretation, it is not a gradual but an instantaneous slowing down, similar to *sostenuto*
Sostenuto: originally meant the holding of a note or chord to its full value (*tenuto*); but it also means holding back of the tempo of a phrase or section
Calando: gradually becoming slower and softer
Smorzando: gradually becoming slower and softer
Morendo: dying away; gradually becoming slower and softer; usually occurs at the end of a piece or section
A tempo: return to the preceding tempo
Tempo primo or *Tempo I*: return to the original tempo
Accelerando (*accel.*): becoming gradually faster
Calcando: gradually more hurried and faster
Stringendo: with accelerated pace and growing excitement
Più mosso: with more motion, faster
Meno mosso: with less motion, slower
Più lento: slower
Più allegro: faster; usually preceded by *allegro* mark
Rubato: See p. 32.

TEACHING TEMPO

The importance of an appropriate tempo should be stressed from the beginning of instruction. Perhaps the best way to start is to help the student become aware of tempo differences. There is ample opportunity for this; beginners' books contain many pieces whose titles imply tempo suggestions. "A Lazy Day" will be played slowly, while "The Fire Engine" asks for speed. Gradually other indicators of tempo determination may be introduced. Choosing the wrong tempo will distort or ruin a piece; this can easily be illustrated by playing a lullaby fast and a polka or square dance tune slowly.

Some teachers believe that all student assignments should be played strictly at the indicated tempo; others may go to the opposite extreme by assigning a composition marked *presto* to a student who will not be able to play it beyond *moderato.* Substantial alterations of the indicated or desired tempo must be avoided, since the tempo determines, to a large extent, the character and mood of the piece.

Speed and excellence may become synonymous in the beginning player's mind. Too often an apt student will play a composition marked *moderato* two or three times faster than warranted, just to display facility. Therefore the importance of *control*, not playing at maximum speed, needs to be stressed.

Many teachers regard the metronome as the best device for helping the student maintain a steady beat. Undoubtedly, the metronome can be useful, although overreliance on it should be avoided, as it is a rather symptomatic treatment of rhythmic instability. Progressive drills (singing, clapping, marching, etc.) can usually instill a sense of beat and rhythm in the student, reducing the need for frequent metronomic assistance. (See "The Metronome," p. 35).

RUBATO

Rubato or *tempo rubato* indicates a flexibility and elasticity of tempo, subtle deviations from the basic metronomic pulse. We distinguish two kinds: *melodic rubato*, in which the melody is played freely against the steady, unchanging pulse of the accompaniment, and *full* or *structural rubato*, in which melody and accompaniment move together in coordinated modification of tempo. Mozart is known to have performed with a melodic rubato; similarly, in jazz and blues a freely projected melody floats over a steady metronomic beat. Chopin and most romantic masters employed both kinds of rubato.

In playing rubato, the student had best not be left to his or her own devices, but rather be helped, at least initially, to think out fully and prepare where and to what extent these tempo deviations are necessary for a sensitive interpretation. It should be determined what elements of form or texture are involved: an ornamental passage, a phrase or phrase segment, or an entire section. In addition to the tempo-modification signs (rit., accel., sostenuto, etc.) other clues often imply a rubato interpretation, such as stress and articulation marks and various mood indications (appassionato, molto cantabile, etc.).

A certain flexibility of tempo is inherent in the performance of nearly all types of music, except perhaps those which are predominantly polyphonic or strictly dancelike and rhythmic in character. The student should also be reminded to avoid such obvious mannerisms of "romantic" interpretation as accelerating toward the climactic point of a phrase and then slowing down toward the phrase-ending cadence, or broadening the tempo automatically in crescendo passages. In all cases, even in pieces of a romantic and sentimental nature, rubato should be employed with taste and restraint; the player should never lose sight of the work's style, structure, and desirable median momentum.

RECOMMENDED READING

Crowder, Louis. "The Rubatometer." *Clavier* May–June 1963.

McEwen, John B. *Tempo Rubato or Time Variation in Musical Performance.* London: Oxford University Press, 1928.

Nadeau, Roland. "Finding the Tempo." *The Piano Teacher* January–February 1961.

Newman, William S. *The Pianist's Problems* (3rd ed.). New York: Harper & Row, 1974.

Nichols, Randolph. "Tempo and Character." *Clavier* March 1976.

Sachs, Kurt. *Rhythm and Tempo.* London: Dent, 1953.

Shenkman, Walter. "Tempo Rubato." *Clavier* May–June 1974.

The Metronome

HAZEL GHAZARIAN SKAGGS

A metronome is an instrument which can be set to sound an adjustable number of beats per minute. When hand operated, like a nonelectric clock, it has a pendulum (rod) marked with a graduated scale from 40 to 208. A movable weight can be set at the desired number of beats per minute. The electronic metronome has a knob instead of a pendulum, that is set at the desired beat.

Although Winkel invented the first metronome in the early part of the nineteenth century, Maelzel patented the invention under his name in 1816, and set up a factory for its production. The following year Beethoven began placing the Maelzel metronome markings on his compositions.

A piece marked ♩=60 or M.M. ♩=60 means that on the Maelzel metronome there are sixty beats to a minute, a quarter note equaling one beat. Below is a chart of the beats-per-minute figures marked on the metronome:

40 to 60 by twos	(40, 42, 44, etc.)
60 to 72 by threes	(60, 63, 66, etc.)
72 to 120 by fours	(72, 76, 80, etc.)
120 to 144 by sixes	(120, 126, 132, etc.)
144 to 208 by eights	(144, 152, 160, etc.)

There are three kinds of metronomes: the hand-operated Maelzel with visible and audible beats, with an optional bell attachment to designate the first beat of the measure; the electronic metronome, with a bulb that may be removed to avoid visual distraction; and a small pocket-watch type from Switzerland. For the student who uses a metronome frequently, the electronic one is the best investment. Unlike the pyramidal table model, it operates in any position and is unlikely to have an uneven beat.

There is no unanimity as to the extent and manner of the metronome's use in the teaching process. It is safe to state that, if used indiscriminitely or too frequently, the metronome can become a crutch and hinder the student's developing an instinct for the right tempo. In addition, a relaxed and expressive performance is impossible if one has to adhere closely to a mechanically precise, uniform beat throughout the piece. This would eliminate the subtle rubato, that fine give and take in tempo, which is the very essence of a meaningful performance.

There are numerous instances, however, when a judicious use of the metronome may be helpful:

- To check tempo markings. Many composers, from Beethoven to our time, have given precise metronome marks at the beginning of their compositions.
- To check occasionally whether or not the rhythmic pulse is steady.
- To facilitate and control the practice of technical exercises (scales, arpeggios, études, isolated passages in certain pieces). This may be done by beginning at a slow tempo and increasing the pace notch by notch (for instance, from ♩=60 to 63, 66, and so on) until the desired tempo is reached.

It should be remembered that playing with a metronome requires a certain skill and self-control, which may need to be developed gradually. In general, a student who has the technical facility to play some simple exercises, such as five-finger drills, is ready to concentrate on listening to the metronome while playing one note at a time with each audible beat. A moderate tempo, somewhere between ♩=84 to 92, might be the best to begin with, as slower and faster tempos are more difficult for the student to maintain. Later, when the student is accustomed to listening to the metronome and playing according to its sound, he or she may try other rates of speed, then two notes to a beat, and so on.

Great composers and outstanding teachers have expressed opposing views on the use of the metronome as a teaching tool. Chopin used the metronome while teaching as a "lie detector, witness or physician for rhythmic ailments." Backhaus, Godowsky, and Grainger recommended that those who need it use it. On the other hand, Rachmaninoff warned against its frequent use, Cortot did not permit his students ever to practice with it, and Debussy was of the opinion that a metronome mark can be considered valid only for the measure over which it stands. Perhaps the most sensitive and at the same time most succinct evaluation of the metronome comes from one of its first users, Beethoven. On the manuscript of one of his songs he wrote the following instruction: "100 according to Maelzel. This, however, is valid only for the first measures, for *feeling also has its tempo* and this cannot be entirely expressed by this figure."

Today's consensus can be summarized as follows: the use of the metronome as an occasional teaching aid is pedagogically sound and, especially in the three instances outlined above, potentially very helpful. However, an overuse or habitual reliance on it should definitely be avoided.

RECOMMENDED READING

Holcman, Jan. "The Misunderstood Metronome." *The Piano Teacher* September–October 1964.

Rhythm

DENES AGAY

There is considerable ambiguity about the correct difinition of this term, as there is about such related concepts as *meter, time,* and *tempo.* To clarify these, let us start with the simplest:

Tempo is the rate or speed of a musical composition or section; it is independent of meter or rhythm. Tempo is indicated by a tempo mark, expressed either by words (andante, allegro, slow, fast, etc.) or by a metronome mark, giving the number of beats per minute. (See "Tempo," p. 29).

Meter and *time* may be considered synonymous; they mean the number and basic grouping of beats within the measure, as indicated by the time signature ($\frac{2}{4}$, $\frac{4}{4}$, etc.).

Rhythm is the relative time length of successive tones and pauses in the flow of music and the resulting sound pattern formed within a metric framework. The concept of rhythm implies an underlying metric foundation (time signature), as illustrated by the following examples:

This succession of notes represents a rhythmic pattern, but one that remains amorphous until it is put into a metric framework by using a time signature. The location of natural accents can now be determined:

For further clarification, here is the first version with pitch added:

Observe how this rhythm and pitch pattern acquires an entirely individual rhythmic profile with a different meter in this charming Mozart Minuet:

To summarize: rhythm is a sound pattern (with or without pitch) formed by the relative length of a group of successive tones and pauses within a specific meter.

NOTE VALUES

In the traditional Western notation system, the basic musical unit is the whole note, which is divided into two, four, eight, etc. equal parts to form half notes, quarter notes, eighth notes, etc.:

American term	English term
whole note	semibreve
half note	minim
quarter note	crotchet
eighth note	quaver
sixteenth note	semiquaver
thirty-second note	demisemiquaver
sixty-fourth note	hemidemisemiquaver

A dot placed after the note head increases the value of that note by one half:

A second dot further increases the value of that note by one-quarter of its basic value:

TIME SIGNATURE

As mentioned, meter is indicated by the time signature ($\frac{2}{4}$, $\frac{3}{2}$, $\frac{6}{8}$, etc.). The lower figure designates the note value which gets one beat; the upper figure shows the number of beats per measure.

Time signatures can be classified as simple and compound. In *simple meter* the beat is represented by a simple note (♩); in *compound meter* the beat is represented by a dotted note (♩.).

In simple meter each beat is subdivided into units of two or multiples of two:

In compound meter each beat is subdivided into units of three or its multiples:

$\frac{6}{8}$ ♩. ♪♪♪ | ♩ ♪ ♬♪♪ |

Meter can also be classified as *duple, triple,* or *quadruple,* depending on the number of beats per measure ($\frac{2}{4}$, $\frac{3}{4}$, $\frac{4}{4}$). $\frac{4}{4}$ is also called *common time*, often indicated by **C** , for historical reasons. During the Middle Ages a full circle (○) was used to mark "perfect" time, a three-unit grouping with symbolic allusions to the Holy Trinity. In contrast, $\frac{4}{4}$, or "imperfect" time, was marked by a broken circle (C), in which our present **C** has its origin. From this evolved the mark *alla breve* (¢). In early notation a stroke through the signature was used to indicate that each note was to be halved in value, which doubled the rate of movement.

In compound meter the student may, at first, count every beat unit; later, the three units are combined into one count.

When a simple beat is subdivided into three equal parts, the resulting group is called a *triplet.*

Likewise, a compound beat may be subdivided into two *duplets*:

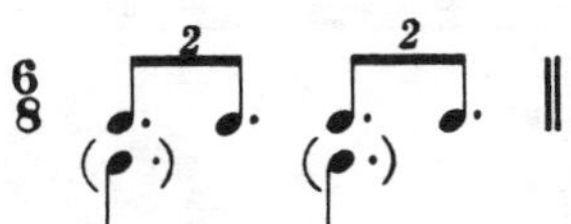

Note values may be lengthened by using ties:

SYNCOPATION

Syncopation is the displacement or shifting of accent to a normally unaccented beat.

The appealing rhythmic tension thus created in the flow of music stems from the interplay between the expected (but unrealized) normal accents and the actually heard off-beat accents. Syncopation can be found in the music of all periods, from early to modern times. It has been an increasingly frequent device since Beethoven; it especially abounds in folk music and in ragtime and jazz, the syncopated idioms par excellence.

Beethoven: *Leonora* Overture

Beethoven: Sonata, op. 31 no. 1

Bartók: For Children, Book 1

Joplin: "The Easy Winners"

RHYTHMIC CONVENTIONS

The composer's notation does not always indicate exact note values and rhythms, in which cases one has to rely on certain performing conventions. Many such irregularities stem from the variable lengthening value of the dot standing after a note. In a melodic passage, the dotted note may be a shade shorter than the notation would indicate:

Chopin: Nocturne

In a brisk piece of music, such as a march or polonaise, it may be held longer:

Schumann: "Soldier's March"

A dotted note with its complementary short note ( ) may become when accompanied by a triplet in another voice. These irregularities occur most often in baroque music and in jazz and blues:

Bach: French Suite no. 4

Another unwritten convention is the shortening of the note duration at the end of a phrase or slur:

Clementi: Sonatina

RECOMMENDED READING

Creston, Paul. "The Structure of Rhythm." *Clavier* November 1971.

Dolmetsch, Arnold. *The Interpretation of Music of the Seventeenth and Eighteenth Centuries*. London: Novello, 1915.

Grove's Dictionary of Music and Musicians (5th ed.). "Dotted Notes," "*Inégales*." New York: St. Martin's Press, 1954.

Sachs, Kurt. *Rhythm and Tempo*. London: Dent, 1953.

Teaching Rhythm

HAZEL GHAZARIAN SKAGGS

A sense of rhythm is the capacity for perceiving rhythmic patterns and the ability to reproduce them. Also, it is a physical experience, felt in the body as a response to music, which begins to develop early in life. Babies often respond to simple music with such movements as clapping their hands and swaying their bodies in time with the music. During the pre-school years (ages two to five) this rhythmic sense is further developed through various forms of rhythmic play. Many children become exposed to the preschool rhythm band; if not, they often have their own pots and pans to drum on at home. Some youngsters may be enrolled in music-readiness programs that further extend their rhythmic responses in a structured program of study. The Dalcroze, Orff, and Kodály methods, as well as dance classes, give children advantages over those who have not had such training.

What children are not taught, however, they often learn by themselves, through such activities as jumping rope and skipping, chanting and reciting rhymes, and ritualistic tapping.

Although children generally come to the first piano lesson without an understanding of rhythm, many nonetheless have a rather well-established sense of it. The teacher's task is to help the student develop this predisposition while playing the piano. Unfortunately, as soon as lessons begin, there is a chance that the student's rhythmic sense may become repressed. When the teacher understands this, steps can be taken to avoid it. First of all, the teacher must remember that rhythmic activity for the child, up to the time of the first lesson, has generally been in the form of play, involving the grosser parts of the body, such as the legs and arms. At the piano the child must reproduce those same rhythms through the weaker, finer finger muscles, manipulating a strange, new contrivance called a keyboard. This is difficult, at times impossible. Not only is the child faced with this physical hurdle, but also with the arithmetic chore of learning note values (and often counting them aloud). If the teacher approaches teaching rhythm without taking into account these realities, the child's spontaneous rhythmic sense becomes more and more repressed.

The wise teacher will try to build on the child's instinctive rhythmic sense, not inhibit it. Generally beginner's books have words, so the first introduction to rhythm may be by the rote procedure of singing and saying words in rhythm.

As the student advances, the teacher may start using words as symbols of rhythmic patterns. One popular system, devised by Hazel Cobb, uses *pie* as the key word.

Any word or group of words created by the teacher may represent a rhythm.

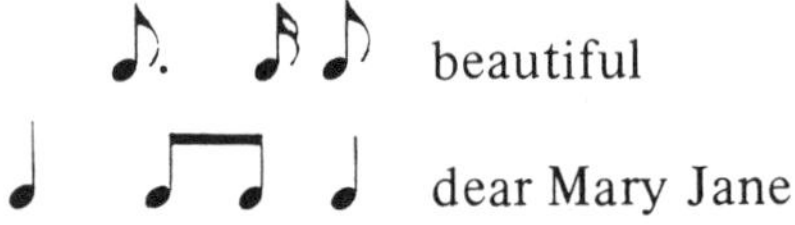

Instead of the words the teacher may substitute a syllable system; here is one with *ta*:

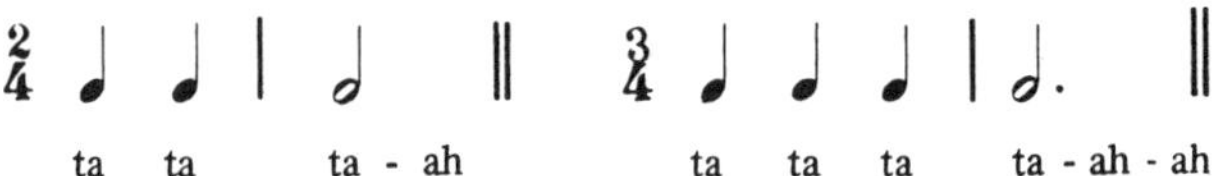

Some teachers use a syllable system until the student feels secure enough technically to change to numerical counting.

Another precounting approach involves saying the actual note values:

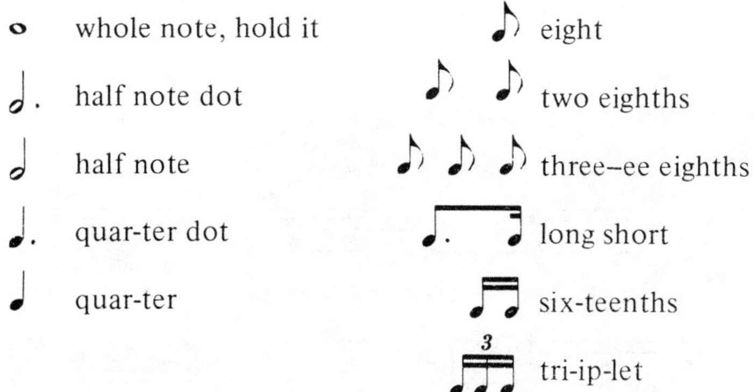

Counting each note according to note value with no regard to its actual position in the measure helps make the learning of note values easier.

When the student is secure in the knowledge of note values and has more technical facility, he or she may then count in keeping with the time signature.

Some teachers are persistent about counting aloud every time the child plays. The teacher of such conviction may pause to consider how it is that the players of brass and wind instruments succeed in keeping time when they are not physically able to count aloud and play at the same time, as pianists are. Yet they certainly function well in ensemble, where rhythmic competence is even more urgent than in solo performance. Also, of what use is counting aloud if the child counts in time with incorrect playing? This is not to say counting aloud is to be discouraged, but to remind the teacher that it can be overdone.

In selecting a beginner's book, the teacher might keep in mind the following considerations to make sure the method gives high priority to developing a physical response to the music being performed: Does the book have songs that the student can play by rote without worrying about note values? Are the words rhythmic? Are there any duets? Are note values introduced judiciously? For example, does the introduction of eighth notes occur on the strong fingers?

Does the book provide for practicing note values with the grosser arm muscles? A piece such as "Ding-Dong Bell" illustrates music that establishes the feeling for the rhythmic pattern

in the arm muscles, which facilitates its transference to the undeveloped muscles of the fingers.

Even if one method book should meet all the above criteria, the teacher may want to devise rhythmic reinforcement through improvisation and games. A fun activity which helps the rhythmic sense grow is playing simple ostinato-bass duets. These may be taught by rote or improvised.

"Frere Jacques"

POLYRHYTHMS

There are various ways to lead the student in the practice of playing two different rhythms simultaneously. Here, for instance, is one sequence of steps that can be followed to practice this pattern:

First, practice one rhythm based on the lesser number of beats (usually in the bass part):

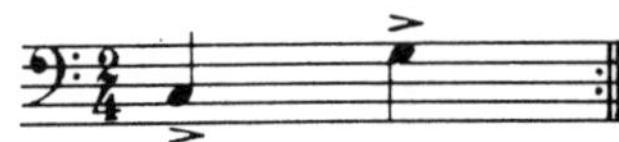

Visualize each beat as consisting of triplets:

Add the other rhythm by playing the two parts together:

Another possible approach is to combine the two parts into a single rhythm pattern and tap the sound with one hand:

Then divide the pattern between the two hands:

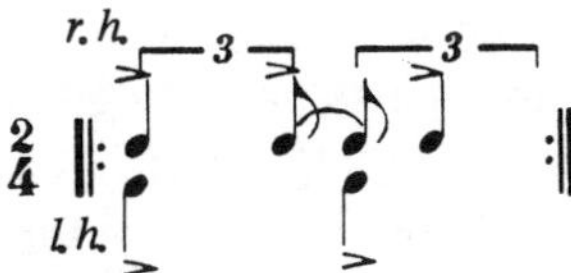

Consider another frequently encountered polyrhythm:

Play with emphasis three beats to the bar:

Visualize the sixteenth-note components of each beat:

Add the other rhythm:

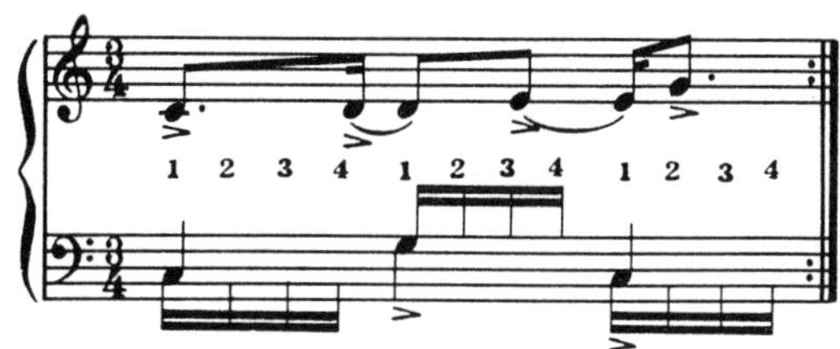

Or, combine the two parts into a single pattern and tap it with one hand:

Then divide the pattern between the two hands:

One can also acquire the facility of playing two rhythms simultaneously by practicing each hand alone with a steady beat until both hands are so secure in their rhythmic parts that when played together, one hand plays automatically while the performer listens for the accuracy of the other hand. Both hands are checked in this manner.

RECOMMENDED READING

Fletcher, Stanley. "Rhythm and Metrical Bookkeeping." *Clavier* March–April 1963.
Goeltz, Lois. "Teaching Rhythm to the Intermediate Student." *Clavier* April 1976.
Marton, Ann. "A Gradual Approach to Learning to Count." *Clavier* February 1973.
Starer, Robert. *Rhythmic Training.* New York: MCA, 1969.

Dynamics

DENES AGAY

Dynamics are degrees and gradations of loudness and softness in the flow of music. The comparative degrees of sound levels from softest to loudest are marked:

pp *pianissimo*: very soft
p *piano*: soft
mp *mezzo piano*: moderately soft
mf *mezzo forte*: moderately loud
f *forte*: loud
ff *fortissimo*: very loud

Some nineteenth- and twentieth-century composers occasionally use:

ppp *piano-pianissimo* or *pianississimo*: as soft as possible
fff *forte-fortissimo* or *fortississimo*: as loud as possible

It should be noted that none of the above terms has an absolute value; the proper meaning of ***f*** and ***p*** must always be decided on the basis of the piece's style and the musical context in which these marks appear. Other factors may also merit consideration: the notation practices of the period and the individual composer, and the type of instrument for which the work was written. For instance, the full dynamic capabilities of the modern piano should not be fully exploited to perform works originally written for the harpsichord, clavichord, or the fragile early piano, all of which were instruments of considerably narrower dynamic range.

Dynamic gradations to louder and softer levels are indicated by either the familiar wedge-shaped signs or the equivalent Italian terms:

< *crescendo* (*cresc.*): gradually louder
> *decrescendo* or *diminuendo* (*decresc.* or *dim.*): gradually softer

Although the graphic symbol (<) and the term *crescendo* are used interchangeably, there is a difference in their meaning. The sign (<) indicates exactly where the increase in volume begins and ends; the sound level attained at the end of the symbol should be maintained until it is altered by a new dynamic indication. The word crescendo, on the other hand, pinpoints only the beginning of the gradation process; theoretically, the volume should be increased until a new sign marks the attainment of the desired dynamic plateau.

Beethoven: Sonata, op. 13 ("Pathétique")

The above rules also apply, in reverse, to > and *diminuendo*.

Often the crescendo or decrescendo mark is followed by a series of dots (*cresc. . . .*) to indicate the extent of increase or decrease in volume. The same end is served by staggering the syllables of the term (*cres. . . cen. . . do*).

più f (louder) and ***più p*** (softer) indicate an instantaneous change in volume and not a gradual one.

fp (*forte-piano*) indicates an abrupt change from loud to soft.

Subito ***p*** indicates suddenly soft; *subito* ***f***, suddenly loud.

Similar in meaning to diminuendo, but also implying a slowing down of tempo, are the following terms:

calando: decreasing, calming down
smorzando: fading away
morendo: dying
perdendosi: becoming lost
mancando: disappearing

The last three terms, very similar in meaning, are generally used at the end of a movement or section.

Accents, in order of their intensity from weak to strong, are marked with the following signs:

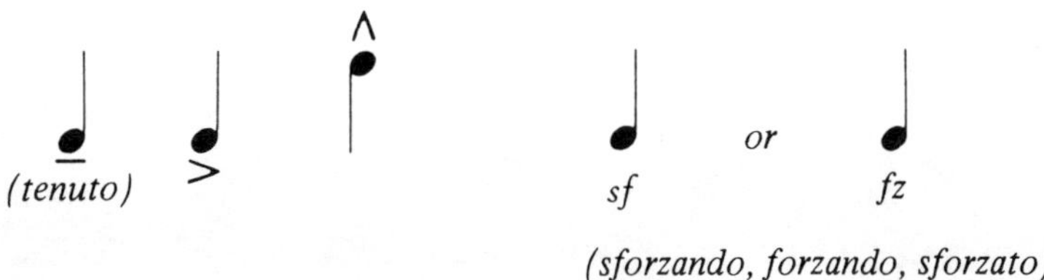

The word *marcato* is used to indicate accents on a succession of notes. *Rinforzando* (***rf*** or *rinf.*) indicates a sudden increase in volume and stress pertaining to a phrase or phrase section, while ***sf*** (*sforzato*) applies only to a single note or chord.

Composers of the baroque period used very few dynamic signs, only an occasional ***f*** or ***p*** ; crescendo and diminuendo were not indicated. Although in the music of this era the principle of terrace dynamics (a contrast between loud and soft sections) prevails, a judicious gradation of sound levels (*cresc.*, *dim.*) does not have to be excluded and is definitely the performer's option. From Beethoven's time and continuing throughout the nineteenth century, the vocabulary and frequency of dynamic markings greatly increased.

The Riddle of the Phrase

DENES AGAY

The *phrase* is the keystone of most musical structures, and *phrasing* is the lifeblood of meaningful musical interpretation. The prime importance of these concepts and the need to define, explain and teach them has been evident for more than five centuries. A substantial library could be filled with the books, articles, treatises, and other scholarly utterances on the subject. How, then, is it still possible to speak of the phrase as being a riddle? It is indeed strange and difficult to believe that today, when all aspects of music—especially the pedagogic processes—are so thoroughly explored, analyzed, and dissected, this basic building block of music is still a somewhat ambiguous concept.

A group of about eighty music teachers was recently asked to determine which is the first phrase in the U.S. national anthem, "The Star-Spangled Banner":

(a) The first two measures (ending on the word *see*)
(b) The first four measures (ending on the word *light*)
(c) The first eight measures (ending on the word *gleaming*)

The overwhelming majority of answers was almost evenly divided between (a) and (b), with a sprinkling of votes for (c). That the phrasing of such a simple song should elicit such differing opinions from professional musicians and pedagogues may be surprising and thought-provoking, yet it is almost inevitable, considering the wide divergence of information available in authoritative writings. The fact is that all three of the above answers—yes, even (c)—can readily be substantiated by many respectable sources.

The elusive nature of the phrase is clearly stated, indeed emphasized, in nearly all scholarly writings on the subject. "The word [phrase] is not and can hardly be used with much exactness and uniformity," states *Grove's Dictionary of Music and Musicians. The Oxford Companion to Music* agrees: "In analyzing any particular composition one theorist might on occasion prefer to consider as one phrase a particular passage which another would prefer to consider two phrases." A more recent source states, "The term *phrase* is one of the most ambiguous in music." Countless others echo the same thought.

As long as the concept of the phrase remains unclear, the meaning of other, closely related, larger form elements, such as the *sentence* and *period*, will also be somewhat vague. "There exists great confusion in the use of the terms," wrote Arnold Schoenberg, which, under the circumstances, must be considered an understatement. For instance, *sentence* is "a group of two or four phrases," according to the *Oxford Companion*, adding that "there is no accepted understanding among musicians on this point." Should you seek further clarification on this matter by consulting other readily available, reputable sources, you might be more confused than enlightened. *Grove's*, the largest music dictionary in the English language, has no entry under "sentence." Neither has *The Harvard Dictionary of Music.* Both contain information on the period, however, and from their definitions one must assume that they regard the two terms as essentially identical and interchangeable. Other equally impeccable sources state that the period is a larger unit, consisting of two complementary sentences. Still others, including Schoenberg, see the sentence and period as form segments of equal length but of different phrase construction.

One could go on indefinitely quoting examples of such contradictory definitions from highly reliable, authoritative sources. Not only are phrase, sentence and period vaguely defined concepts but there is indeed no clear, generally accepted nomenclature of the basic form elements of music. Anyone writing on the subject of musical form has, of necessity, first to select a vocabulary of terms, establish meanings, and identify each term's structural role in the hierarchy of form elements. This subjective approach is made clear by most authors writing on the subject. Such expressions as "by a musical phrase *here* should be understood" or "*in this syllabus* these terms signify" (author's emphasis) very correctly imply that the choice of terms and their definitions are the writer's own and are not necessarily identical to those found in other sources. As a result, the literature of form analysis is replete with a bewildering array of technical names and expressions attempting to describe and designate segments of various lengths in the flow of music. An inventory, by no means complete, of such terms includes:

motive, figure, motive group
einschnitt, zweitakt, incise
phrase, semi phrase (half phrase), double phrase
sentence, half sentence, double sentence

period, double period, thesis-antithesis
theme, subject
section, segment, unit
two-part song form, binary form, three-part song form, ternary form

On the above list perhaps only the motive, the smallest component of the musical structure, is defined with a measure of consistency and unanimity in the corpus of pertinent writings. All the other concepts, including the phrase, sentence, and period, are left vague because of the absence of consensus.

This confusion and ambiguity are due not only to a lack of clear definitions, which are admittedly very hard to achieve. A statement such as "the phrase is a unit of two to eight measures in length (sometimes even more)" may be vague, but is essentially correct. But when the phrase is carelessly defined as being identical with other form elements, the confusion is compounded, and most of the damage is done from a pedagogic point of view. In an older textbook, for instance, one may read that "the phrase is the smallest complete musical sentence." A more recent and in other respects very valuable textbook states that "by phrase we mean a melodic section such as a motive or a theme." A phrase, in fact, is neither a sentence nor a motive. Each of these terms stands for a different form concept and has its own identity and structural role in musical architecture. Regrettably, even the beginning piano student is frequently exposed to such careless terminology. When the youngster is instructed by the method book to "play the following two-note phrases," he or she is led down the path to an early misunderstanding of musical form elements. Two notes connected by a slur may constitute a motive or a figure, but never a phrase. Most sources, their contradictory and confusingly vague definitions notwithstanding, agree on this point. One may play two-note figures to practice *phrasing* (which is probably the kind of drill the method in question intended) but even this wording could be improved by using the term *articulation* instead of phrasing. (See "Phrasing and Articulation," p. 71).

This confusion in terminology has been for too long and, it seems, quite apathetically tolerated by the pedagogic community, which seems to accept the explanation given in most sources for the somewhat hazy status of the phrase: "the infinite variety of situations and conditions found in composition." While this is undoubtedly true, it should not be allowed to stand as a valid reason for the lack of uniform guidelines. The countless ways a thought can be expressed in speech and writing did not thwart the formulation of precise rules of grammar and punctuation. Even other realms of music, such as harmony and counterpoint, which also present a profusion of variety in combinations and patterns, are much more thoroughly and methodically explored and systematized than the domain of the phrase. As a result, so fundamental a question as "what is a phrase?" is being answered in many ways. The purpose of this section is to examine the various representative opinions, to uncover points of agreement, and to add a few observations and practical guidelines.

MOTIVE-PHRASE-SENTENCE

Modern sources generally agree that the three main structural elements of music, in progressive order of length, are the *motive, phrase,* and *sentence*. The following example may illustrate the interrelationship of these three form concepts:

Haydn: German Dance

There are, of course, innumerable ways in which the three elements may fuse, but despite the infinite variety of structural combinations, their relative role in the hierarchy of form elements remains essentially unchanged: motives build phrases, phrases combine to form sentences, and sentences are linked to form the simplest complete pieces of music, the two- and three-part song forms.

Let us now closely examine these three form elements. The smallest component of musical form, and the easiest to recognize (perhaps because it is usually defined with a degree of clarity), is the *motive*: a compact, distinctive group of notes, usually one or two measures in length, which stands out by virtue of characteristic features of interval and/or rhythm. It may consist of as few as two tones or as many as eight. This is a basic generator of form from which the larger units are built through variation, development, extension, etc.

German Folk Song ("Cuckoo")

Beethoven: Symphony no. 5

Grieg: Scherzo, op. 3 no. 6

Here are motives at work, forming the next-larger unit, phrases:

The above phrases are built by repetitions of the same motivic pattern. Phrases can also be formed by the interplay of two or more different motives:

Schubert: Écossaise

Also, motives may be repeated in a varied or developed form to build a phrase:

Chopin: Polonaise

PHRASE CHARACTERISTICS

In examining the motive-phrase relationship in the above examples, one can see that the difference between them is not merely length. The phrase is not only a longer musical line than the motive, but also is a more complete one in the sense that *it terminates in some form of cadence*; the momentum generated by the motivic play comes to a momentary halt, or is relaxed by a point of repose marking the end of the unit.

The division of music by cadences into phrases is often likened to the punctuation of written or spoken language. Just as a sentence is divided by commas, colons, and semi-colons into smaller grammatical units (phrases and clauses), a musical sentence is divided by cadences into phrases; and just as a speaker's voice rises, and falls, and pauses according to the punctuation marks, in music the cadences provide these points of repose and nuances of separation.

The motivic construction of a phrase is not always as sharply defined as in the above examples. Very often a phrase may consist of longer melodic lines, without clear-cut motivic delineations.

Tchaikovsky: Symphony no. 6 ("Pathétique")

Chopin: Concerto no. 1

Beethoven: Sonata, op. 49 no. 2

In these, as in most phrases, the succession of tones and the rise and fall of pitch usually form *a distinctive melodic contour with one or two inherent climactic points*. The progression of the melodic line toward and away from these points of maximum intensity gives the phrase its individual character and expressive content.

Phrases are often described as melodic units of two or four measures in length. While this is true in most cases, it is also a very mechanical and unreliable method of identification. If the tempo of the piece is fast and the measure co.itains only two or three beats ($\frac{2}{4}$, $\frac{3}{8}$, etc.), the phrase will extend to eight or more measures. The momentum of the motivic play itself may carry the phrase over the four-measure mark:

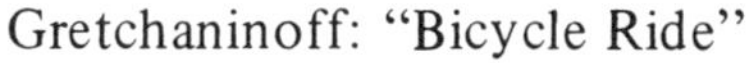
Gretchaninoff: "Bicycle Ride"

Beethoven: Sonata, op. 10 no. 2

The number of measures in a phrase does not have to be a multiple of two. Here are a few, by no means unusual, examples:

Bartók: "Play Tune"
(one-measure phrase)

Mozart: Symphony no. 40
(three-measure phrase)

Haydn: "St. Anthony" Chorale
(five-measure phrase)

Wagner: *Die Meistersinger* Overture
(six-measure phrase)

Beethoven: Sonata, op. 106
(seven-measure phrase)

Identifying a phrase by counting the number of measures is unsatisfactory for other reasons; it evades a closer analysis of the music and may lead to a misconception or a superficial understanding of its structure and design. Only an intuitive understanding or perceptive analysis will clarify the form of a piece and make it come alive in meaningful performance.

On the basis of the preceding discussion and examples, we may describe the phrase as the smallest *complete* musical thought. (The motive is smaller, but too fragmentary, not complete.) The phrase is complete and self-contained in the sense that it has a beginning, a distinctive melodic contour or trajectory with one or two climactic points, and an ending in some form of cadence. Cadences vary a great deal, from a perfect cadence to a subtle breath pause. The key to good phrasing is the ability to evaluate their various degrees of conclusiveness and to identify properly the form segments which they terminate.

On occasion it is quite difficult to determine whether a given cadence ends a phrase or is only a halfway mark within the phrase. Such a halfway mark is characteristic of phrases in which the melodic line is divided into two segments, two *half phrases*. The two halves, which may or may not be motivically related, are usually separated by a cadencelike inflection, or slight *cesura*, observable in the following examples:

Schumann: Little Piece, op. 68 no. 5

To summarize the characteristic traits of the phrase:

- It is a brief but complete musical thought with a distinctive melodic contour, ending in some sort of a cadence
- It is usually between two and ten measures long
- It usually divides into two half phrases and/or several smaller component parts (motives)
- The cadence ending the phrase may vary in intensity, but it is seldom a *perfect* one, with emphatic conclusivity; more often it is a *half cadence*, with a *dominant* harmonic function, which invites a continuation, usually the repetition of the phrase
- In most cases the phrase is repeated at once, with or without changes, to form a sentence

SENTENCE-PERIOD

Here are a few simple musical sentences, consisting of two related, symmetrically balanced phrases, sometimes referred to as "question and answer" or "thesis-antithesis":

Franck: "Puppet's Complaint"

The two phrases of a sentence need not be motivically related:

Nor must the two phrases be of equal length:

Bartók: Hungarian Dance

Sentences may also consist of more than two phrases:

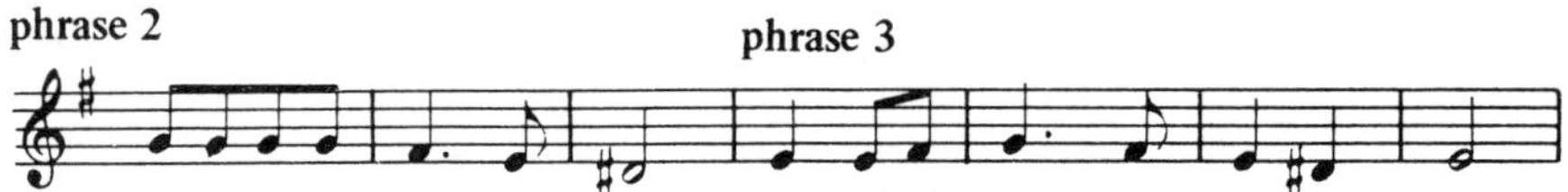

An important exception to the interlocking motive-phrase-sentence hierarchy of musical architecture is the type of sentence which does not divide into phrases. This may happen for one of two reasons. Either the tight continuity of melodic flow does not provide sufficiently pronounced intermediate cadences for phrase endings

Beethoven: Sonata, op. 2 no. 1

or there are intermediate cadences, but they delineate motives rather than phrases.

Beethoven: Sonata, op. 31 no. 3

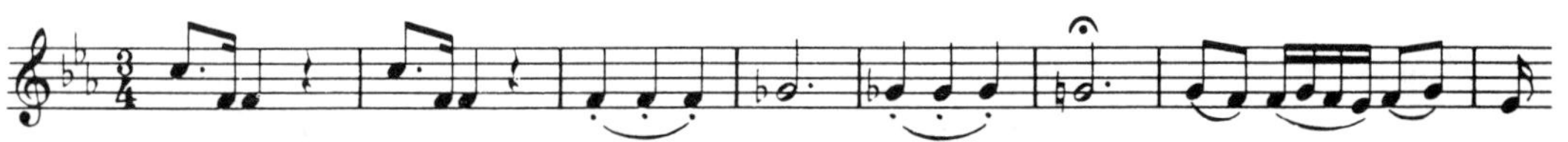

(See also Beethoven's Sonata, op. 14 no. 2, first eight measures of first movement.)

There are other reasons why the phrase-sentence relationship is not always obvious even in the simplest forms and can be determined only by careful analysis:

Bach: Minuet from *Little Notebook for Anna Magdalena Bach*

In the above example, the first eight measures seem to constitute a phrase (they end in a half cadence and are instantly repeated). Closer scrutiny will reveal, however, that these eight measures somehow lack a phrase's characteristic cohesion, and divide rather easily into at least three phraselike segments (measures 1–2, 3–4, and 5–8). It is then better to consider these eight measures a sentence, even though they end in a half cadence and are instantly repeated, ending in a perfect cadence in measure 16. Such a compound sentence may be called a *period*. Two (or more) phrases form a sentence, and two related sentences (the first ending in a half cadence, the second in a perfect cadence) can be designated a period. (This definition, chosen for its relative simplicity and logic, may be at variance with definitions found in other sources.) Other examples include Mozart's Sonata, K. Anh. 135 (547A), first movement, 16 measures; Schubert's Sonata, op. 120, second movement, 15 measures; and Brahms' Symphony no. 3, second movement, 24 measures.

NOTATIONAL INADEQUACIES

The numerous ways in which the phrase and other form elements may interlock to build a musical structure is not the only reason why the analysis of musical forms may be difficult and open to various interpretations. Compounding the ambiguity is our deplorably inadequate notation system, which not only fails to provide a clear, generally valid phrasing mark, but also completely lacks the necessary symbols to notate nuances of musical punctuation. In written music we do not have the equivalents of commas, periods, question and exclamation marks, colons, and semicolons. Throughout history, various composers have made valiant efforts to invent signs and symbols by which the divisions of the musical line could be indicated. Short vertical lines, commas, and brackets above the staff have been tried and are still occasionally used by composers and editors, but none of them has gained general acceptance.

The slur, the only generally accepted sign to indicate a phrase, can not be consistently relied upon, as its main use is to indicate a legato touch and as such is a sign of articulation, often within the phrase. Also, it has been used in past periods in a different manner; for instance, many of the slurs of Mozart, Beethoven, Schubert and their contemporaries were drawn from bar line to bar line, even when a more continuous, extended legato segment was intended:

Schubert: Sonata, op. posth.

This idiosyncratic use of the slur (which Beethoven recognized as such, while deploring "the tyranny of the bar line") is the result of a still prevalent misconception of the role of the bar line, or more precisely the segmentation of music into measures. Bar lines and measures are only sign posts, means of orientation, and do not have any organic role in musical architecture. They can be likened to longitude and latitude lines on a map; they can help to gauge distances in the horizontal flow of written sound, but they are not elements of the underlying musical landscape. The artifice of music is built of motives, phrases, and sentences, not of measures. Centuries ago–and again today–music was notated without bar lines. These lines came into existence at a certain point in the development of orchestral music to facilitate performance, and were first used in orchestral scores even when they were missing from the individual parts. Once introduced, the bar line became more and more a kind of expression mark, a yardstick in the spatial conception of music and a determiner of certain metric conventions, such as the accents on the first beat of the measure. But music is not a succession of measures, set apart by equidistant beats; rather it is a free flow of tones and tone groups (motives and phrases) which usually transcend bar lines.

Another notation factor which often impedes the proper punctuation of music is the connecting beam of eighth and sixteenth notes ( ). The notes tied together by these beams form a metric unit, but–in most cases–not a form segment. For instance, the original notation of this Bach Fugue in B-flat often induces the player to accentuate the first note in the second and third measures.

Bach: Fugue (*Well-Tempered Clavier*, Book 1)

These accents are entirely misplaced, and could be avoided with the following notation:

Composers from Beethoven on have occasionally employed a clearer notation method by drawing or breaking up the beams according to the motivic pattern.

Beethoven: Sonata, op. 10 no. 3

Brahms: Sonata, op. 5 no. 3

Schumann: Concerto, op. 54

FACILITATING ANALYSIS

The failure of our notation system to provide clear and accurate phrasing marks makes the performer's task a complex one, requiring an approach both analytical and instinctive. First, the nature and relationship of the basic components–motives, phrases, and sentences–must be well grasped. Beyond that, one must develop a sense or instinct to feel the flow of music as a spoken language, with its rise and fall of pitch and variety of inflections and pauses at the punctuation marks. True, musical phrasing–the punctuation of music in performance–is not as simple as phrasing in spoken language, because of the paucity of musical punctuation marks. But music does have its cadences, which according to their intensity and placement can act as commas, periods, and even question and exclamation marks. Only by locating the cadences and evaluating their relative intensity can we give the proper contour and shading to a musical thought.

Especially important is the recognition of those cadences which mark phrase endings. To this end the following suggestions and observations may be helpful:

- Examine the beginning of the phrase and note on what beat of the measure it starts. In most cases the phrase will be repeated (in one form or another) beginning on an identical beat a few measures later; the first phrase ends just preceding this beat.

Bach: Two-part Invention, no. 1

- Because phrases usually end in some sort of a cadence–a slight gap, pause, or breathing point in the flow of music–a phrase will never end on a suspended note or on a passing note; both of these imply a need for resolution, a continuation of the tonal flow, and therefore cannot provide that slight repose which is the essence of phrase endings.

Strauss: "Blue Danube Waltz"

In the above example the two dotted half notes are suspensions, which have to be resolved (here, moved down a step) for a phrase ending.

Beethoven: Écossaise

- This example illustrates that a phrase may end and the next phrase begin on the very same note.
- If the outline of the opening phrase is not entirely clear, it is best to find the first definitive (perfect) cadence, usually at the end of a sentence, and analyze this section by locating the subdivisions of the melodic line and weighing the comparative conclusivity of the cadential inflections separating them. For instance, the question whether the first eight measures of "The Star-Spangled Banner" form one, two, or four phrases may benefit by this type of scrutiny.

The consideration of these eight measures as one phrase may be dismissed on the ground that they lack the necessary cohesion; the modulative perfect cadence in measure 4 especially mitigates against such a conception. The possibility of four two-measure phrases cannot be dismissed, but it does not offer an entirely satisfactory solution either, on the opposite grounds: it fragments and disrupts the melodic continuity, especially in bar 6, where a phrase-ending cesura would be rather tenuous. The remaining option—two phrases, ending respectively in measures 4 and 8—offers the soundest constructional perspective on this melodic line.

- Pedagogues often recommend that the student sing or hum the melodic line, which will instinctively lead to the proper delineation of the phrases and their subdivisions. Indeed, this may help in many cases, especially if the student has a sensitive ear for music. A less gifted student, however, will very often divide the melody according to his breath supply rather than the phrase structure.
- Phrasing is both an instinctive and analytical process. Both aspects must be cultivated, and a systematic teaching of form analysis, beginning on the earliest grade levels, should be an integral part of the curriculum.

The joint role of instinct and analysis is well formulated by Lussy, author of one of the most valuable and definitive works on the subject of phrasing: "We must always find out which tones bring to our ears the sense of 'repose,' which is the basis of the idea of cadence. . . . The wise interpreter exercises his own critical sense, his analytical spirit. . . . In short, logic and common sense must prevail and one must take view of the whole of what precedes and what follows."

RECOMMENDED READING

Fontaine, Paul. *Basic Formal Structures in Music*. New York: Appleton-Century-Crofts, 1967.

Keller, Hermann. *Phrasing and Articulation*. New York: Norton, 1965.

Lemacher, Heinrich and Hermann Schroeder. *Musical Form* (Translated and revised by Robert Kolben). Cologne: Gerig, 1967. Distributed by MCA.

Lussy, Mathis. *Traité de l'Expression Musicale* (1873). English condensation by Maurice Dumesnil: "Musical Expression" in *Handbook for Piano Teachers*. Evanston, Illinois: Summy-Birchard, 1958.

McEwen, John B. *The Principles of Phrasing and Articulation in Music*. London: Augener, 1916.

Newman, William S. "What Is Musical Form? (A Problem in Aesthetics)." In *Understanding Music*. New York: Harper & Row, 1952.

Schoenberg, Arnold. *Models for Beginners in Composition*. New York: G. Schirmer, 1942.

Stein, Erwin. *Form and Performance*. London: Faber, 1962.

Tovey, Donald Francis. *The Forms of Music*. London: Oxford University Press, 1944.

Phrasing and Articulation

DENES AGAY

It is important that a performer know the meaning of these terms, the differences between them, and the way they interrelate. *Phrasing* is the proper delineation (separation) of phrases and phrase segments in the performance of music; it involves the carefully weighed observance of cadences through breath pauses, slight rests between the divisions of the melodic line. It is the equivalent of the observance of punctuation marks in spoken language, which dictate the rise and fall and other inflections of the voice at commas, periods, question marks, and exclamation points. *Articulation* deals with the details of performance within the phrase or phrase segment; it is the manner in which individual tones are connected or separated through various types of touch and accent (*legato, staccato, tenuto, marcato,* etc.). It may be likened to the correct pronunciation of individual words in spoken language.

Our notation system does not provide adequate marks for phrasing. The slur, the only generally used mark, is also the legato sign and, in most cases, indicates legato articulation *within the phrase*:

Schumann: "First Loss," op. 68 no. 16

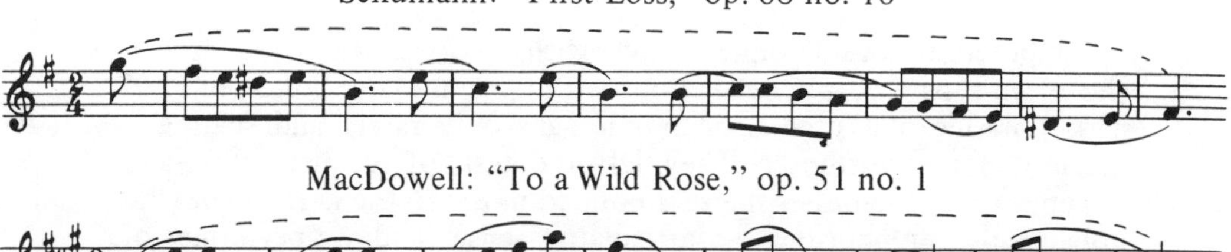

Only where a phrase or semiphrase consists of a continuous legato line is the slur of any value as a phrasing mark; in such cases it also indicates the mode of articulation:

Granados: "Poetic Waltz"

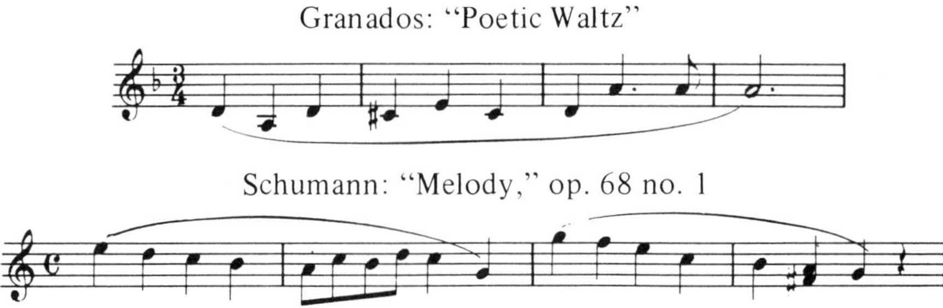

Schumann: "Melody," op. 68 no. 1

The signs of articulation in our notation system are ample and quite explicit. From the time of Mozart and Beethoven, and especially since the romantic period, composers have been giving detailed and reliable notational indications in this area.

Beethoven: Bagatelle, op. 33 no. 6

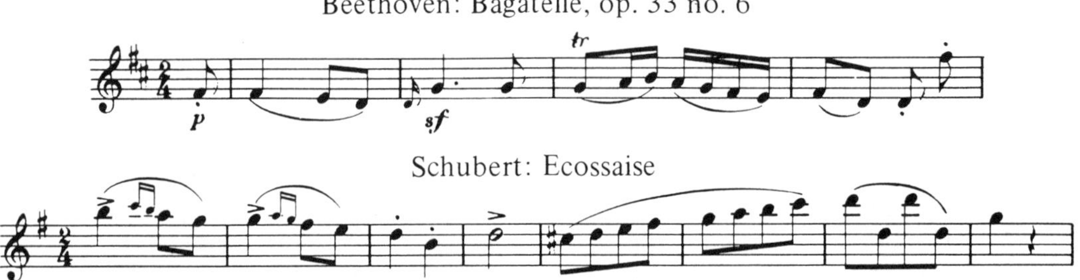

Schubert: Ecossaise

On occasion, both the phrasing structure and the details of articulation are clearly marked:

Brahms: Intermezzo, op. 119 no. 2

Bartók: Folk Song (*Ten Easy Pieces*)

Composers of the baroque period (with the exception of Couperin, who often separated phrase sections with a comma) did not attempt to mark phrasing and used articulation signs only rarely and sparingly, certainly not consistently. They left the task of reconstructing and bringing to life the rather sparsely notated music to the performer, who provided proper phrasing and articulative sense. Today's performer of baroque music has the same task. In so doing, he or she often has numerous options and must choose the articulation pattern best suited to the work's motivic structure and the era's performance practices and conventions.

Examine for instance the first phrase of J.S. Bach's Two-part Invention in C and its various interpretative possibilities:

Bach: Two-part Invention, no. 1

(a) (Urtext notation): Smooth non legato rendition throughout the phrase, with the last note (D) played staccato for proper separation from the next phrase.
(b): One of the extant edited versions which, mistakenly, calls for a mordent on the ornamented note.
(c): Follows the widespread approach of playing sixteenth notes legato and eighth notes staccato.
(d): Possible but somewhat fragmented solution.

Masters of the classical period provided articulation signs quite consistently. However, these marks cannot be accepted at their face value in every instance because of certain contemporary notation habits which may be misinterpreted today. Trying to avoid crossing the bar line with a slur—even when the melodic continuity calls for it—is, for us, one such perplexing notation practice:

Mozart: Sonata, K. 545

Beethoven: Sonata, op. 10 no. 1

In the Mozart, it seems clear that the first two measures form one legato phrase (as do measures three and four) and should not be cut in half, as Mozart's slurs would indicate. Similarly, the natural phrasing in the Beethoven could be better notated by slurs crossing the bar lines, as marked by the dotted lines. It is difficult today to determine the reason for this notation practice. The most plausible explanation is that, in a period when the notation of legato touch in keyboard music was rather new, the masters adopted bowing marks, the legato signs of string music.

Another similar notational oddity in the piano literature of the classical period is the frequent attempt to bridge with slurs the natural cadential gaps between phrases and phrase sections:

Mozart: Sonata, K. 494

Andante

Beethoven: Sonata, op. 13

It is unclear what the masters meant by prescribing such articulation, which doubtless blurs the natural divisions of the melody (indicated by broken lines). Perhaps they presumed that the performer would be aware of the phrase structure, and meant to discourage an exaggerated observation of cadences. In other words, their prime concern may have been the smooth continuity of the extended melody line and the avoidance, even at the risk of some ambiguity, of a fragmented performance. In such cases, today's performer must arrive at a skillful compromise: the natural phrasing structure must be clarified (the contrary notation notwithstanding), but in a subtle manner which also honors the composer's intended goal, the maintenance of a nicely arched long line.

Composers of the nineteenth and twentieth centuries give detailed and, in most cases, entirely precise articulation signs; the phrasing marks, however, have not been nearly as explicit, due mainly to the inherent shortcomings of our notation system.

A clear and meaningful interpretation can result only from an understanding of these two distinct, but simultaneous and interrelated, processes: phrasing and articulation. By phrasing we delineate the long melodic arches of the musical form; by articulation we reproduce the details of design and color within the phrase.

RECOMMENDED READING

Keller, Hermann. *Phrasing and Articulation*. New York: Norton, 1965.

McEwen, John B. *The Principles of Phrasing and Articulation in Music*. London: Augener, 1916.

See also "The Riddle of the Phrase," p. 55.

Fingering

WALTER ROBERT

The anatomic basis of piano fingering is the fact that, in Ernest Newman's words, the pianist's hand consists of a thumb and four fingers.

The musical basis of piano fingering is the fact that piano playing consists of depressing keys successively as well as simultaneously: in other words, playing melodies (of which scales are a special form) and chords.

The ability to use the hands for grasping is one of the chief distinctions between human being and ape. By the development of this ability, based on the opposition of thumb and the other four fingers, human beings have been able to use tools to develop their intelligence, control their surroundings, and think lofty thoughts in abstract terms. However, in terms of developmental psychology, the realization of the fingers as single entities comes comparatively late.

The child is able to make grasping motions very early, but to move fingers individually presents a real problem. Daily life has not habituated the child to use one finger alone; it has not taught that there is a sequence (1-2-3-4-5) by which the fingers should be used, he or she has not learned to discriminate and to decide which finger muscles to activate. The child's joints are flexible and permit any degree of manipulation; a six- to eight-year-old will, for instance, occasionally turn the second finger over the fifth without hesitation, etc. It should not therefore be surprising that piano teachers find it hard to teach "correct"

Reprinted from *Clavier*, February 1973. Used by permission of the Instrumentalist Company.

fingering in the early grades. In fact, there is a certain danger in overemphasizing fingering.

The child who is taught by a method in which every finger is printed or written into the music may rely on the finger numbers alone, without really reading the notes, nor hearing with the inner ear what sounds he or she is going to produce. It is therefore wise to start with an aural approach, to teach note reading next, and to introduce the concept of fingering later, when reading a few notes on the staff at a time is no longer a serious problem.

FINGERINGS IN PRINTED EDITIONS

Composers themselves indicate fingerings only rarely, or not at all, regarding the imposition of their own ideas on a performer as an insult to the pianist's intelligence, as Debussy states in the preface to his Études.

How interesting and how revealing it would be to have Chopin's fingerings, not only for his own compositions, but for the pieces that he assigned to his many students! Even the little that we have of the great masters' fingering indications allows us to gain a deeper insight into their playing style.

Beethoven's few fingerings in his manuscript sketchbooks and first editions have been studied thoroughly by Herbert Grundmann and Paul Mies in their monograph "Studies Concerning the Pianism of Beethoven and his Contemporaries" (H. Bouvier, Bonn, 1966). It seems that Beethoven was strongly influenced in his ideas about fingering, as in all his views on keyboard performance, by Carl Philipp Emanuel Bach.

A study of the principles of fingering by the great masters is still to be written, as far as I know. Such a work would permit deep insights into their playing styles and would contribute in great measure to interpretations.

We are forced then to discover our own principles of fingering, and the best place to start is with the scales.

DIATONIC SCALES

The system of fingering as we know it today was not invented overnight. Couperin, in his *L'Art de toucher le clavecin* of 1716, suggests the following fingering for octave scales,

and for scales with sharps and flats:

J. S. Bach, in his "Notebook for Wilhelm Friedemann" of 1720, prescribes the following *applicatio* (fingering) for the right hand,

and

for the left hand.

J. S. Bach's son, Carl Philipp Emanuel, in his celebrated *Essay on the True Art of Playing Keyboard Instruments*, still gives three fingerings for the C-major scale, ascending and descending, for the right hand, remarking only that he regards the 1 2 3 1 2 3 4 on the whole as the most practical, though in special cases the other fingerings are also usable and practical.

Even as late as 1789, we find in Daniel Gottlob Türk's *"Klavierschule"* the same three choices.

Disregarding minor fanciful deviations, the fingering for major and minor scales is now based the world over on the consideration that we have to play seven consecutive notes, but have only five fingers to do so. Consequently, we "divide" the fingers of a hand into two groups: one of three fingers (1 2 3) and one of four fingers (1 2 3 4). It is time and again surprising to realize how many students are unaware that all diatonic scales have the same fingering.

The only other rule to be observed in fingering diatonic scales is the realization that in playing notes in diatonic sequence, it would be uncomfortable to place the thumb on a black key. The hand's structure places the thumb lower on the keyboard than the other fingers, and the scale fingering must take this into account. The resulting cupped hand makes the passing under of the thumb easy. We therefore shift the 1-2-3–1-2-3-4 grouping away from the tonic, but only when necessary (i.e. when the thumb would fall on a black key); in B-flat major, for instance, we go to the second tone:

C D E-flat	F G A B-flat
1 2 3	1 2 3 4

or we play the 1-2-3-4 group first, as in F major, or we do both, as in E-flat major:

F G A-flat B-flat	C D E-flat
1 2 3 4	1 2 3

In teaching these shifts of the fingering groups, it is best to follow this procedure: have the student play the notes of the scale with one finger, naming the scale tones; do not proceed until he or she is absolutely sure of the tonal material. Then set out to let the student find the most convenient starting point for the 1-2-3—1-2-3-4 grouping by moving his thumb up and away from the tonic. In B-flat the starting point for the 1-2-3 group, as shown above, is the supertonic; in A-flat it is necessary to move up two keys to the mediant.

C	D-flat	E-flat		F	G	A-flat	B-flat
1	2	3		1	2	3	4

in D-flat one again starts with the mediant, but the 1-2-3-4 group has to come first:

F	G-flat	A-flat	B-flat		C	D-flat	E-flat
1	2	3	4		1	2	3

With gifted students one might experiment with an approach to teaching scales not, as customary, by the circle of fifths, but according to the criteria of fingering shifts. Thus, one begins with those scales where the tonic is the basis of the 1-2-3 group; then F major, where the tonic is still the basis of the fingering group, but where the B-flat makes it necessary to have the 1-2-3-4 group first; then scales where the supertonic is the first tone of the 1-2-3 group, e.g., B-flat; and so on, until the really "difficult" scales, like D-flat are reached. (See above.)

In teaching the fingering for the left hand, the same approach is recommended, keeping in mind that the left is the mirror of the right; consequently, the student must first be able to play the left-hand scale faultlessly in descending motion, with one finger only. Then the same rule prevails: the fingering for all diatonic scales, major and minor, is the same. The beginning of the fingering groups is shifted down from the tonic where necessary, and/or the four finger group may have to come first; for example, B-flat:

A	G	F	E-flat		D	C	B-flat
1	2	3	4		1	2	3

The usual system of teaching, which consists of telling the student with which finger to start the scale, does not easily convey the universal validity of the 1-2-3—1-2-3-4 fingering, and leads to the notion that C major is easy, B-flat is hard, and E-flat "impossible."

Ask any student why piano teachers are so concerned about the place of the fourth finger in the scale. Nine times out of ten the student will not know; the simple answer is that the fourth finger occurs only once in each octave and it is therefore easier to memorize its position rather than the position of 1, 2, or 3, which all occur twice.

Another unorthodox recommendation: do not permit the student in the first stages to conclude the one-octave scale with the fifth finger, but insist on one more passing under of the thumb (1 2 3 1 2 3 4 1), to reinforce the awareness of the universal validity of the fingering principle for diatonic scales.

In general, I am opposed to merely mechanical adaptations to novel situations. However, for a first acquaintance with harmonic minor, such a mechanical approach has proved advantageous. Instead of going into long theoretical explanations regarding the interval relations in minor and talking about the raised leading tone with its accidental, the relation of C major and A minor, and the augmented step from 6 to 7, I recommend the following "dumb" procedure. Have the student place both hands (silently) simultaneously on the keyboard, in tone-cluster fashion:

left hand:	C B A	right hand:	C D E
	1 2 3		1 2 3

This accomplished, have the student raise both third fingers and place them on the black keys a half tone below (A-flat, E-flat), then play the cluster:

left hand:	G F E D	right hand:	F G A B
	1 2 3 4		1 2 3 4

Then have the student lower the fingers to E-flat and A-flat respectively. Very soon the tonal material of the harmonic minor scale will be established without long-winded explanations; the correct fingerings should be found exactly as for the major scales.

The descriptions of these approaches sound complicated on paper; in practice they are easily communicated and understood.

OTHER SCALES

No matter how one may think about the music of the twentieth century, is it not about time that piano teachers recognized the incontrovertible fact that the diatonic scale has lost its hegemony over the realm of melody?

Since Debussy at least—that is, for more than three-quarters of a century—the whole-tone scale has become a full-fledged partner of major and minor; rumor has it that the chromatic scale occurs here and there and that even the playing of certain passages in Mozart and Beethoven would benefit if piano teachers would not concentrate exclusively on major and minor scales, if they teach scales at all. The two whole-tone scales are fingered as follows:

that is, the six tones of the scale are played by a group of four plus a group of two fingers.

The chromatic scale with its twelve tones presents problems that can be solved by three basic fingerings:

Fingering (a) is closely related to the principle of diatonic scales; fingering (b), the easiest to learn, avoids the fourth finger, and all the student need remember is that the sequence 1 3 1 3 is altered to 1 2 where the adjacent white keys B-C and E-F make this necessary.

Fingering (c) is the most unorthodox, but permits the fastest "rolling along" and solves the problem of how to play the murderous chromatic runs in the first movement of Beethoven's Sonata in E-flat major for Piano and Violin, op. 12 no.3, to cite only one example.

The rules for the fingering of diatonic double thirds are analogous to the principles enumerated for the single note scales. Of primary concern are the "outer" fingers, that is, the upper notes of the double-third scale in the right hand and the lower notes in the left hand.

The grouping is again into two units: 3 4 5 and 2 3 4 5:

This fingering is valid for the scales starting on C, D, E, G, and A. For the other scales we have to turn the groups around (2 3 4 5 3 4 5); for instance, the right hand in F major

and the left hand in B-flat major.

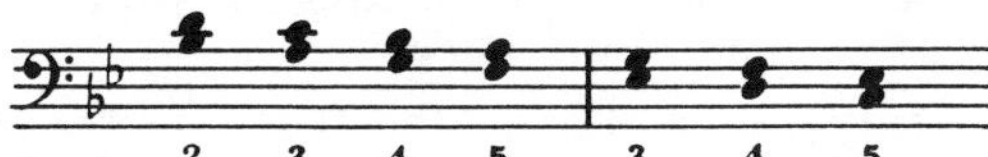

In scales starting on black keys we shift the beginning of the fingering group away from the tonic; for instance the right hand in E-flat major:

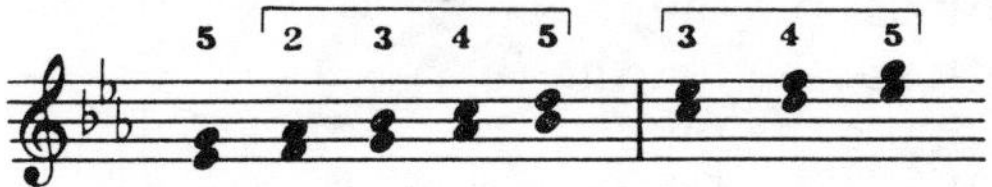

This procedure is analogous to the shift of groups in the single-note scales, as described above.

For advanced players there is also the option to divide the 2-3-4-5 group into two 3-4 groups; for example:

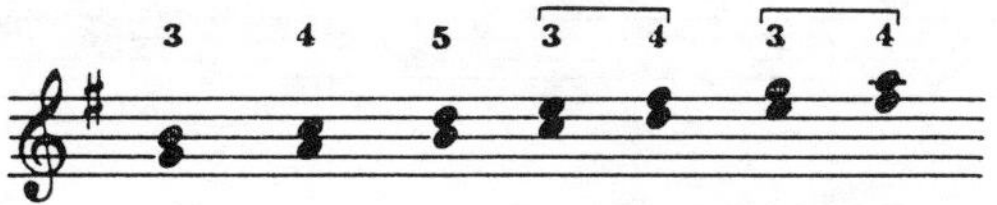

This avoids the bothersome "vaulting" of the second finger over the fifth and thereby permits a smoother and faster semi-legato.

CHORD FINGERINGS

The other pillar of piano fingering is the chord, sounded simultaneously or in broken form. The fingering of chord patterns is not as ironclad as the fingering of scale patterns. It is relatively unimportant which fingering is used in the following examples.

A definite rule, though, can be stated for four-part major tonic triads and inversions, when both hands play together:

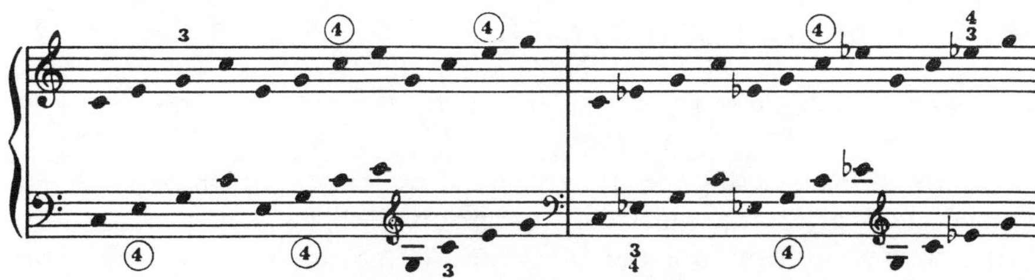

- In the root position (I), left uses the fourth finger.

- In the first inversion (I^6), both use the fourth finger.
- In the second inversion (I^6_4), right uses the fourth finger.

In minor, the only rule is that in the first inversion (I^6), both hands use the fourth.

For four-part dominant seventh chords, broken or in chord form, the best (though not inviolable) fingering principle is:

- In V^7, both use the third.
- In V^6_5, both use the fourth.
- In V^4_3, both use the third.
- In V^2, both use the fourth.

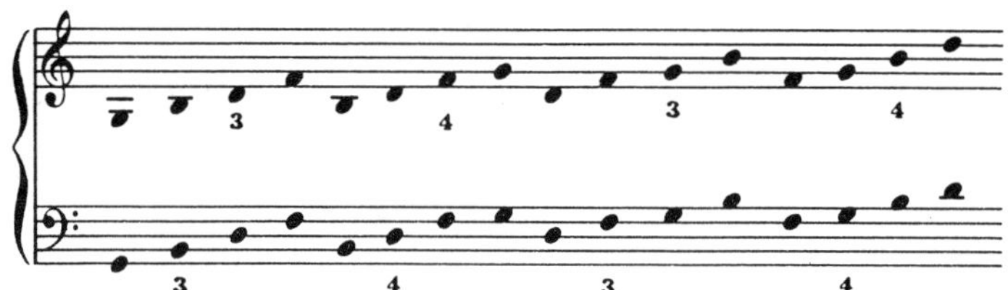

It is unfortunate that the study of chords and inversions, especially in broken form, is often neglected in piano teaching. The classics are full of all sorts of chord breaks, while long arpeggios and scales appear relatively rarely.

ARPEGGIOS

The rule for triad arpeggios starting on white keys is that both hands use the fourth in the first inversion.

Root position and second inversion (I and I^6_4) fingerings can be considered optional, with the following preferences:

Root position: 1 2 3 (right hand)
5 4 2 (left hand)
Second inversion: 1 2 4 (right hand)
5 3 2 (left hand)

In arpeggios starting on the black keys, the right thumb comes immediately after the black key or group of black keys; in the left hand, immediately before the black key or group of black keys. For instance:

This rule is also based on the desire to keep the hand cupped as much as possible.

In dominant seventh arpeggios, the advantage of the cupped hand, which was the reason for much of the above-described practices, is offset by the tendency to avoid a spread between the third and fourth fingers; it is therefore more comfortable to play

rather than

The latter would correspond to the rule of "right thumb immediately after, left thumb immediately before the black key." However, in arpeggios of this type much depends on the opening and closing note, on the tempo, and on the accentuation.

A supreme rule for all arpeggios and arpeggio-like figurations in the context of a composition is: determine the finger for the bottom and the top notes and adjust the fingering for the tones in between accordingly; if desirable, forget about the above-stated rules for arpeggios, which are valid only *in abstracto.*

It cannot be emphasized strongly enough that only an almost automatic response to scale and chord patterns will enable a piano student to use sensible fingerings. "Knowing" the scale finger is not enough; the student must respond instinctively to scale and chord patterns as they appear in the music.

Admittedly, the mastery of scales and arpeggio fingerings is not the most thrilling part of learning to play the piano. The teacher who uses manuals like Herz's *Gammes*; the teacher who drills the student in some mechanical memorizing of "B-flat, E-flat, start with the third finger in both hands; D-flat, G-flat, start with the second in the right"; and the teacher who emphasizes the number of sharps and flats in scales will almost invariably kill what little joy there is in this phase of piano study. The ear must guide the beginning student to find the tonal material of each scale, insight into the principle of fingering must enable him or her to discover the fingering, and skill must make playing the scales and arpeggios automatic.

So far we have considered only the more cut-and-dried aspect of fingering. In fingering scale passages there is usually little choice, even in the context of compositions. Arpeggios and broken chords offer scarcely more than two, at most three, possibilities for sensible fingering. If that were all there is to the problem of fingering, it would be a most dreary chapter of pedagogy.

FINGERING NONTECHNICAL PASSAGES

The problem is much broader, however. Let us take an example at random:

Chopin: Nocturne, op. 9 no. 2

This melody may be fingered

1 5 4543 1 5 or 1 4 3432 1 4 or 1 3 2321 1 3 or
253 23232 25

"It makes no difference," so to say, which of these fingerings is preferred, or does it?

It does, if we regard piano playing as more than pushing down the right keys at the right time. As soon as we take touch, tone color, intensity, curve—in a word, artistic qualities—into consideration, the choice of fingering becomes of paramount importance.

Two schools of piano playing stand in opposition to each other: the school of Czerny, with its idea of equalizing the fingers and using "comfortable" fingerings; and the school of Carl Philipp Emanuel Bach and Chopin, who recognized that there are good and bad fingers.

The Czerny school claims that all fingers can be made to serve equally well and to sound alike. Fingering should therefore use the fingers in their natural order of 1 2 3 4 5 as much as possible: this is regarded as the most "comfortable" fingering.

The other school recognizes the anatomic differences among our fingers and says: let us use the good fingers at least for the most prominent tones of a melody, and arrange the fingerings for the other tones accordingly. There are enough passages where there is no choice anyway, and that is where Czerny's equalized fingers come in.

All the drills to which we subject our students to equalize their fingers (Schmitt, Hanon, Joseffy, Taussig, Czerny, Clementi, etc.) cannot change the anatomically and physiologically conditioned fact that some fingers are naturally more adept at playing the piano than others. No amount of five-finger drill will change the circumstance that the thumb has two phalanges, the other fingers three; that the fourth finger is not activated independently, but "wiggles" together with the third; that the fifth is shorter than the second, third, and fourth fingers; and, perhaps most important, that the second and third are more fleshy at the tip than the fourth and fifth.

Hanon et al. may and do enable us to play five-finger patterns with even rhythm and dynamics and in controlled fashion. Nobody in his right sense implies that five-finger exercises can be dispensed with. But when our aim is not speed and mechanical control, but artistry that breathes life into a melody, then anatomical and physiological facts need to be taken into consideration.

Of course it is not impossible to play that Chopin phrase with almost any fingering, even to play it beautifully with almost any fingering. A good inner ear will overcome obstacles of a material nature, for in piano playing we have to rely on this ability of the spirit to overcome awkward fingerings. There are innumerable cases where we have no choice but to "crawl around," use the fifth finger three times in a row, or leap two octaves and yet "make" as if we were playing legato, with beautiful tone and noble dynamic curve; for example, in this Chopin Waltz:

Chopin: Waltz, op. 42

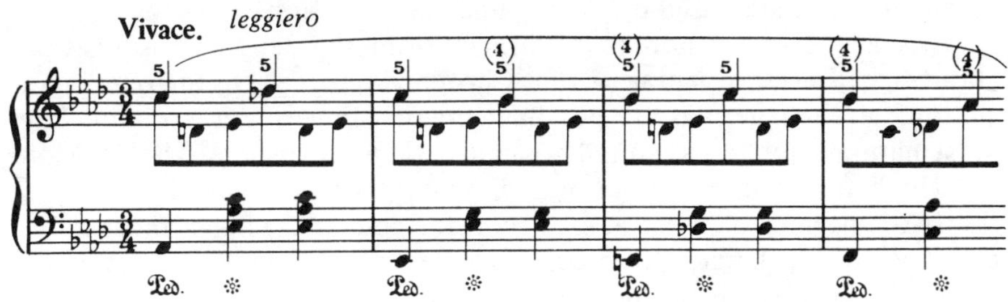

In practically all polyphonic music we have to fight battles of "spiritual legato" versus the material impossibility of playing three melodic lines in one hand with only five fingers. The question is only: is it economic to use that 2-5, etc., fingering for the Chopin Nocturne and thus compensate for the nature-given shortcomings of the fifth and fourth fingers; or by using "good" fingers on the prominent tones, do we better achieve artistic qualities?

The third finger is in the center of the hand; it is therefore capable of transmitting any impulse, whether pressure or stroke, directly to the key without loss of energy; it is also, fortunately, the best-bolstered finger with the broadest tip. Only the fleshy part needs to come into contact with the key; secondary noises like the clicking of the nail on the ivory can be avoided and the key descent can be so controlled that the dynamic level (and with it the desired overtones) can be more easily calculated than with the other fingers.

The fourth finger, being dependent on the third, is much less favored by nature; however, it is a moderately good melody finger, if the hand can be tilted outside so that the second and third fingers rest lightly on it and reinforce it. This is perfectly possible in melodic, homophonic playing if a freely undulating wrist governs the motions of the playing apparatus. Only where the fourth finger has to act under its own power, as in fast five-finger exercises or in polyphonic textures requiring "independence" of the third and fourth, is it a weak finger.

To some extent, it is unfortunate that the fifth finger is called upon to play so much of our melodic lines. It is a short bony extremity; only when it touches the key, not with the tip, but more with the phalanx on the lateral side, can the hand rest lightly on it and give it weight; but it does not have a fleshy cushion like the third finger, so that it is always in danger of making the tone sound percussive.

In many ways, the thumb is really the best melody finger. I believe this is borne out by the phenomenon that we have a sizable number of compositions for the left hand alone, and none, to my knowledge, for the right. In compositions for one hand alone the top voice can be easily manipulated by the left thumb, but could not be handled successfully by the fifth finger of the right hand. The thumb melodies of Schumann and Liszt are based on these same considerations.

What is the conclusion to be drawn from this lengthy disquisition about fingering the opening of that Chopin Nocturne? On the one hand, all four given fingerings are possible; the first fingering is probably the most natural, but is less suited to an artistic performance. The decision on which fingering to use in melodic passages will always be between the two extremes of what is most comfortable and what is most musical. The so-called natural or comfortable fingering will in many cases need a lot of control by the inner ear in order to result in musical playing; the musical fingering will "look" and feel unorthodox at first blush. The final decision will depend on the taste and skill of the player. What is important is awareness, in this as in all things in music. To quote Carl Philipp Emanuel Bach again: "The true method [of fingering], almost a secret art, has been known and practiced by very few. This erring is the more considerable, the less one is aware of it, for at the keyboard almost anything can be expressed even with the wrong fingering, although with prodigious difficulty and awkwardness."

USING UNORTHODOX SCALE FINGERING

Although scales and chords provide the foundation for all piano fingering, there are cases where slavish adherence to scale- and chord-fingering habits thwarts more than it helps. Let me illustrate with an analogy. There is a nice British definition of a gentleman: A gentleman is somebody who knows when he behaves badly. By analogy, one might say that a pianist is a musician who knows when he or she fingers in an unorthodox manner.

One case in point is the use of the thumb on black keys. Because the thumb is used in scales only on the white keys, some pianists have the strange impression that it should not be used on black keys at all. Most students will go to great lengths to avoid using the thumb on black keys. This is silly, for no chord of four (or more) voices built on a black key can be played without using the thumb; since we use the thumb freely in playing chords, why not also use it on black keys in melodic sequences? It is true that the cupped hand is preferable in melodic sequences as well as in scales, but only if other considerations do not prevail.

The necessities of voice leading in polyphonic music and the desirability of using "good" fingers on prominent melody notes whould prevail over the reluctance of using the thumb on a black key.

Another case where we may "break the law" in melodic playing occurs when it seems desirable to return to the eighteenth-century tradition of crossing the third finger over the fourth or the fourth over the fifth. This was a conscious device of Chopin; his Étude in A minor is based on the principle of passing any finger over any other finger. The very first few notes,

show that it is not only defensible, but absolutely necessary to pass the third finger over the fifth: A–B-flat–B-natural–C with 5 3 4 5, then 3 4 3 4 for C-sharp–D–D-sharp–E etc. This so-called Chopin fingering (for which he bothered to write a special étude) should and could be adopted most widely; it is very often the solution for achieving a legato which otherwise can be only approximated by clever use of the pedal and other "optical illusions"! To give only one example: the beginning of the scherzo of Beethoven's Sonata, op. 26 can of course be played with all sorts of fingerings.

The best solution, it seems to me, though, would be to start boldly with the right thumb on the A-flat and play $13\underset{2}{5}3\underset{1}{4}$, which gives perfectly good legato melody line. Or, if this isn't convenient, to start with $23\underset{2}{5}4\underset{1}{5}$ or $23\underset{2}{5}3\underset{1}{4}$. This kind of fingering, crossing over one finger on top of the other, is also particularly appropriate for melodic basses:

Brahms: op. 117 no. 3

Sequences are most easily mastered by using the same fingering on each recurrence of the pattern, rather than by shifting from one fingering to another in order to avoid using the thumb on black keys.

Beethoven: Sonata, op. 22
(third movement)

Another form of 1-2-3-1-2-3-4 "compulsion" prevents students from "leaving out a finger," and would keep them from finding the following desirable fingering:

Beethoven: Sonata, op. 53 ("Waldstein")

Some trills can be better controlled by using 1-3 rather than the orthodox 1-2.

Deviation from the pattern of scale fingerings would be at least defensible where a passage ends on the fifth finger and then either is followed by a rest or turns back upon itself. In many cases, it would be better, I believe, not to play "to the bitter end" with a sequence 1-2-3-4-5, but to turn under once more, as in the following examples:

Beethoven: Sonata, op. 49 no. 2
(first movement)

Beethoven: Sonata, op. 57
(last movement)

Turning under of the thumb does not take time and should not be a handicap. The weak fourth finger might easily come too soon on the accented note, and the thumb is a "good" finger.

Much harm is done by overloading beginners' books with sometimes questionable, sometimes unnecessary, in most cases at any rate stifling, fingering indications. The beginning child will rather read the printed fingering than the notes, especially as long as the piece remains in the five-finger compass. Upon further progress, we will find the conscientious student following the printed indications slavishly, without developing any flair for finding individual solutions; the talented student as well as the "sloppy" learner will not pay any attention to the fingerings anyway.

An entire book could be written about the fingerings found in the editions of the classics. A small but promising beginning was made by Rudolph Ganz, in his addition to Ernest Hutcheson's *The Literature of the Piano.* Ganz torpedoed one of the worst cases of nineteenth-century ballast in many widely used current editions, namely the silly and obsolete finger-change indications wherever repeated tones occur.

The choice of fingering is perhaps not as crucial on the piano as on the cello or the violin. On these instruments, the fingering has a decisive influence on the timbre and the entire musical concept. But it is nevertheless true that on the piano, too, good fingering is of paramount musical importance. A professor at the Paris Conservatoire, Yves Nat, put it most succinctly by saying, *"le doigté parle"*: "fingering speaks."

RECOMMENDED READING

Bergenfeld, Nathan. "Topographical Fingering: An Introduction." *The Piano Quarterly* Spring 1974.

Ferguson, Howard. *Keyboard Interpretation.* New York: Oxford University Press, 1975.

Fielden, Thomas. *The Science of Pianoforte Technic.* London: The Macmillan Company, 1934.

Gât, József. *The Technique of Piano Playing.* London: Collet's Holdings, Ltd. 1965.

Last, Joan. *The Young Pianist: A New Approach for Teachers and Students.* London: Oxford University Press, 1954.

Matthay, Tobias. *The Principles of Fingering and Laws of Pedalling.* London: Bosworth, 1908.

Musafia, Julien. *The Art of Fingering in Piano Playing.* New York: MCA Music, 1971.

Newman, William S. *The Pianist's Problems.* New York: Harper & Row, 1950.

Ortmann, Otto. *The Physiological Mechanics of Piano Technique.* New York: E. P. Dutton, 1929.

Runge, Nancy. "Relationship of Fingering to the Development of Basic Piano Technic and Musicianship." *American Music Teacher* January 1971.

Schauffler, Lawrence. *Piano Technic: Myth or Science.* Chicago: Gamble Hinged Music Company, 1937.

Slenczynska, Ruth. *Music at Your Fingertips* (rev. ed.). New York: Cornerstone Library, 1968.

Pedaling Technique

JOSEPH BANOWETZ

The pedal, in Anton Rubinstein's often-quoted words, is "the soul of the piano," and it is safe to say that every accomplished pianist must be in complete command of pedaling technique. Yet, aside from a few broad rules that often do as much harm as good when applied in an unsophisticated manner, the teaching of pedaling is still largely neglected, misunderstood, and an area too often left to the student's intuition and guesswork. Any discussion of pedaling should include the use of all three pedals found on most grand pianos: the damper pedal or sustaining pedal, sometimes misleadingly termed the *forte* or loud pedal, on the right; the *sostenuto* pedal, in the middle; and the soft pedal (French *sourdine* or *petite pêdale*, German *Mit Verschiebung*, Italian *una corda*), on the left.

THE DAMPER PEDAL

Although the damper pedal was already in use on the newly invented pianoforte by the fourth quarter of the eighteenth century, there are no examples of written indications for its use in any of Mozart's keyboard works, and only two such marks by Haydn, both in the first movement of his Sonata in C major, Hob. XVI/50 of around 1795. Clementi and Beethoven give some pedaling indications, but it is only well into the second quarter of the nineteenth century that such directions become fairly common, although still by no means complete, exact, or systematic. The romantic period has been termed the era of the sustaining pedal, for every composer of this period heavily exploited its possibilities. Works of such twentieth-century composers as Debussy, Ravel,

Rachmaninoff, and Prokofiev are inconceivable in performance without almost constant use of the damper pedal, even though these composers rarely indicate specific pedaling. Many of today's avant-garde composers continue to demand full and imaginative use of all pedals.

The damper pedal has several functions: to sustain and connect tones; to color tones by allowing sympathetic vibrations of overtones when surrounding dampers are raised from the strings; and to create crescendo and decrescendo effects. All of these functions demand from the performer an acutely perceptive ear and a delicate control of the foot. As a general rule, the ball of the foot should never leave the surface of the pedal, while the heel is kept firmly on the floor. Each grand piano's damper pedal has a slightly different "area of effectiveness"; on some instruments the slightest pressure will begin to lift the dampers from the strings, while on others there will be a good amount of free play as the pedal is initially depressed. Once the dampers are fully raised from the surface of the strings, the pedal does not have to be depressed further. There is never an excuse for allowing the pedal to hit as it is released or for slapping it with the foot as it is depressed, even in the white heat of a concert performance, for the resulting annoying thump will be heard throughout a recital hall.

Written marks for the sustaining pedal were indicated throughout the nineteenth century by the rather inexact and bulky *Ped.* and *. The composer usually placed these signs in a haphazard manner, and they were carelessly engraved by the publisher. The contemporary notation given below is more precise and will be used for the musical examples given in the following discussion.

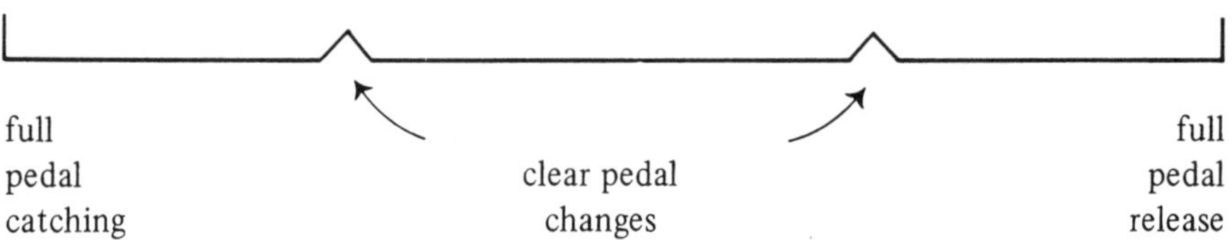

LEGATO PEDALING

The most important technique to master when first using the sustaining pedal is achieving a smooth legato through use of so-called *legato pedaling*. After the pedal catches the first chord, the pedal is raised and then again depressed at the instant the keys sound each new change of harmony. During the time the dampers rest on the strings, the hands must carefully hold down all the notes to be caught with each pedal change.

Chopin: Fantasy, op. 49

The dynamic level in the above example is *piano* and the writing fairly high in register. But when a louder dynamic level is used while playing in a low register, it may be necessary during each pedal change to let the dampers rest on the strings for a split second longer, to stop fully the ringing from each preceding harmony. As before, the hands must remain on the keys during the time the dampers remain on the strings. This delayed manner of changing the pedal is much overlooked even by experienced performers.

Chopin: Sonata no. 2, op. 35
(first movement)

Problems arise in using delayed pedal changes when the hands must immediately move to another position (as in the following example, where the left hand must cross over the right on the second and third beats). Pedaling clarity can still be achieved if the pedal is lifted a split second before the new harmony is sounded. When carefully controlled, this anticipatory changing of the pedal begins to clear out the old harmony, yet does not let the listener perceive an actual gap in the sound. The inaudible breaks in this example not only insure clear pedal changes, but also help give a strong pulse to each downbeat:

Brahms: Rhapsody, op. 79 no. 2

Some passages, as in the following example, call for an atmospheric legatissimo, with the pedal being lifted and then redepressed a split second following the sounding of each new harmony. (The *una corda* indication is Brahms' own.)

Brahms: Intermezzo, op. 118 no. 2

In the following example, the change of pedal with each different harmony should come as the left thumb is played. Lift the pedal somewhat slowly to enhance the desired blending of tones. This type of overlapping pedaling minimizes a break in the melody, while allowing enough time for a reasonably safe crossing over of the left hand. The left fifth finger should always be held until the pedal is changed simultaneously with the thumb.

Franck: Prelude, Chorale and Fugue

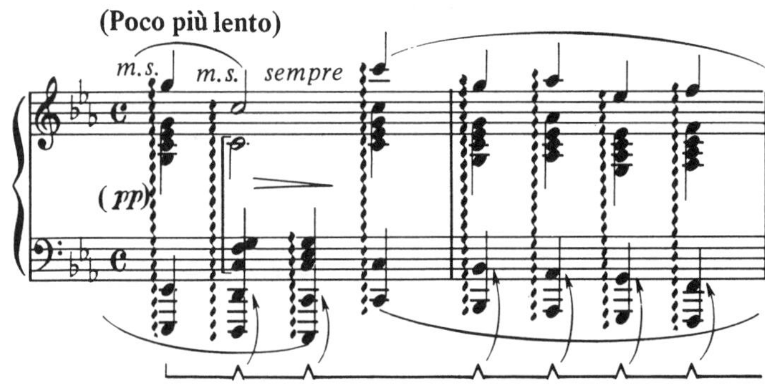

A staccato touch may be indicated in one hand, and in the other a legato that seems to demand the aid of the pedal both for connection and color. This effect in the following example can be achieved by pedaling immediately after the short pizzicato-like tones in the left hand.

Beethoven: Sonata, op. 7
(second movement)

(Largo, con gran espressione)

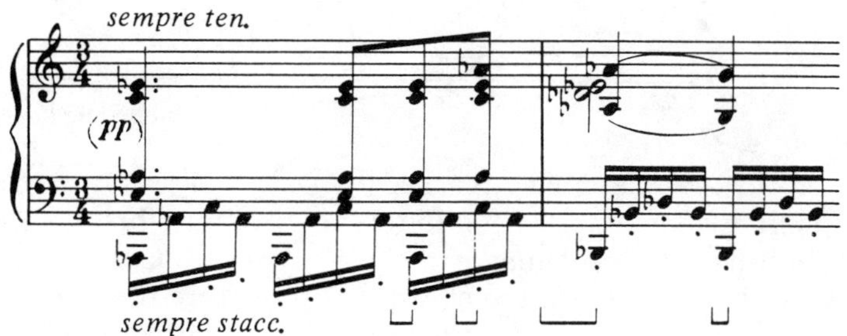

A rapid release of the pedal may be demanded at a staccato that follows a legato use of pedal. Such releases should abruptly coincide with the staccato, without letting the pedal hit as it is raised. Although Brahms gives no tempo indication for this work, a *vivace* would not be out of character.

Brahms: Waltz, op. 39 no. 13

It may be necessary to change the pedal only partially in order to hold a portion of the preceding harmony. This is common in the music of Debussy and Ravel, where often a low bass harmony must be, to some extent, retained to support changing higher harmonies. In the following example, let the dampers lightly slap the strings for a brief instant at each of the following partial pedal changes, then immediately redepress the pedal. The low bass A should still be plainly heard, while most of the preceding harmonies in the right hand are filtered out. Experimentation, practice, and, above all, careful listening by the player will quickly refine this at first somewhat difficult pedaling technique.

Debussy: *L'Isle joyeuse*

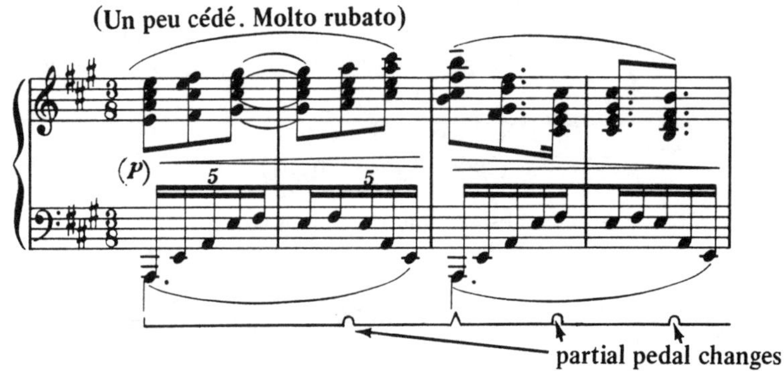

Large chords that cannot be reached by stretching may present pedaling difficulties. The most common type of chord breaking occurs when the left-hand span demands a ninth or more. Customarily, the left hand will begin to break the chord slightly before the beat, and the right-hand melody note will be played on the beat with the highest note of the left-hand chord. But if the pedal is changed on each new right-hand melody note in a normal legato manner, one or more of the low bass notes will inevitably fail to be caught with the pedal. This gap in the bass will be extremely disturbing in slow, sustained passages. It is far better to catch each of the lowest bass notes in the new pedal, while allowing the right hand to have a small break in the legato of the melody by raising the finger a split second before each new pedal change.

Schumann: "*Preambule*," *Carnaval*, op. 9

Another practical solution is to start each left-hand rolled chord on, not before, the beat, and to play the upper notes of the left hand rather softly, in order not to call further attention to the roll. This approach sounds especially well in slower, more lyrical pieces.

Chopin: Nocturne, op. 48 no. 1

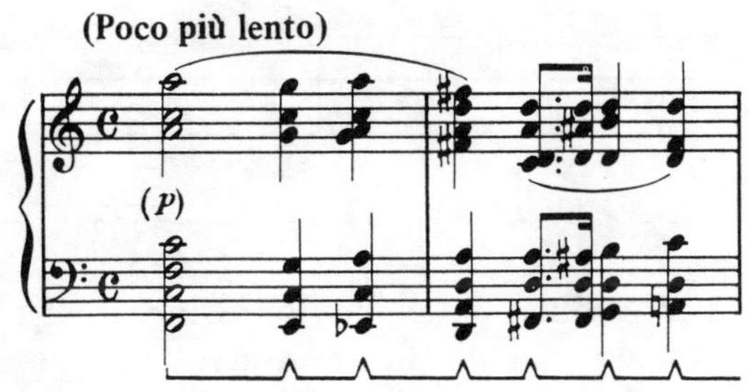

PEDALING FOR COLOR AND SONORITY

When normal legato pedaling is used, the pedal is redepressed a fraction of a second after each new harmony is sounded. But by doing this, the pianist, of necessity, robs the sound of its greatest intensity, when the rich bloom of overtones occurs at the moment of hammer impact if the surrounding dampers are raised. There are many instances when a note or chord is played following a silence. In these situations it is desirable to depress the pedal before playing–anticipated pedaling–to give the tone both its fullest possible richness and truest color.

Beethoven: Concerto no. 4, op. 58
(first movement)

The ingrained habit of always changing the pedal on a downbeat may also rob the performer of the full resonance of overtones.

Brahms: Sonata no. 3, op. 5
(fourth movement)

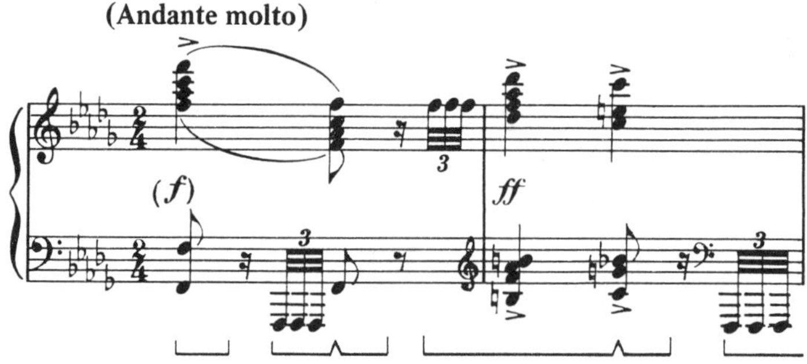

When there is a strong burst of sound following an extremely quiet passage, a change of pedal may not be necessary.

Chopin: Fantasy, op. 49

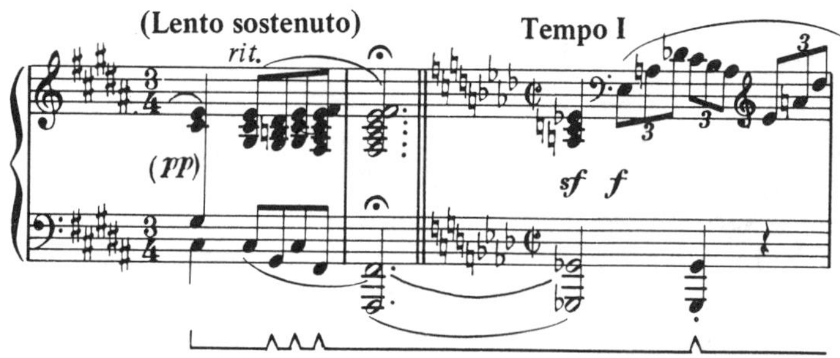

Conversely, it may be necessary to release the pedal early when going to a soft passage which follows a loud dynamic area.

Beethoven: Sonata, op. 57
(third movement)

It may be desirable even when playing staccato chords to use early pedaling for full richness of tone. The pedal must immediately be lifted as the staccato is played.

Beethoven: Sonata, op. 81a "*Les Adieux*"
(first movement)

Strong, short chords may be enriched with a rapid touch of pedal.

Mendelssohn: Rondo Capriccioso, op. 14

The pedal may also serve to color accented chords. In the following example, the pedal should always be released on the rest following each sforzando chord, to avoid creating the sound of a slur extending to the following chord. The metronome indication is from the Clara Schumann edition. Although there is no dynamic sign given by either Robert or Clara Schumann, most artists begin this variation forte.

Schumann: Symphonic Etudes, op. 13
(Etude 4)

Final soft chords may demand a slow raising of the pedal. Begin to lift the pedal a split second early, to allow for the distance the dampers must drop before they actually begin to touch the strings. The fingers should leave the keys first, or else this particular fade-out effect will not be obtained.

Beethoven: Sonata, op. 109
(last movement)

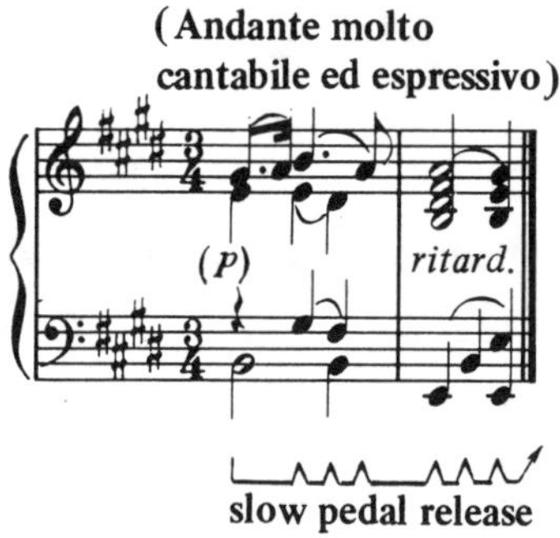

The same gradual lifting of the pedal may be used in slow-moving portato passages to prevent an unpleasant chopping off of the tone.

Beethoven: 32 Variations in C minor
(WoO 80) (Variation 30)

FLUTTER PEDALING

In loud passages at high speed it would be impossible to change the pedal with every note, yet pedal may be desired for color and to avoid dryness. In such situations, a continuous fluttering of the pedal, with the dampers just touching the strings, can be used. The pedal should never be fully depressed nor completely raised. A common notation for this type of pedaling is shown in the following example. Chopin's last dynamic indication is a *fortissimo* some twenty-four bars earlier. But as this *crescendo* leads to a *fortissimo* four bars later, it should probably be started at a *mezzo forte*.

Chopin: Prelude, op. 28 no. 16

Flutter pedaling may also be used to achieve a rapid diminuendo over a single chord or note. The fingers must release the keys to allow the dampers to touch the strings lightly. Depress the pedal early to achieve full resonance when the octave is first sounded.

Schubert: Sonata, op. posth. (D. 960)
(fourth movement)

A similar rapid dampening of the sound is possible if the dampers are brought to rest barely touching the strings. This technique is difficult to master and should be carefully tested, for on some instruments an unpleasant wheezing sound will result from the harmonics.

A diminuendo may be helped with a slow lifting of the pedal over a group of notes.

Schubert: Sonata, op. 143 (D. 784)
(third movement)

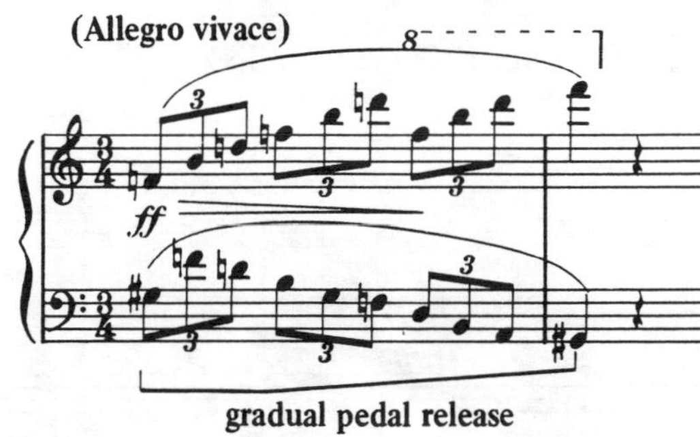

Occasionally a composer may demand a swell on one held note or chord. This would seem to be an impossibility, but can be done in a subtle manner by depressing the pedal immediately after the notes are sounded. The overtones that are released from the surrounding strings as the dampers are raised give the effect of a light crescendo.

Debussy: "*Hommage à Rameau*" from
Images pour piano, Set 1

SPECIAL EFFECTS

High-speed scales may demand unusually long pedaling for color. The following examples will not sound disturbingly blurred if a rapid tempo is taken and a crescendo made to the top of the run.

Chopin: Etude, op. 25 no. 11

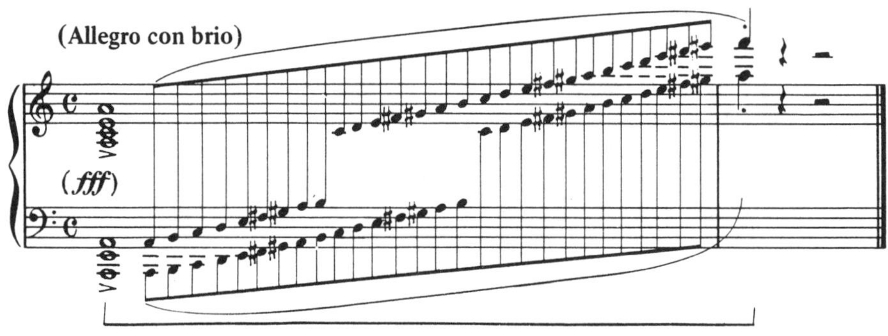

Chopin: Prelude, op. 28 no. 24

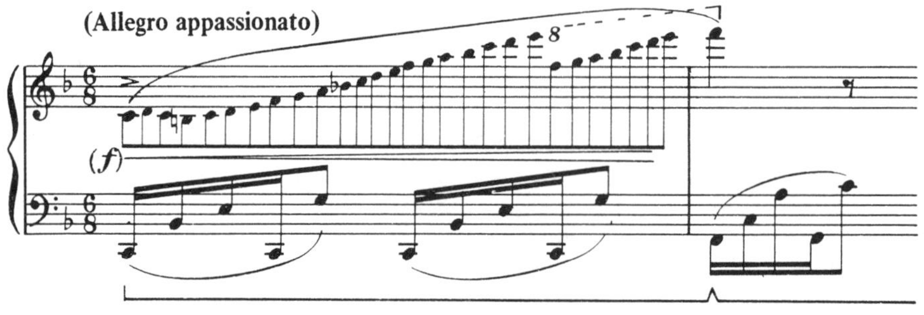

Chromatic runs are more difficult to handle in this manner, especially when they are in a downward direction, and more frequent or partial pedal changes may be necessary.

Mozart-Liszt:
"Reminiscences of Don Juan" (S. 418)

Deliberate blurring for swirling effects may be demanded of the pedal.

Liszt: "St. Francis of Paola Walking
on the Waves" (S. 175/2)

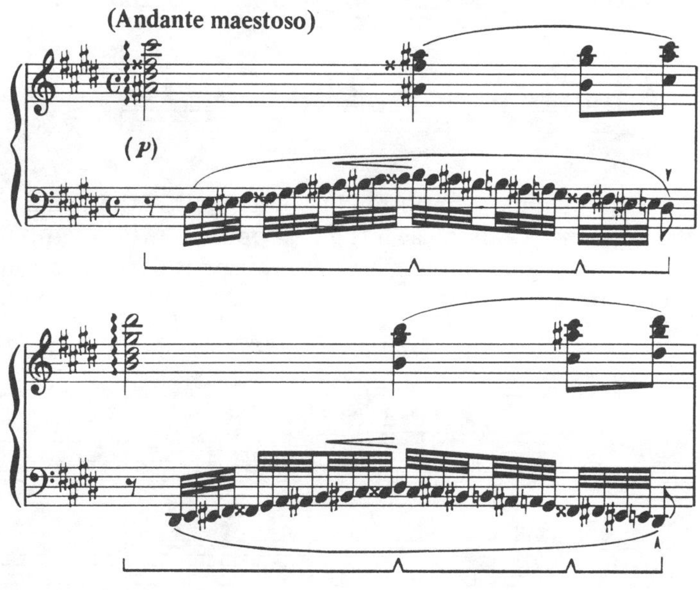

Light touches of the pedal can be highly effective in rapid running passages, to achieve short washes and surges of color.

Chopin: Prélude, op. 28 no. 16

The final movement of Chopin's Sonata, op. 35 demands this kind of pedaling. Rachmaninoff's well-known recording of this work is an example of imaginative pedaling carried to the level of genius.

NON LEGATO PEDALING

The damper pedal may be used in a *non legato* manner to underline the rhythm, as in the following example, where a light touch of pedal is used on each downbeat for color and emphasis. This use of the pedal is one of the few in which the pianist must "keep time" with the pedal by pushing it down simultaneously with the key attack.

Chopin: Mazurka, op. 41 no. 1

A piece in more rapid tempo might sound well if the pedal is held through the first two beats of each bar. Chopin gives no tempo indication for the following example, but an appropriate vivace is found in the Mikuli edition.

Chopin: *Grande Valse*, op. 42

Non legato pedaling may also be used to break the monotony of an overabundance of legato writing. E-177-1

Debussy: Arabesque no. 1

PEDALING A MELODY

There are reasons other than the occurrence of a new harmony for making pedal changes. A passage's melodic shape, direction, register, and phrasing are also important elements to be considered. As a broad generality it is necessary to change the pedal on each new note of a descending melodic line, even when the harmony remains the same. If this is not done, succeeding lower notes tend to sound as parts of a broken chordal harmony, not as individual melody tones. In an ascending melody the pedal can usually be used for longer periods, particularly when the writing is in a higher register.

Schubert: Impromptu, op. 90 no. 4 (D. 899)

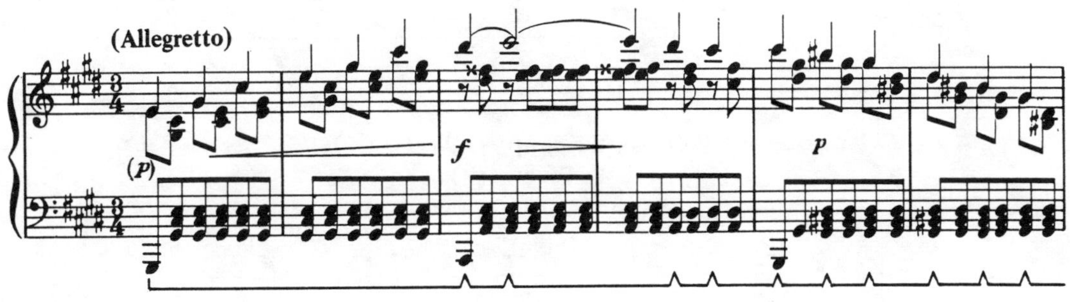

Melody notes which move diatonically at a moderately rapid tempo can often be bound together by the pedal without resulting in unpleasant blurring, especially when receiving underlying support from a clear, less rapidly shifting harmonic fabric. To pedal with the left hand harmony alone in the following example would create excessive blurring.

Chopin: Polonaise-Fantasie, op. 61

As the pedal is changed with the melody notes, other notes may have to be held over with the fingers to avoid disturbing breaks in the harmonic fabric of the accompaniment. This type of holding over of harmonies may be termed "finger pedaling." In the following examples the slurs following each note have been added to indicate which ones are to be held through each succeeding change of pedal.

Chopin: Scherzo, op. 20

Molto più lento
sotto voce e ben legato

Schubert: Sonata, op. 120 (D. 664)
(first movement)

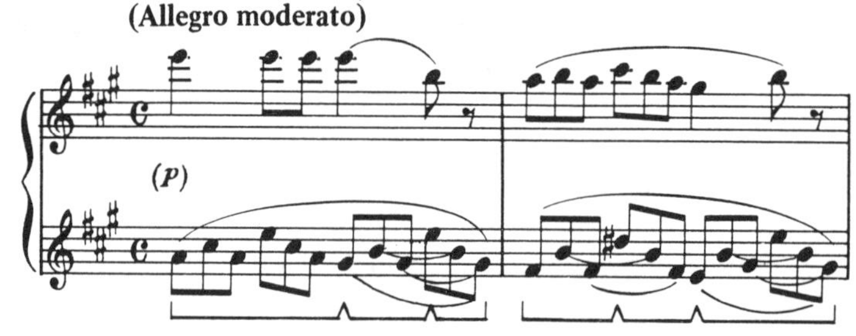

Minute pedal breaks at the ends of phrases can be marvelous aids in highlighting phrasing. Even when a phrase ending is properly tapered in sound, such a break may be desirable to permit the music to breathe during long stretches of legato. This may not always be possible when accompaniment figurations or other factors of continuity must take precedent.

Liszt: Sonata in B minor (S. 178)

(Andante sostenuto)
(pp)
dolce
(una corda)

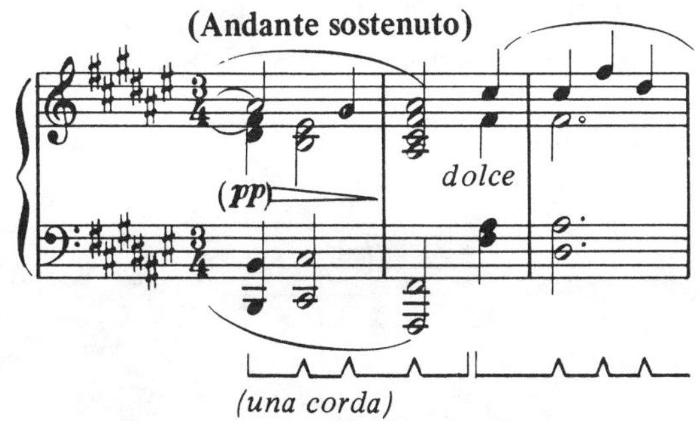

A passage's dynamic level, register and speed must be considered when arriving at a given pedaling, as well as the resonance and size of the instrument being played, and the acoustics of the hall or room. Above all, the ear must be acutely sensitive in reacting to all of these elements. The following passage occurs several times and could appropriately be varied through pedaling in any of the following ways, depending on the dynamic level used.

Chopin: Sonata no. 2, op. 35
(third movement)

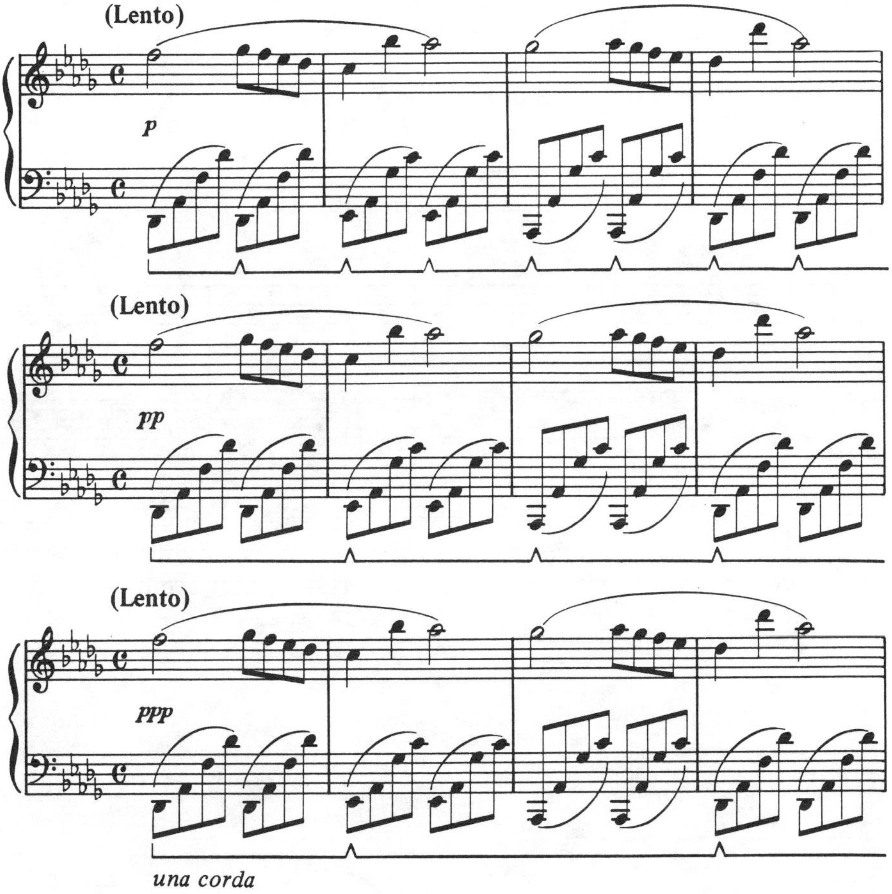

(Lento)
p
(Lento)
pp
(Lento)
ppp
una corda

The next example, if played at an andante, could tolerate the pedal's being extended through each entire beat; but at the prescribed adagio tempo, this section requires pedal changes.

Brahms: Concerto no. 1, op. 15
(second movement)

PEDALING IN CONTRAPUNTAL MUSIC

Although much of the music of Bach, Handel, and others of the period cannot be pedaled without sacrificing clarity of texture, there are many situations in contrapuntal music when use of the pedal is indispensable. The register of the writing, tempo, texture, and technical keyboard layout are all important considerations. Use of the pedal in the following example would be superfluous. Although Bach gives neither a tempo nor dynamic indication, an *allegro vivace* and a *mezzo forte* will not be out of place.

Bach: Fugue in C major
(*Well-Tempered Clavier*, Book 2)

But when a passage contains awkward stretches with uncomfortable adjustments of position, the pedal may prove to be a valuable tool if carefully used. In the next example, Bach gives neither tempo nor dynamic indications. A *lento* and a *piano* may be used.

Bach: Fugue in F minor
(*Well-Tempered Clavier*, Book 1)

Repeated notes may be easier to connect with pedal than with the fingers alone, particularly in baroque works that seem to imitate the rich sound of the organ or the expressive timbre of the clavichord. Again, Bach omits both tempo and dynamic indications; *lento* and a *pianissimo* will best capture this music's deep expressivity.

Bach: Prelude in B-flat minor
(*Well-Tempered Clavier*, Book 2)

When short, varying articulation marks are encountered in different layers of music, care must always be taken not to alter them by careless pedaling. The compositions of Mozart, Haydn, Schubert, and Beethoven are full of such potential hazards. Given the transparent nature of the writing in the following example, the pedal will result in blurring the melody and altering the staccatos and slurs indicated by the composer.

Mozart: Sonata, K. 333 (315c)
(first movement)

In passages having diverse simultaneous musical textures, the pedal should not be used to connect or color in one part at the expense of inadvertently altering the articulation in another. If the pedal is used in the following examples to facilitate a legato in the right-hand melody, noticeable blurring of the left-hand staccato accompaniment will result.

Beethoven: Sonata, op. 27 no. 2
(second movement)

Schubert: Sonata, op. 164 (D. 537)
(second movement)

PARTIAL PEDALING

Thus far, references have been made only to complete changes of pedal, with the dampers' being allowed to come fully to rest on the strings before being completely raised again. But other intermediate positions of the dampers may be used, ranging from their barely being raised from the strings, to their just lightly touching the strings. In any of these intermediate positions there still will be a carry-over of sound but to a lesser degree than if the dampers are fully lifted. At least three degrees of sound releases are useful: one-fourth released dampers, one-half released dampers, and three-fourths released dampers. These fractions refer to the amount of sound that carries over following the initial striking of the hammers on the strings, and are dependent on how far the dampers are allowed to leave the surface of the strings. These fractions are only approximate guides, and they do not refer to the distance the pedal is actually being depressed (this varies from piano to piano), but only to the amount of sound that is meant to linger by depressing the pedal.

To experiment with obtaining these intermediate damper levels, the following effects may be tried:

- To test one-fourth released dampers, play either a scale in moderately rapid tempo or a succession of chromatic chords. There should be no blurring. When these same passages are played without a pedal, a distinct difference in tone quality should be evident.
- To test one-half released dampers, play a scale in moderately rapid tempo. Partial blurring should occur. Staccato chords should still sound staccato.
- To test three-fourths released dampers, play a fairly loud chord. The sound should remain when the fingers release the keys, but with only partial resonance. When played with the pedal fully depressed, the same chord should sound considerably more resonant.

One-fourth released dampers are useful in passages of a medium to rapid tempo which have a dynamic range of pianissimo to mezzo forte, where a slight amount of added resonance is needed to counteract a dry sound resulting from a dead room, small piano, etc. A rapid, full vibrato pedaling in the following examples would give an overly heavy effect. Pedaling on each note is impossible because of the rapid tempo, and pedaling on every other note would create slurs. Using one-fourth released dampers gives a touch of color without blurring.

Beethoven: Sonata, op. 111
(second movement)

Mozart: Concerto no. 20, K. 466
(first movement)

One-half released dampers allow more resonance than one-fourth released dampers and will cause blurring in scales and harmony changes, but in passages with the same harmony they will give the impression of each tone's being partially released after it has been sounded. There will be a marked added resonance over the use of one-fourth released dampers, but without the full blurring and holdover of tones that result from fully released dampers.

Brahms: Concerto no. 1, op. 15
(first movement)

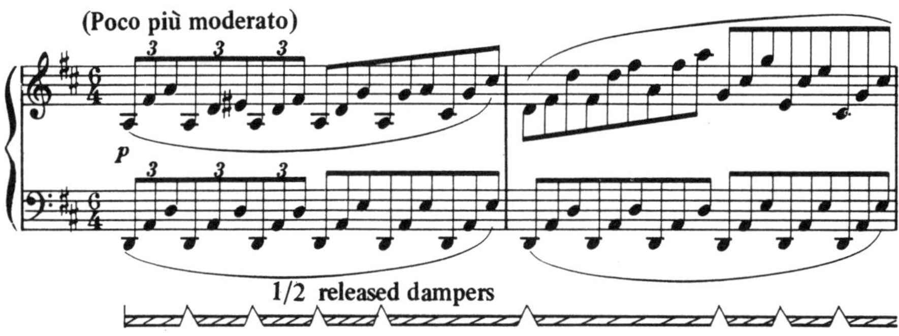

Staccato chords played with one-half released dampers can be made to sound less dry, while not losing their basic staccato character.

Beethoven: Sonata, op. 10 no. 3
(second movement)

One-half released dampers are particularly useful in passages with an Alberti bass figuration, where dryness must be avoided, yet in which even small amounts of full pedaling would prove too heavy. Although Mozart gives no dynamic indication, a *piano* seems appropriate.

Mozart: Sonata, K. 545
(second movement)

An atmospheric light blurring may be obtained through use of one-half released dampers, as if the music is heard from a distance.

Debussy: "*Soirée dans Grenade*"
(from *Estampes*)

Three-fourths released dampers allow the sound to be held in a resonant manner, yet differ from a full raising of the dampers by allowing the tone to be somewhat more transparent.

Beethoven: Sonata, op. 2 no. 3
(first movement)

THE SOFT PEDAL

The soft pedal is an important coloring agent, but this role unfortunately is usually misunderstood or ignored. On upright pianos the left pedal lessens the striking distance of the hammers by moving them a half-inch closer to the strings. This results in an upsetting of tonal and touch control, and in no way fulfills this pedal's true role. Its use on such instruments will not be considered in this discussion. When the soft pedal is depressed on a grand piano, the hammers are moved slightly to one side, so that they strike two instead of three strings on most notes. This results both in a slight loss of volume and, much more importantly, in a change of tone quality. When shifted, the hammers strike the strings in a less packed-down area of the felt surface, to one side of the grooving caused by normal wear. The resulting change of tone to a more velvetlike quality is the most important function of the left pedal, not the relatively small reduction in volume.

The term *una corda* to denote the soft pedal is something of a misnomer. It originates from late eighteenth- and early nineteenth-century instruments, on which it was possible to shift the soft pedal from the *una corda* (one string) position to *due corde* (two strings) and finally to *tre corde* (three strings). This last indication simply means to release the soft pedal entirely. Any accomplished pianist can play just as softly without using the left pedal, so it is a mistake to use it whenever a piano or pianissimo occurs in the music.

As with the damper pedal's being termed the *loud* pedal, calling the left pedal the *soft* pedal is misleading. To call it the *mute* pedal would be more accurate, for the soft pedal should be regarded as functioning similarly to a string player's mute. It should be used only when a muted tone color is desired. The performer should always depress the soft pedal only at a moment when a change of color is demanded in the music, rather than in the middle of a passage or phrase. When a full "singing" tone, or a crisp, sparkling, soft sound is needed, the soft pedal probably should not be used. Soft echo effects give opportunities for effective use of the soft pedal, as in the following example where the *sordini (una corda)* indication is the composer's own.

Schubert: Sonata, op. 143 (D. 784)
(second movement)

(Andante)

sordini

The composer may ask for the soft pedal following a diminuendo. The pedal should not be depressed during the diminuendo, but only immediately before the start of the new phrase. The *una corda* is Beethoven's own.

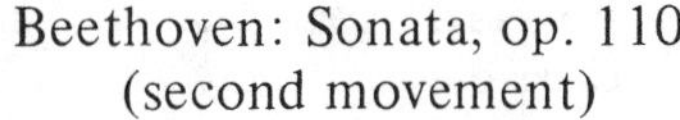

Beethoven: Sonata, op. 110
(second movement)

(Allegro molto)

When the left pedal is released before the soft beginning of a new phrase, it is wise to drop slightly back in sound to match the preceding softer tonal level. In this example the *una corda* and *tutte le corde (tre corde)* indications are the composer's own. Although Beethoven gives no dynamic indication for the *una corda* section, a pianissimo is implied.

Beethoven: Sonata, op. 106
(fourth movement)

THE SOSTENUTO PEDAL

The most ignored pedaling tool is the middle, or *sostenuto,* pedal. Regrettably this pedal usually functions imperfectly or not at all on upright instruments, and even on many grands may be poorly adjusted. The sostenuto pedal was first exhibited by the French firm of Boisselot and Sons of Marseilles at the Paris exposition of 1844, patented in both France and the United States in 1874, but was not widely incorporated by European manufacturers. In the United States, however, Steinway enthusiastically adopted it, and other companies soon followed his example. The sostenuto pedal's role is to prolong certain notes while allowing others to be dampened. When this pedal is depressed, it will catch and hold any dampers that are raised at that moment. The middle pedal must be depressed a split second after the note or notes to be caught are played, as the fingers are still holding them. At this moment it is crucial that the damper pedal not be depressed even the smallest amount, or all the dampers will be caught. Once the middle pedal is fully depressed, however, the right pedal can be used normally to hold and change other harmonies. The sostenuto pedal once fully depressed must never be allowed to rise even a small distance, or additional unwanted tones will be caught when the damper pedal is used.

Use of the sostenuto pedal will not in most cases be indicated in the score, although a few twentieth-century composers ask for it by writing the initials *S.P.* In many piano works, composers seem to think orchestrally, as if certain notes can be held even when the hands cannot possibly accomplish this. The damper pedal may often be able to fulfill this illusionary holding of a note or chord, but in other situations its use will create an ugly blurring that, even with partial pedal changes, creates serious problems for the performer. Here the middle pedal proves to be an invaluable ally of the damper pedal. In the following example, play the bass G-sharp octave quickly before the beat, then rapidly catch it with the *sostenuto* pedal. When this is accomplished, the damper pedal should then be changed on each eighth note. The metronome indication is from the Clara Schumann edition.

Schumann: Symphonic Etudes, op. 13
(Etude 2)

The composer may not actually indicate specific notes to be held, but the performer should nonetheless sense them from the score's harmonic context and style.

Brahms: Sonata no. 3, op. 5
(fifth movement)

The piano music of Debussy and Ravel contains many similar opportunities to use the sostenuto pedal. If the middle pedal is used in the following examples, the changes of damper pedal must still be done in a manner that slightly blurs the harmonic outline, as if the holding of the lower tones by the sostenuto pedal were being accomplished by half-pedal changes of the damper pedal.

Debussy: "*Hommage à Rameau*"
(from *Images pour piano*, Set 1)

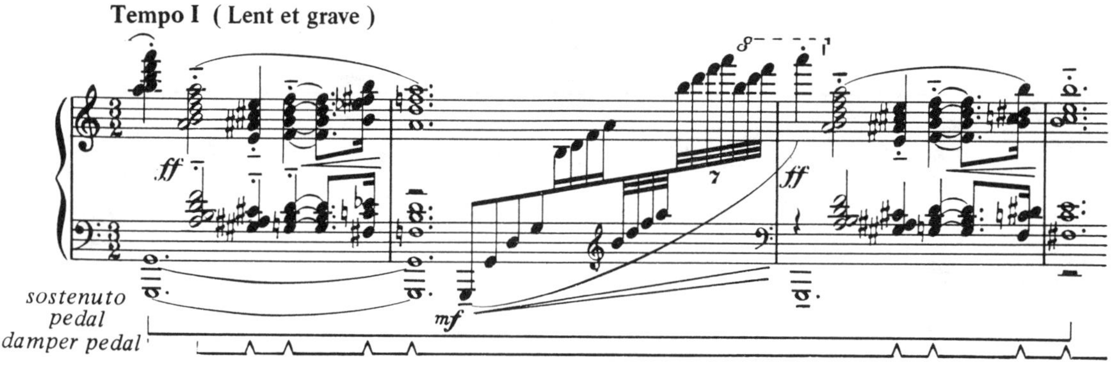

Ravel: *Pavane pour une infante défunte*

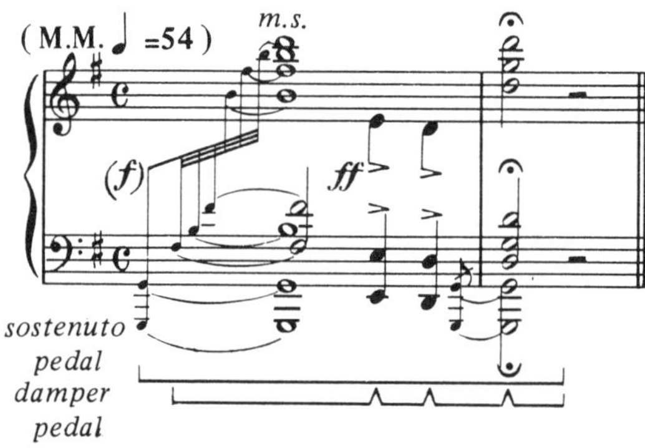

Sometimes the sound of a note or chord in one hand must be eliminated while a note or chord in the other hand is held. A wonderful opportunity for this imaginative use of the middle pedal occurs during the first movement of Prokofiev's Seventh Sonata. In the following example the low Gs must be caught a split second after the release of the staccato C and E in the right hand. This is at first difficult to do in rhythm, but with practice can be managed.

Prokofiev: Sonata no. 7, op. 83
(first movement)

A long pedal point may seem to require use of the sostenuto pedal, but prove to be impossible to catch by itself without other notes' being held that will conflict harmonically. Such a situation occurs near the opening of Liszt's transcription of Bach's Prelude and Fugue for organ in A minor. The low A in bar 10 should be caught with the middle pedal, then held through bar 23. If this were done when the A was initially struck, it would result in the catching of a C in the right hand. The performer may solve this problem by silently depressing the low A just before starting the piece, while at the same time catching the raised damper with the middle pedal. The key should be depressed only until a small resistance is felt. To push the finger clear to the key bed may result in the hammer's striking the string very lightly. Depressing the key approximately four-fifths of the way down is sufficient to raise the damper fully from the string, allowing it to be caught with the sostenuto pedal before actually beginning to play. As this A is not played before bar 10, it will be heard and sustained at its proper time, without catching any unwanted notes above. Neither Bach nor Liszt give either a tempo or dynamic indication; a *moderato* and a *mezzo piano* may be used effectively.

Bach-Liszt: Prelude and Fugue
(S. 462/1)

SIMULTANEOUS SOSTENUTO AND SOFT PEDALING

On occasion it may be necessary to pedal with both the sostenuto and soft pedals, while at the same time using the damper pedal. The left two pedals are played with the left foot, since the right foot should always be reserved for the damper pedal. First depress the soft pedal with the left part of the sole, at the same time placing the heel as far to the left as is reasonably comfortable. Then, depress the middle pedal with a sideways motion of the foot while keeping the heel and left side of the foot firmly in place. The position is not a completely comfortable one, but mastery of this technique is of great value in passages similar to the following:

Debussy: "*Clair de lune*"
from *Suite Bergamasque*

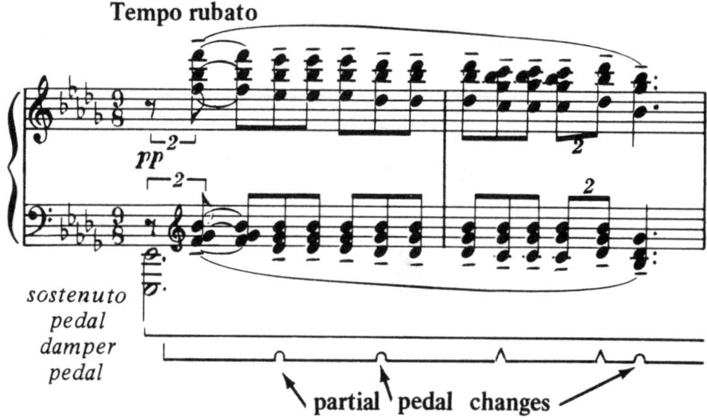

The rather naive argument has too frequently been made that the sostenuto pedal should never be used in performing Debussy and Ravel, since European pianos of their time were not usually equipped with the middle pedal. If this logic is followed, then Bach, Handel, Haydn, Mozart, and even Beethoven should not be attempted on a modern concert grand, for the piano of their day was still in its infancy, and radically different in tone, range, and touch. Artists such as E. Robert Schmitz and Maurice Dumesnil, each closely associated with both Debussy and Ravel, advocated using the sostenuto pedal when performing these composers' music. Every available technique should be used by the performer to convey the composer's intent, as far as it can be ascertained from the written score. The middle pedal is an important aid in this regard.

The foregoing discussion of pedaling only touches on some of the more important aspects of what is a large, subtle and complex area of study. Any of the preceding "rules" has a thousand exceptions. Moreover, every great composer has a unique style of keyboard layout and texture that often radically affects any blanket approach to pedaling. Awareness of these differences can come only from much familiarity with repertory and performance styles. Choice of pedaling will also be constantly affected by the performer's choice of tempos, touch, dynamics, and balance of textures, as well as by the sonority and acoustics of the room and the instrument. A rigidly unvarying pedaling concept for each piece is not desirable, for adjustments must frequently be made on stage to conform to these ever-changing elements. The player must constantly listen and react accordingly. Pedaling is a fascinating study that will always challenge the performer, and its mastery is crucial to any significant pianistic achievement.

RECOMMENDED READING

Bowen, York. *Pedaling the Modern Pianoforte.* New York and London: Oxford University Press, 1936.

Diller, Angela. *First Pedal Studies for the Piano.* New York: G. Schirmer, 1942.

Gebhard, Heinrich. *The Art of Pedaling: A Manual for the Use of the Piano Pedals.* Introduction by Leonard Bernstein. New York: Franco Colombo, Inc., 1963.

Gieseking, Walter, and Karl Leimer. *Piano Techniques: The Shortest Way to Pianistic Perfection and Rhythmics, Dynamics, Pedal and Other Problems of Piano Playing.* New York: Dover, 1972.

Schnabel, Karl Ulrich. *Modern Technique of the Pedal (A Piano Pedal Study).* New York: Mills Music, Inc., 1954.

Ornamentation: Theory and Practice

DENES AGAY

The most important fact to remember about ornamentation is that its roots lie in *improvisation*, and even when notated in various ways and with more or less exactness, the formation of its final shape properly belongs in the performer's domain. Of course, one must be aware of the composer's intentions and know the meaning of the ornamental symbols, but equally important is the realization that these signs are guidelines which allow a variety of interpretations and can come to life only through the performer's creative participation.

HISTORICAL OVERVIEW

Ornamentation is as old as music itself. Some of the earliest musical utterances contain elements of figuration and embellishment which were, of course, improvised. Even today, in idioms such as jazz, gypsy music, and some Oriental music, a profusion of embellishments is largely improvisatory. In Western music from the eighth century on, the earliest music-writing methods, such as the notation of the Gregorian chants, (*neumes*), present the first vague and primitive attempts to commit these extemporaneous vocal figurations to paper. Soon thereafter began the practice of transcribing the various medieval liturgical chants for keyboard instruments in richly embellished variations.

Throughout the Renaissance and early baroque period, ornamentation originating from improvisatory practices became a highly developed and refined art in both vocal and instrumental music. At a certain stage these decorative figurations became so rich and involved that, for the sake of easier and faster notation (and for other, probably didactic, reasons) a methodical classification of ornamental groups and types became necessary. Thus certain standard and quite static formulas of embellishments were crystallized: *gruppetto, trillo, tremolo,* etc. Also, for each type a graphically appropriate design was assigned, from which the now-familiar notation symbols (𝆖, ∽, etc.) derived.

It should be emphasized that during the Renaissance, early Baroque, and beyond, the ornamentation signs–and, indeed the entire note picture–provided only an outline, heavily dependent on the performer's creative contribution. There was (and is) no such thing as a one-and-only, definitive interpretation of these early works. Composers notated sketchily because they wanted the performer to furnish the details of execution. Today such a practice may seem strange; a first-hand account by a writer of that time may throw a better light on this approach to notation.

Tobias Michael (1592–1657), cantor and music director of St. Thomas' Church in Leipzig, wrote in the preface to a collection of his vocal compositions: "I have always been of the opinion that composers would do better, when publishing their works, both vocal and instrumental, not to mingle in or add any embellishments–and this is why. My own experience has been that a skilled musician who not only had natural talent, but has developed a fine manner of performance. . . . can help the piece more with his art and give it character, than if one wrote everything down for him first. . . . I can not agree with those [composers] who want to tie everything together to one manner and still less with those who are not satisfied with anything unless it is of their own making and baking. . . . I stick humbly to my belief that three, four, five or more good manners of performance [of the same work] may be encountered, each acceptable by itself, but quite different from the others."

Michael further elaborates why he does not believe in detailed notation of ornaments: "When an inexperienced performer encounters a work, or one who has no special talent, he will not only bring out the written coloraturas unskillfully, but they will make the work so difficult for him and so unpleasant, that he will either abandon it altogether or present it in such a way that the listener would rather hear it done just simply and without any coloration."

For these very reasons, composers of the early seventeenth century, including Praetorius and Michael himself, published some of their works in both plain and embellished versions, printed one above the other for the choice and convenience of the performer.

From the second half of the seventeenth century, ornaments previously intended to be improvised by the player were written out with increasing detail and care. The leading practitioners of this trend were the French clavecinists, especially François Couperin (1668–1733), whose embellishments are meticulously notated. These French masters attached to their harpsichord publications various "tables of ornamentation" and "explications," whose purpose was to instruct the less experienced player how the ornamental symbols should be interpreted. German writers, J. S. Bach in particular, followed the French lead.

Bach's table of ornaments in the *Little Notebook for Wilhelm Friedemann Bach* is nearly identical to earlier French examples.

It should be noted that well over a century before Couperin and Bach, numerous method books and pamphlets already contained charts and visual aids to help the inexperienced performer. These charts, however, dealt not so much with the proper interpretation of symbols, but with the technique of *diminution,* a type of improvised embellishment in which the written notes are broken up into figurations of lesser note values:

Diminution was widely employed throughout the baroque period and well beyond, not only as an ornamental device, but also as a manner of variation.

PERFORMING BAROQUE ORNAMENTS

The rich ornamentation of baroque and rococo keyboard music is one of the main reasons why the use of this repertory as teaching material is approached with some uneasiness today. There is also another, more subtle reason: pressures stemming from an authenticity-conscious pedagogic community, which, in its often overly pedantic interpretation of stylistic norms, inhibits a relaxed approach to ornamentation. There is a relatively easy solution for this. The subject of ornaments is a somewhat complex one, involving aspects of notation and a degree of familiarity with styles and performance practices of the past; yet it is not too difficult to grasp the basic principles and thereby acquire the necessary confidence to play, teach and enjoy this vital music; as Robert Donington once wrote, the task is "first to know enough, and then to be bold enough, and above all to be creative enough."

To view this matter in its proper perspective, it is helpful to examine *why* baroque keyboard literature is so profusely ornamented. Aside from the fact than an emphasis on decorative elements is a characteristic trait of all baroque art, the rich embellishment of this music was also an acoustical and interpretative necessity. The harpsichord's crisp, momentary, plucked sound made the insertion of filler tones desirable, especially in slower tempos, to sustain the sound of longer notes and to maintain a continual melodic flow. C. P. E. Bach, in his oft-quoted *Essay on the True Art of Playing Keyboard Instruments,* gives three reasons why ornaments are "indispensable":

- they connect and enliven tones
- they impart emphasis and accents
- they make music more expressive

All these reasons are still entirely valid, *as far as harpsichord interpreta-*

tion is concerned. To project a melodic phrase on a harpsichord, more embellishments were needed than on the violin or oboe, which were able to sustain long notes without figurative manipulations. Observe, for instance, how a simple, unadorned theme by Alessandro Marcello, written for oboe, was transcribed by Bach for harpsichord:

Theme by Marcello

Bach: right-hand harpsichord part

The question inevitably arises whether C. P. E. Bach's thinking is applicable and valid when these ornamented works, originally conceived for the harpsichord, are performed on the modern piano, an instrument with decidedly superior sustaining quality, dynamic range, and expressive capabilities, although perhaps with somewhat less clarity and precise acoustical definition of individual tones. One can not escape the conclusion that occasionally some carefully considered adjustments can be made toward simplification. A dense cluster of embellishments may sound clear, expressive, and graceful on the harpsichord, but within a certain texture and in certain tempo muddled, turbid, and heavy-handed on the piano, no matter how well performed. Present-day scholars, in spite of historical precedents to the contrary, usually discourage simplification or omission of ornaments on the ground that this would rob the piece of its specific charm, style, and character. This is true in many cases, but by no means always, especially when baroque music is performed on modern instruments. In such cases we are dealing with a transcription of a piece from one instrument (harpsichord, clavichord) to another (piano), which necessitates taking into consideration the different construction, mechanism, mobility, and acoustical properties of the instruments involved.

In principle, the omission or alteration of ornaments is not contrary to baroque performance practice, which allowed considerable latitude even in the direction of variation (diminution) and improvisation. In spite of this fact, however, present-day performers and teachers are wise to move cautiously in this area, omitting or replacing embellishments only after consideration of all pertinent factors, including the style, texture, and tempo of the piece, and the notation practices of the composer. For instance, J. S. Bach notated his works with utmost care and in great detail, leaving little room or need for interpretive liberties. This does not mean that liberties were not taken, even in such exacting works as the Two-part Inventions. One can view this convincingly in the autograph edition of this work (C. F. Peters Edition), where the first Invention, in C major, appears thus:

Bach: Two-part Invention
(note soprano clef)

The triplets of the second and fourth beats of the first two measures (and repeated in parallel places throughout the piece) will come as a surprise. In a postscript to this edition, harpsichordist and scholar Ralph Kirkpatrick comments that the "decorative alterations. . . were added later and very probably not by Bach, however much they represent the freedom of spirit in which the Inventions were intended to be played." This writer concurs, and adds the following observation: if such conspicuous and basic ornamental additions were accepted in Bach's time, it seems rather unreasonable and hairsplitting to quarrel whether the short trill on the fourth beat of the first measure in this piece should start on the upper auxiliary note or, *horribile dictu*, be played as a mordent. There is no question that the baroque performer did have these options and more, and exercised them to the hilt. *For the sake of authenticity and pure logic, we can not deny the same freedoms and options to the knowledgable player of today.*

WRITTEN AND UNWRITTEN ORNAMENTS

Baroque ornaments may be classified, according to the manner of their notation, into the following three categories:

(1) Written out by the composer in regular or small-size notes. This gives the performer the clearest and most accurate note picture.
(2) Indicated by the composer by signs and symbols (∿∿∿, ∿|, etc.). Their meaning may be ambiguous, all the tables of ornamentation

notwithstanding; they may differ from country to country and according to the individual composer's notation methods. Furthermore, the actual molding and final shape of these embellishments is also dependent on the tempo, texture, and melodic-harmonic context in which they occur.

(3) Ornaments not indicated by the composer in any manner, but expected to be added by the performer, usually extemporaneously. The inherent freedom of baroque performance allowed, indeed demanded, the addition of certain ornaments. Performers should adopt this license with a degree of caution and moderation, and only after acquiring the necessary information about various facets of baroque notation, style, and interpretative principles. The simplest and stylistically safest additions are cadential ornaments:

- If the last note of a piece or section is unsupported by a chord, and especially if it is provided with a *fermata*, a suitable ornament (short trill, mordent, long trill with afterbeat, etc.) may be added to sustain the sound. The last notes in some of the Bach Inventions may be embellished in this manner.
- If the last note of a piece or section is preceded by this typical two-note melodic pattern ♩. ♪ | 𝅗𝅥, the dotted note should receive a trill (as in Bach's Two-part Invention in D major).

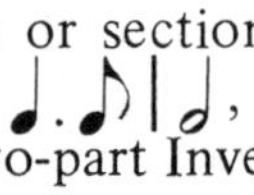

The repetition of a section in baroque music usually implied improvised variations and embellishments. Although this is a more demanding task than the addition of cadential ornaments, a better-than-average student should not be discouraged from doing this, after being thoroughly briefed about the pertinent principles involved. The additions do not have to be improvised; they can be carefully thought out and then written down. The works of Bach and Handel, among others, furnish ample examples of this technique at its best (the Sarabands of Bach's third and sixth English Suites, for instance). On an earlier level, the student may learn a great deal about improvisational additions of all sorts (diminution, figurations, passage work, embellishments, etc.) by playing and analyzing C. P. E. Bach's charming Short and Easy Piano Pieces with Varied Repetitions (edited by Oswald Jonas, Universal Edition).

A REVIEW OF BAROQUE ORNAMENTS

Mordent: a three-note group formed by the rapid alternation of the main note with its lower neighbor:

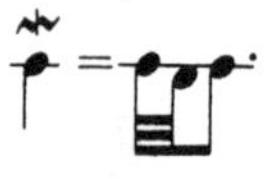

As with all baroque ornaments, the *first* note is considered on the beat.
Long or *extended mordent*:

Upper mordent (*inverted mordent, Schneller, Pralltriller*): a reverse of the mordent, involves the main note with its upper neighbor:

Encountered from the middle of the eighteenth century (C. P. E. Bach) and throughout the nineteenth (see also *short trill*).

Short trill (*shake, Praller*): is normally played:

or

The execution of this ornament starts on the upper neighboring (auxiliary) note. The main reason for this rule is that the upper note usually forms a suspension resolving to the main note, similar to an *appoggiatura,* thus giving added crispness and "bite" to the attack. There are some exceptions to the above rule, which although still somewhat controversial should be noted. The trill can start on the main note if this note itself is a suspension. In such a case starting the ornament on the upper neighboring note would not only dull the incisive quality of the attack but would also often result in faulty voice leading of parallel octaves or fifths.

Another exception occurs when a *legato* melody line approaches the ornament in scalewise motion from above; then the upper auxiliary note is omitted, and a three-note ornament starts on the principal note:

The short trill performed this way is identical to the upper mordent. In slow tempo the upper neighboring note is sometimes tied to the note it precedes:

Trill , *tr* : an expansion of the short trill into a longer one by adding one or more "wiggles" to the symbol. In performance it may be prolonged at will:

or = *etc.*

From this evolved a number of variants:
(a.) A termination is added by a downstroke:

(b.) The beginning of the long trill can be modified by taking the basic ~~~ and placing before it a stroke from above:

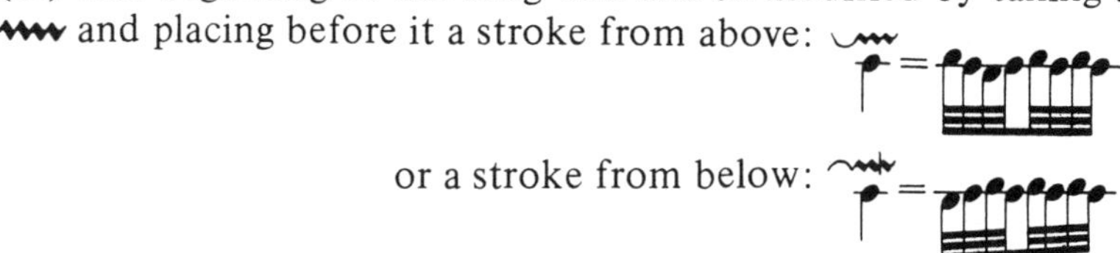

or a stroke from below:

(c.) Both a beginning and a termination may be added:

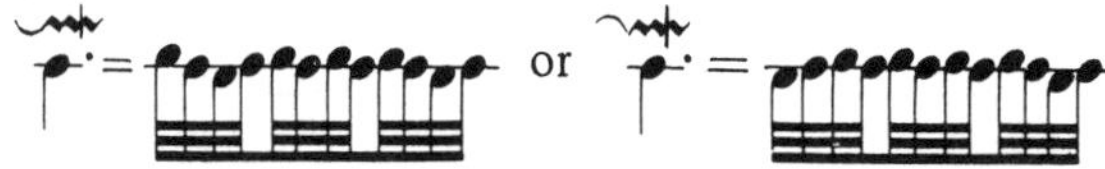

The meaning of the sign *tr* (*trill, trillo*) is often elusive and requires special attention. The sign may indicate a short or a long trill, with or without afterbeat, depending on the period when the music was written, the notation habits of the individual composer, the tempo of the piece, etc. In general the following suggestions may be helpful: in rapid tempo play it as a short trill or as an upper mordent; in slow tempo, or when the sign is over a long note, play it as a long trill with an afterbeat.
Turn ∾ : a four-note group formed by the alternation of the main note with its upper and lower neighbors: or

If placed between two notes (rare in baroque music):

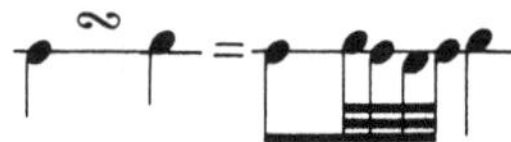

Trilled turn: a frequently occurring late eighteenth century compound ornament, a combination of the turn and the short trill:

Appoggiatura (various symbols): originates from the Italian word *appoggiare* (to lean). This ornament is usually a dissonant suspended note which resolves stepwise upward or downward into the main note to become part of the underlying harmony.

The length of the appoggiatura (the small note) is usually at least half the time value of the main note, but it can be longer, too; for instance:

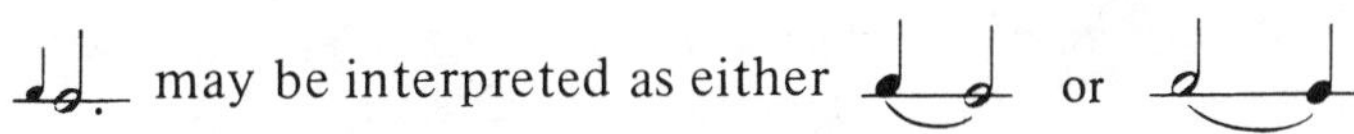

may be interpreted as either or

In the works of certain composers (J. S. Bach and others), appoggiaturas are often marked as follows:

ascending:

descending:

When the appoggiatura leans upon a note which is part of a chord, the solution is this:

It can also precede a trill or a mordent:

or

Acciaccatura: in baroque music, a very short appoggiatura which usually resolves upward:

It also may be interpreted this way: Here the two notes are struck simultaneously; the lower one is released instantly, the upper one held.
In the nineteenth century this ornament acquired a somewhat different meaning as a "grace note" sounded before the beat and moving either up or down toward the principle note: or

In this period the figure may also consist of two or more grace notes:

Slide (*coulé, Schleifer*): a run of two auxiliary notes upward or downward toward the main note. It is notated in various ways:

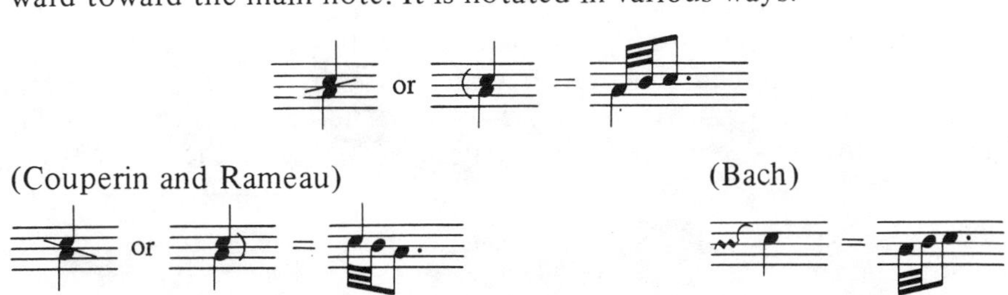

It should be noted that certain slanting strokes in Couperin's work cannot be interpreted as slides, but rather as the joining of the notes into a legato group:

Arpeggio (*broken chord*): the notes of a chord played not simultaneously, but in more or less rapid succession:

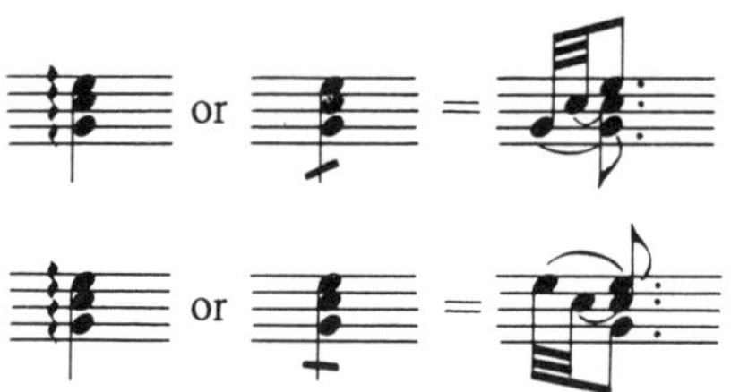

In music originally written for the harpsichord and clavichord, the playing of full chords in an arpeggiated manner can be taken for granted even without specific signs—especially in slow tempos.

The following general rules of baroque ornamentation should be kept in mind:

- The first note of a note group is considered on the beat.
- Trills and turns usually start on the upper auxiliary note.
- The longer the note under the ornament sign, the richer the ornament.
- Baroque ornaments are diatonic, utilizing only the notes of the scale in which the ornament occurs. Any deviation from this is indicated by an accidental placed under the symbol. In modulatory passages, accidentals pertinent to the key can be taken for granted.
- One must never sacrifice musical common sense for the sake of a rule. Should a particular ornament prove to be difficult or awkward when performed on the piano according to the rules, the player may take liberties which, if done with taste and consistency, would not violate the spirit of baroque performance practices. As Thurston Dart wrote, "Ornaments are delicate, instinctive things; if they are not ornamental they are worse than useless, and anxiety about the right way to play them must never be allowed to cloud a performer's sense of the underlying structure of the music they adorn."

RECOMMENDED READING

Bach, Carl Philipp Emanuel. *Essay on the True Art of Playing Keyboard Instruments* (Trans. William J. Mitchell). New York: W.W.Norton, 1949.

Couperin, François. *The Art of Playing the Harpsichord.* Wiesbaden: Breitkopf & Härtel, 1933.

Crowder, Louis L. "The Baroque Period." In Denes Agay, *An Anthology of Piano Music,* vol. 1. New York: Yorktown Music Press, Inc., 1971.

Dart, Thurston. *The Interpretation of Music.* New York and Evanston: Harper Colophon, 1963.

Dannreuther, Edward. *Musical Ornamentation.* London: Novello, 1895.

Donington, Robert. *The Interpretation of Early Music* (2nd ed.). London: Faber, 1965.

Emery, Walter. *Bach's Ornaments.* London: Novello, 1953.

Ferand, Ernest T. *Improvisation in Nine Centuries of Western Music.* Cologne: Arno Volk Verlag, 1961.

Ferguson, Howard. *Keyboard Interpretation.* New York and London: Oxford University Press, 1975.

Grove's Dictionary of Music and Musicians (5th ed.). Article on "Ornamentation." New York: St. Martin's Press, 1960.

Kirkpatrick, Ralph. *Domenico Scarlatti.* Princeton: Princeton University Press, 1953.

Lucktenberg, George. "Ornaments and Embellishments in Eighteenth-century Keyboard Music." In James W. Bastien, *How To Teach Piano Successfully.* Park Ridge and La Jolla: General Words and Music Co., 1973.

ORNAMENTATION IN THE CLASSICAL PERIOD

Ornaments appear less frequently in keyboard works of the classical period than in those of the baroque; ambiguities, however, still exist. In regard to ornamentation, this is an era of transition; many baroque ways persist intermingled with stylistic and notational innovations of the individual classical masters. Only few generally valid observations can be made.

Trills begin on the beat and, in most cases, on the upper auxiliary note, unless this note precedes the main note, or unless the sounding of the main note on the beat is necessary to maintain the melodic flow (scale passages, etc.). To be sure, there were authoritative voices during the eighteenth century which favored beginning the trill on the main note, but it was only from Beethoven's middle period on (around 1800) that this practice became widespread. In the works of Mozart, Haydn, and their contemporaries, trills should begin on the upper neighboring note whenever musically valid and technically feasible.

Trill preparations and terminations are usually written out in small notes. Preparations are played on the beat.

The absence of such small notes does not mean that a prefix or suffix cannot be added. The addition of trill terminations, especially, are at the player's option.

The extent and duration of the trill is often marked by a horizontal wavy line following the *tr* sign: *tr*~~~~~~~~~~
In Beethoven's works the sign of the short trill ⁓ is interpreted, in most cases, as an upper mordent (*Schneller*):

Beethoven: Sonata, op. 13
("Pathétique")

Appoggiaturas are usually written out in small notes; their length is generally indicated by the value of the small note:

Mozart: Sonata no. 3, K. 281

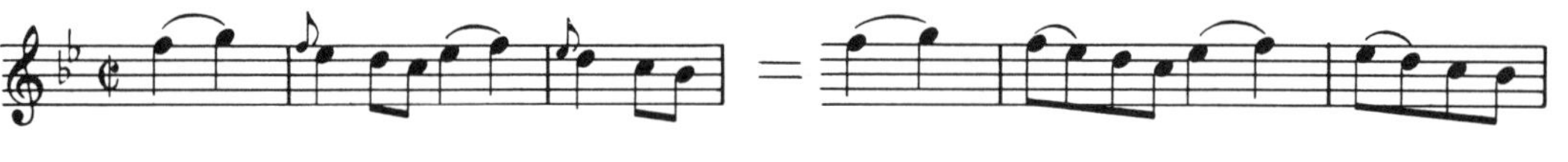

Haydn: Sonata, Hob.XVI:36

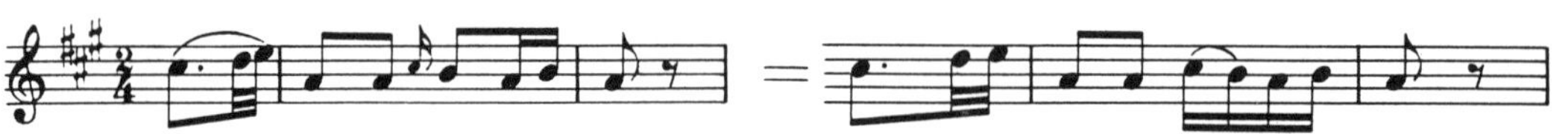

Most appoggiaturas are played *on the beat*, with an accent; there are, however, exceptions. The small note is played before the beat, without an accent, when the main note is marked *staccato* or when the main note itself carries an accent mark.

Why were appoggiaturas in the classical period notated with these ambiguous small notes and not the way the music was meant to be played? In other words, why, for instance, did Mozart notate his Rondo alla Turca this way,

Mozart: Sonata no. 11, K. 331

instead of the way it is played?

Two reasons may be cited:

The first notation makes the harmonic context clear. The small notes are dissonant suspensions resolving into the underlying harmony (A minor).

A more important reason lies in eighteenth-century performance practice which, similar to baroque practice, allowed the performer considerable latitude of extemporaneous ornamentation. If appoggiaturas were written out as played, in large print, the performer may have been tempted to add still more ornaments of his or her own. For instance, if Mozart had notated his Turkish Rondo as it is played, some eighteenth-century players may have felt free to perform it this way:

Mozart's notation precludes such interpretations.

Turns are marked by the conventional sign ∾ or with small notes, in the form of a compound appoggiatura: ∾ or =

The first note of a turn is usually performed on the beat; an exception occurs when the main note is marked staccato or is accented, in which case the ornamental notes should be played before the beat:

Mozart: Piano Concerto no. 15, K. 450

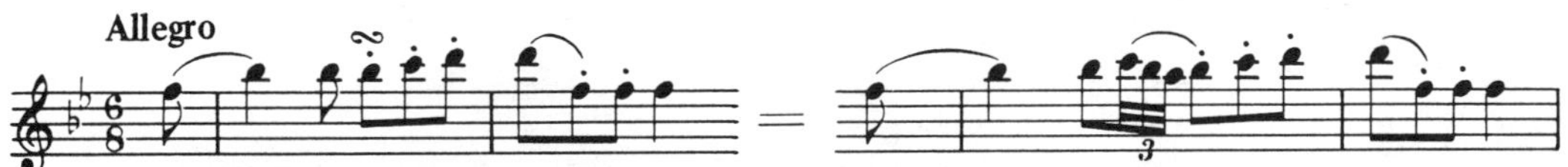

The familiar Haydn ornament is, in most cases, the equivalent of the turn ∾:

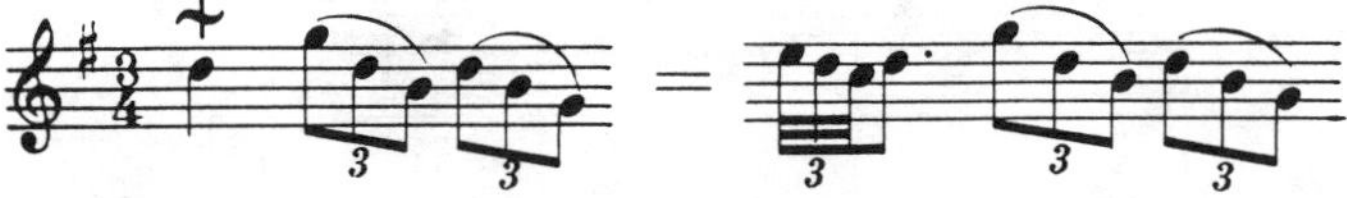

Occasionally it may also be interpreted as a mordent.

Arpeggios are rolled *upward*, at a pace dependent on the musical context. Haydn and Mozart notated arpeggios with a slanting stroke through the chord; modern editions replace this with the familiar vertical wavy line:

In right-hand arpeggios and arpeggio-like ornaments, the bottom note, as a rule, is played on the beat; in the left hand, the top note of the arpeggio usually falls on the beat and the preceding notes are anticipatory.

Mozart: Sonata no. 14, K. 457

Haydn: Sonata, Hob. 16:52

Mozart: Sonata, K. 533

Mozart: Sonata no. 11, K. 331

RECOMMENDED READING

Badura-Skoda, Eva and Paul. *Interpreting Mozart on the Keyboard* (trans. Leo Black). London: Barrie & Rockliff, 1962.

Ferguson, Howard. *Keyboard Interpretation.* New York and London: Oxford University Press, 1975.

Türk, Daniel Gottlob. *Klavierschule* (1789). Facsimile ed. by Edwin R. Jacobi. Kassel: Barenreiter, 1962.

Note: Good *Urtext* editions of classical and romantic masters usually contain detailed pertinent information on ornamentation.

ORNAMENTATION IN THE ROMANTIC PERIOD

Following the trend of the classical era, nineteenth-century composers wrote out ornaments more and more fully, either with regular-size notes in exact rhythmic patterns or with small notes, leaving the final determination of the rhythmic scheme to the performer.

Schumann: "The Poet Speaks," op. 15 no. 13

Chopin: Nocturne, op. 15

Trills begin, as a rule, on the main note, on the beat, unless the main note is preceded by an upper appoggiatura:

If the principal note is preceded by an appoggiatura of the same pitch, the trill begins on the main note; the small note itself is not repeated: E-237

If the principal note is preceded by a double appoggiatura of which the second note is of the same pitch as the main note, the trill begins on the upper auxiliary note.

In general, the main consideration is to link the beginning of the trill smoothly with the preceding tones.

One of the most frequently occurring ornaments in the romantic period is the *upper mordent*, variously notated , , or, rarely, . Depending on the tempo and musical context, it may be performed:

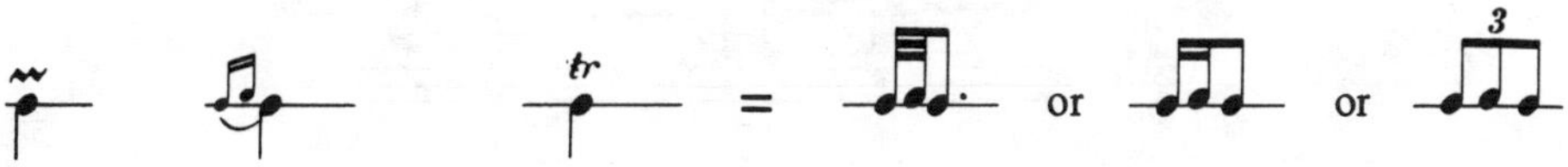

Usually the first note of the figure is played on the beat, but there are frequent exceptions:

- When the principal note is the beginning of a phrase or phrase segment, this note will fall on the beat and the grace notes will be anticipatory:

Chopin: Impromptu, op. 29

- When the main note carries a staccato or accent mark, it is played on the beat:

Schumann: "Harvest Song," op. 68 no. 24

Appoggiaturas are sometimes written out with regular-size notes:

Chopin: Polonaise, op. 26 no. 1

Frequently the composer gives other indications of the ornament's location in the metric scheme. In the following example, the notation makes clear that the appoggiatura precedes the beat:

Schumann: "Warum?" op. 12 no. 3

In most cases, however, the rhythmic positioning of the appoggiatura can be decided only on the basis of the musical evidence at hand. Especially ambiguous is the meaning of the small eighth note with a line across the stem 𝆔. This may be an unaccented grace note:

Schumann: "Reaper's Song," op. 68 no. 18

or a short, on-the-beat appoggiatura:

Chopin: Mazurka, op. 17 no. 4

In the left hand, appoggiaturas are usually played before the beat (with pedal), especially when they serve as a supporting bass:

Schumann: "Album Leaf," op. 99 no. 6

Ornamental groups written out in small notes often follow the outline of the turn, especially in Chopin's music, and should be positioned so that they fall into a natural rhythmic scheme and promote smooth melodic continuity–which in most cases means the small notes are performed before the beat.

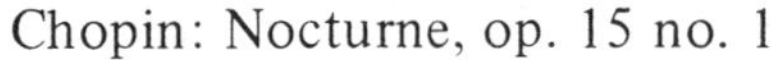
Chopin: Nocturne, op. 15 no. 1

Arpeggios, indicated either by small notes or by vertical wavy lines, are performed in the following manner: in the right hand, the bottom note of a broken chord is usually played on the beat; in the left hand, the top note falls on the beat.

Chopin: Nocturne, op. 9 no. 2

Chopin: Waltz, op. posth.

When there is a separate arpeggio sign in front of both a right- and left-hand chord, the notes of the two chords are broken almost simultaneously, with the bottom bass note slightly anticipated; when the wavy line extends over both staves, the notes should be sounded in succession, at a speed consistent with the mood, tempo, and time element involved:

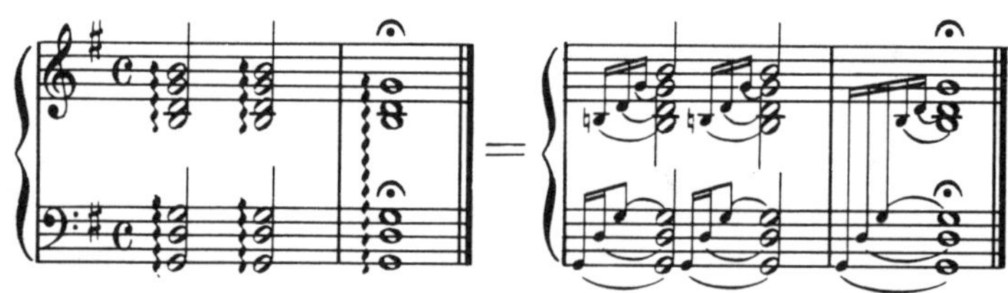

The arpeggio should not impede the flow of melody by delaying a note in the middle of a phrase. For instance, in the following example the third melody note should be played on the beat and should not be dislocated by the arpeggio:

Grieg: "Longing for Home," op. 57 no. 6

There are many instances in the romantic piano repertory when right-hand arpeggios are used in the style of harp or guitar chords; in such cases the top note of the arpeggio is played on the beat:

Rachmaninoff: Serenade, op. 3 no. 5

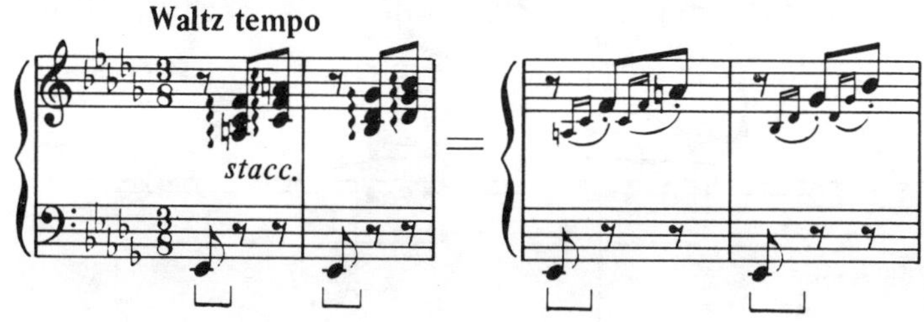

See also Mendelssohn's "Spring Song", op. 62 no. 6.

RECOMMENDED READING

Dunn, John Petrie. *Ornamentation in the Works of Frederick Chopin.* London: Novello, 1921.

Ferguson, Howard. *Keyboard Interpretation.* New York and London: Oxford University Press, 1975.

ORNAMENTATION IN THE TWENTIETH CENTURY

Twentieth-century composers notate embellishments with consistent exactness, which eliminates ambiguity and also restricts the performer's interpretive options. Ornaments in contemporary music are to be played exactly as notated.

Trills begin on the principal note, unless otherwise indicated by the composer. Trill preparations and terminations are indicated in small notes. Often even the rhythmic scheme is spelled out in detail:

Bartók: Sonatina

Ornaments written in small notes are to be played *before* the beat, unless indicated otherwise.

Ornamental groups resembling appoggiaturas, turns, upper mordents, etc. are often written out in regular-size notes, in exact rhythmic patterns:

Prokofiev: "Tales of the Old Grandmother"

Debussy: Arabesque, no. 2

Granados: "The Maiden and the Nightingale"

Arpeggios are generally played upward, as in the romantic period. If another interpretation is desired, the notation provides the necessary information. Some composers, for instance Schoenberg and Křenek, revert to the baroque practice of indicating the direction of the arpeggios with an arrowhead (,). Others provide detailed notation of the arpeggio pattern initially, which is then followed throughout the piece:

Kodály: Piano Music, op. 3

Bartók: Bagatelle, op. 6 no. 7

TWO

THEORY AND BASIC KEYBOARD SKILLS

Theory: The Elementary Aspects

An Overview and Selected List of Texts

HAZEL GHAZARIAN SKAGGS

Theory, according to one definition, is "the abstract knowledge of any art as opposed to the practice of it." In music, the subjects that may come under the heading of theory include form, harmony, counterpoint, composition, ear training, esthetics, and, on the earliest levels, the fundamental concepts of pitch and rhythm.

THEORY IN THE PIANO STUDIO

Whereas piano lessons in the early part of the twentieth century were exclusively devoted to the teaching of performance skills, there is today a growing tendency to teach theory as well. This is often referred to as teaching music through the study of the piano, particularly by group piano specialists. No matter what the teaching approach or method may be, a modern pedagogue must be aware that the knowledge of theory is a precondition of musical understanding and competence. Familiarity with the basic concepts of theory (often referred to as "the grammar of music") greatly facilitates reading, sight reading, and memorization, and helps the student develop independent thinking, instead of blindly following the teacher's step-by-step instructions. And there are other considerations which make understanding music theory so important. The ability to perform on the piano is not the only key to musical satisfaction; a student may enjoy sight-playing, improvisation, composition, or harmonizing simple songs or current pop tunes far better than giving a recital performance of one or two pieces. The only means to acquire these skills is through the study of theory. Moreover, should the student decide to major in music in college, a firm theoretical background will make the freshman year much easier. In some instances, theory may be a prerequisite for entering a college music program.

The extent to which theory is to be included in the studio curriculum unfortunately is predicated upon other matters than the teacher's philosophy of education. The optimum studio situation exists when the parent is willing and able to enroll the child for two lessons a week. The teacher may then devise a complete course of theoretical study, with one lesson devoted to piano performance and the other (perhaps a class) to theory. The teacher blessed with this schedule, if disinterested in theory instruction, may engage someone to give the theory lessons.

If lessons are given only once a week, some teachers may demand a longer lesson (one hour, perhaps) in order to include theory as part of the piano program. As the student becomes more advanced, less time is available for theory; by then, however, a sufficiently broad base of theory can have been covered.

The teacher limited to a half-hour lesson has difficulty "squeezing in" theory subjects, and must use all sorts of devices to cover a maximum amount of theory instruction in a minimum amount of time.

There are a variety of ways to approach the teaching of theory in the piano studio. Some teachers may elect not to use theory books, but to integrate theory with technical drills, harmonization of folk tunes, and interval reading. Below are some examples of this procedure.

Theory through Technical Drill (first year)

- Five-finger exercise: C-D-E-F-G, the first five notes of the C-major scale, transposed to all keys.
- Transposition by ear (do-re-mi-fa-sol)
- Transposition by the pattern whole step, whole step, half step, whole step (W-W-H-W).

Harmonization of Simple Folk Tunes

- "Merrily We Roll Along": harmonize with chords I-V (C-E-G/B-D-G) For pianistic purposes, the inversion works better.
- Transpose to other keys.

Reading through Intervals

- See (read), feel (play), hear fifths and other intervals progressively.
  - Play two-note slurs a fifth apart:

  - Learn a piece with fifths.
  - Improvise a piece with fifths.
- Proceed with other intervals, following the above three steps.

THEORY BOOKS

The use of theory books may save the teacher planning time, give the course of study more structure, and provide visual aids, reinforcement of concepts through written work, and well-formulated tests.

The choice of theory books will depend on the time available for such study. Theory textbooks may best be reserved for one-hour classes in theory; workbooks with single or tear sheets will serve the rushed teacher well, since the student can prepare assignments at home which can be quickly corrected at the lesson.

In selecting a theory book, the following considerations may be kept in mind. Does the teacher:

- Want a theory book that follows the piano method that is being used?
- Want the workbook sheets loose, bound, or perforated? When perforated, the pages may be kept bound or removed when necessary.
- Require a book that is mostly keyboard theory rather than written work?
- Prefer a programmed text so the student can study alone?

The synopses and lists below are not only for selecting the theory book that best serves the teacher's needs, but also as a guide for devising a theory curriculum that will fit the time schedule.

Marvin Kahn: *Theory Papers* (Belwin-Mills)

Book 1: Note reading and notation
Directional reading drills
Rhythms, accidentals
Intervals
Major and minor seconds and thirds
Special sight-reading section

Book 2: The formation and use of chords
Basic chord progressions
Ear-training work
Keyboard harmony drills
Various simple types of bass accompaniment
Ways to supply chordal backgrounds

Book 3: Normal chord progressions
Harmonization of melodies
Basic chords of the key and their functions
Altered chords
Dominant embellishments
Cycle of fifths and dominant sevenths
Analysis
Keyboard harmony drills
Major key signatures

Denes Agay: *Theory Guidebooks (The Young Pianist's Library,* volumes 12-A, B, C). (Warner Bros. Publications)

Volume A: The Keyboard; The Letter Names of the Keys
The Staff; The Grand Staff; Treble Clef and Bass Clef

Notes; Time Values
Bar Lines; Measures; Time Signatures
Rest Signs; Counting with Notes and Rests
Additional Notes on the Staff (Three Cs); Drawing Stems
Sharps and Flats
Further Skills in Note Reading and Writing
The Eighth Note; Review of Time Values; Counting
Tempo Marks
The Natural; Review of Sharps and Flats
All Notes of the Grand Staff; Note Spelling
General Review

Volume B: Ledger Lines
Downbeat and Upbeat
New Notes on the Treble and Bass Staffs
Half Steps and Whole Steps
Intervals; Learning to "hear" Intervals
The Tie and the Slur
Natural Accents
Major Scales; Building Major Scales; Key Signatures
Chords; Triads; Major and Minor Triads
Transposition
A Review of Notes and Time Values
Crossword Puzzle (A Test)

Volume C: A Review of Intervals;
Major, Minor, and Diminished Triads
The Dotted Eighth Note
The Tonic, Dominant, and Subdominant Triads
Review of Key Signatures; The Circle of Fifths
Major and Minor Intervals; Minor Scales
Triads Built on the Notes of the Minor Scale
Review (Notes, Clefs, Counting, Rhythm)
The Three Positions of Triads (Inversions)
Seventh Chords; The Dominant Seventh Chord
Various Chord Positions; Patterns of Accompaniment
Writing Harmonies By Letter Names; Writing Accompaniment
Phrases and Sentences

THEORY BOOKS IN LOOSE SHEETS

Kahn, Marvin. *Theory Papers.* Belwin-Mills, 1954–1958. Book 1, 24 pages; Book 2, 24 pages; Book 3, 48 pages. Includes special sight-reading drills. Each set of papers has a corresponding teacher's supplement in book form, available separately. Contents listed on page 149.

McIntosh, Edith. *Theory and Musicianship.* Carl Fischer, 1955. *Lessons in the Rudiments of Music*, with work sheets; Book 1, 58 pages. *Mu-*

sic Symbols, Books 1 and 2. Preparatory lessons to *Theory and Musicianship*; sixteen lessons in each book, with work sheets for practice in understanding and writing music symbols.

Montgomery, Merle. *Music Theory Papers*. Carl Fischer, 1954–1959. Set 1: "Eye and Ear Training for Nine-Year-Olds"; Set 2: "Seeing and Hearing, for Ten and Older"; Set 3: "Sight and Sound"; Set 4: "Music Composition Papers." 30 pages each.

Weybright, June. *Theory Worksheets*. Belwin-Mills, 1964. Sets 1, 2, and 3, each set 32 pages. May be used in conjunction with the *Belwin Piano Method* by June Weybright. Points for grading are included.

THEORY BOOKS IN OPTIONAL LOOSE-LEAF FORM

Agay, Denes. *Theory Guide Books*, vols. A, B, C (*The Young Pianist's Library* no. 12-A, B, C) Warner Bros. Publications, 1965. Each book 30 pages, perforated for optional removal. Basic workbooks on elementary theory. Each book has a page of "teacher's notes" (guidelines). Contents listed on page 149-50.

Brimhall, John. *Theory Notebook*, books 1, 2, 3. Charles Hansen, 1969. 29 lessons with self-quizzes, writing practice, fill-ins and perforated theory sheets. 30 pages each. Each book has an answer sheet.

Glover, David Carr. *Theory Tablet*. Charles Hansen, 1957. First, Second, Third, Basic Music Fundamentals, Note Spelling, Practical Work Sheets. 24 pages in each tablet.

Schaum, John W. *Keynote Music Speller*. Schaum Publications, 1961. A systematized set of worksheets combine the mental picture of key and note. . . "an effective aid to faster music reading."

Zeitlin, Poldi, and David Goldberger. *The Theory Papers*, Books 1, 2, 3 (*The CMP Piano Library*). Consolidated Music Publishers, 1961-1963. Fifteen lessons per book, with worksheets covering elementary subjects progressively.

THEORY TEXTS IN BOOK FORM

Aldridge, Maisie. *The Bass Clef Book*. Galaxy Music Corp., 1965. 25 pages.

Benner, Lora. *Theory for Piano Students,* Books 1, 2, 3, 4, 5. G. Schirmer, 1962–1968; 51 to 54 pages. Each is a text-workbook, includes musical history, and ends with an examination. *Teachers' Reference* for all five books is available.

Clark, Mary Elizabeth and David Carr Glover. *Piano Theory*. Belwin-Mills, 1968. A programmed text, primer and levels one through six; 32 pages (level 1). There are removable answer sheets in the back. The books are correlated to the *David Carr Glover Piano Library* books. Each one begins with a pretest and ends with a post-test.

Diller, Angela. *Lines and Spaces*. G. Schirmer, 1925. A music writing book, 42 pages (7 pages are blank manuscript paper). This book gives practice in writing and reading notes.

Holt, Hilda. *Note-Speller: A Music Writing Book Progressively Arranged for Beginning Piano Students*. Carl Fischer, 1947. 32 pages (4 pages of blank paper). The drill material includes key signatures, exercises for counting time, circle of keys, and the more remote ledger lines.

Fredrich, Frank. *A First Work Book of Scales and Chords.* Willis, 1963. 32 pages. Besides the scales and chords there are five folk songs to be played both as written and in tonic minor (or from minor to major).

Hirschberg, David. *Theory Is Fun*, Books 1 and 2. Musicord Publications (Belwin-Mills), 1950, 1951. 47 and 48 pages. Covers the usual elementary topics.

Hofstad, Mildred. *A to G, a Very First Musical Alphabet Book*. Boston Music Co., 1955. 24 pages. The book is for very young students. The print is extra large.

Palmer, Willard A. and Amanda Vick Lethco. *Creating Music Theory Papers*, Books 1 and 2. Alfred Publishing Co., 1973. 48 pages each. Both books reinforce and review the contents of the Palmer and Lethco *Creating Music at the Piano*. There are fifty-four flashcards for the student to make in Book 1, thirty-six in Book 2. Games, puzzles, quizzes, etc. are plentiful. Blue and black ink are used.

Paulson, Joseph and Irving Cheyette. *Basic Theory–Harmony: A Text and Work Book for the School Musician*. Pro Art Publications, 1951. 84 pages. Modern (popular) chord names and symbols are used rather than the classical ones. Covers two years of class study work in elementary theory.

Priesling, Dorothy, and Libbie Tecklin. *Language of the Piano*. Carl Fischer, 1956. 88 pages. A workbook in theory and keyboard harmony. Its purpose, in the words of the authors, is "to develop keyboard and analytic skills and to apply these skills to the performance of piano music." This is definitely for serious intermediate students. It is amply illustrated with classical music; classical chord names and symbols are used.

Schaum, John W. *Harmony Lessons*, Books 1 and 2. Belwin-Mills, 1949. 31 pages each. In workbook form; the two books include transposition (melodically and harmonically), intervals, triads, inversions, cadences, harmonizing, and modulation. Answers to *Harmony Lessons* are available for the teacher.

ADDITIONAL THEORY BOOKS

Bishop, Dorothy. *Chords in Action*. Carl Fischer, 1956. 64 pages. The theory in this book can be immediately applied to harmonizing and arranging melodies (mostly folk).

Brimhall, John. *Dictionary of Chords: Piano/Organ*. Charles Hansen, 1976. 33 pages. Includes keyboard-diagram presentation of chords as well as chord notation.

Brimhall, John. *It's About Time: Note Value Relationships, Meter, Rhythm*. Charles Hansen, 1976. 32 pages. Includes workbook pages and self-quizzes for reviewing.

De Vito, Albert. *Chord Encyclopedia* (for all instruments). Kenyon Publications, 1966. 96 pages. This encyclopedia includes chord notation on treble and bass staffs, and keyboard diagrams of the chords.

Newman, Elizabeth. *The Beginner's Own Book: Folk Songs Carefully Graded for Ear-Training, Sight-Singing, Harmonizing and Transposition*. Carl Fischer, 1925 (1957). 53 pages. The first twelve pages are a teacher's guide; the rest of the book contains songs to be harmonized, eight of them in minor keys.

Robyn, Louise, and Howard Hanks. *The Robyn-Hanks Harmony: A Junior Course in Written Harmony, Keyboard Harmony and Ear Training*, Books 1 and 2. Theodore Presser (Oliver Ditson), 1936. 60 pages.

Schaum, John W. *Chord Speller*, for piano or organ. Schaum Publications, 1967. 24 pages.

—— *Interval Speller*, for piano or organ. Schaum Publications, 1966. 24 pages.

Schaum, Wesley. *Rhythm Workbook*, Books 1–4, for piano and organ. Schaum Publications, 1969. Each book 32 pages. Includes workbook pages and self-quizzes for reviewing.

Townsend, Lillian. *Key to the Piano*. Carl Fischer, 1958. 32 pages. This is an easy course in playing favorite melodies. It contains songs only in the key of F within a one-octave range. The student harmonizes these songs with I, IV, and V7 chords.

Zepp, Arthur. *Just Write "Theory in Action": A Supplementary Book for All Students of Music*. Pro Art Publications, 1966. 36 pages. This book tries to actively involve the student in theory through written work that, in the words of the author, helps the student to "think, see, hear, and do."

—— *Let's Learn Chords*, Books 1 and 2. Pro Art Publications, 1957. Book 1, 52 pages; Book 2, 45 pages. For hands that are fully developed, because of the octaves.

—— *Let's Improvise*, Books 1 and 2. Pro Art Publications, 1957. 36 pages each. Book 1 has twenty-two songs for keyboard arranging. It uses major, minor, and seventh chords. Book 2, which also includes twenty-two songs, introduces augmented and diminished chords.

PROGRAMMED TEXTS

Basescu, Bernard. *Music Reading for Beginners*. Bryn Mawr, Pa.: Presser, 1972.

Clough, John. *Scales, Intervals, Keys and Triads: A Programmed Book of Elementary Music Theory*. New York: W.W. Norton, 1964.

Horacek, Leo and Gerald Lefkoff. *Programmed Ear Training* (four vols.). New York: Harcourt, Brace and World, 1970.

ELEMENTARY COMPOSITION

Elementary composition may be a part of the theory program in the piano studio. It is generally introduced through the verse method or through composition assignments which require specific rhythmic patterns, intervals, notes and rests, form, and fingering plans.

Because the young student is already familiar with songs, the verse method is an easy way to begin. The teacher may show how the words of one of the student's beginner pieces may be played in different ways.

A text for the teacher who plans to begin with verse is Sue Shannon: *Composing at the Keys*, Book 1 (Alfred Publishing Co.; Book 2 of this course continues without verse).

Another simple approach to composition might be to give assignments using specific controls, such as fingering plans (for example, the five-finger F-minor pattern), triads, rhythmic patterns, notes and rests, etc. The Frances Clark *Music Tree* series (Summy-Birchard) includes such assignments. Suggesting titles that appeal to the student, showing the work of other students the same age, and praising or at least encouraging his efforts are all positive factors.

A book that can provide guidance and inspiration for both teacher and students is Carola Grindea: *We Make Our Own Music* (Alexander Broude, Inc.). In six stages, the author explains how to teach composition; each contains ample examples of manuscripts in the children's own handwriting.

What does the child gain from composition? First, composition provides a very personal frame of reference. The teacher might now say: "Remember how you took your coda in 'Moon Beams' from the end of theme A; from where does this composer take his coda?" Second, it gives the student better insight into form and theme construction. Third, the student gains a greater awareness and understanding of notation and meter. Fourth, it provides the special kind of joy and sense of achievement that comes only from creative activity.

RECOMMENDED READING

Davie, Cedric Thorpe. *Musical Structure and Design*. New York: Dover, 1966.

Eschman, Karl. *Teaching Music Theory*. Boston: E.C. Schirmer Co., 1966.

McEachern, Jim. *Contemporary Music Theory*. Winnipeg, Manitoba: Educators Research Centre, 1975.

Read, Gardner. *Music Notation*. Boston: Allyn and Bacon, 1964.

Weed, Dorothy. "Theory as Musical Experience." *The Piano Teacher* November–December 1963.

Theory: The Basis of Musicianship

ROSETTA GOODKIND

Teaching theory fulfills one of the important missions of the piano teacher by establishing that the art of playing is more than the mastery of the fingers, by providing the tools for greater confidence and security in performance, and by stimulating the mind and kindling the desire to read between the "lines and spaces" for more intelligent search and discovery.

It is fair to say that while very few piano students pursue a career in music, all are entitled to a complete musical education. It is also generally accepted that ear training, harmony, and structural analysis are primary requisites upon which to build an intelligent performance, since the main function of these subjects is to heighten the sense of hearing and musical understanding.

PRACTICAL RELEVANCE OF THEORY

Of course, teaching theory requires special thought and preparation on the instructor's part, if he or she is to avoid turning the study of this subject into a rather dreary experience amounting to little more than mindless repetitions of unrelated drills. An essential step toward success is to link the study of theory, in a practical keyboard-harmony program, with every piece of music played. Experience has taught us that students respond most enthusiastically to abstract fundamentals when they discover their relevance to the music itself. The time to begin is at the very first lesson.

I have vivid recollections of a harrowing experience of many years ago. At age ten, while performing the Clementi Sonatina, op. 36 no. 5 at a student recital, I had a memory lapse and reached an impasse. It happened as I approached the second theme in the recapitulation. Remembering my teacher's admonition, "Whatever happens, keep going," I did just that! Obviously ill-trained, I repeated the exposition and development four times—turning a three-minute piece into a ten-minute eternity—when a miracle of finger-memory blessedly extricated me from the nightmare. The "open sesame" chords finally brought the piece to a conclusion. With a knowledge of harmony and form I could have been spared all that frustration. I would have been aware that bars 62 to 66 in the recapitulation progress to the key of G and do not modulate to D, as in bars 12 to 16 of the exposition. The memory of that event, and the joy of discovering the "language" of music years later, underscored for me the necessity of piano students to be thoroughly familiar with all the basics of theory.

MUSIC AS A LANGUAGE

Every language has a vocabulary and grammar of its own which one must comprehend in order to be articulate and expressive. Music, like all other languages, communicates through phrases (clauses and sentences) rather than through unrelated tones (isolated words). It is indispensible that our students learn how families of sounds (keys) are arranged in logical fashion (structure), and how these sounds can be communicated with subtlety and depth of feeling (expression).

Alas, how indifferent and inadequate is the training of many average students. Indeed, the talented ones are sometimes even more neglected. For some teachers, lulled by their pupil's musicality, may unwittingly mistake natural flair as an indication of knowledge. Even those with perfect pitch, who can astound others by naming isolated tones, may still be musically illiterate. On the other hand, a student of limited ability trained in musicianship, can frequently give a very creditable performance.

Today's teacher has a rich treasury of instructive materials from which to choose. But the method of presentation and the teacher's attitude play important roles in the student's receptivity or indifference. While enthusiasm, ingenuity, and preparation are the essence of the art of teaching, it takes a patient, dedicated teacher to crack the resistance of a student who would much rather play than think! To generate and maintain interest, attractive materials and appealing ways must be found. Concepts such as chord inversions and the order of keys and signatures can be confusing unless presented in a logical fashion.

Since so much of our music was written by composers of the eighteenth and nineteenth centuries, it is traditional to begin with major and minor tonalities, on which the harmonic vocabulary of those periods is based. First and foremost, it is necessary to teach some of the basics; of course, always accompanied by sound.

THE ELEMENTS OF TRADITIONAL HARMONY

An *interval* is the distance between two notes, or—expressed acoustically—the difference in pitch between two tones. In a harmonic interval the two notes are sounded together; in a melodic interval they are sounded one after the other. Intervals are usually classified as follows:

Minor intervals (major intervals reduced by a half step):

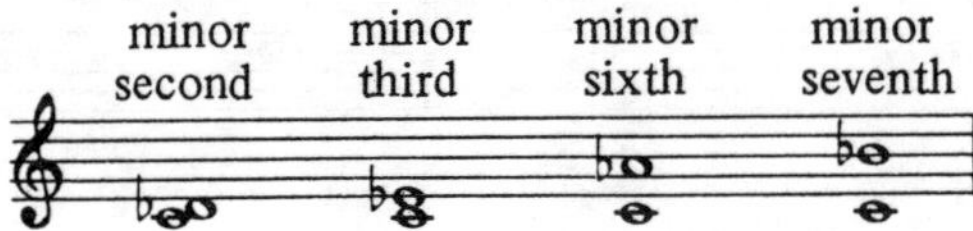

Augmented intervals (perfect and major intervals increased by a half step):

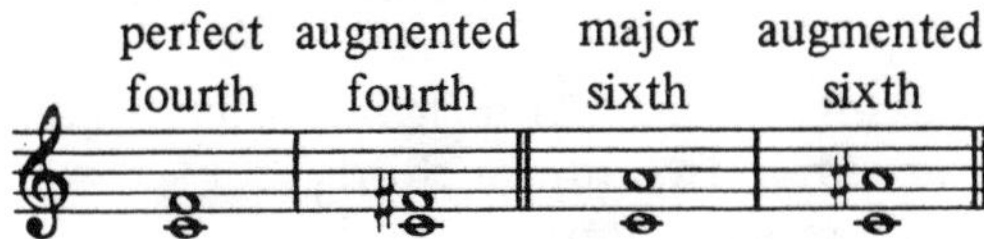

Diminished intervals (perfect and minor intervals reduced by a half step):

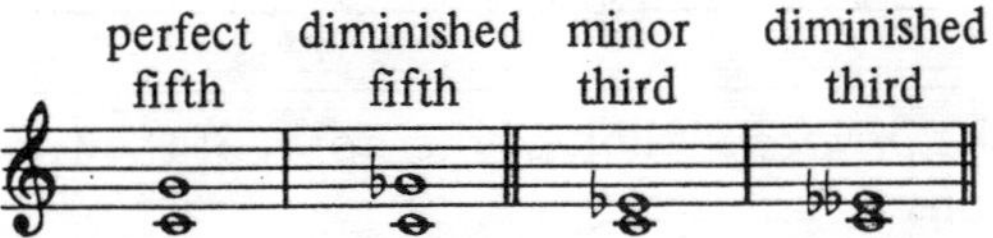

Diatonic scales (major and minor) consist of seven consecutive tones within an octave, arranged in a pattern of whole steps and half steps. Intervals in the major scales are:

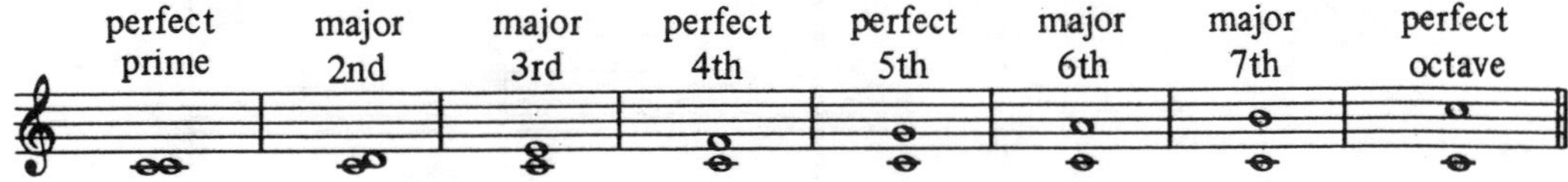

Intervals in minor scales are formed according to the component tones of the type of minor scale in question (natural, harmonic, and melodic).

Triads (three-tone chords) can be built on each of the seven tones of any scale. The triads of the C major scale are:

Of these, I, IV, and V are major triads; II, III, and VI are minor triads; and VII is a diminished triad.

Most frequently used triads:

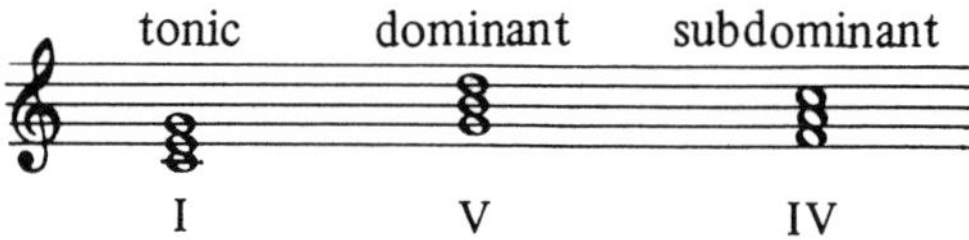

The dominant (V) and subdominant (IV) triads have a strong pull toward the tonic (I).

The four kinds of triads (three-tone chords):

Major triads consist of two harmonic intervals (both thirds): the lower interval is a major third, in which the two tones are two whole steps apart and, above it, a minor third in which the tones are one and a half steps apart.

Minor triads consist of a minor third (lower interval) and a major third.

Diminished triads contain two minor thirds.

Augmented triads contain two major thirds.

Triads may be *inverted*: that is, the notes of the triad may appear in different positions.

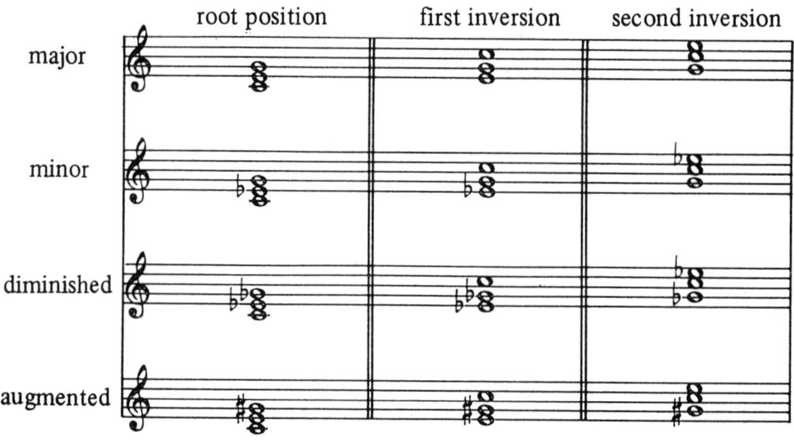

Seventh chords consist of a triad plus the seventh note above the root.

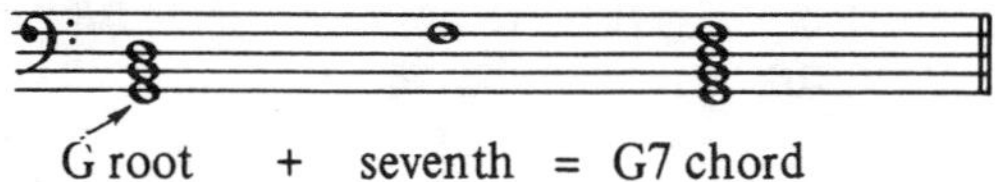

IDENTIFYING CHORDS

Any triad can be named by identifying its root note. When a chord consists of only line notes or only space notes within one staff (close position), the root is at the *bottom.*

An inverted chord consists of line notes *and* space notes. Inversions can be identified by the following notation landmarks:

- In triads, the root note will always be the *top note* of the harmonic interval of a fourth:

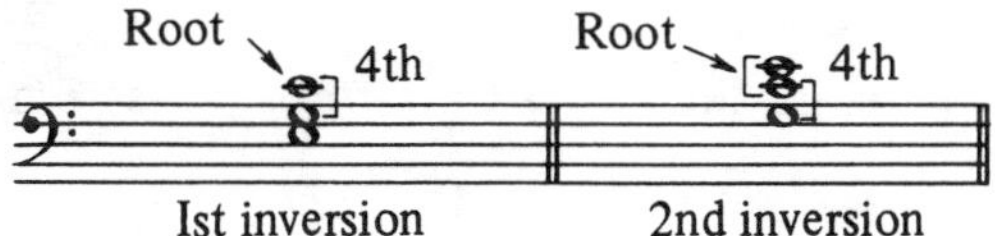

- In seventh chords, the root will always be the *top note* of the harmonic interval of a second:

- A seventh chord can be implied (even though incomplete) by the harmonic interval of a second.

FIGURED BASS SYMBOLS

The numbers under the chords refer to the intervals above the bottom note. When the chord is in root position, the figured bass symbols are customarily omitted. Inversions are indicated in the following manner:

- The number 6 under the bass note means that the root of the triad is at the interval of a sixth above the bass note (first inversion); the numbers $^6_4$ indicate that the root of the triad is a fourth above the bass (second inversion).

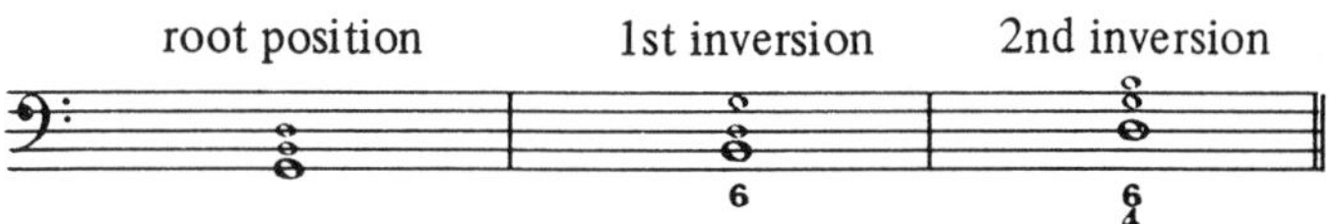

- Figured basses to indicate inversions of the dominant seventh chord:

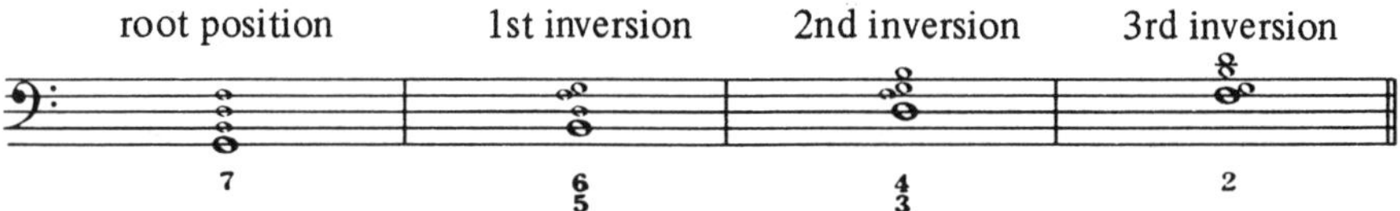

By means of various chord sequences, keys may change within the course of a composition. Such a *modulation* is not difficult to recognize when the student learns how to look and listen for the new tonic. It is also helpful to be guided by visual landmarks, such as the appearance of note alterations through repeated accidentals which necessarily lead into the new tonality.

In summary, here are the basics of harmony that every pianist should know:

- Intervals
- Scales: major and minor (three forms: natural, harmonic, melodic)
- Key signatures: the circle of keys (circle of fifths)
- Triads: major, minor, diminished, augmented (in all inversions)
- Seventh chords: the dominant seventh and its resolutions; other major, minor, and diminished seventh chords.
- Cadences: I-V-I, I-IV-V-I, I-IV-I^6_4-V-I, I-VI-IV-II^6-I^6_4-V^7-I (in all keys)
- Modulations: In a progressive order, to closely related keys at first (C to G, C to F, C to A minor, etc.), then to more distant ones.

So much for the essentials of harmony. But these are only theoretical facts which must be applied and made relevant. How, one may ask, can the teacher evoke a student's willingness to learn something which seems so perplexing and dryly "scientific"? By all means through an appropriate piece of music which contains the specific theoretical concepts to be absorbed. The following steps are recommended. First, enthusiasm for the piece must be aroused by whatever method or approach the teacher chooses: playing the work or parts of it, pointing out some especially attractive, noteworthy, or novel features; relating some interesting data on the work, the composer, the style, etc.

Then the student can be enlightened as to the form, key, scales, important chords, cadences and modulations that might occur. Once a student is motivated through an interest in the composition, abstract drill, involving the above concepts, will be more acceptable. At that point, memorization of all facets can be undertaken. It is unfortunate that so many students devote years to learning scales, chords, and chord progressions only by rote, without ever realizing and learning their implicitly beautiful qualities. Undoubtedly some rote playing is valuable, even necessary, but along with the digital experiences must come a musical awareness. Scales, chords, and other theoretical concepts are not just dry, boring formulas. In the hands of the masters they become tools of the highest forms of musical expression. Think, for instance, of the charming, innocent playfulness of many Mozart scale passages, the exquisite poetic mood evoked by simple broken triads in Beethoven's "Moonlight" Sonata, and so on. Students must be guided to understand this, and to listen with empathy and discrimination; otherwise their study will become a chore, and their playing will lack musicianship and comprehension. As teachers, we must cultivate their ears.

HARMONY AND EAR TRAINING

Harmony and ear training can sometimes be taught more effectively through imagery. If we stimulate the imagination and endow tones with "live" personalities, it is one more step to perceive the tones of a "key" as a "musical family." Tones, like people, need identification. Therefore, we give this "family" a name (the key of D major, for instance) and we identify it with the first and most important tone of its scale (the keytone).

From the earliest lessons, the ear must become involved. Once students are seated at the keyboard, they become impatient to play; any discussion becomes a delay and an intrusion. Have them move away from the piano in order to focus their attention and engage their interest in pure sound. Whatever approach is used, be it improvisation or singing—both excellent—some physical movement is helpful to describe and illustrate on a magnified scale the subtle distances between tones. Many programs have been devised to educate the ear. Some methods relate intervals to familiar tunes. Others, like the Kodály method and Dalcroze-eurythmics, employ hand or body motion.

In order to appreciate fully the often delicate and subtle connection and interplay between tones and tone groups, one must listen and carefully observe the unfolding and constantly shifting tonal panorama. Each tone expresses relative action or repose, depending on its harmonic and rhythmic context. By listening intently and actively it becomes increasingly clear what each tone is doing and what its role is in the tonal fabric. Is it at rest or is it moving? And if it is moving, where is it headed?

An ongoing program of ear training should be continued in depth throughout piano studies, to include intervals, chords, scales, and rhythm.

Students are intrigued to learn that the basic harmonic material used by the great masters of tonal music (I-IV-V chords) is identical to that found in popular and folk music. It is here that we can stimulate imagination by indicating the importance of hearing and becoming acquainted with the versatility of chords. When sensitively played, each chord can convey an emotion or influence the direction of the harmonic sequence. For not only do chords serve to establish keys and act predictably at cadences, but they also have an important impact on the character and interpretation of the melody.

The student's interest and appreciation will be heightened if the teacher can convey the emotional and esthetic qualities and characteristics of various chords. The following are random examples of the many ways one can attempt to savor the effect of certain harmonies, tonal sequences, and cadences.

The mercurial "mood changes" by shifts from major to minor and vice versa; the "urgency" of the diminished seventh; the "excitement" of a modulation; the "serenity" and secure "homecoming" feeling of the tonic; the "grandeur" of the $^6_4$ chord and the "anticipation" aroused by its use approaching a cadenza; the "surprise" of an evasion (V-VI); the "colorful subtleties" of chromaticism; the "foreboding" of an augmented chord (sharped fifth); the "elegance" of changing harmonies under one melody tone; and so on.

EXPLORING MUSICAL FORMS

Structure and harmony are inseparable. Introducing the subject of analysis in an interesting way is a challenge. Students must be led into thinking as well as listening, but care must be taken not to overwhelm them with more information than can be absorbed comfortably.

For a "new" intermediate or moderately advanced student, I would begin by selecting a piece at least one level below his or her ability. Technical problems would only complicate matters. We don't wish to discourage or deflate the ego of someone who comes to that first lesson playing a Beethoven sonata without the vaguest notion of what is really in it structurally and harmonically. This is a delicate time in the teacher-pupil relationship. Because Clementi and Kuhlau sonatinas are lovely compositions and clearly representative of late eighteenth-century style and structure, they make good choices for first keyboard harmony lessons. Also, it is expeditious to have a repertory of reasonably tempting pieces (in easy signatures) to satisfy the craving for "bigger sounds," such as Heller's Études nos. 46, 26, and 24 from "Fifty Selected Studies" (G. Schirmer). Thereafter, structural and harmonic analysis can be integrated into the presentation and assignment of each piece. A familiarity with the elements of form (motive, phrase, sentence) is, of course, a prerequisite for analysis, and the student's secure grasp of these concepts must be established as a first step.

Since organization and preparation are the mainstays of good teaching, we must do our own homework before assigning a piece, in order to:

- select suitable material for study
- know its style, form, and all its component elements
- decide the manner in which we may want to stimulate the student's interest in the work, such as preplay, verbal information, etc.
- assign exercises that will reinforce the student's facility in all technical and interpretative aspects

In this fashion the teacher explicitly clarifies and gives a theory lesson on the work at hand. Many of these elements will become clearer as they are directly illustrated in analyzing Friedrich Kuhlau's Sonatina in C major, op. 20 no. 1.

TECHNICAL AND THEORETICAL REQUIREMENTS
(For Playing the Kuhlau Sonatina, Op. 20 No. 1)

- Scales (in two-octave range): C major, G major, C minor (three forms)
- Triads and inversions: I, IV, V, V^7 in above keys, plus A-flat major and F-sharp diminished triad.
- Chord progressions (cadences):

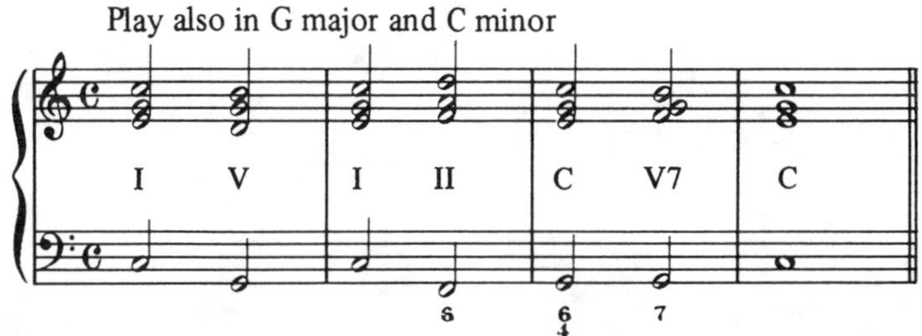

- Modulation (C major to G major):

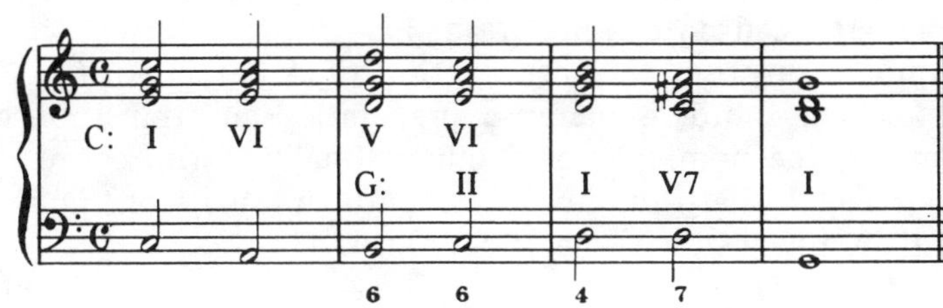

- Finger drills: Hanon, Ex. no. 1, to be played in above keys to familiarize fingers with the keyboard topography of scales involved.

MELODIC AND HARMONIC ELEMENTS
(In Kuhlau's Sonatina, Op. 20 No. 1)

- Scales: G major (measure 24); C minor melodic (m. 42); C major (m. 73)

- Melodic material based on chord tones:

In right hand:	C chord (ms. 1-2) C chord, second inversion (m. 3)
In left hand:	C chord (ms. 9-10) G chord, first inversion (ms. 11-12) C minor (ms. 13-14) D chord, first inversion (ms. 15-16)

- Chord tones in Alberti bass accompaniment: ms. 1–6, 17-20, 32–38, 50–55, 66–69
- Upper and lower neighbors of chord tones shaping melodies: ms. 7, 18, 19, 22, 23, etc.
- Roots of I, IV, V chords used to establish the key of G major (ms. 21–24)
- "Divided" chords: second inversion of C-major triad (m. 9), root position of G^7 (m. 11) in the right hand
- Suspensions and resolutions: the first note in m. 4, a C carried over from the previous measure, creates a suspension within the G^7 chord which resolves to the chord tone of B

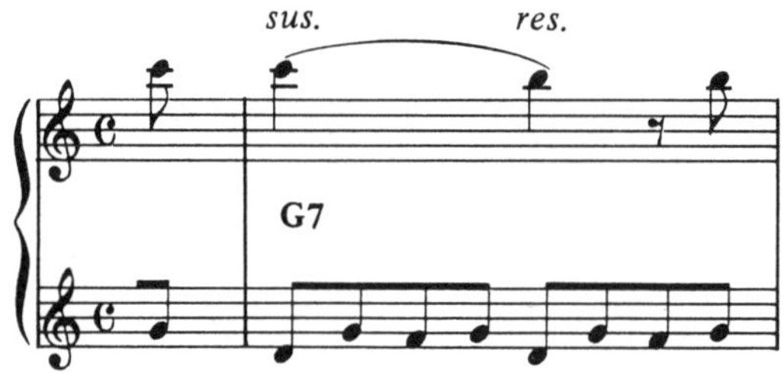

- Passing tones (between chord tones): ms. 18, 48–49
- Modulation: the dominant seventh chord of the new key (D^7 in m. 15–16) leads into G major (m. 17)
- Harmonic surprise: the introduction of A-flat major (m. 39), an unexpected chord, is merely a preparation and transition toward G major, the dominant of C-minor tonality. Both chords–A-flat major and F-sharp diminished seventh (m. 40)–are "pulling" cadentially toward the G-major chord (m. 41)

GLOSSARY OF ABBREVIATIONS AND TERMS
(Kuhlau's Sonatina, Op. 20 No. 1)

Capital letters indicate chord names (C-C major, Cm-C minor, etc.). Numerals under the staves indicate scale degrees and inversions.

CT	Chord tone
LN	Lower neighbor of chord tone
UN	Upper neighbor of chord tone
PT	Passing tone between chord tones
Sus.	Suspension of a tone within a given harmony
Res.	Resolution of a suspended tone into a chord tone
Alberti bass	A bass accompaniment for the left hand, consisting of a broken chord pattern; named for Domenico Alberti and used by many composers of the eighteenth and nineteenth centuries
Antecedent phrase	The first phrase of a musical sentence
Consequent phrase	The second or answering phrase in a musical sentence
Bridge	A short transition (usually modulatory)
Cadence	A sequence of two or more chords leading to a point of rest (temporary or final)
Coda	A closing statement, to reinforce an ending
Extension	The lengthening or development of a given theme
Period	A term used to indicate two consecutive, complementary sentences or phrases
Phrase	Shortest complete musical thought; equivalent to a clause or sentence in speech
Semicadence	Halfway point of rest
Transition	A connecting phrase that helps bind one section to another
Variation	Something new added to an already stated melody to embellish it and add new interest

Kuhlau: Sonatina, Op. 20 No. 1 (First Movement)

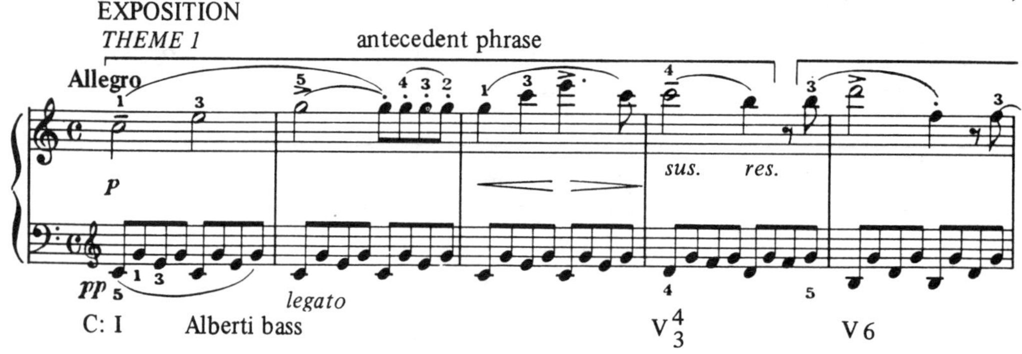

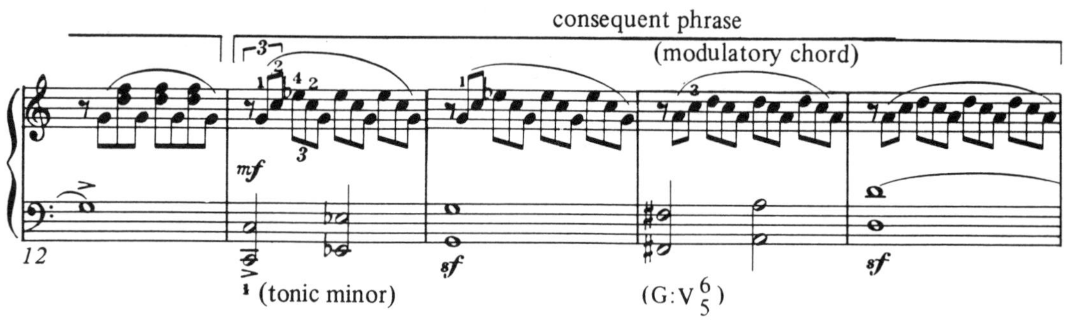

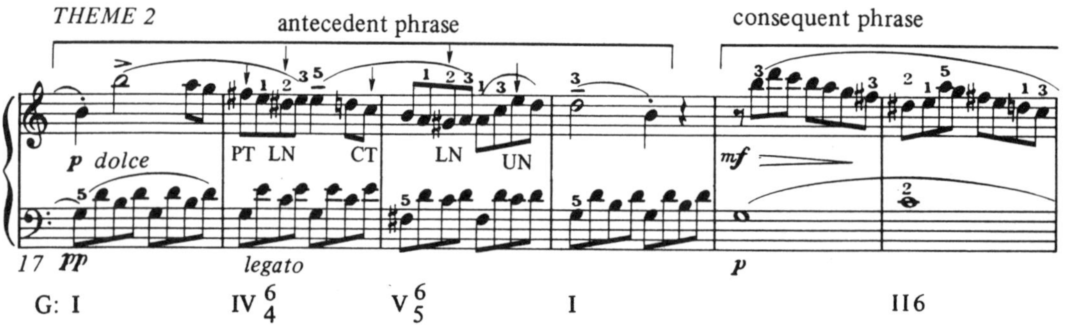

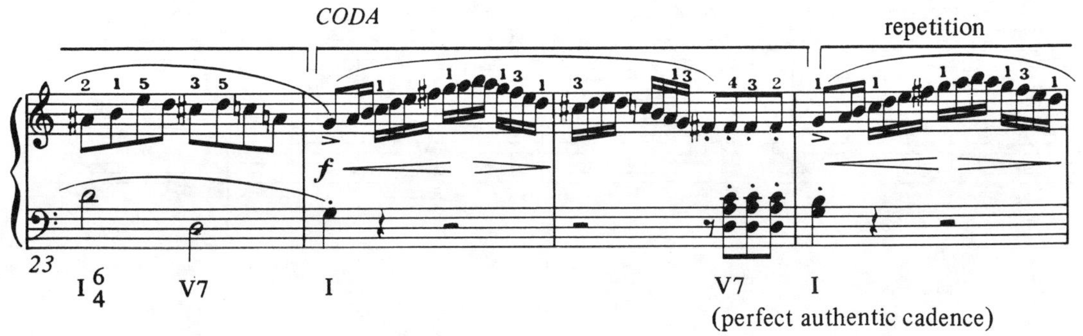
CODA
repetition
23
I 6 4
V7
I
V7
I
(perfect authentic cadence)

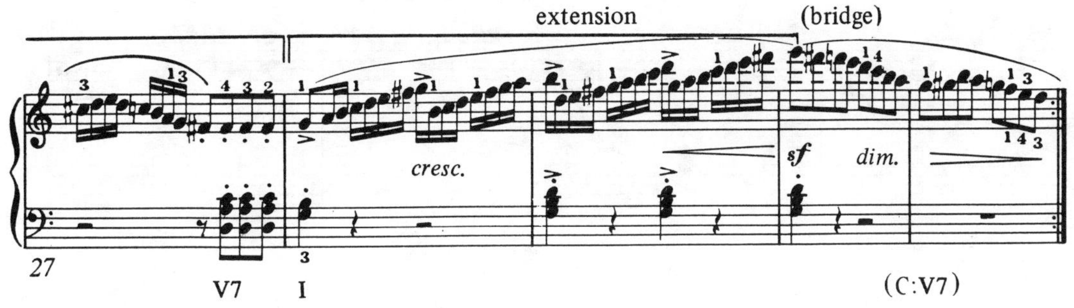
extension
(bridge)
cresc.
dim.
27
V7
I
(C:V7)

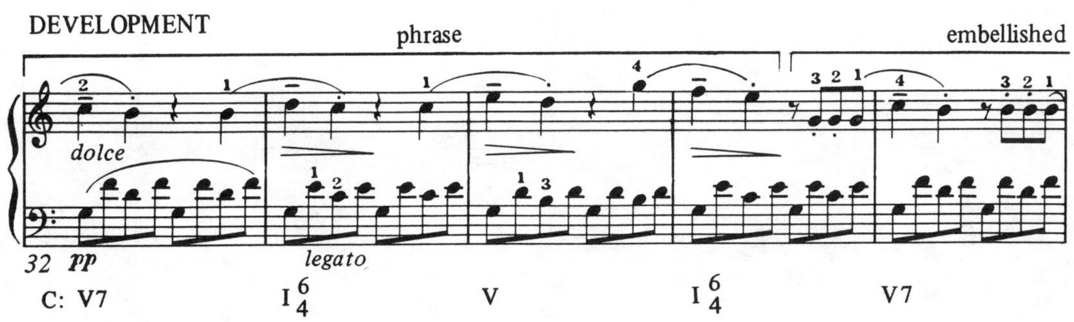
DEVELOPMENT
phrase
embellished
dolce
32
legato
C: V7
I 6 4
V
I 6 4
V7

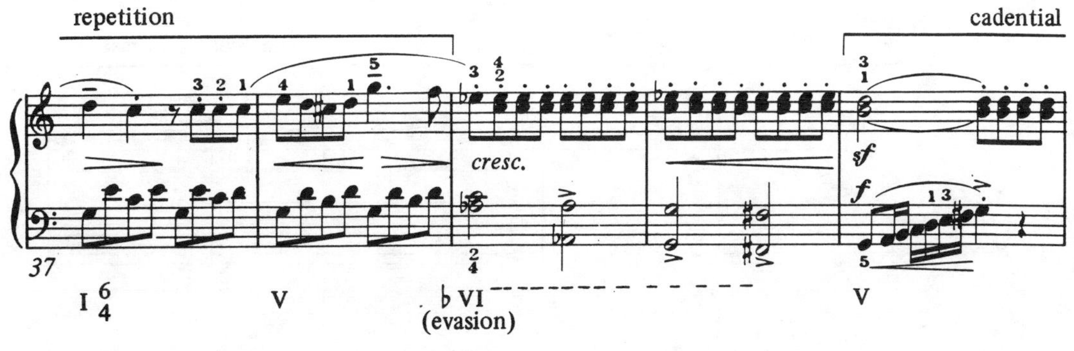
repetition
cadential
cresc.
37
I 6 4
V
♭VI
(evasion)
V

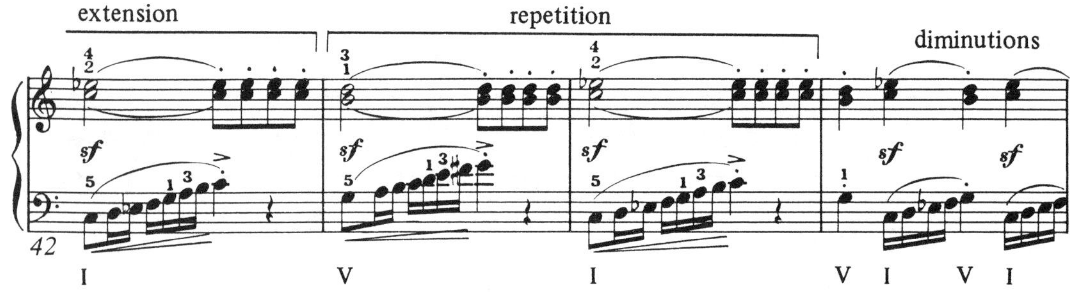
extension
repetition
diminutions
42
I
V
I
V I V I

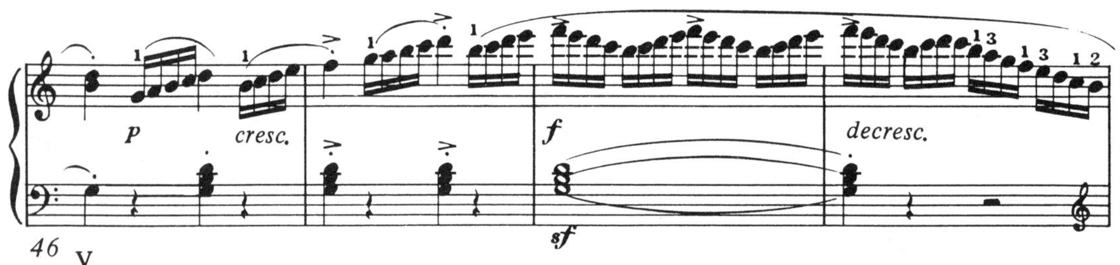
bridge to recapitulation
p
cresc.
f
decresc.
46
V

RECAPITULATION
THEME 1
antecedent phrase
consequent
p
pp
legato
50
I
V4 3
V6

phrase
antecedent phrase
mf
p
55
I
II6
I
V 6 5

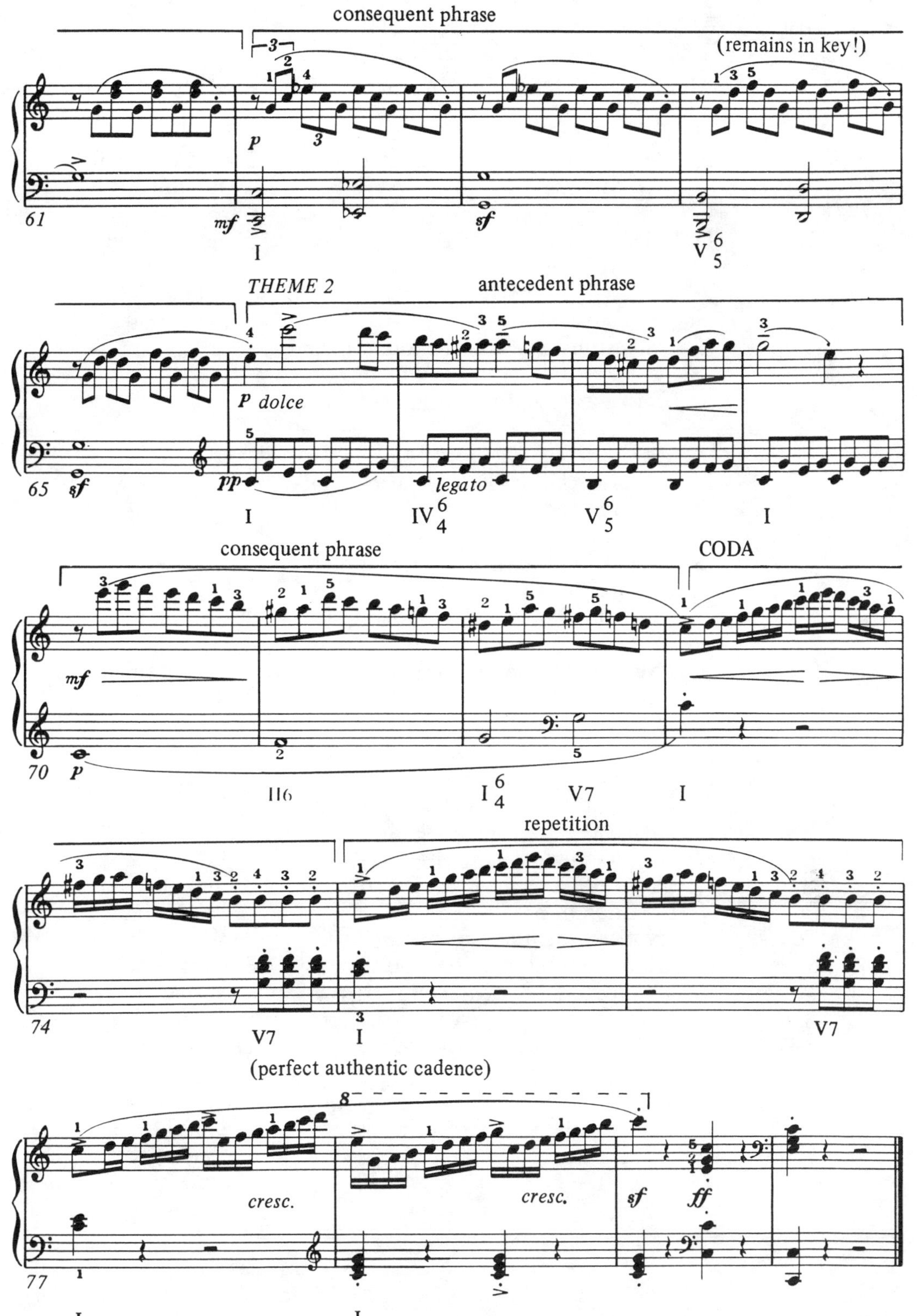
consequent phrase
(remains in key!)
61
p
mf
sf
I
V 6 5
THEME 2
antecedent phrase
p dolce
65
sf
pp
legato
I
IV 6 4
V 6 5
I
consequent phrase
CODA
mf
70
p
II6
I 6 4
V7
I
repetition
74
V7
I
V7
(perfect authentic cadence)
cresc.
cresc.
sf
ff
77
I
I

ANALYSIS OF EXPOSITION SECTION OF KUHLAU SONATINA, OP. 20 NO. 1 (A SAMPLE OUTLINE TO ANALYZE OTHER WORKS)

Measure	Hand	Harmonic Elements	Structure
1-2	R	Melody in broken chord (C root position)	First theme—key of C (ms. 1-8).
3	R	Melody in broken chord (C second inversion)	A musical sentence consisting of two phrases
1-8	L	Alberti bass outlining chord sequences: $I-V^7-I-II^6-V-I$ in key of C	
4	R	Suspension and resolution C-B in G chord	
8		Semicadence (G chord)	
9-12	R	Divided chords ($I^6_4-V^7$), accompaniment for broken-chord melody in left hand	
13-14	L	Theme restated in C minor (tonic minor)	
15-16		Modulation through dominant seventh (crucial measures)	Transition to key of G
17-20	L	New key (G major); chord sequence $I-IV-V^7-I$	Second theme (G major) Contrasting melody
18-19	R	Melodic figure using scale tones, passing tones, LN, and chord tones	
21-23	R	Same as above, supported by root tones in left hand ($I-II^6-I^6_4-V^7-I$)	
24-28	R	Scale of G, securing the key by repetition of phrase	Closing theme
25-26	L	Notice cadential root notes (D^7-G)	
28-29	R	Recognize modulation: look for repeated accidental (F-sharp)	Extension of closing theme
30-31	R	Bridge modulating back to main key (C); notice F-natural	Transition to repetition of exposition and/or development section

RECOMMENDED READING

Des Marais, Paul. *Harmony: A Workbook in Fundamentals*. New York: W.W. Norton, 1962.

Diller, Angela. *Keyboard Music Study*, Book 2. New York: G. Schirmer, 1937.

Harder, Paul. *Basic Materials in Music Theory*. Boston: Allyn and Bacon, 1970.

Hardy, Gordon and Arnold Fish. *Musical Literature: A Workbook for Analysis*. New York: Harper & Row, 1963.

McIntosh, Edith. *Theory and Musicianship*, Books 1, 2, and 3. New York: Carl Fischer, 1963.

Priesing, Dorothy and Libby Tecklin. *Language of the Piano*. New York: Carl Fischer, 1959.

Roeder, Carl M. *A Practical Keyboard Harmony*. New York: Schroeder & Gunther, 1939.

Scovill, Modena. *Keyboard Harmony*, Book 1. New York: Carl Fischer, 1939.

Scales, Modes, and Related Terms

A Glossary

DENES AGAY

Scale: an orderly succession of tones, ascending or descending according to a predetermined pattern of intervals, usually whole steps or half steps. Scales are classified as *diatonic* (major and minor), *chromatic, whole tone*, and *pentatonic*. *Modes* (modal scales) have often been classified as diatonic, but majority opinion today regards them as belonging to their own category.

Diatonic: a category of scales to which the *major* and *minor* scales belong. The term is also used to describe the tonal character of passages, chords, and entire works which use only the unaltered tones of the major and minor scales. Although various types of minor scales involve note alterations marked by accidentals, they are, according to present usage, considered diatonic in character.

Major scale: a step-by-step succession of eight tones in the following pattern of whole steps (W) and half steps (H):

The following example illustrates the diatonic relationship of major scales. On the fifth degree of any major scale a new scale may be started whose key signature is one sharp more or one flat less.

Each scale has the same tonal relationship of whole steps and half steps; only the starting note (keynote) is different. Each scale is thus an exact transposition of any other.

Minor scale: differs from the major scale in that the third tone is a minor third above the keynote, whereas in the major scale the distance is a major third. This gives the two scales and the respective tonic triads their distinctive sound. There are three types of minor scales: natural, harmonic and melodic.

Natural minor scale is formed by taking seven consecutive tones of any major scale *starting on the sixth degree*:

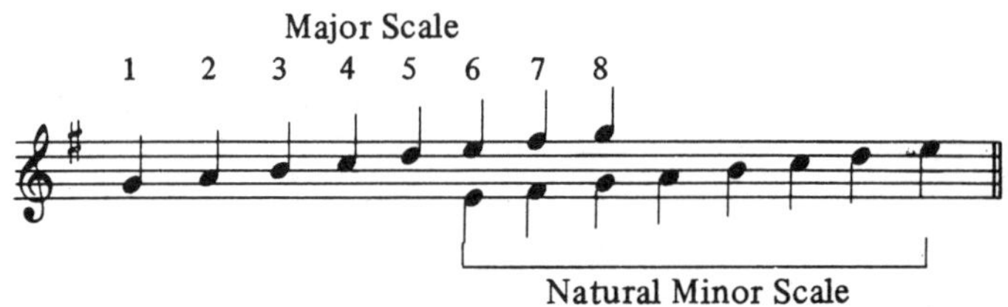

The above two scales–G major and E minor–are called *relative* scales, because they share the same key signature (one sharp).

Harmonic minor scale is formed by raising the *seventh degree* of the natural minor a half step:

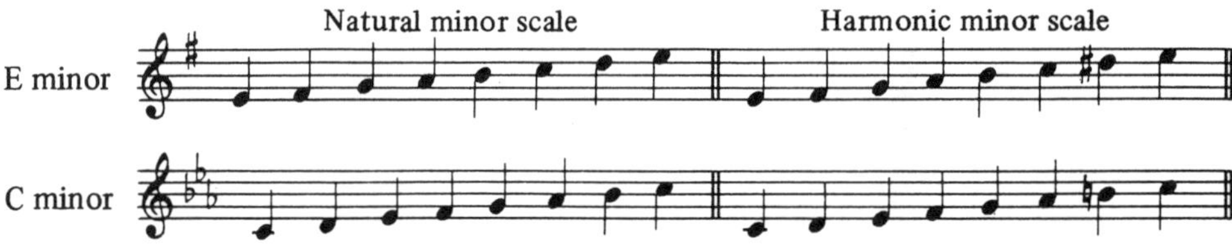

The accidental altering the seventh degree is not part of the key signature.

Melodic minor scale has an ascending and a descending form. Going up, it is formed by raising the *sixth* and *seventh degrees* of the natural minor a half step; going down, the tones are identical to the natural minor:

As mentioned, certain major and minor scales are called *relative* by virtue of sharing the same key signature (C major and A minor, F major and D minor, etc.). Major and minor scales may also be related by having the same keynote; these are called *parallel* scales (C major and C minor, F major and F minor, etc.).

The most frequently occurring minor scale is the harmonic, followed closely by the melodic. The natural minor, which is identical to the Aeolian mode, conveys a more vague and somewhat archaic feeling of tonality. It does not appear often in postbaroque keyboard literature.
Key signature: the number of sharps or flats appearing at the beginning of each line of music, indicating the prevailing key (scale) of the composition. A given signature may stand for either a major key or its relative (natural) minor. The absence of sharps or flats means either the key of C major or its relative minor, A minor. The sharps and flats are placed on the staff on the line or space which represents the note to be altered:

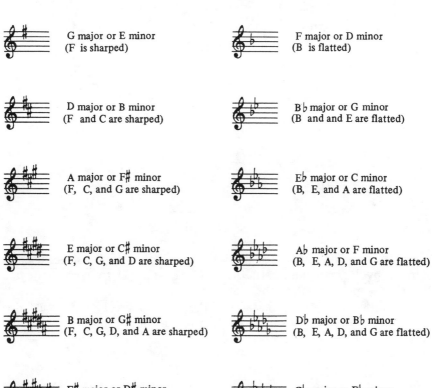

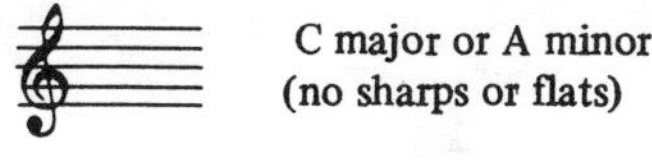

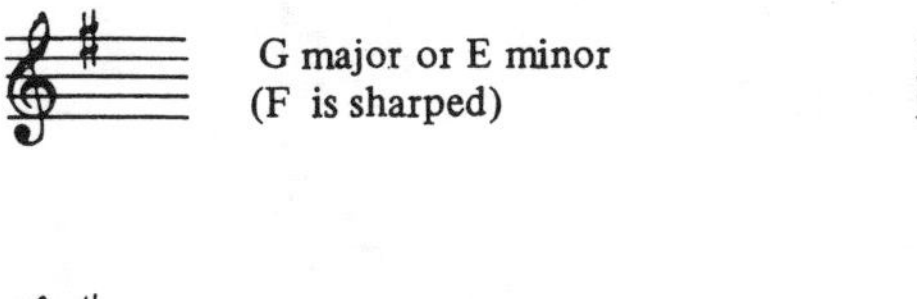

F major or D minor
(B is flatted)

D major or B minor
(F and C are sharped)

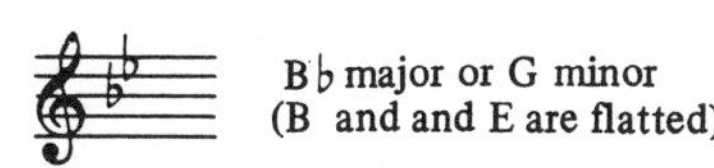

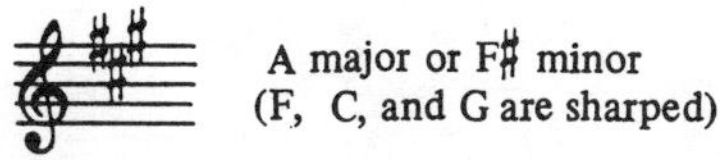

A major or F♯ minor
(F, C, and G are sharped)

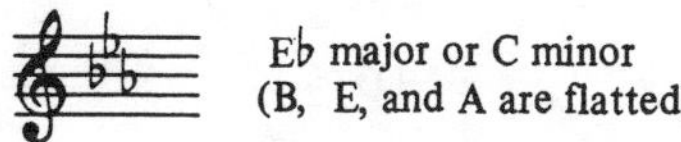

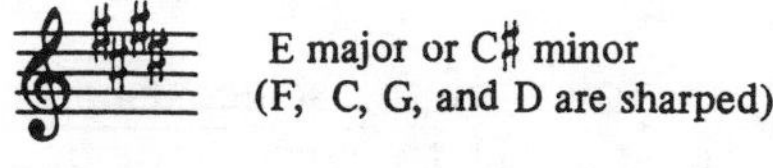

E major or C♯ minor
(F, C, G, and D are sharped)

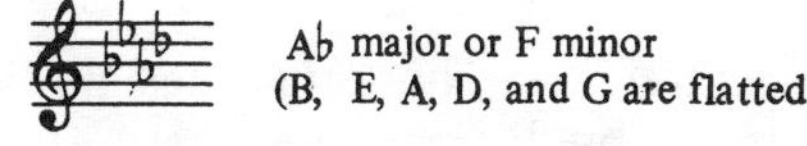

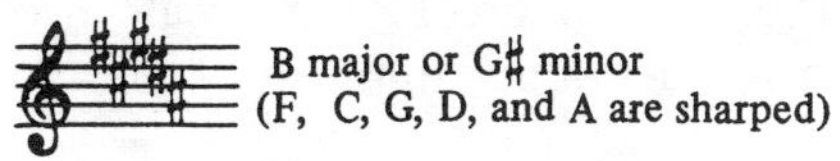

B major or G♯ minor
(F, C, G, D, and A are sharped)

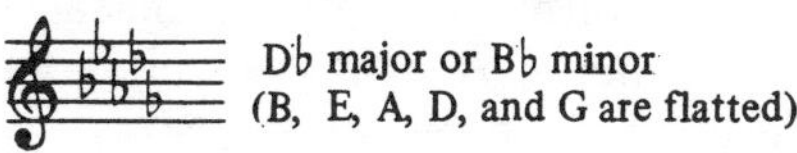

D♭ major or B♭ minor
(B, E, A, D, and G are flatted)

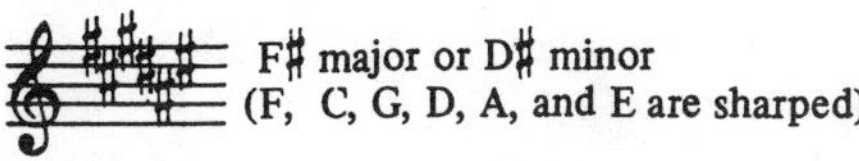

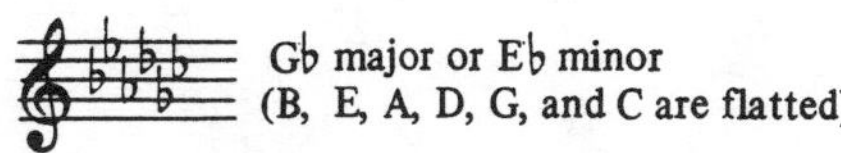

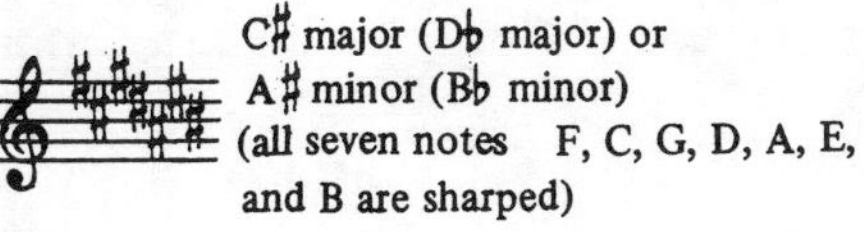

C♯ major (D♭ major) or
A♯ minor (B♭ minor)
(all seven notes F, C, G, D, A, E, and B are sharped)

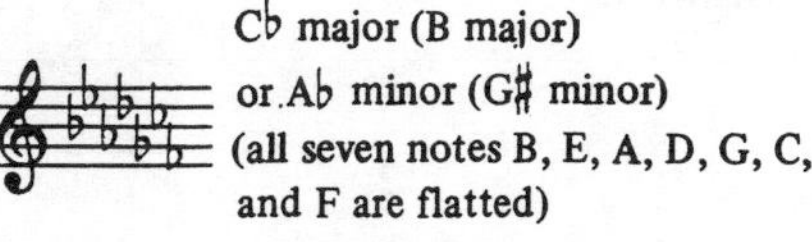

C♭ major (B major)
or A♭ minor (G♯ minor)
(all seven notes B, E, A, D, G, C, and F are flatted)

The increasing number of sharps and flats in the signatures above follows a pattern which can easily be illustrated. Going up from the focal point of middle C (representing the keynote of the C-major scale) by fifths, the sharps increase one by one (G major has one sharp, D major two sharps, etc.) Going down from middle C by fifths, the flats increase one by one (F major has one flat, B-flat major two flats, etc.).
Circle of fifths is a key-signature chart illustrating this order of scales according to the increasing number of sharps and flats. Capital letters indicate major scales; lower-case letters minor scales.

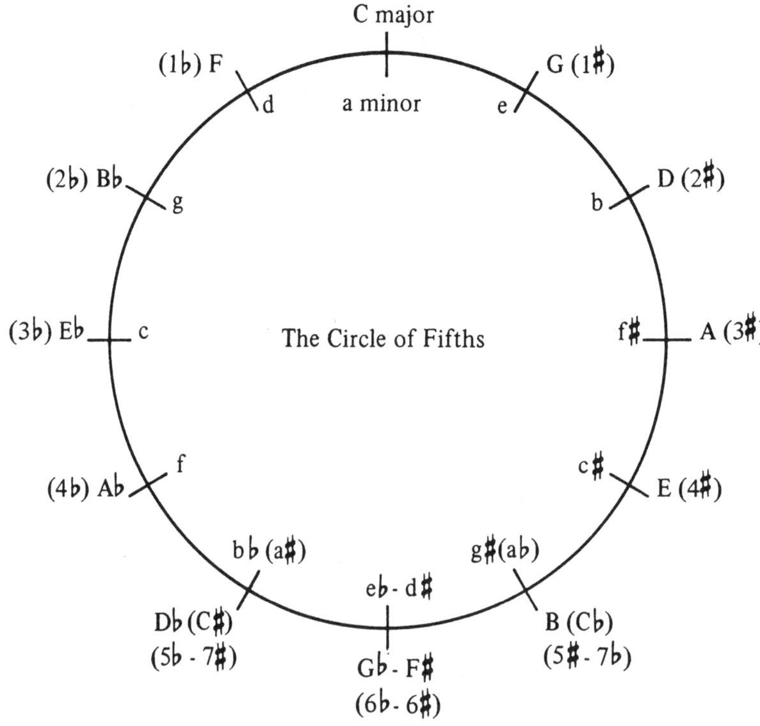

Scale degrees: Numerical designation of the tones of the scale, usually marked by Roman numerals, from first degree (I) to seventh degree (VII). (The eighth tone of the scale is degree I.)

In addition to a numeral, each of the seven degrees of the scale also has a name, referring specifically to the harmonic function of chords built on these various degrees.

I	II	III	IV
Tonic	Supertonic	Mediant	Subdominant

V	VI	VII
Dominant	Submediant	Subtonic (Leading tone)

Another kind of designation for the scale degrees is *solmization*, in which the following syllables are used to identify the seven tones of the scale: *do, re, mi, fa, sol, la, ti, do*. This nomenclature has its origin in a system devised by Guido of Arezzo in the early eleventh century. He got the idea from an ancient hymn to St. John the Baptist, in which six successive lines of the text start on six successive tones of the hexachord (a mediaeval six-tone scale):

The name of the seventh tone, originally si, was added in the sixteenth century, derived from the initials of Sancte Ioannes (St. John), the last two words of the hymn. Later, the name of the first tone, *ut*, was changed to *do* for easier vocalizing. For similar reasons the last tone's name was changed to *ti*.

Solmization as a means of identifying scale degrees is used today in two ways. In the *fixed do* method, the syllables refer to the seven degrees of the C-major scale; *do* is always C, *re* is always D, etc. In the *movable do* (as in the *tonic sol-fa*) system, the terms apply to the seven degrees of the diatonic scale, regardless of what scale it may be. In other words, *do* is always the keynote, *re* the note above it, etc.

Key: the tonal resources of a major or minor scale; or perhaps more precisely, the tonal framework within which a piece of music is written, utilizing the tones of a given major or minor scale. It should be remembered that there is a difference between *scale* and *key*. The D-major scale, for instance, is D–E–F-sharp–G–A–B–C-sharp. A piece is in the key of D major if it uses the tones of the D-major scale, in any order and in any melodic and harmonic combination. (*Keys* also refer to the levers of the piano [white and black] which are depressed to produce a tone; *keyboard* is the entire set of keys.)

Tonality: the melodic and harmonic organization of a given work resulting in a definite key identity, major or minor. It also means the modulatory key scheme of a larger work, cadentially gravitating back to the home key.

Polytonality: the simultaneous presence of two or more keys within a work. *Atonality* is the lack of tonal focus. A piece is atonal if it can not be identified as belonging in any key.

Chromatic scale: a step-by-step succession of the twelve tones within the octave, each a half step higher when ascending, lower when descending.

The generally accepted notation method of this scale is as illustrated above: ascending, the diatonic tones are raised by sharps; descending, they are lowered by flats. There are, however, frequent exceptions to this rule, mainly to emphasize underlying harmonic functions. Examine, for instance, the following two chromatic examples, where the harmonic contexts decide whether a tone is notated as A-sharp or B-flat.

Whole-tone scale: stepwise succession of six tones, progressing only by whole steps, instead of by a pattern of half steps and whole steps, as in the major and minor scales and modes. There are two whole-tone scales within the octave:

The whole-tone scale may start on any of the twelve tones. The lack of a magnetic keynote and the absence of a distinct tonality give this scale and its derivative chords a vague, indecisive character, which made them suitable colors on the palette of impressionist composers (Debussy, Ravel, and others).

Pentatonic scale: an ancient scale, abundantly present in the folk music of many cultures, is a progression of five tones:

This pattern is transposable into any other position. The black keys of the piano, played in orderly succession up and down, produce tones of the pentatonic scale.

Modes: also called ecclesiastical or church modes, are types of scales which were prevalent in the middle ages and dominated melodic and harmonic thinking until the seventeenth century, when they were grad-

ually replaced by the major and minor scales and tonalities. This does not mean that music based on modal scales is extinct today. Indeed, an interesting and appealing modal flavor permeates many folk and popular songs of our time. In addition, composers from Beethoven to Bartók and beyond have used and still use modality as a source of inspiration.
For pianists, modal scales have easily recognizable earmarks: they all utilize only notes played on the white keys. The principal and most frequently encountered modes are:

For our ears, attuned to the sound of major and minor tonalities, each one of the modes conveys a distinct, somewhat archaic flavor. The Dorian mode resembles the natural D-minor scale, differing only by the raised sixth degree (B-natural instead of B-flat). The Phrygian mode resembles the E-minor scale, with the second degree lowered (F-natural instead of F-sharp).The Lydian mode is close to the F-major scale, with the fourth degree raised (B-natural instead of B-flat). The Mixolydian mode sounds like the G-major scale with the seventh lowered (F-natural instead of F-sharp).
In the sixteenth century two other scales were added to the system of modes: Aeolian (A to A on the white keys; identical to the natural minor scale)

Ionian (C to C on the white keys; identical to the C-major scale)

Very seldom used and of only theoretical interest is the Locrian mode (from B to B on the white keys).

In the works of the masters, classics to moderns, the modes often appear in a transposed position. Keyboard music of the baroque (especially the early baroque) provides profuse examples of this. The player therefore should not be confused if he or she encounters key signatures which do not fit any major or minor key. For instance, the four principal modes, transposed so that each has the tonic note of C, will have the following key signatures:

Glossary of Musical Forms and Dance Types

DENES AGAY

Album Leaf: A dedicatory musical thought to be entered in an autograph album. A short, simple piano piece of intimate character.
Allemande (*Alman*): A dance form in moderate $\frac{4}{4}$ time, usually starting with a short upbeat. It is the first movement of the baroque suite, unless preceded by a prelude. Although the term is the French word for "German," the dance itself should not be confused with the later, Viennese form known as the German dance.
Alternativo: In eighteenth-century instrumental music, the term has the same meaning as the trio of a minuet or scherzo.
Arabesque: A term borrowed from the decorative designs of Moorish architecture, meaning a composition of rather fanciful melodic contours.
Bagatelle: A short, light piece, usually written for the piano. In this sense, the term was first used by Beethoven.
Barcarolle: A romantic instrumental piece in swaying $\frac{6}{8}$ time, suggesting the boat songs of the Venetian gondoliers.
Binary and *Ternary Forms*: The *binary form* consists of two sections, with either or both sections repeated (A-B). Many folk songs, hymns, popular songs, as well as numerous dance forms of the baroque and classical periods fall into this category ("America," "Greensleeves," Minuet from *Don Giovanni*, etc.). In *ternary form* there are three distinct sections, of which the third is a repetition of the first (A-B-A). The minuet and scherzo movements of sonatas and symphonies have this construction (with the trio section representing part B), as well as many waltzes, nocturnes, songs without words, etc. of the romantic era.

Some confusion arises when, in the second half of a binary form, a phrase or section of the first half is repeated, suggesting an A-B-A (ternary) structure. The repetition of the first section, or of part of it, at the end of a piece does not necessarily indicate a three-part form. The deciding factor is the nature of the cadence immediately preceding the repeated portion of part A. If this cadence is not a full and conclusive one—if it somehow suggests a continuation in the flow of melody—then the succeeding section, even if a repetition of part A, can not be regarded as a self-contained, independent unit, but only as a concluding segment of part B, resulting in a binary, not ternary, form.

For a simple example one may examine the phrasing structure of "Oh! Susanna": $\|: a^1 - a^2 :\|: b - a^2 :\|$. This is unquestionably a two-part form, despite the recurrence of the opening strain. Two miniatures from Schumann's *Album for the Young*, "Little March" and "The Wild Horseman," provide further illustration of the same point; the first piece is binary, while the latter is ternary.

Bourrée: Originally an old French folk dance. Since the seventeenth century it has been an optional movement in the baroque suite in lively $\frac{4}{4}$ time, usually with an upbeat of a quarter note or two eighth notes.

Cakewalk: A sharply syncopated dance of the ragtime era (c. 1896–1916) in $\frac{2}{4}$ or $\frac{4}{4}$ time. (♬♪ ♫ and similar patterns are typical.)

Canon: The most exacting polyphonic form, in which a melody line sounded by one voice is strictly imitated in one or more other voices, either at the unison, octave, or another chosen interval.

Canzon (*Canzona, Chanson*): Originally a song, a vocal piece. From the sixteenth century on it also has designated an instrumental form. Sometimes it is called *Canzone da Sonar*, a song to be sounded on an instrument. The canzon is usually polyphonic in texture but has no definite form. It is the ancestor not only of the fugue, but also of the baroque sonata.

Canzonetta: Literally "a little song." An instrumental piece suggesting the mood and character of an Italian air or folk tune.

Capriccio (*Caprice*): In general, a lively instrumental piece in free style. During the baroque the term is almost identical with the fantasia, and in the nineteenth century with the scherzo.

Chaconne and *Passacaglia*: Closely related baroque instrumental forms in slow triple meter. In essence, they are both a series of variations, either on a short, four- to eight-measure basso ostinato melody or on an harmonic sequence of similar length. During the early baroque the terms were interchangeable; according to eighteenth- and nineteenth-century definitions, however, variations on a bass melody are called passacaglia and on a set succession of harmonies chaconne.

Choral Prelude: A polyphonic instrumental piece, usually written for the organ, in which the main theme, a hymn, is interwoven with and surrounded by contrasting melodic passages in one or more other voices.

Courante (*Coranto*): A lively dance in triple time; usually the second movement of the baroque suite.

Csárdás: A Hungarian dance in $\frac{2}{4}$ time, usually consisting of two sections, slow (*lassú*), followed by fast (*friss*). The latter may start at a moderate tempo and gradually accelerate to the end.

Divertimento: During the Italian baroque, a light instrumental composition in one or several movements. Haydn used the term as a title of some of his clavier sonatas and string quartets. Mozart wrote many divertimentos for various small instrumental groups.

Écossaise: Although the word means "Scottish" in French, this dance probably did not originate in Scotland, but was born in the ballrooms of Paris during the late eighteenth century. Like the contredanse and English dance, it is in lively $\frac{2}{4}$ time and usually consists of two eight-bar sections, each repeated.

English Dance (*Anglaise*): Generic name for various lively dance forms of the eighteenth century, supposedly emulating the character of English country dances. The meaning of the term is very close to the contredanse and écossaise.

Étude: An instrumental piece, usually built on a single figure or motive, designed to develop the player's technical ability. Some composers of the nineteenth and twentieth centuries, especially Chopin, were able to combine the didactic purpose of this genre with a truly meaningful and poetic musical substance.

Fantasia (*Fantasy*): The term covers a wide variety of instrumental forms, all of which have in common a certain freedom of construction and often a quasi-improvisatory character.

Foxtrot: The basic American dance of the early jazz era (c. 1910–1930). The tempo is moderate to fast in $\frac{2}{4}$ or $\frac{4}{4}$ time, with strong accents (♩♩♩♩).

Fugue (*Fuga*): A polyphonic piece conceived for two or more parts (voices). The voices enter successively with the same theme in alternating tonic and dominant keys (subject and answer). Each voice, after stating the subject, usually continues with different thematic material (countersubject), which is heard simultaneously with the entry of the subject in another voice. As a rule, the subject and countersubject appear several times in each voice during the course of the piece. Often digressing thematic passages, called episodes, connect the entry of themes in the different voices. The first section of the fugue, to the point where the subject has been stated once in each voice, is called the exposition. The fugue does not have a strict form. There can be great variety and freedom in its construction, as evidenced by the works of its unsurpassed master, J. S. Bach.

Gaillard (*Galiardo*): See Pavane.

Gavotte: A graceful, old French dance in moderate $\frac{4}{4}$ time, usually beginning on the third beat of the measure. It is an optional movement in the baroque suite and is frequently followed by a second gavotte, called *musette*, after which the first section is repeated.

German Dance: A term interchangeable with *ländler*. A type of country waltz in moderate $\frac{3}{4}$ time, much cultivated by the Viennese classics.

Gigue (*Giga*): The last and liveliest movement of the baroque suite, in $\frac{6}{8}$, $\frac{9}{8}$, or $\frac{12}{8}$ time. Its origin is obscure. The word derives from the Italian *giga*, an early fiddle, but the dance itself probably came from the jig, a sixteenth-century English-Scotch-Irish country dance.

Ground, Ground Bass: A series of variations over a persistently repeated, unchanging bass line (*basso ostinato*), usually four to eight measures in length. Closely related to the chaconne and passacaglia.

Hornpipe: A lively English dance during a period extending from the sixteenth to the nineteenth century. It derived its name from a primitive instrument—a pipe made from the horn of an animal—which often accompanied this dance.

Humoreske (*Humoresque*): A good-humored, capricious instrumental composition, usually in one movement.

Impromptu: A character piece, usually written for piano by romantic composers. The term, which means "improvised" in French, suggests a certain spontaneous and extemporaneous quality. The finest examples of the genre are Schubert's and Chopin's.

Inventio: J.S. Bach's title for his short, masterfully constructed keyboard works in imitative, two-voice counterpoint. (Bach calls his Three-part Inventions Sinfonias.)

Ländler: A country waltz of the Austrian, Bavarian, and Bohemian regions.

Loure: Originally, the name of an old, bagpipelike French instrument. As an occasional movement in the baroque suite, it is a dance form in slow or moderate $\frac{3}{4}$ or $\frac{6}{4}$ time with heavily accented dotted notes.

Mazurka: A Polish dance in $\frac{3}{4}$ time. It is of moderate tempo, usually slower than the waltz, with accents on the second or third beat. Chopin's Mazurkas are the finest stylized examples of the genre.

Minuet (*Menuet*): A graceful French dance in $\frac{3}{4}$ time which became popular during the reign of Louis XIV, mainly through the works of Lully. The dance retained its popularity throughout the seventeenth and eighteenth centuries. Always in triple time, originally it was of moderate tempo, stately and refined in character; as such it became part of the baroque suite around 1700. In the second half of the eighteenth century, in a somewhat changed form, it was incorporated into the classical sonata and symphony. With Haydn and Mozart the minuet's tempo became livelier, its restraint and grace often replaced by a more robust, country-dance quality, akin to the ländler. With Beethoven the tempo further quickened and the form developed into the scherzo.

Moment Musical: A term, first used by Schubert, for a short, lyric piano composition.

Motive: See "The Riddle of the Phrase," p. 55.

Musette: An eighteenth-century French bagpipe; a dance piece with a sustained drone bass imitating the sound of this lusty instrument. It is usually a companion piece of the gavotte.

Nocturne: A "night piece"; lyric, instrumental composition of a quiet, reflective mood. Chopin's are outstanding.

Novelette: A lyric piano piece usually including a trio. The term was first used by Schumann.

Ordre: See Suite.

Partita (*Partie*): An eighteenth-century term for the suite. Occasionally it also meant a set of variations.

Passepied: An old French round-dance. During the reign of Louis XIV it was introduced into the ballet, and later became an optional movement in the suite. It is in triple meter, of gay, spirited character, and it usually begins on the third beat of the measure.

Passacaglia: See Chaconne.

Pavane: A rather slow, dignified dance of Italian or Spanish origin. It was popular in the sixteenth century and is often found among the works of English virginalists. The pavane is usually followed by the galliard.

Period: See "The Riddle of the Phrase," p. 55.

Phrase: See "The Riddle of the Phrase," p. 55.

Polka: A lively dance in $\frac{2}{4}$ time. It is probably of Czech origin, and became extremely popular during the second half of the nineteenth century.

Polonaise: A Polish dance of a stately, processional character, in $\frac{3}{4}$ time. It originated in the sixteenth century, probably from court ceremonies, and it appears frequently among the works of eighteenth- and nineteenth-century masters. Chopin imbued the form with an intensely lyric and often heroic substance.

Preambulum: See Preludium. Another name for the baroque prelude.

Preludium (*Prelude*): Literally, a piece of music which serves as an introduction to another piece (such as a fugue) or a group of pieces (as in the baroque suite). It is often written in a free form, in the manner of an improvisation. Since Chopin, the title prelude is used for a short, independent composition, usually of a lyric, and sometimes descriptive, character (Debussy).

Rhapsody: A fantasylike instrumental composition, usually in one movement, formed of loosely connected contrasting sections (Liszt's Hungarian Rhapsodies, Gershwin's Rhapsody in Blue). Brahms' rhapsodies are more tightly organized, almost sonatalike constructions.

Ricercata (*Ricercare*): The word comes from the Italian verb "to search out." It is a polyphonic instrumental composition in strict imitative style, a forerunner of the fugue.

Rigaudon (*Rigadoon*): A lively dance in $\frac{2}{4}$ or $\frac{4}{4}$ time, similar to the bourree. It probably originated in the south of France and is an optional movement in the baroque suite.

Rondino: A little rondo.

Rondo (*Rondeau*): A musical form of French origin in which a main theme (rondeau) alternates with two or more secondary themes (couplets, episodes). See also p. 318.

Rumba: A Cuban dance of African origin, which became popular in the U.S. and Europe around 1930. The tempo is moderate to lively in double time, with strongly syncopated rhythmic patterns.

Samba: A rather fast Brazilian dance in duple time, usually starting with an upbeat of three eighth notes. The rhythm is strongly syncopated. It became popular in the U.S. around 1940.

Sarabande: A stately and solemn old Spanish dance in triple meter. As a part of the baroque suite it usually serves the function of a slow movement.

Scherzino: A little scherzo.

Scherzo: The Italian word for joke or jest. An instrumental piece of humorous, playful character in $\frac{3}{4}$ or $\frac{3}{8}$ time. It is usually the third movement of a sonata, symphony, or string quartet, and has the form structure of the minuet, from which it evolved. (Pattern A-B-A, scherzo–trio–scherzo.)

Sentence: See "The Riddle of the Phrase," p. 55.

Serenade (*Serenata*): Originally, evening music to be played under the window of the courted lady. The term came to denote a great variety of instrumental forms in one or several movements, for either a solo instrument or various instrumental groups.

Siciliano (*Siciliana*): An instrumental or vocal piece of pastoral character in calm, $\frac{6}{8}$ time. It presumably derived from a Sicilian dance, and was a very popular musical form during the eighteenth century.

Sinfonia: The Italian word for symphony. It usually denotes orchestral pieces of various kinds. Bach uses the term as the title for his Three-part Inventions– short, masterfully constructed keyboard works in imitative counterpoint.

Sonata: The name derives from the Italian word *sonare*, "to sound" on an instrument, in contrast to the cantata, which comes from *cantare*, "to sing."

There are various types of baroque sonatas differing both in the number and the construction of the movements. The earliest examples of this form closely resemble the suite. In Kuhlau's "Biblical" Sonatas, the first keyboard works of the genre, each movement is headed by a descriptive programmatic title. Domenico Scarlatti's sonatas, true gems of the high baroque, consist of one movement in binary (two-section) form. In the sonatas of Pergolesi, Paradisi, Galuppi, and Kirnberger, the polythematic character of the first movement and other architectural features of the later, full sonata are more and more discernible. The clavier sonatas of C.P.E. Bach are in three movements, fast-slow-fast, and lead directly to Haydn, Mozart, and the supreme master of the form, Beethoven.

Sonatas of the romantic and contemporary literature tend to deviate from the classical pattern. They are more free, and often more fantasy-like in construction.

Sonatina: A short sonata of simple design. It may consist of one, two, or three movements.
Songs without Words (*Lieder ohne Worte*): Mendelssohn's title for forty-eight piano pieces, songlike in form, mood, and character.
Suite, Partita (*Partie*), *Ordre*: A set of contrasting, stylized dance movements, usually all in the same key. Most often it consists of an allemande, courante, sarabande, and gigue, in that order. Occasionally the set is preceded by a prelude and frequently there are other dance movements, such as minuet, gavotte, bourrée, and passepied interpolated between the sarabande and gigue.
Tango: An Argentinian dance in duple time which became extremely popular all over the Western world around 1910. It is similar to the Habañera, but faster and with more pronounced syncopated rhythms.

Tarantella: An exhuberant Italian dance in fast $\frac{6}{8}$ time, often in alternating major and minor sections.
Ternary form: See Binary and Ternary Forms.
Toccata: A free-style keyboard piece, usually in rapid tempo. The word comes from the Italian *toccare*, "to touch," implying a certain lightness and brilliance in execution.
Trio: Originally, a piece played by three instruments. Also, the middle section of a minuet, scherzo, or other instrumental piece in ternary (A-B-A) form.
Variations: One of the earliest of extended instrumental forms, in which a musical thought (theme) is repeated a number of times, but always in a more or less modified version (variation). Each variation usually retains some melodic, harmonic, or structural relationship to the theme. There are many different types of this form, from the chaconne and passacaglia of the baroque to the more freely constructed variations of modern times.
Waltz (*Valse, Walzer*): The most popular dance of the nineteenth century and, in different stylized versions, a much-cultivated instrumental form of romantic composers. It is a close but more sophisticated relative of the ländler and German dance. Always in triple time, its tempo, mood, and character can vary greatly.

The Fundamentals of Music Notation

DENES AGAY

The ability to write notes and symbols neatly and correctly is one of the basic requirements of musical literacy. This skill, the learning of which is—or should be—an integral part of every student's education, facilitates a quick perception of pitch relations, rhythmic divisions, and reading in general. It also can promote musical creativity. Many students who are taught and encouraged to improvise and even compose little pieces do so happily and with ease, but encounter extreme difficulty in putting into notes what they have created.

To commit a musical idea to paper requires not only a fair grasp of theory, but also a knowledge of at least the elementary rules of music orthography, the correct shape and proper placement of notes and symbols on the staff. This skill can be learned easily and painlessly if it is started early in the instruction process and continued with diligent consistency. The first steps—the most important basic guide-lines—are listed here. Numerous good elementary books provide ample opportunities for written exercises in this area; a selective list of such publications and other textbooks on all details of correct music notation are given at the end of this chapter.

Treble Clef
Draw it in two steps, starting on top; it ends on the second line of the staff. At first, practice each step separately.

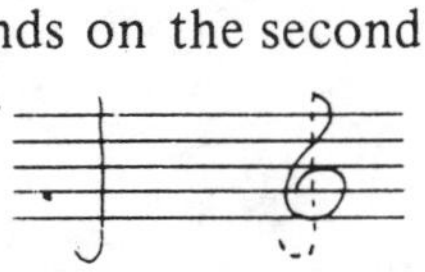

Bass Clef

An inverted C, starting on the fourth line of the staff; place the two dots in the third and fourth spaces.

Time Signature

Make the two figures equal in size. They can be placed either vertically or diagonally, separated by an oblique line.

Notes

Note heads should be of uniform size.

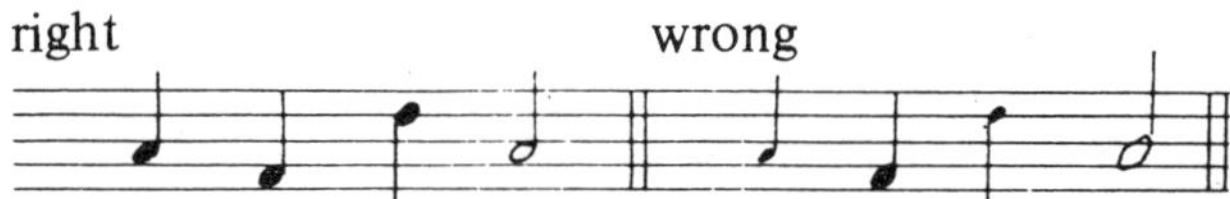

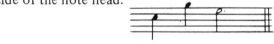

Stems should always be vertical and straight.

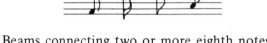

All notes below the third line of the staff have stems extending up on the right side of the note head.

Notes on or above the third line have stems extending down on the left side of the note head.

The flags of single eighth notes, sixteenth notes, and shorter units are always placed on the right side of the note stem, regardless of the stem's direction.

Beams connecting two or more eighth notes or sixteenth notes should be drawn neatly and straight. Generally the note farthest removed from the middle (third) line of the staff will determine the direction of stems and placement of beams.

Dots are always placed in spaces, never on lines. A dot after a line note is placed in the space just above the note.

Rests

Whole rest: a small rectangular block hanging from the fourth line. It indicates rest for a full measure, regardless of the time signature.

Half rest: same design as the whole rest, but resting on the third line.

Quarter rest: a slanted letter Z with a little tail.

Eighth rest, sixteenth rest, etc.: drawn like fancy figure 7.

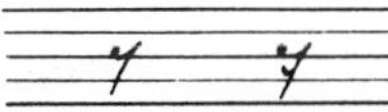

Accidentals (Sharps, Flats, Naturals)

Sharp (♯) is drawn with two double strokes
Flat (♭) is also drawn in two steps
Natural (♮) may be drawn in three steps

Ledger Lines

These must have the same equidistant spacing as the lines of the staff.

right wrong

Ties and Slurs

Tie (connecting two notes of the same pitch) is always placed at the note heads, opposite the stems.

right wrong

Slur (grouping two or more notes as a legato or phrasing mark) is placed above the notes, if all the stems in the note group extend down:

If all stems in the note group extend up, the slur is drawn below the notes

If the stems of notes extend in both directions, the slur is placed above the notes

Double Notes and Chords

Notes sounded simultaneously must be placed vertically under each other, except the notes forming the interval of a second, which are placed diagonally, the lower note on the left.

The direction of the stem is determined by the note farthest from the middle (third) line of the staff.

Writing the interval of the second and chords containing seconds requires special attention. The lower note of the interval is always on the left, and the stem is between the note heads. When three or more notes are involved, put as many notes as possible on the correct side of the stem.

Horizontal Spacing

Notes should be evenly spaced and their note values considered. Whole notes and half notes must be given more horizontal space than eighth notes or sixteenth notes.

RECOMMENDED READING

Boehm, Laszlo. *Modern Music Notation*. New York: G. Schirmer, 1961.

Donato, Anthony. *Preparing Music Manuscript*. Englewood Cliffs, N.J.: Prentice-Hall, 1963. (Also Amsco paperback.)

Rosenthal, Carl A. *Practical Guide to Music Notation*. New York: MCA, 1967.

Read, Gardner. *Music Notation: A Manual of Modern Practise.* (2nd ed.) Boston: Allyn and Bacon, 1964.

Sight Reading: The Basics, Step by Step

DENES AGAY

Sight reading—the ability to read and play music at first sight—is a basic pianistic skill and the ultimate test of note-reading ability in general. Its importance cannot be emphasized enough. A child's first school task is to learn to read. Only after a child knows how to read can he or she proceed to other subjects and further detailed studies. Similarly, in piano study the ability to read and play music easily and effortlessly is of prime importance. It is not only an essential factor in the attainment of sound musicianship, but also a potential source of a lifetime of musical enjoyment.

To read and play music at first sight is the result of a rather complex series of body functions:

(1) the eyes see the note picture;

(2) the brain interprets the received image on two levels, aural and tactile, and accordingly transmits the proper muscular impulses for the desired keyboard contact;

(3) the hands and fingers play, thus transforming the visual and aural impression into sound.

Let us examine these three interlocking and very nearly simultaneous functions more closely. It should be noted first that in order to see the note picture well, the page of music should be placed at a proper distance from the eyes, with adequate lighting. The student's eyesight should be ascertained; this is especially important with small children, who quite often are unaware of their nearsightedness and the need for corrective lenses.

HOW THE EYES MOVE

The manner in which the eyes move while reading has been well determined through exhaustive research. Modern pedagogy and reading techniques have established that while reading a line of print, the eye does not focus on individual letters one by one, but on groups of letters, words. Consequently, the movement of the eyes from left to right is not steady and continuous, but rather happens in a series of jumps. At every stop the eye takes in the next letter group. This is why in modern education the child first learns to read words as complete patterns and picture symbols before learning the whole alphabet and before being introduced to spelling. For instance, *dog* or *cat* are each complete word pictures which evoke the animals' image without a consciousness of the component individual letters. The larger the "eyespan"—the amount of material the eyes can take in at one glance— the fewer jumps the eyes will make per line, and the better and quicker the reading will be.

Reading music involves a somewhat similar eye function: the eye does not focus on individual notes, but rather on a group of notes, which by virtue of certain characteristics (pitch contour, rhythmic pattern, chordal design, etc.) forms a recognizable visual pattern and musical unit. There are, however, fundamental differences between reading words and reading notes. In reading piano music, the eyes must move not only horizontally from left to right, but also, to a lesser extent, vertically, in order to take in the notes and symbols of the two staves, chords, and polyphonic textures. An even more important difference is that in a line of print, words are clearly separated, ready for the mind to grasp and interpret, while in music notation there is no such visually clear, matter-of-course separation of note groups; the mind has to organize the individual notes into recognizable patterns, such as motives, phrases, measures, chords, etc. Finally, a pianist not only has to read (see and perceive) the note picture, but also has to make an instantaneous physical response by generating the prescribed sound through the ten fingers on the keyboard. These differences have important ramifications as to the methods and techniques of sight-reading training.

To enable the mind to group individual notes into meaningful patterns, a knowledge of the various musical elements, such as notation, harmony, and form, is necessary. A keen ear, quick perception, good muscle coordination, and an intuitive understanding of the logic in the organization of musical materials are tremendous assets in achieving sight reading fluency even without much hard and disciplined work. But it is also a fact that those less endowed with natural talent may also attain an impressive reading skill through systematic, step-by-step study.

PERCEPTION OF SINGLE NOTES

The first step and the most urgent goal in teaching sight reading is the instant recognition of single notes on the entire range of the grand staff and the location of these notes on the keyboard. Any progress toward sight reading efficiency will be thwarted if this elementary capacity is missing. Slides of single notes, projected on a screen at a steady cadence and played by the student at sight, is an ideal method of practicing and testing his skill, but excellent results may also be obtained with flash cards. The teacher holds up the cards and the student plays the notes without hesitation.

During these elementary drills, note recognition and keyboard familiarity may be facilitated by establishing a few visually logical, easy-to-spot notes on the staff as landmarks. In the early stages such strategically located pilot notes can guide the student and help orientation on both the staff and the keyboard. The pilot notes used most frequently are the five Cs of the grand staff:

The G of the treble staff and its upper octave, and the F of the bass staff and its lower octave, are also used often as landmarks, because of their relationships to the respective clefs.

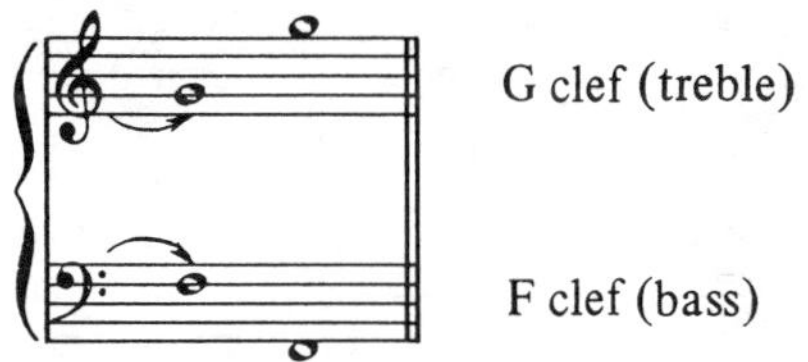

These two groups of pilot notes can easily be combined and studied through the following chart:

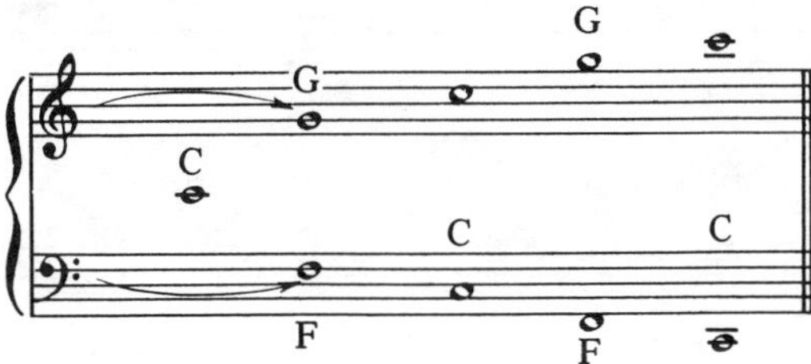

Observe that the Cs an octave above and below the middle C are in the second space from the top and bottom; the Cs above and below the grand staff are both on the second ledger line; the Gs of the treble staff are on the second line from the bottom and on the space just above the staff; the two Fs of the bass staff are on the second line from the top and on the space just below the staff. It should be emphasized that middle C as a focal point of orientation is not meant to imply a "method" or "approach" to note reading, but merely to illustrate the visual logic in the placement of these pilot notes and their symmetrical location on the grand staff in relation to middle C, which should facilitate memorization of these landmark notes. The reading and playing drills, however, do not have to emanate from middle C; in fact, they can and should involve all notes of the grand staff and the corresponding compass of the keyboard.

A cardinal requirement in the attainment of proficient sight-reading is the player's looking at the notated page and not at the keyboard or at his hands. The main reason for this is to maintain the continuity of eye movement from left to right, which is essential for the uninterrupted perception of note groups in advance of the instant of playing. This habit and skill of looking only at the music while playing and feeling the location of the keys under the fingers without looking, must be developed from the very beginning, starting with simple keyboard drills. The characteristic design of the keyboard, with its orderly grouping of two and three black keys, provides good tactile landmarks for locating the keys and playing without looking. The following preliminary exercises may be suggested as first steps in acquiring this "keyboard feel." The notes should be played without looking at the hands and only after the keys are located and securely felt under the fingers.

The location of white keys can easily be related to the black-key groups: the Cs just to the left of the two black keys, the Fs just to the left of the three black keys, the Ds between the two black keys, and so on. All white keys should be located and played with separate hands (and later with both hands) up and down the keyboard. The following exercise may serve as a pattern. The small notes in parentheses indicate the pilot keys, which should be felt, but not depressed, before playing the large note.

Play the above example with the right hand two octaves higher. Through all early sight-reading drills, note recognition on the staff and the tactile perception of corresponding keys should be constantly coordinated.

TWO-NOTE IMAGES (INTERVALS)

After the student is able to recognize and play single notes without hesitation, he or she is ready to drill for the next goal: the instant perception of two-note images in the form of melodic and harmonic intervals. Again, the use of flashcards is recommended, showing first the smaller intervals (seconds, thirds, fourths, and fifths)–step by step–involving the entire range of the grand staff. It will help the student to point out that the lines and spaces of the staff provide good visual clues in gauging the distance between the two notes of the interval.

Seconds move from line to the next space, or from space to the next line:

Thirds move from line to the next line, or from space to the next space:

Fourths move from line to space, or space to line, with a line and space in between:

Fifths move from line to line, skipping a line, or space to space, skipping a space:

To acquire a tactile perception of these intervals on the keyboard, little exercises in five-finger positions are recommended. The following sample drills should be played not only in the given G position, but also starting on A, C, D, E, F and B, first with separate hands, then with both hands.

The teacher can improvise many other useful drills to promote keyboard sensitivity even without written music. For instance, with the student's two hands in five-finger position—the fingers touching, say, A–B–C♯–D–E—the following instructions can be given:

- Play the notes as they are called out: E, B, D, A, C♯, etc.
- Play B; now play the upper interval of a fourth; now down a third; up a second; down a fourth; up a fifth; etc.
- Right hand play the note on the third line; third space; fourth line; etc. Left hand play the note on the second line; third space; third line; etc.

There are many well-known, simple folk songs and play tunes which lie within five-finger position and can be assigned for sight-reading purposes ("Aunt Rhody," "Lightly Row," "Love Somebody," etc.). These too should be played and practiced in various keys.

From the beginning, aural aspects of interval study should be integrated with the function of the eyes and the physical responses of the hands. In other words, the student should be able not only to read the notes and play them, but also to *hear* them. To fix the sound of an interval in the student's mind, it can be helpful to relate that sound to a portion of a well-known tune where that interval occurs. The opening strains of the following melodies may serve as samples:

Seconds: "Frère Jacques," "Deck the Halls"
Thirds: "On Top of Old Smoky," "This Old Man"
Fourths: "Down in the Valley," "Here Comes the Bride"
Fifths: "Twinkle, Twinkle, Little Star"
Sixths: "My Bonnie"

MAJOR AND MINOR TRIADS

Staying within the five-finger range, the reading and playing of major and minor triads can be practiced. In root position these triads are notated on three consecutive lines or spaces of the staff:

For keyboard practice, place hands in any five-finger position and play only the keys under the two outer fingers and the middle finger (left hand: 5-3-1; right hand: 1-3-5). Also, play the following exercise with both hands, in all major and minor keys, starting first on the white keys, then on the black ones.

When hearing a triad, the student should be able to identify it as major or minor and be able to sing its component notes. In the beginning he or she may be reminded to associate the major triad with the first three tones of the "Blue Danube" waltz or "The Star-Spangled Banner." In reproducing the tones of a minor triad, it may help to recall the well-known "Halloween theme" or the song "Black Is the Color of My True Love's Hair."

To repeat and consolidate all the foregoing note-reading and playing drills, very easy little pieces in five-finger position can be assigned. The five-finger positions do not necessarily have to be identical in the two hands, and may shift within a piece. These simple pieces should engage the already acquired skills step by step, starting with melodies in which notes or note groups are played alternately by the left and right hand, or played in unison, followed by pieces with gradually differing parts in the two hands. A graded sequence of such miniatures can be assembled by the teacher from various elementary collections and piano primers. Well-edited sight-reading books, written specifically for this purpose, may also be found.

LARGER INTERVALS – CHORD INVERSIONS

The larger intervals, sixths, sevenths, and octaves, may be practiced next, coordinating their visual perception on the staff, their feel on the keyboard, and the recognition of their sound. Here, too, certain visual clues may be followed:

Sixths move from line to space, or from space to line:

Sevenths move from line to line, skipping two lines, or from space to space, skipping two spaces:

Octaves move from line to space, or from space to line:

The following little melody, involving the larger intervals, may be played in various keys:

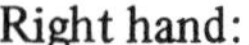

Practicing the perception of three-note images, both in the form of triads (including inversions) and melodic sequences, is the next logical step in sight-reading training. Recognizing triads is easiest when the chord is in root position, notated on three consecutive lines or spaces of the staff. Reading and playing the inversions of the triad require a little more scrutiny and practice. Again, a few visual characteristics may be pointed out. While the outer notes of a triad in root position are always a fifth apart, the outer notes of both inversions are a sixth apart. (Some sources, quite logically, use the following terms: Root Position, Second Position, and Third Position.)

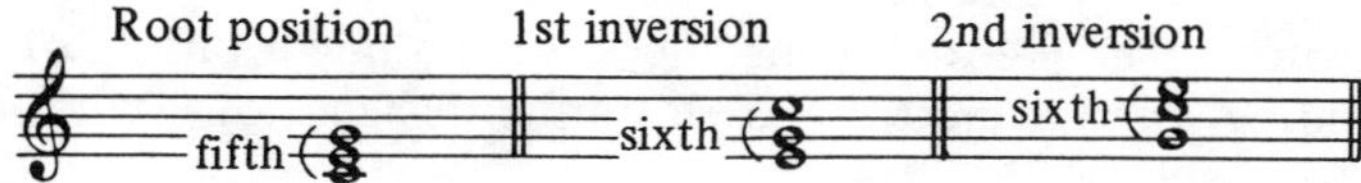

Visually, the two inversions can be quickly distinguished by the location of the middle note. In the first inversion this middle note is a third apart from the bottom note; in the second inversion it is a fourth apart. In other words, the two intervals forming a triad are—from the bottom up—a third and a fourth in the first inversion, a fourth and a third in the second inversion:

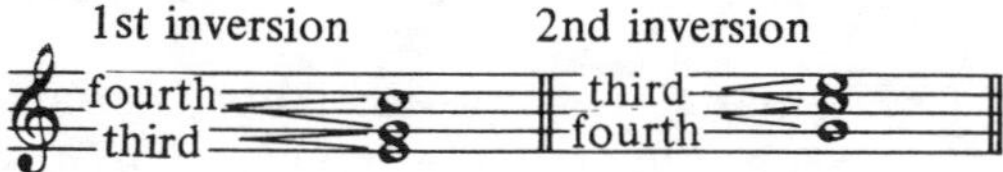

The root of the triad is always the upper note of the fourth.

The following exercises, played in various keys, can promote keyboard familiarity with triads and their inversions (fingering is the same in all keys).

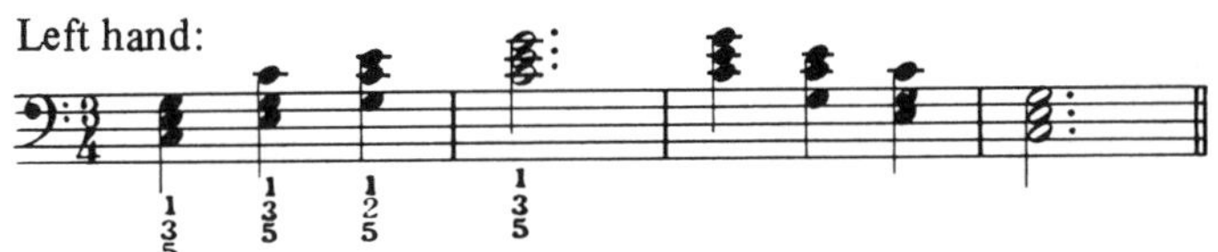

Melodic sequences of three or more notes usually appear in a metric and rhythmic framework. The reading of these note groups involves not only pitch recognition, but also the perception of these notes within the context of a specific meter and rhythmic pattern. The following note sequence of F–G–A, for instance, can assume a variety of identities depending on the metric and rhythmic designations, without any variations of pitch:

For the sake of a systematic, step-by-step approach and especially in the training of slow readers, it may be advisable to first practice the reading of three-note groups without any metric and rhythmic connotations. In this manner the student can concentrate first on pitch recognition only. As a sample, here is a sequence of progressively arranged note groups which can be put on flash cards on both the treble and bass staffs. The cards should be shown sequentially, with the same length of viewing time allotted for each.

FOUR-NOTE IMAGES (SEVENTH CHORDS)

Sight-reading the seventh chord and its inversions implies the vertical perception of four-note images. An analysis of the manner in which these chords are notated can furnish certain hints toward easier recognition. In root position, the notes of the seventh chord are placed on four consecutive lines or spaces of the staff; the bottom and top note form the interval of a seventh:

In all three inversions of the seventh chord, when the notes are written on one staff (close position), the bottom and top notes are a sixth apart:

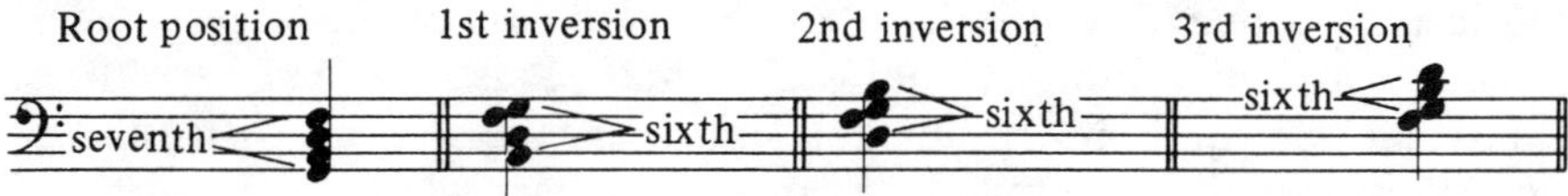

To recognize a given inversion, one has to look for the two notes which form the interval of a second. This interval is instantly recognizable in any chordal structure because of its diagonal placement on the staff (F and G in the above examples). In the first inversion this interval is on top, in the second inversion it is placed in the middle, and in the third on the bottom. The root of the chord is always the upper note of this diagonally notated interval:

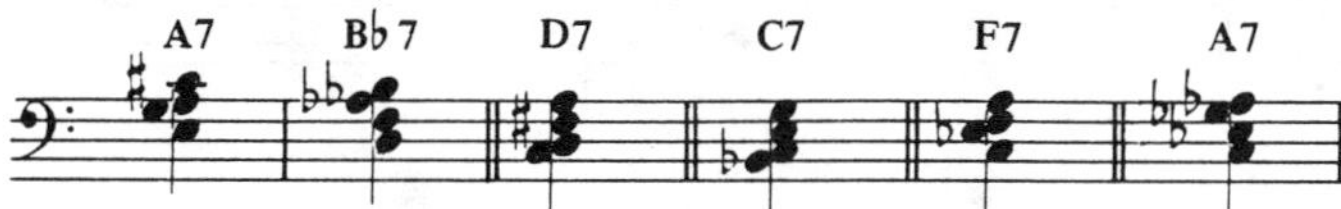

The seventh chord, especially the dominant seventh, often occurs in an incomplete form, with the fifth of the root missing:

EXPANDING THE EYE SPAN

If the student is able to sight-read fluentlv and securely all preparatory materials presented so far, the next desirable goal is to expand his eye-span, the number of notes and symbols the eyes can take in at one glance. As mentioned, a cardinal requirement of good sight reading is the player's ability to "look ahead" and read not just one note at a glance, but a group of notes, the same way one reads complete words rather than individual letters. Our notation system provides no distinct delineation of cohesive note groups, and the reader's split-second judgments must determine what notes belong together and can be perceived through successive eyespans. In view of this, it is not enough to tell the student to look ahead; he or she should also be given suggestions how far ahead to look, or more precisely, *what to look for.*

Bar lines are the most obvious signposts in the horizontal division of notated music, which would suggest that the reader's eye can move from bar line to bar line and absorb note images measure by measure. This is certainly the simplest and most obvious yardstick to go by, and it can, indeed, often bring satisfactory results; as a general approach, however, it is entirely too mechanistic and musically unreliable. A much safer, more intelligent, and ultimately more efficient way to read music is to perceive at one glance *organic elements* of the larger musical structure at hand: motives, phrases or half-phrases, which very often transcend bar lines. It is inevitable, of course, that even with this approach one reads occasionally from bar to bar, when notes within a measure are also a cohesive form element (motive, figure, etc.), as in the following examples:

Gruber: "Silent Night"

Bar lines may also be relied on as horizontal signposts when reading long, uninterrupted note sequences, which occur often, especially in baroque music:

Rameau: Minuet

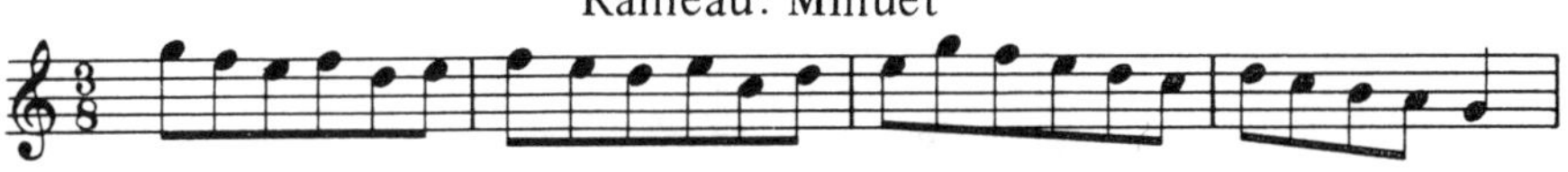

Such bar-to-bar perception may also be justified and supported by the harmonic context of the melodic line:

J.S. Bach: Fugue

The foregoing examples notwithstanding, the eyes of a good sightreader should not move measure by measure, but rather follow the natural divisions of the musical line, regardless of the placement of the bars; the eyes should seek out the "breathing spots" (cadences, cadence-like inflections, pertinent long notes, and rests) and thus determine the note group to be perceived by one eyespan. It is immaterial whether such a note group takes up exactly a measure, transcends the bar line, or amounts to less than a measure, as the following three examples respectively illustrate:

Le Couppey: Rondino

Hüllmandel: German Dance

Gretchaninoff: "Tiresome Lesson"

In the complicated process of sight reading, the player must not only read ahead to take in notation in advance of the moment of playing, but also *remember* what has just been perceived in order to play it at the next instant. This is why organic form elements (motives, phrases, etc.) are ideal note groups for easy perception; they are, by definition, memorable sections of the musical context. Indeed, they must be, as the basic building blocks of the musical artifice. It is their repetition and elaboration which fuels the forward momentum in the development of the larger forms.

PITCH CONTOURS – RHYTHM PATTERNS

To recognize these form elements instantly, one has to look for certain distinctive, memorable features in the note image. The two most obvious of these are a *characteristic pitch contour* (the graphic outline of the rise and fall of successive notes on the staff), which in most cases also represents a *distinct rhythm pattern*.

The melodic contour will be a straight line when a note is repeated and will climb or dip at various degrees, depending on the interval between the successive notes. Observe, for instance, the outline of the following melody; brackets indicate logical eyespans:

French Folksong

Also, review the examples on p.202-04 and notice how melodies are formed by notes repeating, moving stepwise in seconds, skipping by thirds, or progressing by larger intervals. Very often the succession of notes outlines broken chords, or furnishes other important clues to the harmonic content which, if perceived, will greatly facilitate reading and playing the piece.

Hummel: Écossaise

Haydn: German Dance

A sequence of tones forms not only a melodic outline, but also, in most cases, a rhythmic pattern, the perception of which is equally important, if not more so, from the standpoint of sight reading. In order to recognize such patterns and reproduce them through finger action on the keyboard, a secure sense of rhythm is essential. This sense—the ability to feel and maintain a steady pulse and to coordinate this underlying beat with the notated rhythm patterns of the music at hand—must be nurtured and developed from the very start. Systematic drills, singing in cadence, counting, clapping, and stepping exercises are described in many easily available articles and books.

Although the beginning reader's eyespan may often not be wide enough to encompass motives or phrase sections as a whole, training and practice should be directed toward this aim. Certain practical suggestions may help the student; for instance, he or she should be reminded to look for *repeated features* in the note image. Once a note image is absorbed and remembered visually, aurally, and kinetically, its sequential recurrence will trigger the appropriate sensory function and finger action more or less automatically. Repetition may involve a single note, various intervals, melodic figures consisting of three, four, or more notes, scale and arpeggio-like passages, solid and broken chords, and other accompaniment figures. Observe the repetitions in the following examples:

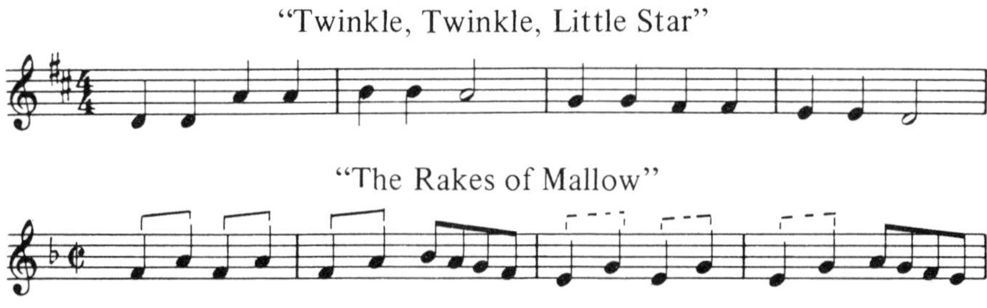

Watching for repetitions of melody segments and rhythm units can lead the student through the first steps in form analysis, which is an important part of sight-reading training. A good start might include reading and playing folk songs, play tunes, and simple, appropriate small pieces in steady tempo, observing the repetitions and variations of melody and rhythm. In the following excerpts, brackets indicate eyespans; identical letters over the brackets signify exact repetitions; figures 1 and 2 after identical letters mean that the rhythm is exactly repeated, but the melody is slightly altered.

"Ten Little Indians"

Shostakovich: March

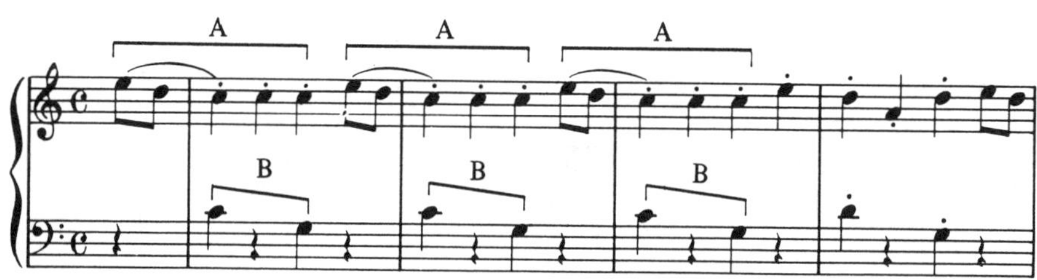

Schmitt: Sonatina

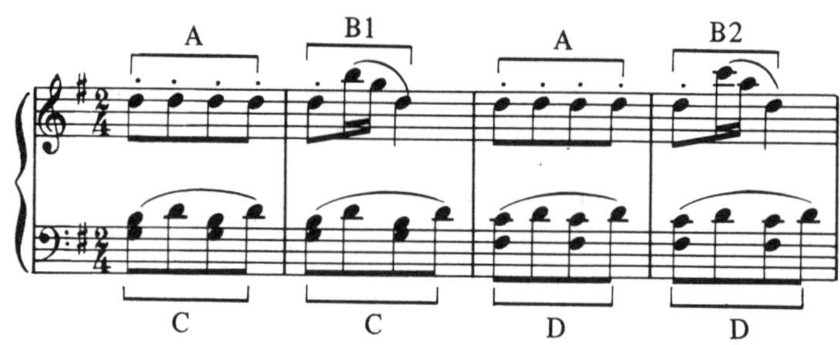

A quick preliminary scanning of a piece in advance of playing is recommended, in order to discover as many characteristic aspects of the note image as possible. In the following excerpt, for instance, each of the three rhythmic features occurs sequentially three times. Sight reading this piece will be immeasurably facilitated if this fact is ascertained prior to the playing.

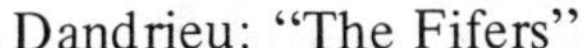

In the following example the perception of the following salient features will be helpful:

Measure 1:	(right hand)	Repeated notes
	(left hand)	Broken F-major triad repeated
Measure 2:	F-major scale	
Measure 3:	(right hand)	Stepwise motion upward
	(left hand)	Broken intervals, with the lower notes moving stepwise down, and the upper note repeated.

Beethoven: Sonatina

A knowledge of elementary harmony is a necessary precondition for good sight reading. This enables the student to recognize the chord basis of arpeggio figures, the scales that yield the runs and passages at hand, and, in general, helps to put melodic contours in their harmonic context. This automatically facilitates the perception of accompaniment features and voicings. Furthermore, a familiarity with chord sequences within frequently occurring cadences will let the player *anticipate* certain harmonic functions, without the necessity of deciphering every note of a chord. In the following example, the right-hand chord in the second measure does not have to be read note by note; the dominant-tonic sequence, implied by the left-hand notes, together with the lowest note (G) and the shape of the chord in question, make safe the assumption that a G-major triad with a doubled octave should be played:

Scales, arpeggios, and cadences should be practiced in every key, major and minor, following a progressive plan. Scales can be grouped according to fingering patterns: first C, C-minor, G, G-minor, D, D-minor, A, A-minor, E, E-minor, and B, B-minor, followed by F, F-minor, and then the scales starting on black keys. Similarly, arpeggios can be grouped according to the configuration of their component white and black keys, taking first the ones starting on white keys. Simple cadences, such as the following, should be practiced in all keys and all inversions.

All drills must be played slowly, accurately, and without looking at the hands.

Practicing scales, chords, and arpeggios will help to develop a sense of harmony, facilitate transposition, and foster the student's technical ability and the adoption of good fingering habits—all very important skills in achieving sight-reading competence.

TRANSPOSING

It has been repeatedly emphasized that the student should be guided toward "feeling at home" in all keys; hence the frequent suggestions for transpositions. In this area, a few obvious reminders to the student will be helpful to overcome initial hurdles. Before playing the piece in the new key:

(1) Ascertain the new key signature.
(2) Play the scale and a few simple cadences in the new key.
(3) Observe the distance between the keynotes of the old and the new key; this will indicate the interval by which every note will have to be shifted. If there is a choice between two intervals (depending on whether the shift will be up or down), it is usually wiser to choose the *smaller* interval. For instance, when transposing a piece from F to D, one can go up a sixth or down a third; the latter will usually be preferred.
(4) Look at the starting notes of both hands in the original key and determine what these notes will be in the new key.
(5) Put hands in the proper new position and play by shifting the notes (or rather the note groups) in the proper direction by the predetermined interval.
(6) Be constantly guided by your ear, or more precicely, by the memorized sound obtained when having first played the piece in the original key.

THE SIGHT-READING REPERTORY

All foregoing drills and exercises or similar ones meant to enlarge the eyespan, to acquire tactile security on the keyboard, and learn basic concepts of form and harmony, are essential for systematic sight-reading study. In addition, an ample, carefully selected repertory of interesting pieces should be assembled for daily sight-reading use. There are numerous publications specifically designed for this purpose; also, the teacher may select materials from the large number of method books and teaching collections containing suitable pieces on all grade levels. In assembling such a repertory, the following guidelines may be kept in mind:

- Grading should be leisurely to give ample opportunity for gradually engaging all body functions—visual, tactile, and aural.
- Only interesting, appealing, well-written pieces should be selected.

Hackneyed construction, awkward voice leading, or illogical harmonic sequences will fail to evoke the desired anticipation and proper conditioned responses; they will only serve to confuse the player's musical sense.

- It should always be clear to the teacher (especially in the early grade levels) what specific purpose the piece at hand serves (interval reading, rhythm perception, chord study, keyboard familiarity, eyespan expansion, etc.).
- Pieces for sight-reading should be easier than the student's regular study materials, with grade difference varying according to individual circumstances. In the early grades a half- to one-year lag will be sufficient for the average student. In the intermediate grades, sight-reading pieces may be one or two grades easier than the regular fare. Players with obvious reading problems should be given a remedial course starting on levels two or three grades below the technical capability. In some extreme cases it may be necessary to start systematic reading from the beginning level, regardless of the student's playing ability.
- An ample repertory of graded duets must be at the teacher's disposal for daily use. Playing duets is an important part of sight-reading training. The player must maintain a steady forward momentum and rhythmic flow; if he or she falters, the continuity of sound is carried by the other player, so that there is time to find one's place again and regain composure. Best results can be achieved with materials in which *primo* and *secondo* are on approximately the same grade level, so that the student can alternate playing the two parts. These duets may be written for either one or two pianos, and many solo pieces may be played as duets. Baroque keyboard music—inventions, fugues, and various dances—are especially suitable for this purpose.

GENERAL SUGGESTIONS

To summarize, a good sight-reading repertory should contain a great variety of well-written, appealing, carefully graded pieces, assigned to the student according to individual needs, in a methodical, step-by-step fashion. The student will benefit from the following general suggestions for reading and playing by sight:

- Before starting to play, be sure to know the piece's *title, tempo mark,* and *key signature.* This may seem to be an elementary and superfluous reminder, but it is not. All too often the student plunges into playing before being aware of these essential facts about the piece. A title by itself can often convey not only the mood, but even the approximate tempo and basic rhythm of the work. Consider, for instance, nocturne, tarantella, pastorale, rag, gavotte, etc. Also, certain tempo indications (andante cantabile, allegro giocoso, solid blues tempo, for instance) impart much more than a measure of speed; they condition the player for the appropriate physical responses.

- Before starting to play, ascertain the starting position of both hands and, with a quick glance, try to perceive conspicuous repetitive and other characteristic features of melody, rhythm, harmony, and accompaniment patterns.
- Always look and think ahead. Do not read note by note, but try to perceive note groups (motives, phrases, phrase sections) with one glance. Phrase endings, cadential long notes, and pauses are ideal spots for scanning the next note group.
- Always look at the music and not at your hands; you should feel the location of keys under your fingers without looking. To practice this, try to play pieces or sections that you know by heart, with closed eyes or in a dark room.
- When reading chords, start from the bottom up. The bottom note, together with the graphic appearance of the chord notation, can give you a good clue to the harmonic function and position (root or inversion) of the chord.
- Play more slowly than indicated, if necessary, but maintain a steady pace; do not hesitate or stop. If you make a mistake, be aware of it, but keep going. (An important qualification should be kept in mind by the teacher: sight reading and playing which is consistently full of errors and omissions cannot be accepted; it means that the student is not ready to sight-read on that particular grade level and should be assigned easier materials.)

OMITTING "NON-ESSENTIAL" FEATURES

Writings on sight reading usually emphasize that not all elements of the note picture are equally important, and that the player must give preference to those elements which are more essential than others. In other words, certain notes which as background or ornamental detail may be judged secondary may be omitted as long as a steady pulse is maintained and the main structural features (form, rhythm) are unimpaired. This is a valid procedure, except on the elementary grade levels, where an insistence on reading and playing *everything* contained in the note picture is of utmost importance. Only in this manner, through reading and playing every note in a graduated sequence of drills and pieces, can the beginner learn to recognize the organization of music, both horizontally and vertically, and acquire the basic skills of coordinating the functions of eyes, brain, and hands. In the intermediate grade levels, after the fundamental aspects of sight-reading techniques (note recognition, keyboard feel, elementary form and harmony concepts) are learned and assimilated, the student should be allowed, indeed encouraged, to become a constructively selective reader, an "expert skipper" by perceiving only the essential and omitting the nonessential. In doing so, the following priorities may be listed, in order of their importance:

- a steady, uninterrupted pulse
- rhythmic accuracy, which also implies good articulation and phrasing
- note accuracy, particularly in the lead voices
- a correct grasp and rendition of harmonic context, regardless of the shape, form, or voice distribution of the individual chords
- expression and musicality
- a perception of secondary features, such as accompaniment patterns, figurations, ornamental details, etc.

The amount of time required for sight-reading practice will vary according to the student's needs. As a rule, at least a short segment of each lesson should be devoted to it. If the student is a fairly good reader, a few minutes will suffice; poor readers will require more time at each lesson, in direct ratio to their reading deficiencies. During the lesson the pupil should sight-read from a systematically graded supply of materials, selected by the teacher. At home, a part of every practice period should be spent on sight reading. For this the teacher may assign a variety of ungraded materials ranging from easy to just below the student's technical level. Collections of appealing pieces—classic to modern, original and arranged, hymns, familiar tunes—presenting varied forms, tempos, rhythms, and harmonic sequences, are ideally suitable for this purpose.

Teaching sight reading is an exceptionally difficult and challenging task. Numerous basic musical skills are involved, all of which have to be cultivated and developed gradually and continually. Once the student is trained to a degree where these skills become intuitive, enabling him or her to sight-read with confidence and even a dash of flair, the teacher's reward is at hand: the student has become a musician.

RECOMMENDED COLLECTIONS OF GRADED MUSIC

Agay, Denes. *Fun with Sight-Reading* (3 books). (YPL No. 10-A, B, C). Warner.

Deutsch, Leonhard. *Piano: Guided Sight-Reading*. Nelson-Hall.

Johnson, Thomas A. *Read and Play* (10 books). Hinrichsen.

Last, Joan. *Rhythmic Reading* (5 books). Bosworth.

RECOMMENDED READING

Bishop, Dorothy. "Sight Reading in the Piano Class." *Clavier* January–February 1964.

Bryant, Celia Mae. "Sight Reading—An Art!" *Clavier* March–April 1962.

Havill, Lorena. "Sight Reading Can Be Taught." *Clavier* February 1971.

Jones, Marjorie Dana. "Sight-Reading All-Important." *Étude* March 1957.

Schumann, Judit. "Remedial Sight Reading." *Clavier* February 1969.

Wildman, Arthur. "Increase Your Sight Reading Skill." *The Piano Teacher* July–August 1964.

Memorization and Performing from Memory

DENES AGAY

To understand fully and put into proper perspective this important phase of the piano student's education, it is best first to clarify the concepts involved. *Memory* is the *capacity* of recall of things learned or experienced in the past. *Memorization* is the *process and discipline* by which we may obtain this faculty. In other words, memory is the result, the end product, of memorization.

Let us use here a very contemporary parallel. The information storage unit of an electrical computer, aptly called "memory," can, at the push of a button, activate impulses to furnish needed answers and information. But it can do so only if properly "programmed"; that is, if the right types and amounts of data are stored in advance within its maze of components. Similarly, the human brain, this most complicated and miraculously proficient of all computers, is able to remember, to recall and re-play anything and everything that was previously stored in its "little grey cells" through various physiological means, by the process of memorization.

The memorization process can be, and at its best should be, conscious and planned, but it also can be subconscious, an automatic byproduct of other learning functions, mental and physical. When we play a strain of music, certain impressions remain embedded in our minds even without a conscious effort. These impressions, usually concurrent and interlocking, fall into three categories: *aural* (the sound of the music), *visual* (the image of the note picture), and *tactile* (the feel of the keys under the hands). As we play the strain repeatedly, some elements of melody, harmony, rhythm—certain graphic configurations of the notation, and some motion patterns of hands, arms, and fingers—become more and more implanted in our memory banks, and at a certain point we are able to play the piece from memory.

Such involuntary memorization is especially characteristic of the way young children usually learn to play "by heart." Their fresh, uncluttered minds absorb the necessary information by rote, one might say. They do not set out to memorize; they simply play the piece repeatedly and in the course of it automatically retain, usually by aural and tactile means, the mental imprints to be recalled and reactivated later. This subconscious, reflexlike memorization is, of course, not restricted to children; adults too, to a somewhat lesser degree, assemble musical memory data the same way. However, a memory acquired solely by such automatic responses is usually not secure and trustworthy. If such reflexlike recall fails momentarily during a performance, a breakdown is inevitable, unless there are consciously assembled patterns, data, and memory aids available to come to the rescue.

THE IMPORTANCE OF ANALYSIS

This, actually, is at the heart of the matter. *The basis of memorization is analysis*, a planned, systematic effort to organize the various aspects and elements of the music into distinctive patterns, images, and relationships which the mind is able to store, retain, and reconstruct better and more easily than a jumble of indistinct bits of information. Since music by its very nature implies tonal organizations of various kinds (form, harmony, rhythms, etc.) its analysis seldom offers any problems. The basic concepts (scale, interval, triad, phrase, etc.) are given and defined; to memorize we must discover and understand these concepts' specific character and interrelationship within the piece and judiciously select and spotlight pertinent elements for remembering.

Analysis can and should begin at an early stage and proceed gradually, from the simplest and most obvious analytical premises to more complex ones, parallel with the acquisition of theoretical knowledge. At the very beginning of instruction, for instance, playing the C-major scale can easily be memorized by the simple formula of beginning with C and playing eight white keys in succession. This is an analytical pattern of sorts, albeit an elementary one. It is also of very narrow usefulness; it does not help the student memorize any other scale. So in due course—and as soon as possible—the player should become familiar with the major-scale pattern of whole steps and half steps, which provides a helpful matrix to adopt the proper visual and tactile associations toward memorizing all major scales.

In the earliest grades, the analytic tools can be only the theoretical concepts already familiar to the student. For example, in examining the following little piece for the purpose of memorization, the student should know about note values, intervals, major scales, and phrases. The important features to remember are:

- the predominance of melodic thirds in the melodic contour (bars 1, 3, 5, 6, 7)
- phrase A is repeated in bars 3 and 4 (phrase B) a sixth lower
- phrase C is repeated in bar 6 (phrase D) an octave lower
- phrase A and phrase B are repeated–by right and left hand respectively–in bars 7 and 8

Tonal organizations in the works of baroque, and especially of classical and romantic composers are readily apparent because they are built on familiar concepts and elements. The exposition of the first movement of Mozart's C-major Sonata (K. 545) is presented here as a sample for analyzing works in the classical mold. The following resumé of salient features (memory aids) should be checked point by point:

- the three themes, all of which contain broken-chord patterns: main theme (ms. 1-2), second theme (ms. 14-15), third (closing) theme (starting on the second beat of m. 26, ending on the first beat of m. 27)
- the harmonic functions of the broken chords forming the Alberti bass in ms. 1 to 4
- the up-and-down scale passages in bars 5-8, gradually descending (starting note is A in m. 5, G in m. 6, etc.); the accompanying bass notes also descending stepwise (F in m. 5, E in m. 6, etc.)
- the G–C–G–C broken-chord sequence and corresponding melody notes in m. 11
- the melodic contour formed by the encircled notes and the D ostinato in the left hand, in ms. 13-17

- alternating broken-chord patterns is ms. 18-21 (the starting note of the right hand pattern is always identical to the preceding note on the same staff ; the starting note of the left hand broken triad is always a third [tenth] below the preceding melody note.)
- The G–D7–G harmonic underpinning of the closing theme (ms. 26-27)

Mozart: Sonata, K. 545

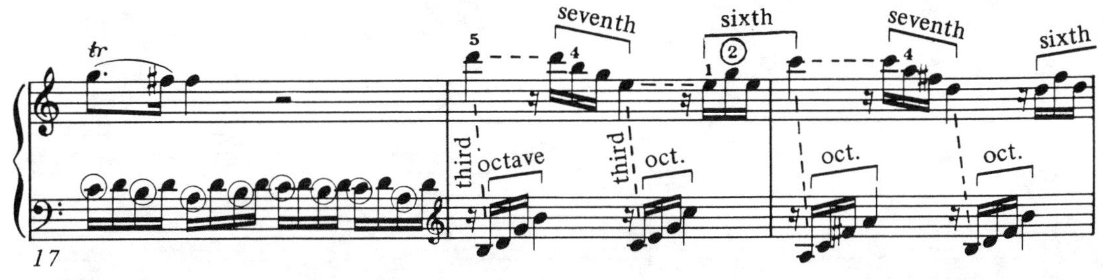

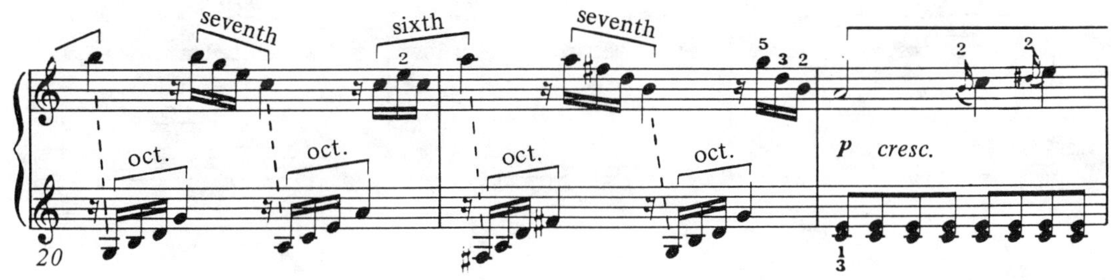

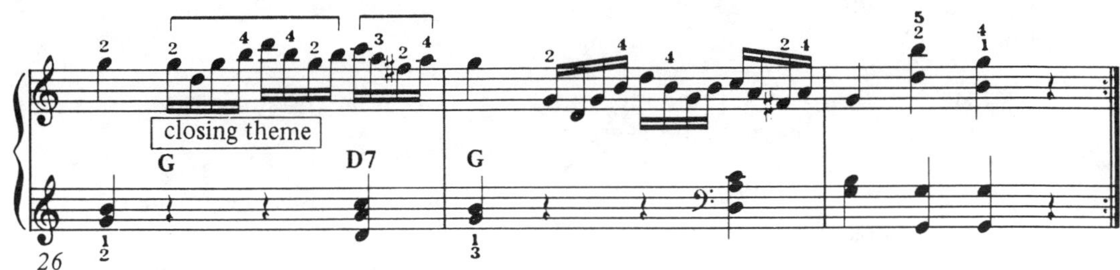

Memorization of contemporary music may require closer scrutiny, as its organization may not be as obvious. However, astute analysis of modern works will usually disclose characteristic features of pitch, interval, and rhythm which can serve as guiding patterns for memorization.

Bartók: Bagatelle, op. 6 no. 2

In the above example the repeated seconds (A-flat–B-flat) continuing through six measures are immediately evident and easy to remember. With a few more searching glances we are also able to discern an important pattern in the left-hand part, which becomes more apparent if the phrase is notated in the following manner and dissected into two divergent parts, one ascending and the other descending (by half steps):

The developing pianist should keep in mind the following main steps in the process of memorization:

- Have a clear and definite idea about the work as a whole: its form, style, mood, texture, and tempo
- Follow good practice habits (see page 14), which include a good deal of analytical involvement. Learn to play the piece from beginning to end securely, confidently, without mistakes *from the score*; have a thorough grasp of the work in its totality and details, and have firm technical control over each and every measure
- Subject the piece to a still closer analysis, section by section, noting and storing all pertinent features of the component elements which can serve as memory aids
- Play a memorized piece repeatedly, at judicious intervals, to insure secure retention

PSYCHOLOGICAL FACTORS

Memory is a mental capacity which is as complicated as it is fragile; stress on mind or body can easily affect it and impair it. Concerns, uncertainties, and anxieties associated with playing from memory, especially in public, are well-known, commonplace symptoms plaguing not only inexperienced players but celebrated artists as well. The source of this unwelcome proclivity is not so much the fear of not being able to memorize a score, but rather the apprehension of not being able to recall every part of a memorized piece during the course of performance.

How can the teacher help in alleviating these anxieties?

The first step is to bolster the student's confidence by assuring the student that he or she is well equipped to play and memorize the piece, and conveying that a degree of anxiety is a natural phenomenon shared by nearly everyone performing in public. Then, once the piece is thoroughly learned and memorized, the student should be provided with opportunities to play the memorized piece on a number of occasions for small, friendly audiences in an informal setting, as psychological preparation for public performance at a more formal recital or concert.

If a student has severe anxieties about performing in public, and especially if he or she already has had one or two unfortunate experiences with memory lapses, other alternatives should be explored to spare the student unnecessary anguish and a seriously adverse affect on his or her musical outlook and motivation. One possibility is for the student to use the score while performing. Sometimes the mere presence and availability of the score is enough to calm apprehensions and generate confidence. In any case, it should be the student's choice whether to play at a recital from memory or from the score. The student who prefers the latter, even with the aid of a page turner, should be free to do so without embarrassment.

Although performing from memory has become the predominant custom of our time, it has not always been so and is not a universal practice. Chamber-music players, many organists, nearly all piano accompanists, and some piano soloists have the scores in front of them while performing, without the slightest impairment to the fluency, musicality, and sensitivity of the performance. Students, parents, and audiences should be made aware of this, and realize that a performance should be judged solely on its musical merit, regardless of whether it was played from memory or from the score.

When evaluating the pedagogical role of memorization, one should not lose sight of the significant distinction between the *memorization process* and a *public performance from memory*. Memorization is an important part of the student's education. It teaches analysis, leads to a thorough understanding of and identification with the music, and, in general, sharpens the musical mind. Performance from memory is a desirable but entirely optional corollary; it is a public demonstration of materials learned, which should, by all means, be encouraged and guided, but never insisted upon especially in the presence of possible negative psychological factors.

RECOMMENDED READING

Bryant, Celia Mae. "Memorization." *Clavier* October 1963.

Matthay, Tobias A. *On Memorizing and Playing from Memory*. New York: Oxford University Press, 1926.

Novik, Ylda. "Reading and Memorization Techniques Leading Toward Performance." In James W. Bastien, *How To Teach Piano Successfully*. Kjos, 1973.

Rabson, Grace Rubin. "The Influence of Analytical Prestudy in Memorizing Piano Music." Dissertation, Columbia University, 1937.

Thrope, Louis P. and Harvey S. Whistler. "Memorizing Piano Music." *The Piano Teacher* July–August 1959; September–October 1959.

Improvisation

SYLVIA RABINOF

Music existed centuries before notation. Bards and minstrels sang, performers blew, plucked and beat on primitive instruments, all without the guidance of written systems. How did they manage? They improvised. They responded to the lyrical impulses which welled up within them under the stir, the stress, the moods of melancholy or excitement, the whole emotional spectrum of their daily lives. It was an outpouring, spontaneous and extemporaneous, of the basic human need to fashion and articulate ingratiating sounds for the entertainment and delight of others as well as oneself. History abounds with accounts of these early musicians. The songs, if we may so characterize them, were delivered as a quasi-accompaniment to a poetic text, extolling virtue, valor, love, hope, sacrifice.

Did the advent of notation make improvisation obsolete? It did not; however, about a hundred years ago the art went into decline. Extemporization in the world of so-called serious music became neglected, if not lost. Today the only forms where one can find it are folk music, jazz, pop, and organists' improvisations at church services or concerts. But this was not always so. In Bach's time, for example, keyboard improvisation was part and parcel of standard harpsichord instruction, an accepted discipline that was taught along with scales, technique, and repertory. Baroque performers had to be expert in adding a correct, melodically and contrapuntally satisfying "filler" above a given figured *basso continuo.*

Bach's illustrious successors—Mozart, Beethoven, Chopin, Liszt, and others—utilized this ancient technique to realize their conceptions at the very instant of the creative process. They relied not only upon preconceived ideas but often invented them to meet the exigency of the situation. This might arise on a challenge, as in the celebrated duel between Mozart and Clementi, to determine which one could come up with more ingenious variations on a random subject; or it might be an occasion for the introduction of harmonic or contrapuntal material into a work already in progress. But most often, and with reference to the most popular of all solo instruments, the piano, improvisation meant composing at the keyboard on the spur of the moment. One may ask whether this can produce great work; the answer is to be found in the achievements of the past. Equally significant is the fact that improvisation was not only used but taught. It enjoyed a status comparable to all other accepted and traditional functional devices for making and producing music—theory, harmony, counterpoint, etc.

Improvisation is the embodiment of rhythm, melody, harmony, and form—the basic elements of music. It synthesizes the human factors that enter into the creative function: experience, imagination, intuition. It links theorist, composer, and performer by combining these attributes in the pursuit of a common objective. It is the amalgam that helps bring into being "the compleat musician."

WHY TEACH IMPROVISATION?

What has this to do with the piano student, whose task is to sit at the keyboard and render the music as well as his or her skill permits? The answer is that the ability to improvise will help make the student a better performer. It is not only a question of filling in missing interludes (as where cadenzas are called for) or of adding ornaments; rather it is a matter of improving both technical and interpretative faculties. Improvising gives a superior tactile relationship to the keyboard, an aural awareness, and a sense of "at homeness" in any key, better memory and sight-reading ability, a gift for compositional analysis, security, and poise. But over and above all else, it enhances his musicianship to the extent that understanding, imagination, and creativity make possible. Whatever the student's aptitude, improvisational facility will sharpen his insights. It will ignite a deeper awareness of the problems that must be resolved if artistry, rather than mere fluency in performance, is to be achieved. Phrasing and dynamics, the gamut of technique and interpretation, all these now become clearer.

Can improvisation be taught? And if so, how? The answer to the first question is that it not only can be taught and learned, but, with diligent effort, mastered. It may be studied privately or in class; the latter may be more effective, since it encourages ensemble playing, which fosters alertness, strong rhythmic feeling, the virtues of listening, and playing accurately and together with other members of a group. Improvisation is accessible to all ages, regardless of the student's proficiency. There are, however, preconditions: the student must be able to play a one-octave C-major scale with both hands and a simple, early-grade piece (such as Clementi's Sonatina in C major) and have a thorough understanding of simple time signatures, pitch names, and accidentals in both clefs.

Like any skill, improvisation must be practiced regularly, more at the keyboard, of course, than on paper; it should not be an academic exercise. For the beginner there is the understandable need to overcome timidity or reluctance. Improvisation is a step beyond acquiring a musical vocabulary: it is applying that vocabulary creatively. Therefore the process should be gradual, a progression from very simple rhythmic and melodic patterns to larger and more complex forms.

Successful improvisation calls for the cultivation of correct habits from the very first lesson. Exercises in learning the fundamentals of music are a necessary part of study, but to avoid a preoccupation with formalism the exercises must be followed by improvisational practice. Many of the skills necessary for fluent sight reading now become involved: planning (the mind must always be ahead of the fingers), concentrated listening at all times, playing at a comfortable tempo, counting aloud (in the earliest stages), not going back to correct errors or hesitating or pausing at any point. A basically strong rhythmic pulse is vital, as is a feeling for the phrase as a whole and the sense of "going somewhere" and returning, at the conclusion, to the tonic or "home tone." Together with assignments at the piano, written ones should document each step. At first the student should play his or her improvised melodies and then also write (at least some of) them, in clear, correct notation. Clean playing and legible writing are essential from the start, the latter to help the beginner visualize the work.

THE FIRST STEPS

Music is a language, and the most elementary musical sentence is a four-measure melody. The improviser's very first step should be to think and "conduct" in the air, counting aloud, a four-measure phrase in $\frac{2}{4}$ meter, ending with a held half note in the fourth measure. This should be followed immediately by playing a melody with the right hand in C major, using the same rhythmic pattern and ending on the keynote C. The sense of conclusion and "returning home" in the fourth measure is helped by always employing a slight retard. Here, for instance, is a sample rhythmic pattern:

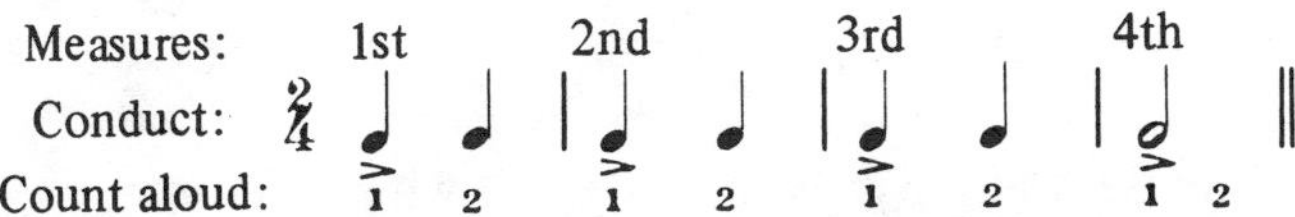

Play the following examples; improvise the missing notes by following the rhythmic pattern given above the staff and call out the measures (1st, 2nd, 3rd, 4th) on the downbeats.

The successful improviser never settles for one melody. At least five original melodies should be played, at a leisurely pace, using the same rhythmic pattern and ending on the keytone. The next step is to conduct five four-measure melodies in $\frac{3}{4}$ meter in C major, first conducting the whole phrase in the air, counting aloud.

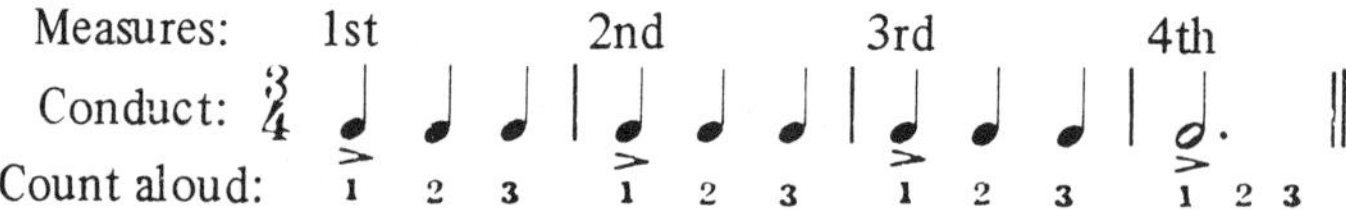

In the following examples of melodies in $\frac{3}{4}$ meter, improvise the missing notes, following the rhythmic pattern above the staff and calling out the measures (1st, 2nd, 3rd, 4th).

This in turn should lead to improvising several four-measure melodies in $\frac{4}{4}$ meter in C major, first conducted rhythmically in the air.

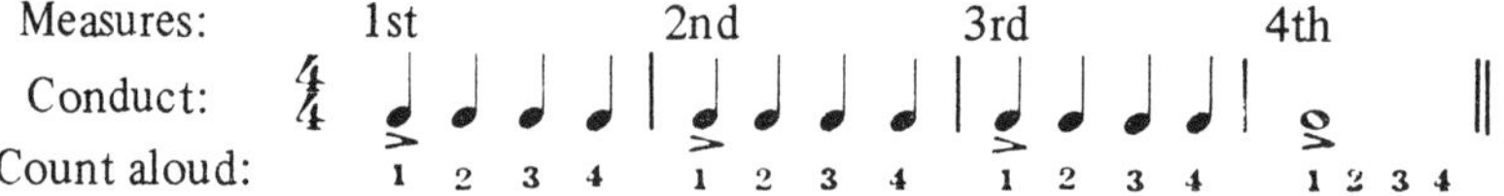

Again, improvise the missing notes, following the rhythmic pattern above the staff and calling out the measures.

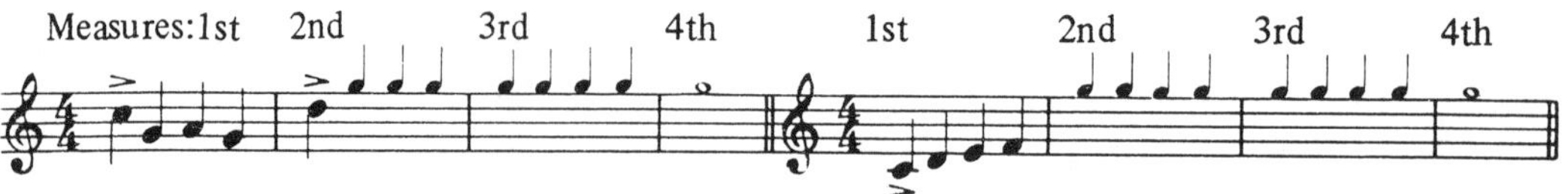

From this point progress should be smooth. Melodic improvisations must be pursued in the three meters ($\frac{2}{4}$, $\frac{3}{4}$, $\frac{4}{4}$) in various keys, and also transposed into other keys. The student should be drilled in simple rhythm patterns involving quarter notes and eighth notes, clapping and counting aloud; then these patterns should be introduced to four-measure melodies beginning on the first, third, or fifth tone of the key. The one-measure rhythmic pattern should appear in the first, second, and third measures, but the melody must come to a rest at the fourth measure.

The following is a chart of twelve rhythmic patterns (four each in the meters of $\frac{2}{4}$, $\frac{3}{4}$, $\frac{4}{4}$). Improvise four-measure melodies in different keys (D, A, F, B♭ , etc.) played by either hand or by both hands in unison.

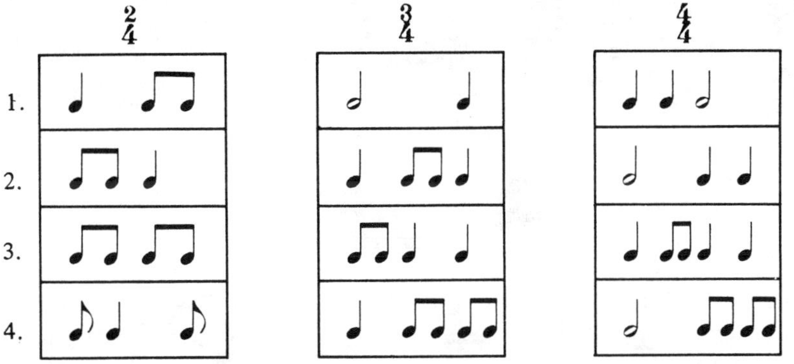

The following are examples of melodies based on some of the rhythmic patterns given above; add the missing notes.

Continue improvising at least two or three four-measure melodies on each of the twelve patterns.

"BORROWED" MOTIVES – SEQUENCES

As the improviser gains in experience, he or she may utilize a ready-at-hand device which will prove great fun: borrowing simple motives from the classical repertory. Motives are the distinguishing features of melody, the "signatures," so to speak. But while they consist of tonal and rhythmic fragments, they comprise in themselves complete thematic ideas. The motive is a characteristic note group of one or more measures. The one-measure motive is, of course, the simplest, and is found in the very first measure of a composition, identifying it somewhat like names identify people.

Bach: Minuet from *Little Notebook for Anna Magdalena Bach*

Example of improvised melody

1st 2nd 3rd 4th

Burgmüller: Arabesque

Observe the similarity between the first two measures (a and b) in the second example above. The second measure is closely related to the first: the same rhythm pattern, the same tonal relationships. The only difference is that the motive in the second measure starts one tone higher; it is a *sequence* of the first note group. Sequences are vital in the construction of music; they are the frequently used devices to expand a motive or figure into larger form units. A melodic sequence is the repetition of a note pattern one or more times, starting from a pitch up or down the scale in stepwise progression.

Here are a few preliminary exercises to illustrate how sequences can be utilized. In the next example the first measure contains the sequence pattern. Play it up and down the scale; the left-hand part underscores and reinforces the stepwise progression.

Four-measure melody using a rhythmic variant of the above pattern:

Improvise four-measure melodies based on the following sequence patterns and their rhythmic variants:

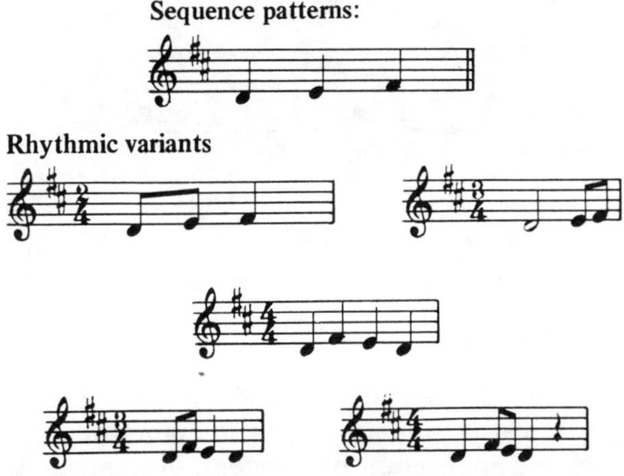

All the above patterns may also begin on the third tone of the scale, instead of the keytone:

The next step in creating melodies is to experiment with one-measure motives, expanding them in various ways. Let us take, for instance, the following two melodic units (one measure each):

With these two motives and various alterations on them (inversion, sequence, variation), it is possible to compose hundreds of different melodies. Here are just a few:

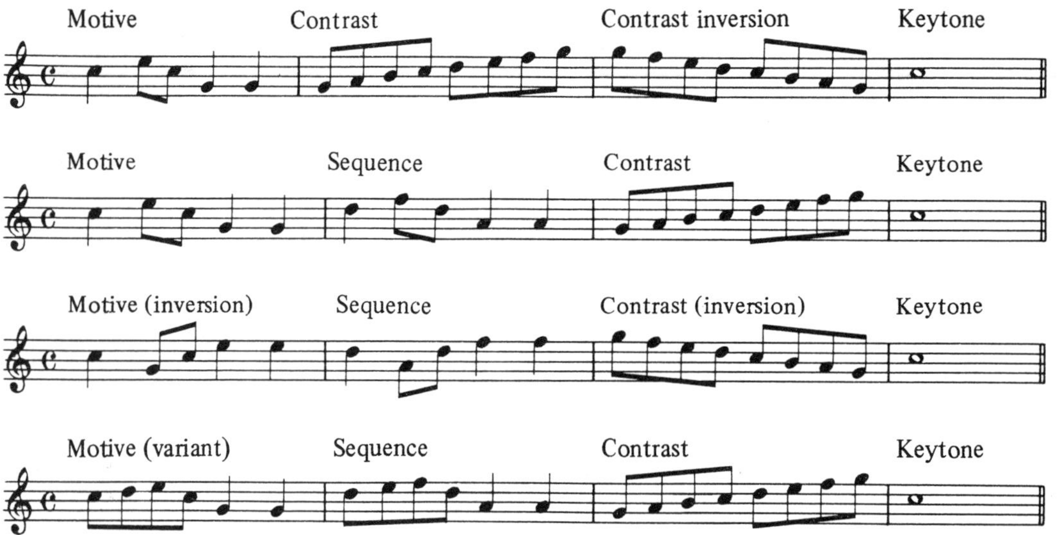

The student should first create other four-measure melodies based on the above components and then invent original motivic materials with which to construct improvisations.

ACCOMPANIMENT STYLES

Much space has been given to the development of the melodic craft, the spark of the creative impulse which illumines all other elements. This brings us to the application of harmonic accompaniment to melodies, beginning with the routine practice of the full authentic cadence I-IV-V-I in major keys, which must be played with the left hand, one chord to a measure. The right hand executes the melody based on the triads, resting on the keytone in the fourth measure. At all times the harmony must guide and determine the melody and not the other way around.

With practice and the deployment of passing and neighboring tones, a variety of rhythmic patterns, and other devices, the melody becomes more interesting. In contrast to the preceding example, for instance, this one employs passing tones, a rhythmic pattern, and a sequence.

Rhythmic styles in the left hand animate the accompanying chords as they are broken up, resulting in miniature compositions. The following are popular accompaniment styles:

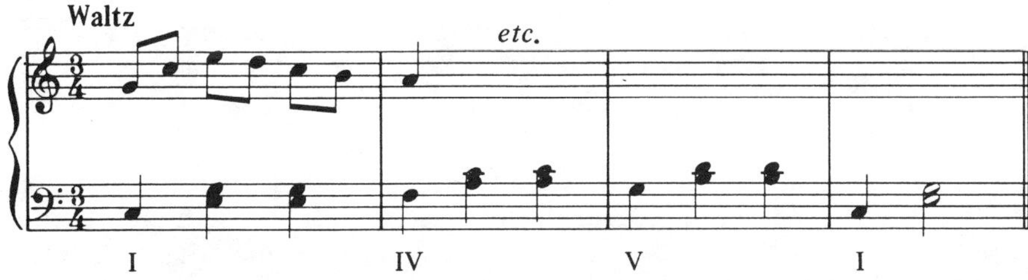

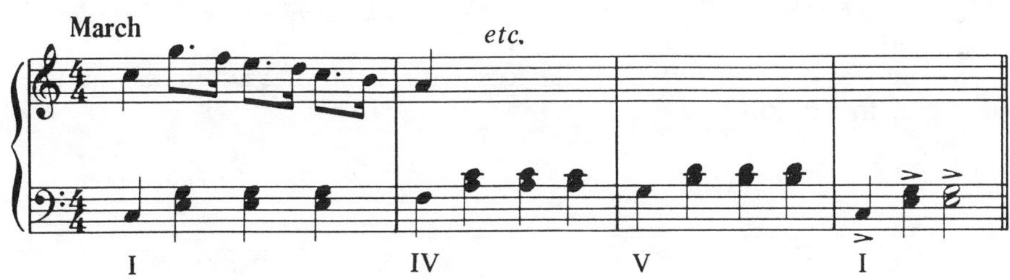

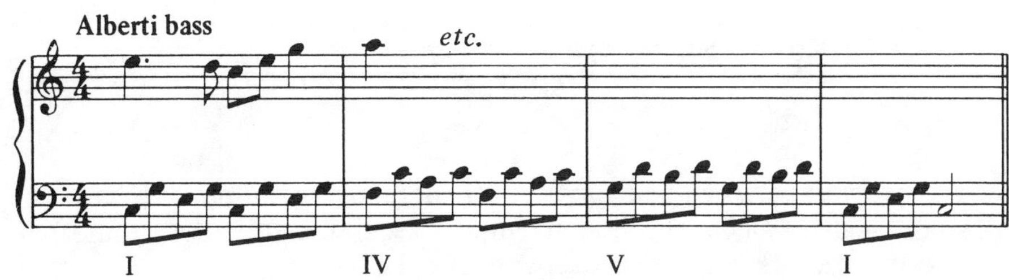

Psychologically, titles implement the feeling of achievement. Teachers should encourage students to write small pieces headed by appropriate mood titles.

"A Swiss Miss"

ENLARGING THE FORMS

To proceed to a larger form: the eight-measure sentence, which consists of two complementary four-measure phrases.

Note that the fourth measure, although still a resting figure, no longer settles on the keytone, which in this case brings the sentence to its close in the eighth measure. Improvise several other melodies which fit the above chord sequence. (Remember that the starting note can be either the keytone, third, or fifth tone of the scale.) Transpose your improvisations into other keys.

Fill in the missing tones in the following example; an eight-measure sentence in a minor key. (Use harmonic minor.)

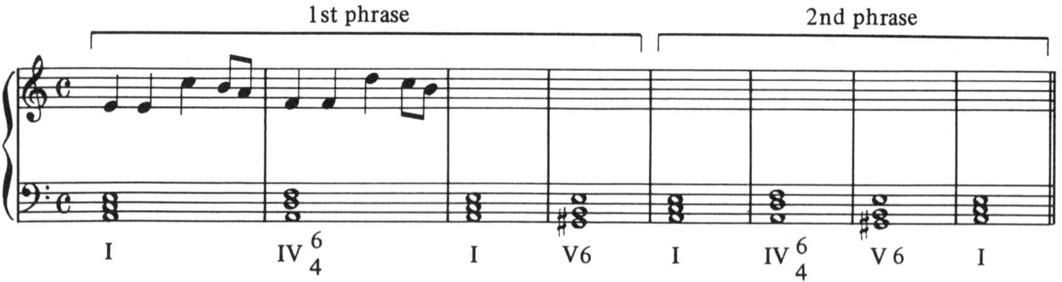

To attain experience and facility, all the above examples, as well as the similar little pieces the student improvises independently, should be played in various keys and accompaniment styles.

The next step in the expansion of musical ideas leads to the very important two-part song form (binary form), which consists of two complementary musical sentences (A-B). It is the smallest complete musical form, a frequently occurring musical construction in all periods. Many charming examples of this form can be found among the minuets, German dances, and écossaises of the classical masters.

The following example of an improvised binary form uses successive triads based on the notes of the major scale, ascending and descending. As a preliminary exercise only the bass notes should be played, rather than the full chords, with the student calling out the number of the chords (as marked under the staff) while a melody is improvised with the right hand. To memorize the succession of these chords, the following clues should be kept in mind: the two bottom notes of the triads always move in thirds and the distance (interval) of the top note from the bass is indicated by the number above the chord.

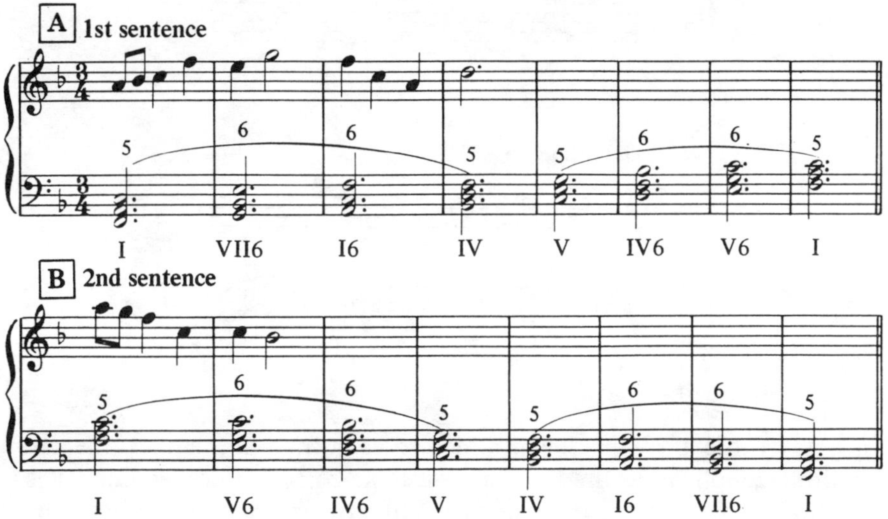

For easier memorization the chord progressions may be practiced in groups of four measures. Melodies should be improvised in $\frac{3}{4}$, $\frac{4}{4}$, and $\frac{6}{8}$ meters, and several accompaniment styles should be employed to add variety and color to the forms and textures. Here are a few sample patterns to be applied to the above chord sequence:

Tango

Tarantella

Nocturne

Andante

* * * etc.

I VII6

Barcarolle

Andantino

etc.

* * *

I VII6

An octave note (*) has been added to each triad in the nocturne and barcarolle, duplicating the bottom note. The correct voice-leading rules of orthodox harmony (avoidance of parallel fifths, etc.) are not observed here for didactic reasons: to supply the beginning improviser with a logical sequence of block chords which lie comfortably under the left hand. Also, the inversion of the diminished triad (VII^6) in the second measure may be changed to V^6 or V to serve a more traditional cadential function.

The above binary form and its variants should also be improvised in minor keys, based on the triads of the harmonic minor scale, in the same sequence as above.

Add Melody:

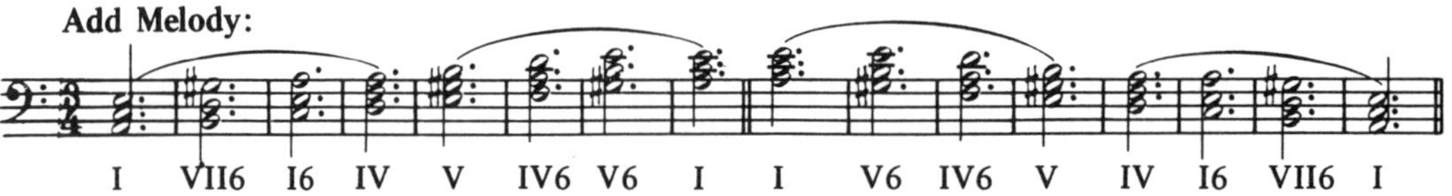

Still another binary form follows, which gives an opportunity to use all the major-scale triads in an easily memorized sequence. Add the melody and play it in various keys; the practice suggestions outlined in connection with the previous binary form are also valid here.

Add melody

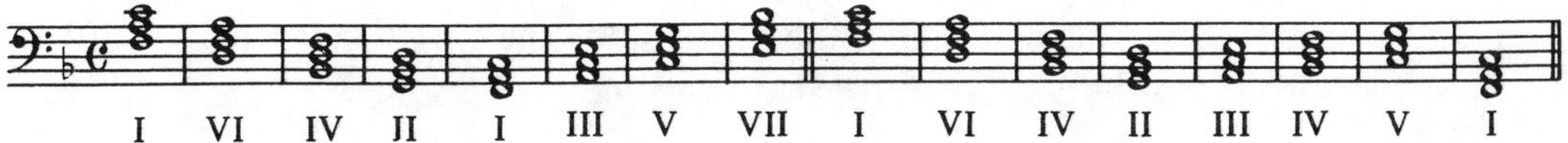

There are many devices available to the student to make improvisations more effective. One of them is *open harmony*, the virtue of which is that chords take on a richer sonority. This is achieved simply by omitting every other triad tone:

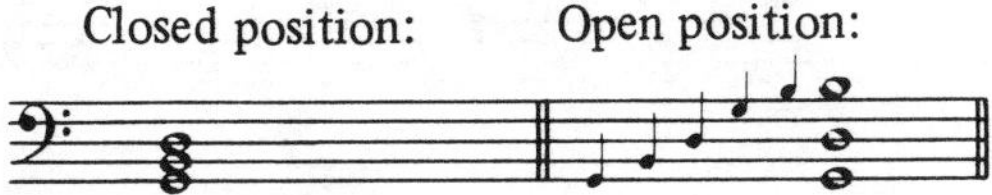

Facility is accomplished by practicing major and minor triads (and, later on, their inversions) as an exercise in open harmony up and down the chromatic scale:

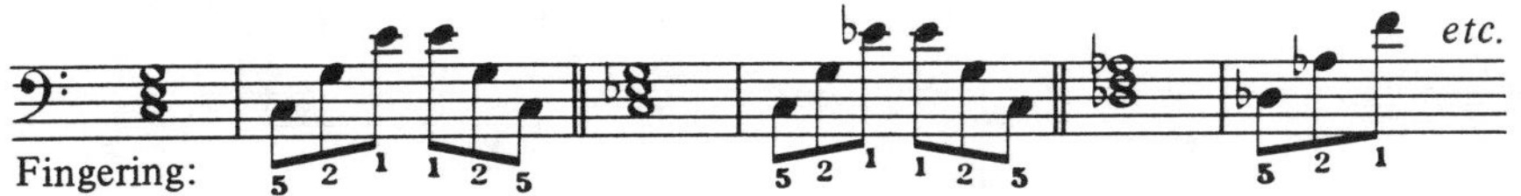

Open chords may now be adapted to all the harmonic forms. Andante would be the appropriate tempo:

Three Andante Styles

A word is in order here about an all-too-prevalent misconception about "playing by ear": that it is somehow a form of musical illiteracy. This attitude overlooks its enormous benefit to the performer in ear training, which is especially helpful in improvisation. This nonconformist procedure enables the player to invent variations on familiar tunes, a popular pastime and creative device of composers through the ages.

To a greater or lesser degree, everyone can play tunes by ear—even if it is only with one finger. But whatever the measure of skill, one can improve one's facility with persistent effort, so the player does not grope for the right notes and will eventually come up with a tolerable production.

There are guidelines which can help. For example, once a tune has been mastered in the right hand, the player adds the I, IV, or V triad in the left hand, on the first beat of every measure.

"Auld Lang Syne"

Here are some comparatively uncomplicated variations:

- Divided-chord accompaniment:

- Transferring major into minor: The third and sixth scale degrees are flatted; triads of the harmonic minor scale are played in the left hand—I and IV, which are minor triads, and V, a major triad.

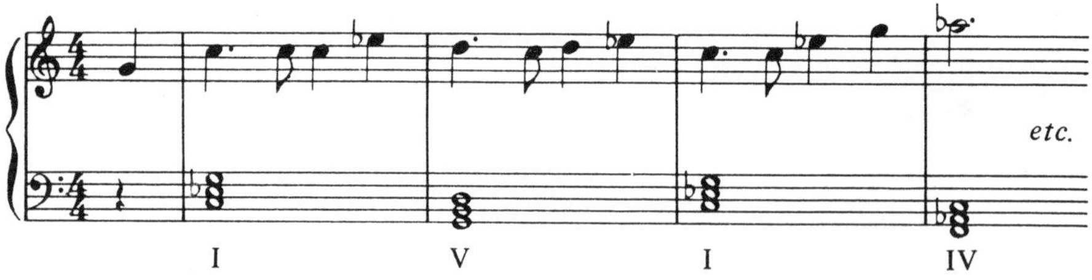

(The left hand may also play divided chords.)

- Alberti bass (for "music box" effect, play two octaves higher and use pedal):

• Tango:

• Nocturne:

• Changing $\frac{4}{4}$ meter into $\frac{3}{4}$ meter: Each $\frac{4}{4}$ measure becomes two $\frac{3}{4}$ measures when each note on the first and third beat of the original melody is converted to a half note.

• If the melody is in $\frac{3}{4}$ (as in "Happy Birthday"), it can be converted into $\frac{4}{4}$ by holding each note on the first beat of the measure one beat longer.

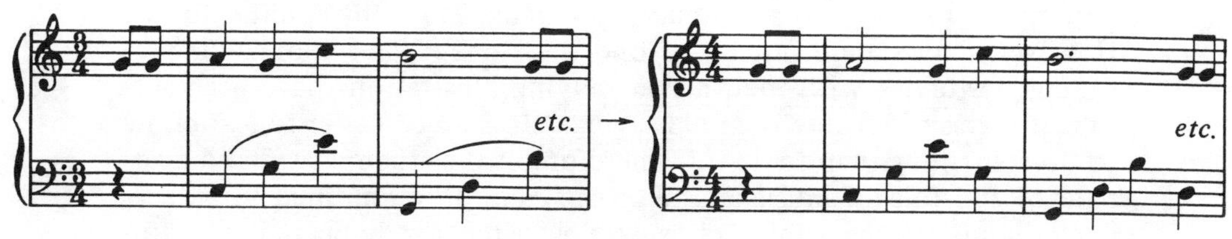

We now turn our attention to a more advanced stage, the three-part song form, or ternary form (A-B-A), a time-honored and much used musical structure on which some of the most popular music of all ages is based. Ternary lends itself to the most striking possibilities. For example, if it is coupled with an exercise in modulation to directly related keys, one may come up with the following graceful and appealing mazurka. Note that section B is based on the four-measure authentic cadence I-IV-V-I over a pedal point. Chords in small notes are not to be played; they are cued in only to guide the construction of melodies. In addition to quarter notes and eighth notes (♫), the melody in the right hand may employ triplets (♫) or dotted eighths (♫) on any beat throughout the piece.

Mazurka

The scope and goals of this section must exclude a study of the larger structures: rondo, fantasy, sonatina, sonata, and contrapuntal forms. However, they should not be beyond the student's reach once the preceding postulates with their accompanying illustrations have been sufficiently grasped. There is an old saying: "It is much easier to learn how to do something than to do it." Therefore, if the student wants to graduate to the role of musician, he or she cannot be confined to an academic study of the subject, however persistent or dedicated. The student needs practice and still more practice on actual improvising; he or she must learn by doing.

Music may be compared to a foreign language in that a knowledge of either involves aural as well as visual elements. In the case of music, improvisation is comparable to conversation. In learning a foreign language, it is clearly not enough to be able to recognize the characters or the meaning of words. One must be able to speak the language, and that means more than repeating the textual material of a primer. A point is reached when the student must strike out independently and use the vocabulary to express his or her own thoughts, and not those of the textbook. Similarly in the case of music, a facility for improvisation will make a true musical conversationalist. The great challenge of our time, to music teachers and students alike, is the revival of this wonderful skill.

RECOMMENDED READING

Berkowitz, Sol. *Improvisation Through Keyboard Harmony.* Englewood Cliffs, N.J.: Prentice-Hall, 1975.

Lloyd, Ruth and Norman. *Creative Keyboard Musicianship: Fundamentals of Music and Keyboard Harmony Through Improvisation.* New York: Dodd, Mead, 1975.

Rabinof, Sylvia. *Musicianship Through Improvisation.* Bryn Mawr, Pa.: T. Presser, 1966.

Wollner, Gertrude P. *Improvisation in Music.* Garden City, N.Y.: Doubleday, 1963.

THREE

APPROACHES TO SPECIFIC TEACHING TASKS

The Very Young Beginner

HAZEL GHAZARIAN SKAGGS

Traditionally, up to a decade or two ago, the optimum age range for beginning piano study was considered to be seven to nine. This was mainly because of the then largely accepted belief that a child's nervous system and kinetic sense is rarely fully developed before the age of six or seven. This is still considered true, but, as numerous modern music education systems (Dalcroze, Kodály, Orff, Suzuki) have demonstrated, it is not an overwhelmingly valid reason to forego all learning and instruction at an earlier age. Indeed, it is a widely accepted belief today that generally children aged three, four, or even younger have many basic and continually developing faculties, active and passive, related to music, which can be—and many insist should be—nurtured and cultivated, both to achieve the child's full educational potential and to prepare for a sounder, easier and more enjoyable instrumental study.

The instruction of very young children does require special preparation on the piano teacher's part. The first and most important aspect of this preparation is acquiring familiarity with the various stages of the very young child's intellectual and physical development, including the average capacity to hear, understand, absorb, imitate, re-create, etc.

What musical activities can children between the ages of four to six do? Making allowances for various maturity levels and differences in individual capabilities, children in this age bracket can

- maintain a steady beat (stepping, clapping, singing)
- synchronize various simultaneous activities (singing-clapping,

marching-singing)

- recognize and classify sounds in terms of pitch (high-low), volume (soft-loud), duration (long-short), tempo (fast-slow)
- have a degree (however limited) of digital dexterity and muscle coordination for keyboard contact
- have a sense of direction, aural and spatial (up-down) and a sense of distance (step, skip, same note)

APPROACHES TO PRESCHOOL TEACHING

How do we utilize these capabilities? There are three possible options:

(1) Teach piano using materials that progress in small, very gradual steps.
(2) Begin with a preinstrumental approach and introduce the piano later.
(3) Combine the piano and preinstrumental course so that there is a separate lesson for each or a combination of the two in one lesson.

About fifty years ago, authors of methods began writing primers to take care of younger beginners' needs. Today we still use such primers (Thompson, Aaron, Schaum, Richter). They begin very simply, using one hand at a time (alternating hands) and introduce notes and simple note values gradually. Verses encourage children's singing the tunes they play.

Most of the pieces are in five-finger position. Generally, playing begins with the stronger fingers (one-two-three) and gradually proceeds to the weaker part of the hand (four-five). Double notes, if any, are restricted to fifths and possibly thirds. (The teacher may introduce very simple five-finger exercises and technique games.) When the child has gained some confidence, pieces are introduced in which the left hand plays one-note accompaniments for the right hand's note groups. By the end of the book the child is playing very simple pieces, hands together. Generally these books have large print, are oblong shaped, and contain many pictures. Essentially, each primer is the same in methodology as the grade-one book that follows it. Often the child needs more very simple elementary material to fill the gap between the primer and grade-one book. Collections of simple pieces are very useful at this point.

With the current increased emphasis on early education, new approaches have been incorporated into primers. For instance, in Nathan Bergenfeld's *The Very Young Beginner* (*Acorn Basic Lessons in Piano*, 1977), music reading is introduced with the modified staff:

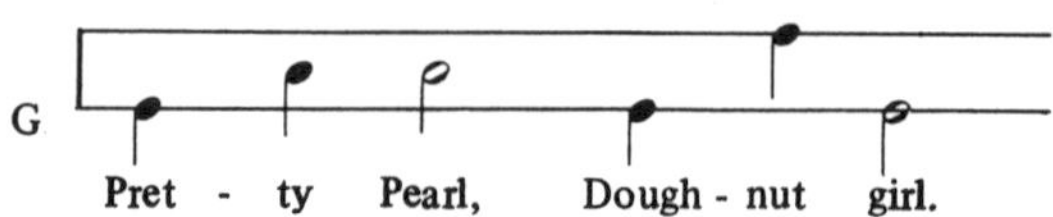

Other books, including the *Discovery* 1-A book of *Music Pathways* by Olson-Bianchi-Blickenstaff (Carl Fischer, 1974), use the modified staff. *Time to Begin* from *The Music Tree* by Frances Clark and Louise Goss (Summy-Birchard, 1973), before introducing the modified staff, devotes a considerable part of the book to familiarizing the child with keyboard-related pitch concepts through the use of note pictures. For instance, a piece of music such as

is represented by

A less structured kind of reading is introduced in *The Little Avant-Garde*, a piano method for the preschooler by Stephen Covello (Schroeder and Gunther, 1971). The child improvises within a certain framework shown in pictorial form. One line indicates middle C; the notes either below or above middle C are left to the child's choice.

A preschool course that encourages improvisation and transposition is Robert Pace's *Kinder-Keyboard* (Lee Roberts, 1977); the *Teacher's Manual* is a guide to using *Kinder-Keyboard* effectively. *Music for Moppets* by Helen Pace (Lee Roberts), like *Kinder-Keyboard*, offers a creative and imaginative program for the preschooler. The *Teacher's Manual* to *Music for Moppets* is not only a teaching guide but also a text to help teachers with a background in early-childhood education and group instruction organize and successfully teach a preschool course.

A preschooler's kit that encourages improvisation and writing is *Piano Is My Name* by Minuetta Kessler (Musical Resources). The young child reads from a very simple and attractive "Dash-a-Note" system. Halfway through the course, a transparent "C-Thru Grand Staff" transforms these Dash-a-Notes to their proper position on the staff.

SUZUKI

The Suzuki method, developed at first for the study of violin by Shinichi Suzuki in Japan, is based on listening, rote learning, and elementary technique. These are nurtured by both the teacher and the parent, who serves as the home teacher. Listening begins at birth. When actual piano study begins, part of the child's assignment consists of listening to the piano music contained in *Suzuki Piano School*, vol. 1. (Records are available for both volumes.) When the child begins to play the piece, he or she already knows the music by ear. Listening is the key to success in this method. The *Suzuki Piano School* vol. 1 and vol. 2 (Summy-Birchard) provide explanatory notes concerning the method and study materials.

All above materials may be used in either class or private lessons. Many teachers recommend class for the younger child, since it is easier to play games, clap, and sing in a group than in a private lesson. Small children enjoy being with their peers, and learn quickly from each other.

Many educators believe that the preschool child is best suited for a preinstrumental course than for direct study of the instrument. A survey of these methods can be of tremendous value for the teacher, who may decide to give such a special preliminary course to preschoolers or include some of the methods and ideas in the regular piano program.

EURHYTHMICS

Eurhythmics is a method created by Emile Jaques-Dalcroze. It aims, in Lisa Parker's words, to "develop the ear through carefully structured games involving the student's mind, body and spirit, and to awaken creativity through the use of improvisation in all areas of the work." It is as suitable for preschoolers as it is for students of all ages. The student in the Dalcroze course develops better concentration, memory, coordination, and body awareness, all important in piano study. Information on workshops for teachers and reading material may be obtained from the Dalcroze Society of America, Box 6804, Pittsburgh, Pennsylvania 15212.

ORFF

The Orff-Schulwerk, developed by the German composer Carl Orff, concentrates on preparing the preschooler for instrumental study through a one-year rhythm and melody course. It consists of clapping and stamping out rhythms, reciting rhythmic canons, singing melodies, and some improvising. Orff instruments (specially designed glockenspiels, xylophones, and metallophones) may be combined with simple percussion instruments (castanets, rattles, triangles, etc.) and recorders. Suggested class size is between twelve and fifteen, but eight may be large enough. No practice is needed at home. Information regarding Orff workshops, music, and method books, and Orff instruments is available from Magna-Music-Baton, Inc., 6394 Delmar Boulevard, St. Louis, Missouri 63130. Teacher training for this course may be completed in ten days of intensive work.

KODÁLY

The Kodály method, originated by the Hungarian composer Zoltán Kodály (1882–1967), may not be appropriate for the preschooler, since it stresses singing and ear training. Syllables (do, re, mi, etc.) and hand signals are used. The repertory consists of folk songs of the child's native country, then international folk music, and later classical music.

Detailed information on this method, its literature, and teacher training can be obtained from the Kodály Center of America, 525 Worcester Street, Wellesley, Massachusetts 02181.

CARABO-CONE

Madeleine Carabo-Cone has based her method on the basic fact that preschoolers learn and think in concrete, visible terms. A sensory-motor method adapted from the observations of Jean Piaget, it prepares children for music study through a series of games in which they become the elements they study. For instance, one child may be note C, another child E, and another G, and the three together will sound out a C-major triad. Information may be obtained from Carabo-Cone Method, Carnegie Hall, 881 Seventh Avenue, Studio 862, New York, New York 10019.

READINESS

It is best for the teacher to determine through an interview whether the child is ready for formal piano study of one or two lessons a week, perhaps of half-hour duration each. The prospects of success are strengthened if he or she is able to do all of the following:

- sing and enjoy listening to music
- go to the piano and pick out little tunes previously heard, or improvise
- show an interest in learning and knows how to learn
- concentrate long enough to play the piano for about ten minutes at a time
- have someone at home who can help his or her practicing (this is important; assistance at home will be necessary unless the child can come to the studio daily for short lessons)

However, any child ready for nursery school may enroll in preinstrumental classes. Generally these classes require no home practice.

The preschool studio, since it will be mostly for groups of very young children, will require the same equipment as the group piano studio. (See "Group Piano Teaching,"p. 265). In addition to the standard equipment, the teacher may find useful a keyboard floor, pertinent wall charts, and colorful decorations. A list of suppliers of such materials and games is given below.

- Aspasia, 9272 Shannon Avenue, Garden Grove, California 92641: Funtastic Music Theory Games, "colorful, durable, washable, attractive, and easy to play."
- Ability Development Associates, Box 887, Athens, Ohio 45701: Suzuki materials, textbooks, records, music.
- Market Place, 1045 Borden Street, Prince Rupert, British Colum-

bia V8J IV6: Giant floor staff, magic keyboard chart, "Opus I" game kit (an assortment of 27 separate theory games).

- Music in Motion, P.O. Box 5564, Richardson, Texas 75080: flashcards for chords, intervals, rhythm, etc.; vinyl rhythm shade, large vinyl floor mat with grand staff, magnetic music board.
- Musical Resources, 30 Hurley Street, Belmont, Maine 02178: Game, "Staftonia."
- Peripole, Browns Mills, New Jersey 08015: A vast catalog of musical instruments for education and recreation including those for Orff Schulwerk; records for rhythmic games.
- Sine Music Co., P.O. Box 445, Dubuque, Iowa 52001: flashcards.

Some teachers prefer to make some or all of their own props and game equipment.

Classes for the very young may have special bonuses for the piano teacher. They permit an expansion of teaching hours, since preschoolers are available during the morning hours. This means added income. And gratification in working with young children has its own special rewards. The teacher is a very important person to these young students, and each first event in their young lives is excitingly new. To share their experiences and watch their growth can be refreshingly satisfying.

Teaching preschoolers does require special preparation and training. An interested teacher should have some background in child development and group methods. Workshops in teaching preschoolers will be of great value. These workshops provide not only the expertise for organizing and teaching a preschool program, but also provide the impetus, confidence, and inspiration to become involved in the imaginative and amusing world of young children.

RECOMMENDED READING

Bastien, James. "Teaching the Very Young Beginner." *Clavier* May–June 1974.

Barrett, Betsy. "Kindergarten Musicians." *Clavier* December 1966.

Mussen, Paul H., et al. *Child Development and Personality*. New York: Harper & Row, 1969.

Nash, Grace. "Kodály and Orff." *Clavier* September 1968.

——— "Orff Exercises." *Clavier* September 1967.

Owens, Janet Russell. "Before Piano Lessons, What?" *The Piano Teacher* March–April 1959.

Parker, Lisa. "Dalcroze: The Method." *Clavier* September 1974.

Piaget, Jean. *The Origins of Intelligence in Children*. New York: W.W. Norton, 1963.

Pierce, Ralph. "Music for the Preschooler." *The Piano Teacher* July–August 1965.

Standing, E.M. *Maria Montessori: Her Life and Work*. New York: Mentor-Omega Books, 1962.

Steck, Sue Ann. "Piano Lessons for the Very Young." *Clavier* February 1976.

Zipper, Herbert. "Orff and the Piano Teacher." *Clavier* September 1967.

The Adult Beginner

HADASSAH SAHR

It scarcely seems necessary to define the word *adult*. Yet for the piano teacher, an adult can be anyone of several people: the eighteen-year-old high school graduate or college student who "likes" music and wants to take some piano lessons; the young woman whose children are now in school and who wishes to resume lessons after a hiatus of many years; the individual in a field other than music who wishes to embark on some sort of artistic study, has decided that the piano is the instrument he or she has always wanted to learn to play and is now ready to begin; a person whose children are grown, who is looking for new interests to develop, and who thinks learning to play the piano would be rewarding; the retired individual who now has the time to pursue his or her musical interests and wants to learn to play the piano.

For the person who teaches adults, there are some psychological aspects to keep in mind. The adult who chooses to study piano is usually strongly motivated and often has many attitudes and ideas about the piano. He or she frequently possesses a background of musical experiences, though not necessarily all good and not necessarily related to the piano. These musical experiences influence his or her attitude toward studying music and the reasons for choosing the piano to learn to play.

Sometimes these experiences include a childhood period of piano study, which was disliked. Coming back to piano study at a later age, the adult is full of hope that this time learning how to play will be successful and enjoyable. The teacher can assume a strong attachment to both music and the piano. It is important that a teacher find many ways of encouraging good practice habits and positive attitudes, at the same time helping the student build technique and musicianship. The adult student often has many questions about music. A teacher must deal with these questions and should be prepared to offer information that is both pedagogically and psychologically appropriate.

SPECIFIC APPROACHES

For example, when a teacher talks about a major scale or a major key, an adult may ask, "How many kinds of scales are there?" It can be very stimulating to the students if, instead of being given an answer such as "We're only going to talk about the major scale now, because you can't learn to play more than one kind at a time," the teacher describes in a few words what a scale is, illustrates it on the keyboard, then points out that the major scale is only one of many. The teacher might add that different cultures have their own tonal systems; that the major and minor scales have predominated in the music of Western culture for the past three or four centuries. He or she can then illustrate at the piano by playing scales made up of different tonal patterns (chromatic, pentatonic, etc.), which helps to dispel the idea that a major scale is the "one and only." It is still important to learn to play the major scale, but the idea of a scale is placed in a different framework when discussed from a historical and cultural point of view.

The adult student frequently reveals a whole range of attitudes toward playing the piano. For example, many adults are perfectionists; the idea of making a mistake is acutely disturbing to them. But a mistake in playing the piano is thought of more in terms of playing wrong notes than wrong rhythms. In their minds it is all right to hesitate while playing through a piece if by so doing, no wrong notes will be played. This causes problems when students are learning to read music, because they tend to think, "I must first be sure I know what notes to play. After that I'll think about the rhythm."

Many beginning adults think that learning to read music is chiefly a matter of learning the names of the lines and spaces of the music staff. A common notion seems to exist that finding the notes on the keyboard will come automatically, and rhythm is something to think about after the notes have been learned. Even after the adult beginner has learned the different note and rest values, maintaining a steady beat, with a feeling for the pulse, can be very difficult. For some students this goal is unattainable within the first few months of piano study, despite all the pedagogic techniques available. In other words, it is difficult for some students to learn to read music and play it on the piano no matter how well it may be taught.

Reading by interval, recognizing tonal patterns, seeing rhythm patterns, reading and thinking in groups of notes rather than individual notes—these are all aspects of reading that the teacher must constantly keep in mind, but with the realization that it takes most students a considerable amount of time to integrate such details into music reading.

For many students, playing the piano and reading music are two separate activities. The muscular skills involved in playing the piano are distinct from the intellectual understanding necessary to read music. Often a student must concentrate on reaching some degree of muscular control before turning his attention to various aspects of reading skill. This often causes considerable frustration, since the adult student is usually capable of understanding much more about music more quickly than he or she can develop the skills necessary to produce it.

HARMONY

Many adults are fascinated by harmony. With children, it is enough to teach how to find and play a major chord; it is not necessary to talk about other kinds of triads for quite a while. However, it is often quite desirable to have the adult beginner find and play several major chords at the first or second lesson, in order to understand that such a chord can be built upon any key, black or white. The next step is to show the student how to find and play some minor chords, which are taught in relation to the major ones; for example, to form a minor triad, start with the major triad and lower the middle note a half step.

Often the difference in sound and tone color between these chords is fascinating and understandable enough to the student that the teacher will want to illustrate two other kinds of triads, diminished and augmented—not only as chords to be assigned and learned, but also as colors to be heard, ones that the beginner can find at the piano.

Basic principles of reading music can be described to the adult beginner in terms that one would not use so quickly when teaching a child. Words such as *pulse, beat,* or *pattern* already have meaning for adults; the teacher needs to apply the meaning of those words to music. In describing and illustrating them, the teacher can expect a more intensive kind of concentration and understanding from the adult student. It is important to remember that the beginner will probably not develop technical skill any more quickly, but one can and should use an adult vocabulary even though teaching piano skills at an elementary level.

Fundamentals of music theory can be taught to the adult beginner more quickly than to a child beginner. The way in which a teacher decides to do this depends to an extent on the student's responsiveness. Many students show great interest in music of the rock-pop-jazz idiom, and a large amount of music theory can be related to music in these styles. For example, it is possible to teach the basic chord vocabulary using letter names only. All triads and seventh chords can be taught this way. Understanding key relationships requires more prolonged study, and many adults are not ready to embark on such work if piano is primarily a recreational study.

Learning chords by their letter names first is much easier. Usually, students are delighted to realize that the entire chord vocabulary grows from the twelve basic triads that they can find and play on the piano.

This is not to imply that once they know the twelve triads they can play anything; rather, that the immense variety of sounds in the music they hear (except for much contemporary music) grows from the relatively simple beginning of the three-note chord, built in thirds, that we call a triad.

The structure of the triad is not difficult to explain and illustrate. At first, it is not necessary to describe it in terms of intervals of major and minor thirds. One can say:

> This is what we call a C-major triad. Notice the spacing between the notes. It looks evenly spaced, but if you count the number of notes between the bottom and middle notes of the chord, and the number of notes between the middle and top notes, you will notice that they are not the same. The former consists of four half steps, the latter of three half steps. Whenever you find this particular tonal relationship you have a major triad. And you can build that tonal relationship starting from any one of the seven white keys or the five black keys of the piano octave.

It is also a good idea to include the following suggestions:

> In addition to learning to find and play these chords, it is important to learn how to spell them. It is customary to spell a chord from the bottom note to the top one. Thus the C-major triad is spelled C–E–G. The D-major triad is spelled D–F-sharp–A. The bottom note is always called the root of the chord, and is the note after which the chord is named.

Some readers may note that this is not a very complete explanation, and that the subject of intervals is slighted. The above description is an example of how one can present chords initially to an adult beginner. It does not include all the available information. It is a way to start learning about chords, and usually can be related to some knowledge that the adult student already has. The beginner can thus find various harmonic colors on the piano and at the same time learn the principles underlying the structure of the chords being played.

TECHNIQUE

Certain technical exercises to help the student develop both playing and reading skills can be assigned quite early during the course of study —perhaps during the second or third month, depending on individual circumstances and capabilities. One of the most useful early technical exercises is learning to play the pattern of the first five notes of the major scale in any key. Another way of saying this is: "Learning to play the first five notes of all the major scales." But the latter statement implies that one is going to learn at least twelve scales. The former statement suggests there is one pattern to learn, which can be played starting from any note on the keyboard.

It is helpful to point out the differing combinations of white and black keys that occur in the various scales. For example, the first five notes of the C-major and G-major scales are all white keys, the first five notes of the D-major and A-major scales include one black key (the third note); the first five notes in the keys of D flat and A flat include a white key in the middle and black keys on both the bottom and top. This need not be presented as information to be memorized, but rather as things to notice as one plays. In learning this exercise, students are also being helped to understand the concept of that characteristic "family of tones" called a key (in more technical terms, the concept of tonality).

STUDENT SENSIBILITIES

A teacher needs to recognize that students have different study patterns and that they often have strong feelings related to learning to play the piano. Many are genuinely apprehensive that they will not do well; many feel almost apologetic about their wish to learn, saying, "I really am not very talented. Do you think it is possible for me to learn to play?" Or, "Is it foolish of me to want to take lessons?" Many students are nervous about playing for another person.

It is important for the teacher to establish and maintain a nonpressured environment in which the student has the freedom to develop piano skills and musical interests at an individual rate. A teacher is really teaching a number of different yet related aspects of music: how to read music (or better ways of reading music), how to play an instrument, elements of music theory, introducing a variety of music literature. It is not possible, or even desirable, to emphasize all aspects equally at each lesson. The preferred alternative is to be sure that all are dealt with over an extended period of time.

A teacher should provide a continually changing variety of music to study and play. The music must be simple or the student won't be able to play it, but it also has to be interesting or the student won't enjoy it. The student's attitude toward what he or she plays and the quality of concentration will be better if he or she enjoys—or at least sees the value of—the material assigned.

Among the most satisfying moments in teaching a beginner are those when the student can pick up a piece of music he or she wants to play, look it over, study it a bit, and then make sense out of it on the piano without any instruction whatsoever.

SUGGESTED GUIDELINES FOR BEGINNING LESSONS

The purpose of these suggestions is to indicate some ways in which a teacher may cover a considerable amount of basic information in the first few lessons. They should not be considered as conventional lesson plans. The order in which they are given can be changed, except in the first lesson, where nos. 1 and 2 are necessary in order to proceed with 3, 4, and 5.

The terms *objectives* and *procedures* have been used to help the teacher separate the aim of *what* is being taught from *how* it is achieved. Often it is necessary to use several procedures in order to achieve one particular objective. Each teacher will want to use those procedures most appropriate to the particular student being taught.

All the material suggested here can be arranged in ways other than the ones given here. For example, it is possible to introduce some of the rhythmic concepts in the second lesson; reading pitch need not precede reading rhythm.

First Lesson

(1) (Objective): To get acquainted with the piano keyboard; to learn the names of the white and black keys.
(Procedure): Have the student feel the groups of two and three black keys in different registers of the keyboard. Have student find the black-key groups with eyes closed; find some high sounds, then some low sounds.

(2) (Objective): To get acquainted with the fingers on both hands as they are used on the keyboard (fingers are numbered from one to five, the thumbs on both hands being number one.)
(Procedure): Have student hold out both hands and move different fingers as you call for them by number.

(3) (Objective): To learn the pattern for the first five notes of the major scale; to find and play this pattern starting on C and D, and possibly on G and A.
(Procedure): Teach the pattern by rote. Describe it to the students in words such as these: "We're going to play five adjacent white keys, starting from C. The five keys appear to be the same distance apart from one another, but if you look at the piano keyboard carefully, you will notice that there is a black key between the first and second keys, the second and third keys, and between the fourth and fifth keys, but not between the third and fourth keys."

Continue your explanation by illustrating what a half step and a whole step are, then teach the pattern through the following diagram: (The numbers represent the first five scale tones; W = whole step; H = half step.)

$$1^{W}\,2^{W}\,3^{H}\,4^{W}\,5$$

(4) (Objective): To learn two songs that are contained within this five-

note pattern: "Merrily We Roll Along" and "Drink To Me Only With Thine Eyes" (the first phrase).
(Procedure): These songs should be played in at least two keys, so that the student experiences transposition. You may want to teach some students only one song at the first lesson.

(5) (Objective): To have student find and play major chords, starting with the C-major triad.
(Procedure): Show how the C-major triad is found within the five-tone scale pattern (every other note). Indicate the fingers to use, point out the name of the chord and how it is spelled. Have student play the chord as an accompaniment while you play, and both of you sing, "Frère Jacques" or "Row, Row, Row Your Boat."

If the student plays the C-major triad rather easily, add the D-major triad at the first lesson. Relate this chord to the first five tones of the D-major scale, illustrating how the chord can be found within the scale pattern.

Second Lesson

The first part of the second lesson consists of a review of each item taught in the first lesson:
(1) Drill the names of the black and white keys. Ask student to play A's in different registers of the piano; then D's, B's, etc. until fluency has been achieved.
(2) Have the student play the five-note pattern starting from C, then from D, then suggest two new keys, G and A.

Have the student play the right hand alone, then the left hand alone, then together. Make appropriate suggestions about hand position, how the fingers should look, the shape of the hand, the flexibility of the wrist, how the arm should feel.
(3) Review the two songs. If the tempo and pulse are not even, and if the sound can be improved, make appropriate suggestions.
(4) Find and play the chords learned at the first lesson.
The second lesson may well be the time for introducing note reading. A first, brief explanation of how music is written, and how the alphabet is used, might go as follows:

"Below is a picture of a music staff: "

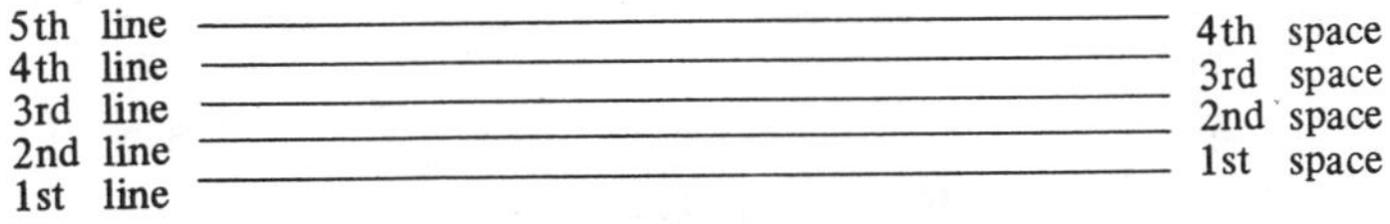

5th line
4th space
4th line
3rd space
3rd line
2nd space
2nd line
1st space
1st line

"A music staff consists of five parallel lines and the four intervening spaces formed by these lines. For convenience of identification the lines are numbered from one to five, starting from the bottom, and the spaces are numbered from one to four, also starting from the bottom."

"Since the piano has a wider tonal range than any other instrument (except the organ), music written for it cannot be represented by notes written only on one music staff; two staves are necessary. In the picture below you will see two music staves. Each staff has a clef sign at its left. The upper staff has a treble-clef sign, and the lower staff has a bass-clef sign."

"The notes represented by the lines and spaces in the treble clef are in the upper half of the piano (the right-hand side). The notes represented by the lines and spaces in the bass clef are in the lower half of the piano (the left-hand side). Each line and each space represents one white key, unless there is an additional symbol—a sharp or a flat—to alter that note."

"Together, the treble and bass clefs represent all the notes on the piano: from the second G below the middle of the piano to the second F above the middle of the piano. The treble and bass clefs together are often referred to as the *grand staff*. In the picture below you see a portion of the piano keyboard underneath the grand staff. Each white key is identified by its letter name, and a line is drawn from each one to the line or space in the grand staff which corresponds to that note."

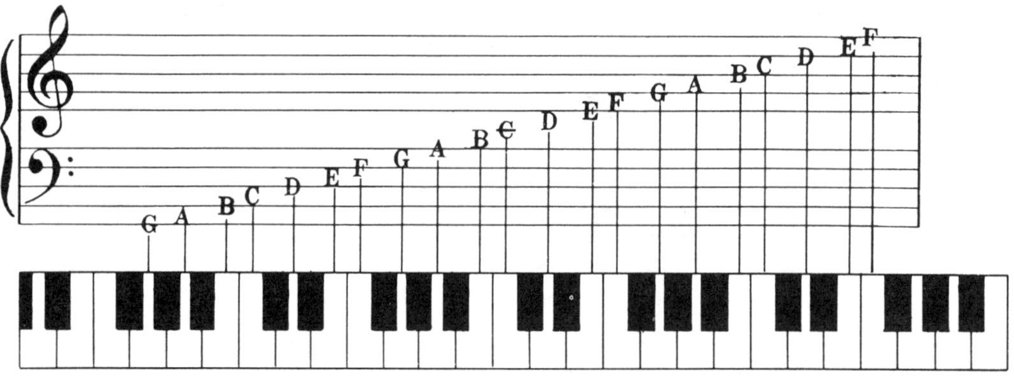

There are different ways to learn the names of each line and space and relate these names to the corresponding piano key. You should choose whichever way, or combination of ways, is most effective and useful for the particular student you are teaching.

For example, you might want to use flashcards for quick drills in naming and playing individual notes. These can be used both at the lesson and during practice sessions. Or it might be helpful to separate the notes on the lines from the ones in the spaces and have the student study each group separately.

A third way is to have the student look at different short pieces of music, and name and play the notes evenly in as rapid succession as possible. (For this drill, note values and rhythm need not be taken into account.)

Third Lessson

After a review of the material taught in the previous lessons, the subject of rhythm can be presented. This consists first of a general presentation of the way music is "pictured" on the page, pointing out all elements concerned with rhythm: measures, time signature, the various note and rest values. A simple piece of music can be used to draw illustrations of the rhythmic elements in music notation. For example:

Agay: "Greeting from Jamaica"
(From "The Joy of First Year Piano.")

The student's attention might first be drawn to the time signature ($\frac{4}{4}$), then to the observation that the whole piece is eight measures long. Next, the various note and rest values could be pointed out (quarter notes, half notes, whole notes, quarter rests, half rests).

Next, attention should be given to the way in which the note and rest values in each measure add up to four beats. Make it clear that, while the treble and bass clefs are read and played simultaneously, the note and rest values in each clef separately add up to four beats; otherwise it might appear to the novice that they are eight beats in each measure.

Immediately after explaining and illustrating all the rhythmic elements, the teacher should play the piece, asking the student to join in counting. The student should also be guided in following the music on the page as it is played, to get a sense of how it feels to coordinate the various aspects of reading music.

This example might be followed with a piece in another meter; for example:

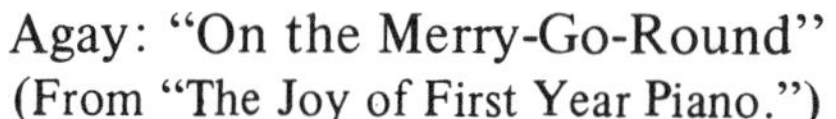

A similar procedure can be followed with this piece:

- the time signature is $\frac{3}{4}$
- the piece is sixteen measures long (or contains sixteen measures)
- there are quarter notes, dotted half notes, and rests that last an entire measure
- each measure contains three beats or counts

After these points have been made, the piece should be played following the same procedure suggested with "Greetings from Jamaica."

It is helpful to have a table of note and rest values at hand:

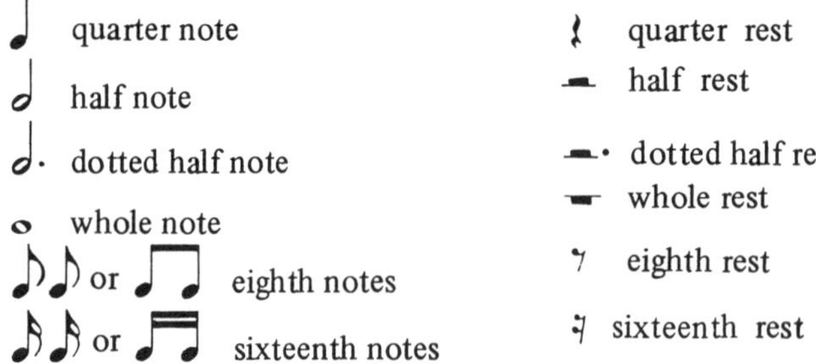

In addition, the student should be given an opportunity to gain experience in reading and clapping some simple rhythm patterns. For example, here is a rhythm pattern made up of quarter notes, half notes, and a whole note in a phrase with a time signature of $\frac{4}{4}$.

The teacher can illustrate the way it sounds by clapping the pattern and counting. Then the student joins the teacher, both of them clapping and counting. This can be done with other simple rhythm patterns in $\frac{2}{4}$, $\frac{3}{4}$, and $\frac{6}{8}$ time. This need not all be done at one lesson, of course, but would be covered during several lessons.

Immediately after reading, clapping, and counting one or more such pattern, the rhythm pattern of a simple melody can be treated in the same way. In this manner the foundation is laid for developing skill and ease in reading both the rhythm and tonal patterns of a piece.

The amount of time spent on various aspects of reading music will vary, depending on the individual learning capacities of different students, and each teacher will need to decide what works best in each specific situation.

Teaching an adult to read music and play the piano is an ongoing process; more than one season is needed to reach a substantial achievement. However, this does not preclude the possibility of a student's having a sense of accomplishment after a short period of study.

The imaginative and resourceful teacher will continually discover additional ways of teaching the basic materials of music in response to the variety of personalities, attitudes, and learning styles presented by adult students.

RECOMMENDED READING AND SOURCES

Agay, Denes. *The Joy of First-Year Piano*. New York: Yorktown Music Press, Inc., 1972.

Bastien, James and Jane Smisor Bastien. *Beginning Piano for Adults*. Park Ridge, Ill.: General Words and Music Co., 1968.

Catron, Betty Schien. "Class Piano for Senior Citizens." *Clavier* December 1977.

Clark, Frances. *Keyboard Musicianship for the Adult Beginner*. Summy Birchard, 1976.

Glover, David Carr. *Adult Piano Student*. New York: Belwin-Mills, 1970.

Noona, Walter and Carol. *The Adult Pianist*, vols. 1-3. Dayton, Ohio: The Heritage Music Press, 1979.

Pace, Robert. *Music for the Piano for the Older Beginner*. Lee Roberts Music Productions, 1967.

Robinson, Helene. *Basic Piano for Adults*. Belmont, Calif.: Wadsworth Publishing Co., 1964.

Strangeland, Robert. "The Art of Teaching: Do We Practice It?" *Piano Quarterly* Winter 1974–1975.

Wurlitzer Music Lab–
courtesy of Joseph M. Chopp, Manager, Educational Services–Wurlitzer

Group Piano Teaching

HAZEL GHAZARIAN SKAGGS

The terms *group piano* and *class piano* are often used interchangeably, even though the two approaches differ in procedure and in numbers of students. A group generally consists of from three to ten students, while a class might comprise ten to thirty students. The procedure for group piano involves utilizing group dynamics—the student's interaction through participation. In the hands of a skilled teacher, group dynamics creates the motivation to explore, discover, and finally learn. Without this interchange, a group of students might be classified a class even though the number of students is three to ten.

When the teacher is more concerned with the development of musicianship through the piano than with performance skill, the term *class piano* is generally applied. Classification may be as follows:

private	one student
semiprivate (paired)	two students
group	three to ten students
class	ten to thirty students or more

Group lessons are generally one hour long, but they may be longer for more advanced students and shorter for beginning students.

The choice of approach will depend on the teacher's training, personality, and preferences, as well as on local and economic circumstances.

In some instances, group piano is regarded as suitable only at the beginning level or for the average student. Private teachers often reject class piano for performance while utilizing it for all other activities, including improvisation, theory, and ensemble. Some music schools find class piano adequate, but reserve such classes for students not majoring in piano. Other teachers believe so strongly in group teaching that they maintain total group instruction meets the needs of all students, regardless of advancement, talent, or age.

Although a teacher may not wholeheartedly favor group teaching, a shortage of teachers in an area might make it expedient to consider the possibilities of organizing groups. In such situations, the teacher could feel that group lessons are better than no lessons at all.

Economic factors may also necessitate group lessons for some students. Since the fee is considerably lower than for private lessons, some families would be able to provide instruction that they otherwise could not afford.

METHODS OF GROUPING

Any method, private or group, may be used exlusively or in combination. In recent years the idea of overlapping the private lesson with the semiprivate (paired) lesson has been gaining popularity. For example, student A has a twenty-five minute private lesson, then the next twenty-five minutes of the lesson are shared with student B. When student A leaves, student B remains for another twenty-five minutes, this time alone with the teacher. Rather than overlap lessons, some teachers have the paired students remain together for the entire session. A great many teachers use a paired lesson for performance, while classes of about ten students are devoted to theory, improvisation, and ear training. Others use both private and group lessons in different combinations; for example, both types each week or a weekly private with a monthly class lesson. Often the kind of combination of group and private is predicated on the students' availability for such combinations and the parents' ability to bring students to the studio more than once a week.

In the overlapped lesson, it is best that the students be of about the same level, and not more than a grade apart in school. In lessons that are totally semiprivate, the pairing must be even more compatible, because in essence the lessons are based on shared experiences rather than on group dynamics.

In beginning group piano, children of about the same age are generally placed together. As individual differences in advancement appear, the group becomes heterogenous until students are reclassified. In a studio with limited enrollment, this reclassification sometimes does not occur until the following season.

The teacher in a private studio, unlike the teacher in a large school with a pool of two or three hundred beginners, is forced to place all available beginners together, regardless of age or talent. Later, in continuing classes, there may be a span of a grade or two between the least and most advanced students. A teacher may divide enrollment into four sets: beginners, second- and third-year levels, intermediate, and advanced. Groups are then formed from each of the four sets on the basis of one or more of the following: age, grade level, talent, ability, and interests. Unfortunately, top priority must be given to scheduling a lesson that does not interfere with the student's extracurricular and private study activities.

ADVANTAGES OF GROUP STUDY

When children are together, learning can be fun. They enjoy playing for an audience of peers, they look forward to the learning games, they make new friends, and they learn from each other. The private student has only the teacher as a model, whereas in the multiple setting, children are challenged by the realistic models of their equals.

With more than one child, greater ear training, ensemble playing, and critical verbal expression are possible. Individual repertory assignments enable group members to become familiar with a much greater portion of the piano literature than private students can. In James Mursell's words, watching the music while other students play "is as valuable a technical drill as any of the ordinary exercises for developing dexterity." Every lesson resembles a recital class: the students are performing for an audience of peers, learning to accept criticism from each other and gaining self-assurance. There is always a complete lesson of active listening, with constant repetition reinforcing the various concepts. Playing together, in unison or ensemble, improves the student's rhythmic fluency. Because playing games is exciting, attention spans become longer. Relaxed in a friendly setting, students participate in a give-and-take which is essential to learning. Most important of all, the stimulation of being part of a learning team provides motivation for practicing.

However, when the group lesson becomes a series of short private lessons, all the advantages of such study are nullified. A child in a group of six gets only ten minutes or even less; the results are grossly inferior to private study. Furthermore, the uninvolved students may become bored, daydream, or create a disturbance. Neglect may also occur when so many students are enrolled in the group, that each student does not have ample opportunity to participate. When interaction is at a minimum, learning is also at a minimum. Additionally, students in such a group may feel that the teacher is not personally interested in them.

DISADVANTAGES OF GROUP STUDY

Even with an ideal teacher in an ideal group situation, a child accustomed to being the center of attention at home might be happier with a teacher's total attention. For this type of child, particularly one having difficulty adjusting to being part of a class in school, the private lesson may be preferable.

Also, the needs of a talented student seriously interested in performance become so different from those of the group that it is then best that the lessons be private. Generally, the private lesson provides the most appropriate setting for students preparing for frequent or lengthy auditions and public performance.

ADVANTAGES FOR THE TEACHER

Some teachers find group piano more stimulating. It relieves them from the monotony of saying the same thing over and over again privately to each child. The teacher sees the children's behavior in relationship to their peers rather than on the adult-child basis of the private lesson. This, the group teacher believes, provides a more complete picture of children as they really are.

The group instructor is often a teacher of concepts, and elects the group approach in order to create opportunities for learning through active participation (group dynamics). In private lessons, the group teacher contends, the child is passive and learns only by imitation. According to some educational psychologists, learning by imitation is undesirable. They recommend that children explore and discover concepts under the teacher's leadership so that they become thinking students rather than imitative ones. Essentially this is what the group teacher of concepts strives for: the thinking, independent student, not one who constantly needs the teacher as a crutch. The group setting provides the means for developing such a student.

A personal advantage for the group teacher is that the teaching day is shorter. While it takes five or ten hours to teach ten students privately, it takes the group teacher from one to three hours to teach the same number. Unlike school-teachers, piano teachers generally begin working in the middle of the afternoon, so the private piano teacher's day is not over until middle or late evening. This commitment to night hours often conflicts with family routines and social interests. The group piano teacher, however, with reduced teaching hours, enjoys the benefit of completing work earlier in the day.

Another advantage accruing to the group piano teacher is that the problems of makeup lessons are eliminated. An entire group cannot be rescheduled, just as a school day cannot be rescheduled to accommodate individual members. Often attendance improves. Furthermore, the dropout rate is less, since students enjoy being part of a team.

DISADVANTAGES FOR THE TEACHER

If group work is to be successful, the teacher must be willing to devote many hours to preparation. This, depending on the method, might involve long hours of typing and administrative chores. Teaching more than one student at a time demands an alert, quick teacher prepared for whatever interaction may take place. Since any kind of fumbling, sitting back, or searching for materials can trigger the onset of chaos, the teacher must be energetic, in good health, and emotionally strong enough to cope with discipline problems. These can be harassing even when quickly settled.

If the studio is located in a quiet residential area, the increased traffic and commotion that result with students' arriving and leaving may disturb even the best of neighbors. Also, it is possible that in some areas group teaching is viewed—unjustifiably, to be sure—as a method representing lower standards, commercialism, and mass education.

For the teacher who desires a part-time occupation to carry on at home, without investing in a professional studio and waiting room, group piano may not be a wise choice. And in part-time work, grouping becomes even more difficult because not enough students are enrolled in each category.

The class teacher's training and background are essentially the same as the private teacher's, except that courses in group-teaching methods are recommended, as well as additonal courses in education, psychology, and testing. The ability to type is useful, if not necessary.

Personal qualifications are also the same for both types of teacher. The group teacher must also enjoy working with more than one student at a time, have the skill to bring about desirable group interaction, and be able to cope with organizational work and discipline problems. A good memory is a tremendous asset since there is little time to continually consult a lesson plan and the printed music when the group is present.

TEAM TEACHING

Team teaching may be initiated to take advantage of combining skills and energies. In team teaching, two or more teachers plan, teach, and evaluate the same group of students, and each teacher provides that part of the program in which he or she specializes. For instance, one teacher may have an extensive background in Dalcroze, another may be a specialist in piano technique, and still another may be successful at teaching elementary composition. If the three are capable of combining their efforts, the results can well surpass that of an individual teacher assuming the entire task alone.

Team teaching in the private studio, however, is an ideal not too often realized. It is difficult to find persons who are not only willing to work with each other, but to use their talents without competing with each other for first place in the eyes of their students and colleagues.

FEES AND MATERIALS

Fees for group lessons may range from one sixth to exactly the same as a private lesson, depending on group size, local conditions, and the teacher's objectives and qualifications. Those group teachers who set higher fees believe that they are justified because more time is required for lesson planning, more energy and know-how is demanded during the teaching hour, and often a greater investment has been made in the studio equipment and space. These teachers generally emphasize performance as well as musicianship, and their groups are kept small, possibly from three to six students.

Materials may be the same as those for private instruction, except that it is advisable to use collections rather than single pieces, so that when individual assignments are made, all students will have the music to follow at the lesson; they may also sight read the other students' assignments at home, or even be sufficiently motivated to learn them as extra projects. Class students generally require more music, since there is apt to be more weekly variety in the lesson than in private study.

COURSE OF STUDY AND ACTIVITIES

The curriculum does not differ from that of private study except that the very setting of the group encourages more ensemble work and the sight reading of duets, trios, and quartets. Generally group-piano teachers favor the multiple-key approach, the song approach, and stress more of the musicianship phases of study such as improvisation, keyboard harmony, analysis, and ear training.

The group lesson is so planned that all take part every moment of the class hour. Short pieces, short drills, and short comments keep each member alert and ready to participate at all times. The teacher does not lecture but leads, drawing out information from all members of the group. Variety of activities keeps the lesson moving at a rapid pace, giving the children little chance to withdraw.

Discussions are not recitations. No student is put on the spot, but all are encouraged freely to respond in order to reinforce the old and learn the new. The following example illustrates the review of the G-major key and the introduction of its relative minor. The teacher at all times serves as a guide in exploring and discovering new concepts.

Teacher: Why did you say this piece is in the key of G?
Student 1: It has one sharp.
Teacher: Could it be in another key besides G?
(No one answers. Finally:)
Student 3: No, it has to be in G.
Teacher: Well, let's see why.
Student 3: It has one sharp.
Student 2: It ends on G.
Teacher: Any other reasons?
(By now several students are bursting to tell why.)
Teacher: Everybody, why?
All students: The left hand begins with the G chord.
(Since the students are working on simple folk tunes, the answer is acceptable for their level of advancement.)
Teacher: And that means?
Student 4: It starts with the G chord and ends with G, and so it must be in the key of G.
Teacher: Now turn to page 63. This piece has one sharp too. In what key is this?
Everybody: G.
Teacher: Does it end on G?
Student 4: No.
Teacher: What does it end on?

Student 1: E.
Teacher: I wonder why.
(The children are puzzled. The teacher plays the piece.)
Teacher: Does it sound like the key of G?
(The teacher now plays some of the first piece in G. Students decide that it doesn't. Finally:)
Student 4: It sounds sad.
(Several students decide the piece sounds "minor," just like the piece they had a few lessons before.)
Teacher: Then this piece is in a minor key?
Students: Yes. (They all agree.)
Teacher: Can any one guess what minor?
Student 3: E.
Teacher: Why?
Student 3: It begins with an E chord.
Teacher: E-what chord?
Student 4: E minor.
Teacher: Everybody, what chord does it end with?
All: E minor.
Teacher: So a piece with one sharp may be in what key?
All: E minor.
Teacher: And?
All: G major.
Teacher: We say G major and E minor are related. Why?
(No one answers.)
Teacher: What do they both have?
Student 4: One sharp.
Teacher: In the . . .
Student 3: . . . key signature.
Teacher: How many sharps or flats does the key of C major have?
All: None.
Teacher: Think carefully. What minor scale has no sharps or flats in the key signature?
(No one answers.)
Teacher: G's related minor lived how many steps away from G? (The teacher points to G on the keyboard.) G is the number one note of G major and we move down. . .
Student 1: . . . three steps. G, F, E.
Teacher: Yes, three letter names or what?
(No one answers.)
Teacher: G to F-sharp is what?
Student 2: Half step.
Student 4: It's three half steps down.
Teacher: Yes, G to F-sharp, then F-sharp to F, and . . .
All: . . . F to E.
Teacher: So what is the related minor of C?
Student 2: A minor?

The teacher now encourages the students to figure out more relative minors. Each time, the sameness of key signature is stressed. At this point the minor-third concept (three half steps) may also be introduced; the lesson on relative minor scales and minor thirds ends at this point.

Taking turns could be tedious for the child not at the piano unless the teacher instructs the listening. The teacher might say, "This time when Mary plays the piece, shut your eyes and count how many times you hear the theme," or "This time I want you to raise your hands whenever John plays the number-five chord." The listening period may also be used to reinforce rhythms either by clapping, conducting, or using rhythmic band instruments. When there is extensive repertory work for a recital or auditions, the teacher may assign written work or individual assignments for waiting students to practice on silent keyboards. Also, older students may listen and serve as judges, writing their criticism of the student's performance. As mentioned, watching the music as it is played is also beneficial.

Assigned solo work may be played in unison as well as solo. Playing together in unison is difficult and requires careful rhythmic preparation. Exercises, scales, duets, trios, and quartets all provide good opportunities for playing together. The students may also sight read solos and ensemble pieces. When the music is difficult, one student might play the right-hand part while another plays the left. Any kind of ensemble playing strengthens rhythmic accuracy and fluency.

Occasionally the teacher may ask a student to select a piece and learn it without assistance. (This is done in private lessons too.) Such an assignment not only helps the student establish the habit of seeking out material he likes to play, but also gives the confidence to function independently. In evaluating the choice of material, the teacher gains further insight into the student's personality. For instance, if a student picks a hard piece, it indicates ambition and a desire to be challenged. The selection may also reveal the student's taste.

For some students, self-study work may well set the pattern for playing the piano even when there are no lessons, such as during the summer months and later in adulthood. It also provides another means of determining how successful the teacher has been in guiding the group toward independence.

GAMES – REWARDS – DISCIPLINE

Flashcards: Each student keeps the cards he or she identifies correctly. At the end of the game the students count the number of cards they have and possibly decide on winners.

Signature drills: Two teams play; speed counts. One member from each team is at the blackboard when the teacher calls out a key. The first one to place the key signature on the staff earns a point for the team.

Playing together: Students are playing in unison; the teacher listens attentively only to piano 1 and directs all criticism to pianist 1. The students alternate at piano 1. The rotation from piano to piano is fun for the students, particularly for younger ones.

Playing editor: The teacher writes a melody containing discernible errors on the blackboard. Each error corrected wins a point for the student.

Rhythm game: The teacher taps a rhythm. The first student to write it correctly on the board gets a point.

Keep the beat: Students take turns tapping the rhythm, one measure at a time, of an eight- or sixteen-bar phrase. A student who loses a beat drops out. The one student left is the winner.

The group teacher believes that the rewards of studying together are greater for the student because acquiring skills in the natural social setting of the group heightens the student's sense of satisfaction and achievement. The group teacher, however, must be mindful that inasmuch as praise is more meaningful in front of one's peers, harsh criticism is difficult to endure when not given in private. Such negative remarks as "You are wrong; that was a silly thing to do! Correct your mistakes!" must be avoided. Instead the teacher might take a positive approach: "You're right except for this spot. Why did you play the third finger? Isn't it easier to keep it all the same as the beginning?" Since group behavior will be modeled after the teacher's, such an approach will provide a more harmonious group spirit.

The reward of excessive praise had best be eliminated, since there is no place for the star system in group piano. Rather, every child must be encouraged and every child must shine for his or her contribution to the group. Each child has some asset that even the most talented lacks.

The group setting provides an opportunity to win points in much the same way that a baseball team does. Students work toward accumulating points both at home, through practice, and at the lesson, through participation. These points may serve as symbols of individual achievement. The teacher who avoids competition in the studio will not approve of any system of awards.

The exponents of group piano seldom mention the problem of discipline. Even the ideal lesson plan coupled with ideal leadership cannot compete with an impending birthday, an intense desire to be home with the new puppy, or an emotional disturbance. Therefore, the teacher must be prepared for whatever eruptions occur. The following guidelines might help the teacher to keep order:

- Discontinue an activity when students are distracted.
- Alter the lesson plan (completely if necessary) to fit an unexpected mood.
- Speak softly. Children respond in kind; disruptive attention-seekers had best not be reinforced by negative reaction from the teacher. Rather, such behavior may be eliminated by the teacher's paying attention not to their misbehavior but to their successful participation in the lesson.

STUDIO EQUIPMENT

An astute teacher who has faith and confidence in the group approach will succeed in spite of sparseness of equipment. One piano with a bench might be sufficient, but two pianos will greatly facilitate teaching. The kind of equipment selected will depend on the approach used. It is best for the inexperienced teacher to furnish the studio after the method of instruction is determined. Electronic pianos provide an extension of the varieties of group procedure. For instance, students equipped with earphones may work out new or old problems alone before presenting them to the group for discussion. With electronic pianos there can be group performances in unison, with some of the pianos turned off so that the teacher is attentive only to one or two of the performers (students take turns in being heard). The same procedure may be worked out with silent keyboards; one student plays at the piano while the rest of the group plays along in unison on their silent keyboards. The teacher observes the fingering and hand position of all students, but directs criticism on tone, rhythm, notes, etc. to the student at the piano. Each student gets a chance to play at the real piano.

Since they do not respond to finer details of touch, electronic pianos will be inadequate for the teacher who wants to offer a great deal more than the basic aspects of reading and playing in the group program. Audio-visual aids such as music projectors, films, and cassettes are always an asset, if properly used, as adjuncts of a well-planned, imaginative curriculum. Investment in such equipment requires careful consideration, as it too often happens that they are bought and seldom used. Blackboards, placed where they may be seen by all, serve many purposes: communication, drill work, visual display, and an opportunity for learning games. They may also constitute a source of mischief, and in the home studio cause an undesirable film of chalk dust, its thickness depending on the kind of materials used.

Because more than one child is involved, the logistics of scheduling and smooth operation make the availability of a waiting room imperative.

After a teacher has considered all the pros and cons and evaluated personal assets, training, ability, personality—as well as the physical plant of the studio—the decision may be made as to what degree the conversion to group piano is desirable. There may be a test period of one or two group sessions a week, or all teaching may be converted to a combination of the private and group method. If the teacher is sufficiently determined to make group piano succeed, then the private lesson may be totally eliminated. The latter approach, although risky, has one important advantage: the parent and student realize at once that the teacher strongly believes that the group approach is preferred, particularly if that teacher keeps the enrollment at the same level as it was in the years of private lessons.

HISTORICAL BACKGROUND

Although group piano is still not the preferred approach by the majority of teachers, its history is fairly long. As early as 1815 class piano was in existence in Dublin under the master Johann Bernhard Logier. There is evidence that at least two American teachers were curious enough to go abroad to join his classes. Logier's innovation apparently spread, for in *Dwight's Journal of Music* (1860) two anonymous letters discuss piano classes conducted in Mississippi, southern Tennessee, and Virginia.

In 1887 a new philosophy very much akin to contemporary group piano was presented by Professor Calvin Bernard Cady. He believed that some factors of musicianship could be taught only in a small group.

It was not Professor Cady's ideas, however, that gained popularity in the United States, but rather class piano patterned after teaching methods used in the classroom. In 1913 class piano was incorporated in the public-school curriculum in Boston. By 1930 it had reached its apex, with 880 school systems offering classes with eight to thirty students in a class. Fees ranged from nothing to thirty-five cents a lesson.

Decline rather than further growth followed because of the persistent failures of class piano in public education. These were blamed on the lack of trained teachers. Today only a few large cities, including Dallas and Denver, have piano classes, but private studios, universities and colleges, and conservatories have become more and more involved with teaching piano in groups.

One explanation for the failure of group instruction to achieve overwhelming acceptance may lie in the fact that teaching privately is so comfortable, so traditional, so accepted, and so appropriate, especially for those who teach only part time, that it continues to perpetuate itself. Most important of all, and a fact no teacher can ignore, is that the Artur Rubinsteins and Van Cliburns are products not of group method, but of private instruction.

Many teachers, in their enthusiasm for the group method, are inclined to denigrate the private lesson and exalt the group approach as a magic wand that can turn lazy students into eager, practicing ones. This is not the case. As far back as 1931, the versatile and erudite writer on music, John Tasker Howard, wrote (*Parents' Magazine*, June 1931):

> I have argued in favor of class lesson but I am not for all class lessons—only good ones. By good ones I mean those in charge of a capable teacher, trained both in class methods and in piano pedagogy—a teacher who likes children and who loves music—who thinks of mechanics not as an end, but as a means for producing music. And that applies to all teachers whether they give class lessons or teach privately.

In the final analysis the success of any approach, whether group or private, depends upon the teacher's inner resources and personality. There can be no arbitrary conclusion as to which method is superior. The decision to use either or both rests entirely with the individual teacher's preferences and objectives.

RECOMMENDED READING

Bennett, Beulah Varner. *Piano Classes for Everyone*. New York: Philosophical Library, 1960.

Bishop, Dorothy. "Group Teaching." *Clavier* March–April 1962.

——"Equipping the Music Studio for Piano Lessons." *Clavier* May–June 1965.

Couchane, Lillian. "The School Piano Class for Teenagers." *Clavier* April 1967.

Denegar, Donald. "Musicianship as Developed in the Class Lesson for Private Students." *Clavier* May–June 1964.

——"Problems of Grouping." *Clavier* March 1968.

Enoch, Yvonne and James Lyke. *Creative Piano Teaching* (Chapter Four: "College Group Instruction"). Champaign, Ill.: Stipes Publishing Co., 1977.

Hartman, Nancy. "Common Errors Made by Group Teachers." In Enoch, *Creative Piano Teaching*. Champaign, Ill.: Stipes Publishing Co., 1977.

Kern, Alice M. "Criteria for Selection of Materials for Class Piano." *Clavier* March–April 1965.

Mehr, Norman. *Group Piano Teaching*. Evanston, Ill.: Summy-Birchard Co., 1965.

Mursell, James L. *Principles of Musical Education*. New York: Macmillan, 1931.

Pace, Robert. *Piano for Classroom Music* (2nd ed.). Englewood Cliffs, N.J.: Prentice-Hall, 1971.

Rezits, Joseph. "Organizing the College Piano Class." *The Piano Teacher* January–February 1964.

Richards, William. "How Group Teaching Started." *Clavier* October 1963.

——"Zoning Laws and the Music Teacher." *Clavier* November 1974.

Robinson, Helene, and Richard L. Jarvis, editors. *Teaching Piano in Classroom and Studio*. Washington, D.C.: Music Educators National Conference, 1967.

Skaggs, Hazel Ghazarian. "The Private Lesson on Trial." *The Piano Teacher* November–December 1962.

——"Some Aspects of Converting to Group Piano." *Clavier* November–December 1963.

——"The Truth About Group Piano." *The American Music Teacher* March-April 1964.

Werder, Richard H. "Piano Classes–More Work, but Worth It!" *Étude* August 1952.

The Piano Teacher and the Handicapped Student

ANITA LOUISE STEELE

Teaching piano to the handicapped student, who is slower to learn by traditional methods, need not overwhelm the piano teacher. It is true that the effects of a learning disability, physical handicap, mild retardation, or an emotional problem may interfere significantly with the student's ability to learn, and techniques that are effective with other students may not succeed. This does not mean, however, that the student cannot learn. Teaching the handicapped is a challenge which will require patience and careful planning, for the unique characteristics of each student will demand an individualized approach.

The teacher of a handicapped student should therefore:

- be prepared to assess the particular strengths and limitations of the individual's learning style
- be willing to define standards of achievement appropriate for the individual
- set reasonable objectives for the student
- break down each learning task into easily attainable steps graduated in difficulty
- adapt or create teaching materials with consideration to the individual's handicap
- provide the student with a good measure of support and encouragement throughout each stage of the learning process

---

The material presented in this section is collected primarily from the experiences of the author and other music therapists on the staff of the Music Therapy Program at The Cleveland Music School Settlement.

Instruction should begin with an inventory of what abilities the student has and what limitations the handicap imposes. A determination can then be made as to what initial abilities can become the foundation upon which to build other skills. The teacher will also gain a better idea of what problem areas are best avoided and to what degree materials will have to be altered.

Some of this information may be obtained from the parents, school teachers, music therapists, or others who have worked with the student. A great deal can also be learned from the teacher's own observations in the private piano lesson. The following are among the questions which should be answered in order to assess the student's level of ability.

(1) What is the handicapping condition?

(2) What areas of functioning are affected (mobility, coordination, vision, hearing)?

(3) Can the student discriminate right from left; match letters; read and comprehend what is read; follow a line of printed material from left to right unassisted; look at the teacher when spoken to; follow verbal directions; move the fingers of each hand independently; stay seated for five, ten, or fifteen minutes; etc.

The student can be evaluated on these and other skills through prepared music activities which are both fun to do and which fit his or her age and interest. For instance, the action song "Hokey Pokey" can be used to determine whether or not a younger child can distinguish the right hand from the left. Directions given in the song instruct the child to "Put your right hand in/ Put your left hand out/ Put your right hand in / And shake it all about." (Techniques used with the older student should be more subtle.) During the evaluation the teacher should remain objective, encouraging, and noncritical. The opportunity for correction and further instruction will come at a later time.

THE FIRST LESSONS

It is most important that the first piano lessons be structured so that the student will achieve a degree of immediate success. Most beginning piano literature unfortunately presupposes the ability to read notation fairly quickly in order to play a melody line. This presents quite a problem for those handicapped students who require an extended period of time in which to learn staff notation.

Because of the student's special needs, the teacher must choose another set of symbols to indicate pitch or location of keys on the keyboard and devise materials. Colors, numbers, or letters can be used to serve the same purpose as notation (at least at this very elementary level). If the student is familiar with upper-case letters, the letter names of the keys can be written by the teacher or the student on small pieces of masking tape or self-adhesive labeling tabs (available in small quantities from office supply stores), placed on the octave C^1 (middle C) to C^2.

A familiar tune with a limited range is written down for the student with the appropriate letter name given below each note; for instance:

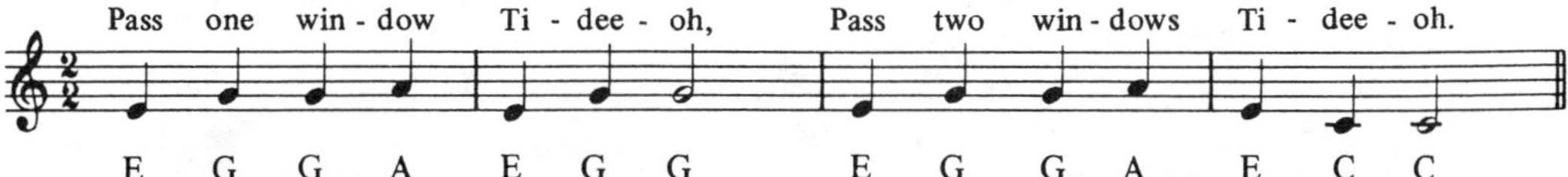

(Other suitable tunes which can be written in the key of C include "Mary Had a Little Lamb," "Skip to My Lou," "Hey Lolly Lolly," "Michael Row the Boat Ashore," "Born Free," "This Old Man," "Camptown Races," etc.) The student is taught to play the tune by:

- pointing the index finger of the left hand to each letter in sequence
- matching the letter by pointing with the index finger of the right hand to the same lettered key on the piano
- depressing the key with the right index finger

Some students may need to be taught the steps involved in using the second finger of the left hand as a "pointer." This training can begin by actually moving the student's left hand, with index finger extended, from letter to letter across the line of music. Gradually the teacher withdraws assistance until the student can point and play independently. If the student can not point to each letter, perhaps because of a physical disability, the teacher can point instead.

The student is encouraged to play each tune written in this manner at a comfortable speed; precise rhythm is not a concern at this time. An approximation of the correct rhythm can be made by singing as the melody is played or by having the student sing the melody several times before playing. By singing as the student plays, or by using the sustaining pedal, the teacher can extend the sound of individual notes which the student may play quite slowly, in order to make the tune more obvious.

Certain students may have difficulty following a line of music from the left to the right and moving from one line to the next. To assist the student, the teacher can place different colored dots made with marking pens or colored stickers at the beginning of each line. As the first line is finished, the student is told to find the red dot placed to the left of the next line of music. Gradually the color cues are removed and the student need only be reminded with "Find the next line" or "Next."

A handicapped student whose intellectual ability is impaired may remain at this *point-match-play* stage for many weeks or months. The teacher should consider giving the student Richard Weber's *Musicall* book for the keyboard, which follows the general approach just outlined (Richard Weber, Musicall, Inc., 17 West 60th Street, New York, New York 10023). The *Musicall* book is one of the very few published materials for this beginning stage of music learning. (The book is also available for string and band instruments.) Although it is not difficult for the teacher to write material at this level, the published book is attractive, contains a group of favorite children's tunes, and places in the hands of the student his or her very own, "real" book.

As Dr. Weber suggests in his *Musicall* series, the learning experience can be further extended to include playing with both hands. The student is taught to duplicate the melody line with a finger of the left hand. To help the student discriminate which keys are to be played by the right and left hands, different colored letters (blue for the right and red for the left) are printed on self-adhesive tape (half-inch strips of masking tape will do) and placed on the keys. The letter names under the notes in the manuscript can be colored to coincide with the letter names placed on the keys to provide an even stronger cue.

Some students can be taught to play a simple accompaniment with the left hand. The harmonizing chord can be indicated by placing the appropriate upper-case letter (enclosed by a circle or square for easy reading) above the place in the melody line where chord changes occur.

The nature and complexity of the accompaniment may vary according to the student's ability. A student with adequate finger dexterity may be able to finger a major triad in the root position as a block chord (for example, C, E, G to represent the C-major chord). A student with coordination problems might execute the same accompaniment as a major third (C and E) or as a single note on the tonic C.

Additional material can be given to the student by assembling a book with pieces written out by the teacher and selected by the student. In this way it is possible to supplement the student's repertory with current tunes. The themes of any number of favorite popular and folk songs can be written, with a few modifications, in the keys of C, F, or G. "Kum Ba Ya," "Born Free," and the chorus of "Country Roads" are among the many which younger students enjoy. Naturally, in the beginning stages the pieces should be transcribed to avoid the extensive use of sharps and flats. (The *Musicall* book introduces only one black key: B-flat.) If keys must be used beyond a one-octave range, a short horizontal line can be placed above the letter written on the tab and placed on the keys in the higher octave. (C^2, D^2, and E^2 above middle C would be written under the notes and on the tabs as $\overline{C}$, $\overline{D}$, and $\overline{E}$.) Memorization of the sequence of keys within the octave will often result from playing by the point-match-play method over a period of time. The lettered tapes can then be removed from the keys either gradually or all at once.

READING NOTATION

The introduction of staff notation should be approached thoughtfully, with consideration given to the student's basic academic and developmental level. The pace at which the student progresses, and therefore the rate at which the teacher can introduce new material, will not be the same as with other students. Not all students will learn to read notation well enough to advance their playing ability. Some students will be able to read the treble clef well enough to play simplified music and to execute basic harmonies with the left hand from chord symbols. Others will be quite capable of learning to read from the grand staff and will do so as well as the nonhandicapped musician.

Although a basic method for teaching notation may be generally accepted among music teachers, there are perhaps as many variations in approach as there are students to be taught. Alterations which need to be made in teaching the handicapped student will be influenced by the degree to which the student's particular disability interferes with the learning process. (The teacher may find that with certain students the teaching process is slower but does not require major alterations in methods or materials.) If the capable student is to advance beyond the letter-matching method of playing melodies with basic harmonization, success will depend in great measure on the instructor's ability to match skillfully a given approach to the student's ability level.

A frequent problem encountered in teaching notation to the handicapped child is that the size of the printed notes is, in most cases, too small for the learning needs. Although some beginning graded series present first pieces on a larger than normal staff, even this may not be large enough for a student with visual perception or eye-hand coordination problems. If the teacher asks the student to place a finger "on the line" or "in the space," the distance between the lines and spaces must be large enough to accommodate the student's response. Added advantages to a larger staff include the fact that the notes must also be larger and the number of notes per line reduced. The teacher may find it necessary during the initial stages of teaching notation to stencil a supply of different-size manuscript. As the student's ability to discriminate between the lines and spaces improves, the size of the staff paper can gradually be reduced.

Some students may be confused at first by the number of lines and spaces making up the grand staff. Until they learn the system of reading notation, it will be difficult for them to "see the tree for the forest." It may be easier for them to begin with fewer lines and spaces. A study of Grace Nash's approach to the musical development of the young child (*Today with Music* [Teacher's Edition], Alfred Publishers, 1963; *Music with Children* [Series I Elementary, Teacher's Book], Kitching Educational Division of Ludwig Industries, 1963) suggests one method by which this may be done.

Working with only a two-line staff, the student learns to distinguish between the first (E) and second (G) lines and the space between (F). The student learns a number of simple tunes composed of G and E which can be sung, played, and written on the two-line staff.

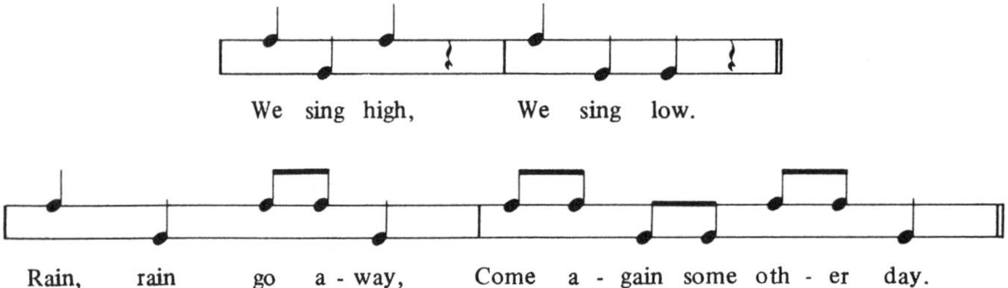
We sing high, We sing low.
Rain, rain go a - way, Come a - gain some oth - er day.

To make the presentation more interesting, the student may be given the opportunity to compose pieces with lyrics, which he or she then writes down and plays at the piano. Brightly colored circles (colored self-adhesive filing labels obtained from an office-supply store or circles cut from colored construction paper) may be used as note heads and given to the student to place on the appropriate lines or spaces. At this stage the teacher may choose to use somewhat oversized, two-line manuscript which has been duplicated ahead of time, or lines may be drawn on the blackboard.

A variety of percussive and melodic instruments such as the metalophone (an instrument similar to the xylophone but with finely tuned metal bars rather than wooden ones), xylophones, and glockenspiels are an integral part of the Orff method (see p.250)and Nash's elaboration upon the basic Orff idea. These instruments are particularly helpful in teaching the handicapped since the bars are removable, permitting the use of only the number of bars with which the student can work successfully. As the student advances, additional bars can be added to encompass a full range of several octaves. The larger metalophone and wooden xylophones (available in soprano, alto, tenor, and bass ranges) are more suitable for students with fine motor coordination problems, since the bars are wider and therefore easier to strike. The published materials of Nash, Orff, and others offer a wealth of simple tunes composed within a five-note range. These and other simple beginning pieces can be played on the bars by rote or by reading notation.

Notation may be presented in the order of E, G, A, D, C etc., according to the Nash approach, or the teacher may choose to use middle C as the more traditional starting point. Once the student is reading from the two-line staff, other lines and spaces can be introduced. To stimulate interest, the student may be given the opportunity to compose pieces using the notes he has learned, and experiment with playing a beginning piece on the xylophone or performing the piece composed for the xylophone on the piano. (It is often very pleasing to the student to learn that he or she can play more than one instrument.)

If necessary, an additional cue may be provided the student by the use of the Curwen-Kodály system of hand signals, which identify a

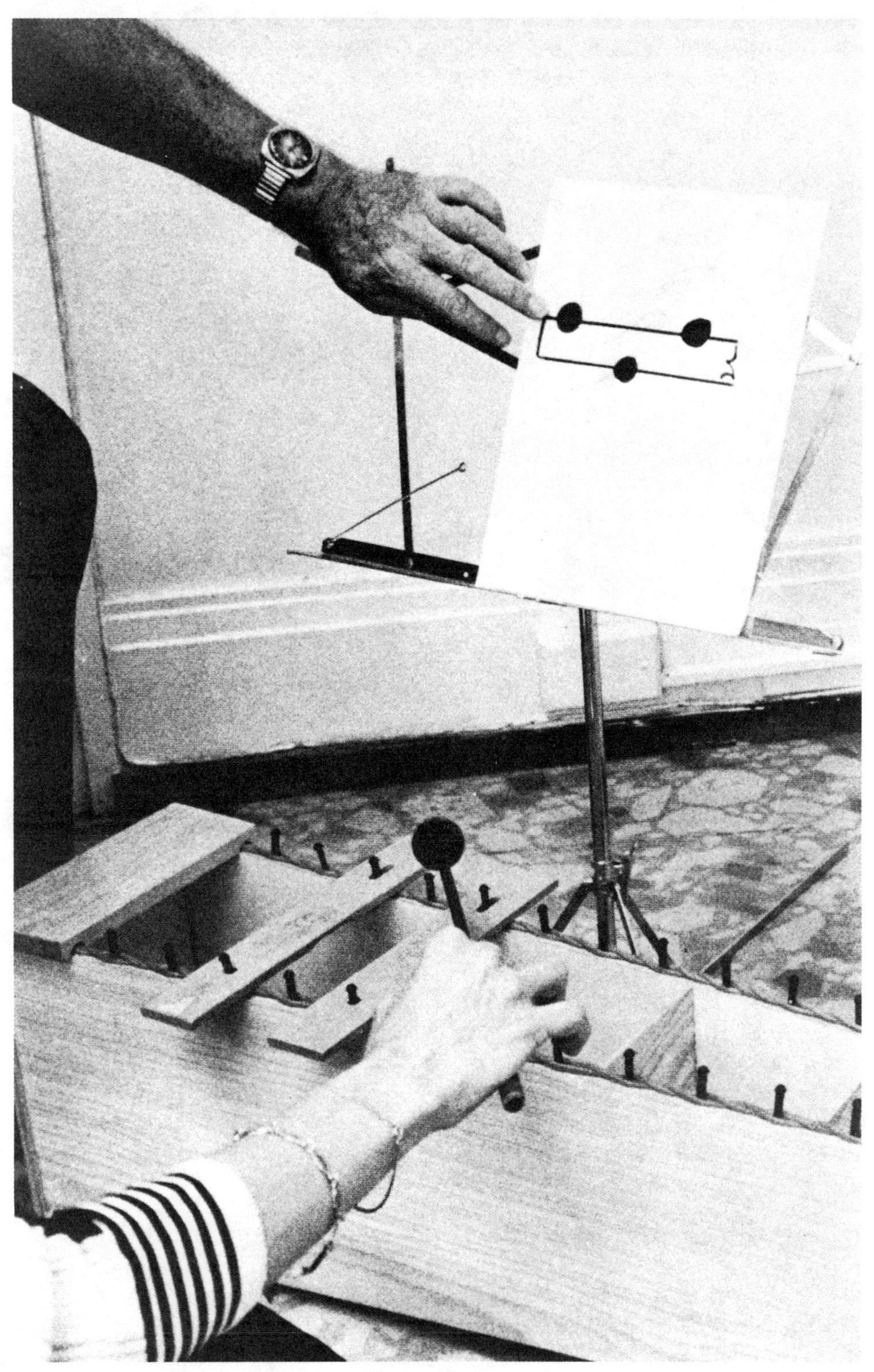

particular position of the hand with each of the eight degrees of the scale. (Outlined in Wheeler and Raebeck, *Orff and Kodály Adapted for the Elementary School*, William C. Brown Co.).

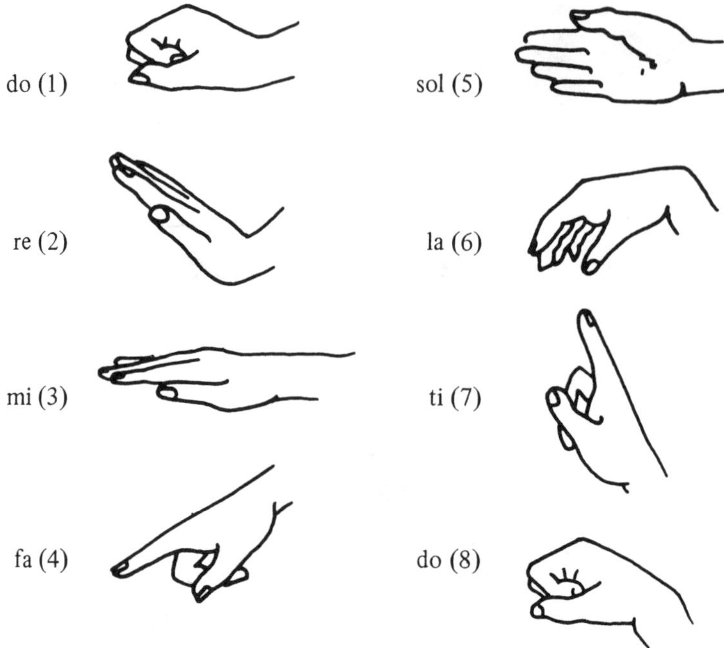

Until this time in the teaching program, the letter names of the piano keys may have been printed on tabs placed on the keys. For those students who learn to locate middle C and to determine the location of other keys from it, these tabs can gradually be removed. If the Curwen-Kodály hand signals have been taught, these can be used to help remind the student of the letter names until skill in determining successive location of keys by moving up or down from C or F, or some other designated starting point, is achieved. Until the student can identify the keys in sequence and in random order, the letter names of the keys should be reviewed at the beginning of each lesson.

Although the student has begun to read notation, some part of the lesson can still be devoted to playing familiar melodies which have the letter names printed under each note. (The lettered tapes on the keys may no longer be necessary.) The repetition of this and other previously successful activities will help ensure continued enjoyment of the lesson, particularly during the more difficult beginning stage of reading notation. As long as the student is playing—regardless of the method used—familiarity with the keyboard and finger dexterity should improve.

If a student is academically prepared, notation can be taught more traditionally through interval relationships using C, E, or any other note as the starting point. Tracing each line of the staff with a different color is a technique which may be used to help the student who has problems identifying the lines on the staff. Gradual removal of the color cues will depend on the individual's timetable of absorbing and learning.

Music therapists are often required to teach beginning notation in steps progressing so slowly that failure is virtually eliminated. The following approach might be useful for the piano teacher of the slower student.* Construction paper or light cardboard is cut into pieces the size of playing cards. Individual cards are prepared for the five notes middle C through G on the treble staff and the five from middle C down to F on the bass staff. Two sets of cards have the letter names of the notes printed below each note; two other sets have no letter names. Matching sets are made so that both the teacher and the student can have one complete set of each type of card, one with the letter names under the notes, and one without.

The teacher first presents the lettered cards to the student and rehearses the identifying visual characteristics of each note (for example, "Middle C is on a line all by itself"; "D is below line number one"; "E is on line number one"; etc.). These visual characteristics will aid the student in making correct differentiations between notes once the letter names are removed from the cards. Next, using a medium-size staff, the teacher draws in sequence the same notes presented on the cards (with letter names under the notes). The student must now select a card from the teacher's hand, identify it and point to the same note from among those drawn on the music paper. (At this point the primary skill required is that the student be able to match the card with its identical representation on the manuscript paper.) The teacher now switches to the set without the letters as the student learns to identify the notes. As skill improves, the letters beneath the notes on the paper can also be removed.

In a further elaboration of the game, the teacher strikes a bar on the xylophone (avoiding sharps or flats) or plays a white key on the piano, and instructs the student to find the corresponding note on the manuscript paper. The teacher must, of course, indicate the appropriate clef and with which hand the note is to be played. Teacher and student can also exchange roles, with the student playing the note and indicating whether or not the teacher identified it correctly.

Moving to the piano, the teacher assists the student in placing the right thumb on C and each finger on the appropriate white key. The student is instructed in playing C through G with the five fingers of the right hand and C through F with the five fingers of the left in ascending and descending order. The manuscript paper is then presented and the teacher points to each note as the student plays the appropriate key and says the letter name. The final step in the sequence is for the teach-

*This approach to teaching beginning notation was developed by Linda Gerstle, music therapist at The Cleveland Music School Settlement, to teach a cerebral palsied student.

er to point to one note at a time, in random order, on the music paper for the student to identify and play on the piano. The piece of manuscript with each note identified is placed to the side, within sight of the student, to be used temporarily as a reference chart.

PLAYING WITH BOTH HANDS

Special problems may exist for the handicapped student in reading the grand staff (that is, the two staffs simultaneously). People with learning problems or birth defects often have disabilities affecting more than one area. Although not described as having a visual impairment, the student may have difficulty focusing eyes or coordinating movements which involve both eyes and hands. The instructor will need to provide assistance and training in order to establish a sequential pattern of looking at the music ("Look"), placing a finger over the correct key ("Find"), and pressing the key down ("Play"). If matching letters, the student is told to look at the music ("Look"), point to the letter indicating the key to be played ("Point"), place the finger over the key ("Find"), and press down the key ("Play").

If the two hands are playing together, the teacher may need to train the student to see the notes as each occurs on a vertical plane. Sitting to the left of the student, the teacher's left hand is placed palm down, to the left of the printed notes to be played, with the fingers pointing to the right. The third finger of the teacher's left hand is placed beside the first note of the treble clef. The student is told to find that note on the keyboard.

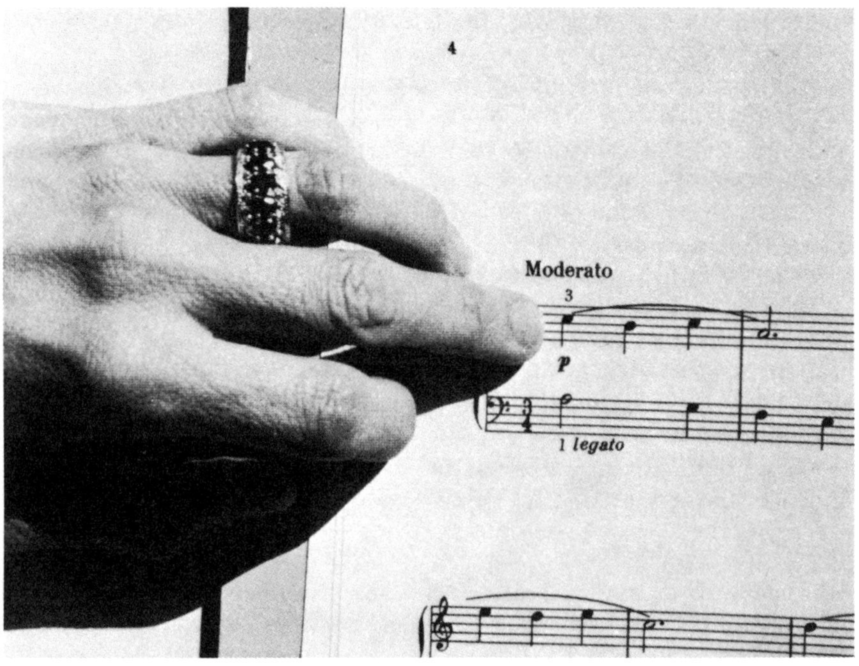

The teacher then uses the second finger of the left hand to point to the first note of the bass clef, directing the student to find that note.

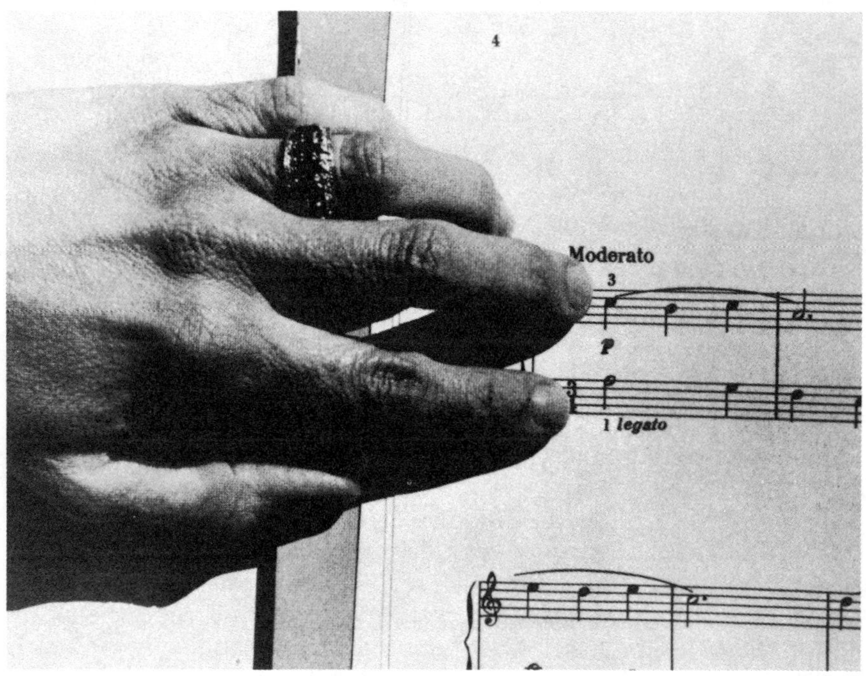

Once both notes are located, the direction to "play together" is given. Although the process may seem laborious it will help train the student's eye-hand coordination, which will eventually become more automatic.

Students with even a minimal learning problem may have difficulty discriminating between the right and left hands. Before beginning to play, the teacher and student may need to identify the right hand and associate it with the treble staff in the piece to be played. If further cues are needed, a small red mark or self-adhesive tape can be placed on top of the student's right hand. A similar mark can be placed to the left of the treble clef at the beginning of each line of music. A stronger visual cue could be given by placing a red mark above each measure written in the treble clef and a mark of a contrasting color placed below each measure of the bass clef.

The student's ability to read notation and to transfer these learned concepts to the keyboard rests largely on the ability to make rather refined choices. The student must be taught to capitalize on the visual cues which help in making these judgments. Pointing first to the treble clef and then to the bass clef, the teacher can offer the following explanation: "Use your right hand when the notes are written *up* here in the treble clef. Use your left hand when the notes are written *down* here in the bass clef." In the very beginning some students may be helped by a notation method (although orthographically not correct) in which all notes in the treble clef have stems pointing up, and all stems in the bass clef have stems pointing down. Here, then, "stem up" means play the right hand, and "stem down," the left. These instructions will see the student through most traditional beginning material. When the student advances to more difficult music in which, on occasion, the right hand plays in the bass clef and the left in the treble, the teacher then introduces the information needed to play the particular passage. With many handicapped students, including the mentally retarded, it is not necessary to explain all the "rules" and exceptions which govern playing. It is generally better to introduce only that amount of information the student requires to play the immediate repertory.

HAND AND FINGER PLACEMENT

Along with the introduction of basic notation, the teacher may work more directly on developing the correct placement of the hands and fingers over the keys, to the extent that the student is capable. Positioning of the hands and fingers may be introduced much as it would be with the average learner. The teacher would begin by molding the student's fingers into the playing curve. (It may be suggested to the students that they pretend to catch a ball with their hands and then put their hands, palms down, over the keys.) The teacher then assists the student in placing each finger of first the right and then the left hand in the five-finger position beginning on middle C. (The first finger of each hand touching middle C.) To help the student depress the correct key with the correct finger, the teacher can gently stroke the top of the finger the student is to use. As that finger releases the key, the teacher touches the next finger.

A short exercise involving all the fingers can be demonstrated by the teacher and performed by the student. Rhymes which are sung as a sequence of keys are played can be used to make an interesting exercise for the younger student.

Right hand:	C, D, E, Has a tree. Full of apples, As can be.	*Left hand:*	C, B, A, Loves to play. In the fields, In the hay.
Right hand:	C, D, E, F, G, Cat goes up a tree.	*Left hand:*	C, B, A, G, F, Come back down my pet.

Simple exercises beginning with the right thumb on middle C and the fifth finger of the left hand on C an octave lower can also be used to develop finger facility, much as one would do with any student. (For instance, C, D, E, F, G/Cat goes up a tree; G, F, E, D, C/Come back down to me!) These exercises can first be done by each hand separately and then with both hands, if the student is capable. Other ideas for exercises of increasing difficulty can be taken from available published materials or from the teacher's own files and adapted to the needs of the handicapped student.

The student with fine motor problems affecting finger coordination will find it difficult to execute the correct hand position and to move each of the fingers independently. The teacher should accept the student's best efforts and patiently work toward developing strength and control. When such problems exist, correct hand position should not be a prerequisite to further playing.

SELECTING BEGINNING MATERIAL

At this point, the teacher is ready to select a beginning book. John Thompson, *Easiest Piano Course*, Part One, (Willis Music Co.) is one which introduces note recognition gradually. The entire book deals with only five notes in the treble clef (middle C to G) and five notes in the bass clef (C to F). Middle C, for example, is presented in various pieces, first as a whole note, then as a half and later a quarter note, over a number of pages. Each short piece has a teacher's accompaniment which counterracts the boredom of playing only one note repeatedly. Bonnel Nunez, *Pixie Piano Playbook*, Book 1, (Willis Music Co.) might also be considered for the very young. Many teachers believe that rhythmic patterns should be composed first of quarter and eighth notes, followed by half, dotted half, and whole notes. It is the opinion of these teachers that the more frequent movement of the hands and fingers is more natural and, therefore, easier for the student to perform. If the teacher finds this to be true for the handicapped student, it is suggested that study from the Thompson book begin with the quarter note Cs (page 11) and progress backward to half and whole notes. The remaining material can then be taken in order.

Because the handicapped learner may advance much more slowly in acquiring each new concept to the keyboard, additional playing material will be needed at each level of difficulty. There are several ways in which this can be done. Examples can be drawn from different books, illuminating the same problem in different contexts. The teacher may also find it more suitable to construct the student's own book of teaching pieces, tailor-making the teaching program for the particular student. Another way to reinforce the learning of a specific concept is to have the student compose a piece incorporating the note or musical concept immediately following its introduction in the lesson. These pieces can be placed into a collection of the student's own works.* Additional interest can be created by having the students study and perform each other's compositions.

When selecting published material for the handicapped, the teacher

*This particular idea has been formalized in an experimental teaching program for elementary age (nonhandicapped) students and their parents, developed by Richard H. Kauffman, director of the Extension Program of The Cleveland Music School Settlement.

should do so with even more care than in selecting materials for other, often more capable, students. Frequently the page of music, made visually appealing by the use of pictures and combined with written instructions for the teacher, can prove distracting. Too much material within the student's visual field can interfere with the ability to focus on that which is most important to playing. If music is being written down for the student, a straightforward, uncluttered presentation of the music is probably best.

Selecting appropriate music for the older handicapped student presents a special problem for the instructor. It is important to keep in mind that although a person may be mentally retarded or physically handicapped, and does not perform academically, socially or musically at the same level as others that age, he or she has lived in this world for a given number of years. This student will very likely have musical preferences similar to those of most other people the same age.

Although the teaching approach may be the same as that used with a younger person with similar disabilities, the character of the materials will be different. Even in the very beginning stages, tunes with titles such as "Marching to the Zoo" might be renamed "Football March" or whatever seems appropriate to the individual's age and interests. The more advanced and older student with limited piano skills might be able to use some of the Richard Bradley popular music materials (Richard Bradley, *Second Pop Book*, Screen Gems, Columbia Publications) and duets arranged by Denes Agay (*Duet Recital*, vols. A and B, *Broadway Classics*, vols. A and B, Warner Bros. Publications.)

The use of teacher accompaniments to augment and enhance the student's playing is important in all stages of the teaching process. Not only can the playing of duets be fun, but the experience is one which enables the handicapped student to engage in an activity with someone. If the student's parents play an instrument, the teacher can arrange music which the parents and child can play together at home. In playing duets the student is able to share music and to perform as a partner. As many musicians will no doubt agree, playing duets can be a very exciting experience, since together the performers produce a musical response which neither party could accomplish alone.

Music therapists who often work with the severely handicapped are well versed in "instant duet" techniques. As the teacher plays a familiar tune based primarily on the I-IV-V chords, he or she calls out a harmonizing single note for the student to play. With a little creativity the teacher can discover any number of ways in which duet playing can take place as early as the very first lesson.

RHYTHMIC NOTATION

Teaching rhythmic notation can be approached apart from its direct application to playing piano. Because of the amount of concentration and coordination required to play correct notes *and* rhythm, it is probably unrealistic and unnecessary to require this of the student all at once. The handicapped person may be better able to integrate these skills after each has been learned separately, and are later interwoven as application is made gradually to playing piano.

The first step in teaching rhythmic notation is to teach the student to respond rhythmically without the complication of reading notation and making specific responses on the keyboard. Rhythmic-imitation games, in which the student is presented patterns of increasing difficulty to clap, can be effective teaching devices. To gain the student's attention in a follow-the-leader activity, the teacher may repeat the following rhyme:

> Listen, listen, you will see!
> Do what I do after me. Do this: ♩ ♩

The teacher claps two quarter notes and the student repeats the pattern. Other patterns of increasing difficulty can be introduced,

stopping as soon as the student begins to make errors, at which point there should be a return to simpler patterns.

This activity (also useful in developing the student's listening skills) can be made more fun by exchanging roles, permitting the student to execute rhythmic patterns for the teacher to imitate. Borrowing again from the Carl Orff approach, the teacher and student may engage in "rhythmic conversations" as a means of developing listening skills and practicing the steady performance of rhythmic patterns. Using a variety of simple rhythm instruments such as wood blocks, bongo drums and small tambourines (available in local music stores or from instrument supply catalogues) on which to produce the rhythm patterns can make the exercise even more interesting for the students.

The student may enjoy learning short, simple patterns (combining quarters, eighths, and rests) which are set to piano accompaniments performed by the teacher. If the student has difficulty maintaining a steady beat, the teacher may find it helpful to instruct the student to watch the movement of the teacher's left hand as the steady beat of the accompaniment is played with somewhat exaggerated movement.

To accompany the playing of a march or other tune in $\frac{4}{4}$ meter, the student can be instructed to clap hands or hit the drum on the quarter beat while counting aloud "One, one, one, one," or "One, two, three, four." Audible counting provides an additional cue which may be needed in order to maintain a steady rhythm.

Teaching the student to read rhythmic notation involves teaching the visual symbols used in written music to represent duration. A very simple approach begins with a single stem (|) which is identified as a "walk" and associated with one sound (a clap or a beat on a drum) made by the student. The double connected stem (⊓) is called "running" or "run, run" and is associated with two quick responses, performed first by the teacher and then imitated by the student. The quarter rest is performed by having the student "throw away the sound" with arms extended to each side and backwards. Once the student can correctly respond to notated patterns on nonmelodic instruments, a transfer can be made to the music played at the piano.

The teacher may find the system of counting all quarter notes as "one" and all half notes as "one-two" appropriate for some students. (This approach could easily be used with the Thompson method referred to previously.) Traditional counting ("one, two, three, four," "Ta, ti," etc.) may be introduced later if the student demonstrates an ability to understand and use these systems. The point to keep in mind is that a teacher's convictions as to how counting should be taught to the average student may have to give way to how it must be taught in order for the handicapped student to learn.

FINGERING

Fingering is introduced first by placing the fingers of the student's right hand over the keys C through G. As the fingers are positioned, the teacher touches the top of each finger in succession and asks the student to name the correct number of the finger being touched, and to depress the key. Later this process is repeated in random order, requiring more concentration from the student to respond correctly. At this point the student is directed to look at the fingering numbers placed underneath or above the notes of the pieces being played. As the student plays, the teacher continues to touch the correct finger until the student's attention to fingering improves.

Fingerings indicated in published materials must often be altered to accommodate the coordination difficulties of many handicapped students. The teacher will need to analyze the student's finger dexterity, determine the most suitable fingering sequence, and reinforce its consistent use.

Dependency on fingering and counts printed in the music can also present a problem. If overdone, the student will be inclined to play by the finger numbers placed next to the notes rather than being guided by the notes' location on the staff, thus inhibiting the acquisition of note-reading skills. The teacher may even decide that for some students it is best to remove all prescribed fingerings from the music. If reading notation is within the student's capability, the teacher will want to be certain that the student is actually reading notes, not just finger numbers.

Fingering exercises and games can be used to promote the learning of finger numbers. One very simple activity involves numbering each finger as the palms of the hands are placed together. The teacher and student then take turns calling out the number of the pair of fingers to be moved. The numbers are called more quickly and in random order as the student's recognition improves. Other keyboard games can be easily designed and practiced with the help of the parents at home.

On 3-by-5 index cards are drawn those notes which the student can read, with a finger number for each note indicated. (Duplicates of the notes may be made with different fingerings given.) One person chooses a card from the hand of the other player. If the person choosing the card can locate the correct key which corresponds to the note on the card, and can play it with the indicated finger, a point is earned. The first person continues to play in this manner until a turn is lost by incorrectly identifying a note or by playing the key with an incorrect finger. Another suggestion to develop correct fingering is to keep a count of the errors made in fingering a selected piece. On repeated playings the student tries to lower the count and thus improve the fingering record.

To develop independent use of the fingers, Edna Mae Burnam's *Dozen A Day Preparatory Book* (Willis Music Co.) can be quite useful. This collection of fun-to-play exercises can often be introduced to the student by rote, since the first exercises consist of patterns using the first five notes in the key of C. (Later, those students who learn to read notation can read the exercises for themselves.) Each exercise is introduced by a simple stick figure engaged in an activity suggested by the title of the piece. The book first presents material of only one line, then two and finally four lines or a full page as the level of difficulty is gradually increased.

For the very capable student, Denes Agay's *Fifteen Little Pieces on Five Note Patterns* (Boston Music Co.) can be used to focus the student's attention on keeping each finger over a specific key and decreasing unnecessary finger and arm movement. This collection of short pieces using the five fingers of both hands also familiarizes the student with various contemporary sounds.

A CLOSER LOOK AT TWO SPECIAL GROUPS

Frequently found among those studying with the private piano teacher are the *learning disabled* and the *visually handicappped*. The following sections acquaint the teacher with the symptoms and learning needs of these two groups. It is also suggested that the teacher's knowledge and understanding of these problem areas be increased through further research and study, and by consulting specialists such as psychologists, music therapists, and special educators. The references at the end of this chapter can serve as channels for initial orientation.

The Learning Disabled Student

According to the Association for Children with Learning Disabilities, the learning disabled are those children and adults who exhibit a disorder in one or more of the basic psychological processes involved in understanding or using spoken or written languages. Their disability may be expressed as a disorder of listening, thinking, talking, reading, writing, comprehension, speech, or mathematical computations. Discrepancies exist between the student's capability and achievement; the learning difficulties do not stem from retardation, emotional disturbance, physical handicaps, or visual or auditory impairments.

The term *learning disabled* applies to a very select group and should be reserved for those who have been professionally evaluated and diagnosed. The piano teacher may be alerted, however, to the possibility of a specific learning disorder by noticeable deviations from expected behavioral or social adjustment, deficiencies in motor and perceptual development, and discrepancies in academic performance.

Although a student with a specific learning problem will not evidence all possible symptoms of learning disabilities, the teacher should realize the many manifestations of this disorder. The learning-disabled student often has difficulty understanding written or verbal information, recording it, storing it for future use and retrieving it when the information is needed. Problems in perceiving similarities and differences may create difficulty in (1) discriminating between lines or between spaces (first-line E may be confused with second-line G in the treble clef, and first-space F with second-space A) and (2) identifying notes appropriate to the clef (first-line E in the treble clef may be confused with fifth-line A in the bass clef). The student may have trouble distinguishing between crescendo < and decrescendo > markings and in determining which hand is to be playing in each clef.

The student may have unusual difficulty distinguishing among sounds as well as among visual stimuli. He or she may not be able verbally to classify pitches as higher or lower, same or different, eighth or quarter, or melodic passages as having been played moderato or ritardando, although the student may be able to reproduce the pitches or passages. There may be difficulties with such concepts as high/low, loud/soft, fast/slow; remembering the directional relationship between a notated passage and the location of keys on the keyboard; and understanding the use of ledger lines (all ledger lines may look to the learning-disabled student like middle Cs). If conceptualization is poor, the child will probably have difficulty understanding explanations of "touch," "playing with feeling," or "phrasing." Problems with retention and the placing of events in proper sequence may result in difficulty remembering the order of notes for the lines and spaces or the order in which the sharps and flats occur. Memorizing music or listening and then repeating a rhythmic or melodic pattern may be a highly frustrating task.

The student may not approach a learning task in what the teacher would consider to be a logical, systematic manner. An initial approach to reading notation for simultaneous playing of both hands might be to play notes in the treble clef first and then those in the bass clef, not conceptualizing the fact that the two clefs make up the grand staff and are to be read and played together. Teaching this child to follow the movement of notes from left to right across the page and to observe the movement of notes between clefs (indicating alternate playing of hands) may require more than casually calling attention to the way in which it is to be done.

Incoordination may be observed as difficulty synchronizing the movement of the eyes with that of the hands in order to create smooth, legato playing. If independent finger action is inhibited, the precise execution of difficult rhythmic passages may be impossible, and the speed with which the student is expected to play a well-prepared piece will have to be modified.

Behaviorally, the learning-disabled student may appear unusually disorganized, and generally sensitive to criticism and to real or anticipated failures. On the other hand, the student may reveal little of himself or herself, choosing not to volunteer information and responding only when required to do so, and then only when certain that the response will be correct and accepted.

The student's learning problems may be further complicated by an inability to ignore extraneous stimuli, to concentrate when others are in the room or when sounds from other sources can be heard. The student may be unable to settle down and begin the lesson quickly, perhaps insisting on looking through all the pages of a book on the piano before beginning the lesson. Compulsive fascination with a particular irrelevant subject and an urge to repeat details of a relatively unimportant conversational matter are also manifestations of this problem.

The child with a learning disorder is often described as "immature," becoming easily excited and "silly" in situations which hardly faze other children. Because of social immaturities and lack of expertise in human relations, the student may be perceived by other children as naive, which impairs the development of new friendships.

The response of some students with a specific learning disability to traditional teaching methods may be excellent. Others may require only more time than their peers to learn. In certain cases, however, it will be necessary to alter the teaching approach and adapt materials as suggested previously.

The Visually Impaired Student*

There are many degrees of visual impairment. The most severely handicapped are those considered "legally blind," whose vision is 20/200 or poorer with correction in the better eye, or with a visual field of less than 20 degrees. Generally, visually handicapped students may be taught by the skilled piano teacher with only a few adaptations in standard teaching approach.

Orientation to the keyboard consists of teaching the student to locate groups of two and three black keys, with C to the left of two black keys. The student will respond quickly to this method, and identification by touch is, after all, the ultimate objective with all musicians. Because the blind student must rely on memorization of material, the teacher should include theory instruction from the very beginning.

*Summary of an article by Catherine D. Knoll, "Guidelines for Teaching Blind Students," *American Music Teacher* April–May 1978. Used by permission.

Depending on the degree of impairment, the student may learn music by reading Braille notation, large print or "bold notes," as well as from recorded instruction. (See Appendix 2 for agencies from which music and other materials can be obtained.) The Braille system requires the student to feel and read the symbols for notation with the fingers of one hand as he or she plays the piano with the other. Small sections of from one to four measures are memorized, and the teacher then instructs the student in playing each section until the whole is achieved. The teacher does not have to be proficient in reading Braille notation in order to coach the student who uses this system. With some study, the teacher can keep ahead, particularly with the beginning student. Phrasing, dynamics, and other technical markings can be recorded on tape for the student to use in conjunction with Braille notation. Care should be taken in regard to the amount of material assigned, since so much of it must be memorized. A balance must be maintained between challenging the student and keeping expectations between reasonable limits.

Some students cannot use Braille music because of a poor sense of touch, which may be the result of certain physical complications such as diabetes. Such students will need to rely heavily upon verbal dictation from a cassette tape. Music can be divided into numbered measures and dictated systematically, using special codes indicating fingering, octaves, rhythm, and other details. The following measure could be dictated as follows:

> Measure 5. Beat 1: Treble clef: quarter F1. Bass clef: dotted half, block chord, F2, A2, and C1. Beat 2: Treble clef: quarter A1. Beat 3: Treble clef: quarter C2.

Many students with partial vision will be able to read bold-print music, some of which is available through the Library of Congress and other publishers (see Appendix 2). The teacher and student can also recopy their own music on a large hand-drawn staff, using a dark marking pen on white paper.

Teaching rhythmic concepts to the blind student may require special attention because the student cannot see symbols and patterns in the printed music. The teacher will need to introduce the playing of simple, and later more complex, rhythmic patterns at the keyboard (also clapped or performed on rhythm instruments) with one and both hands.

The greatest hurdle which the sighted teacher must overcome in teaching the blind is discomfort in the presence of the visually handicapped. Once misconceptions and prejudices are eliminated, a rewarding and successful learning experience for both student and teacher can develop.

PARENTS

There are occasions when a student's learning problem is not identified by the parents. Experience instructing the student over a period of time, however, may lead the teacher to suspect a learning difficulty. The teacher will then want to discuss these observations with the parents and ask for their suggestions. Frequently instructional guidelines are available for students who have received a formal diagnostic evaluation by a qualified professional or who have been seen previously by a music therapist. If the parents are not aware of a learning problem, the teacher may suggest that the student be seen by a specialist who could provide further assistance. Regardless of whether a condition exists which inhibits learning, the subject is one which must be approached with great care, tact, and sensitivity. The teacher may in fact wish to obtain professional advice concerning how best to handle a discussion of this nature before meeting with the parents.

The degree to which the teacher involves parents in the teaching of the handicapped student must be judged on an individual basis. Factors influencing this decision include the student's age, ability to function independently, individual needs, feelings about the matter, and relationship with the parents.

If the student is to be given assistance at home, one or both parents should be coached during some part of the lesson as to what their responsibilities are to be and how they are to be carried out. On the other hand, if more independence is desired, then it is the student who must be coached during the lesson in how to practice effectively at home.

SUMMARY

It will strike the reader that certain instructional problems encountered in teaching the handicapped, and the approaches suggested, are in some ways similar to those of the normal teaching situation. It is true that some of the difficulties experienced by the handicapped student seem to differ only in degree from those of the average learner. There are many problems, however, which are more complicated and require special attention and handling. The sensitive and skillful teacher develops a sense of what can reasonably be expected of each individual as instruction progresses. Standards of achievement and performance are determined, but relative only to the particular student in question.

The individual with a handicap such as mental retardation may require frequent repetition in order to learn even simple concepts. The ability to generalize something learned in one situation or set of conditions may also be impaired. Additional time is needed to learn what to another would be an automatic transfer.

Consistency of approach is vital when teaching a person with any type of learning problem. If the instructor employs descriptive terms or special words to cue a response, these terms should be paired repeatedly with the response expected of the student. The simple direction "Check" may be used following the incorrect playing of a note to signal the student that an error was made and to look again at the given notation.

Preparing the handicapped student to play with both hands simultaneously can be facilitated by the use of simple verbal cues: "Check right" (find the note for the right hand), "Check left" (find the note for the left hand). Depending on the time signature, the following words spoken in rhythm signal the student to play on the first beat of the next measure.

	(1)	(2)			
$\frac{2}{4}$	one,	together |	(play)		
	(1)	(2)	(3)		
$\frac{3}{4}$	one,	two,	together |	(play)	
	(1)	(2)	(3)	(4)	
$\frac{4}{4}$	one,	two,	three,	together |	(play)

Simple, clear-cut statements help the student focus attention on the task while receiving the necessary assistance and instruction from the teacher.

Most of us will never fully understand what it means to have a desire to learn and yet to be hindered by a disability. As teachers, we are obligated to become sympathetic to the psychological and emotional strains experienced by the handicapped student engaged in the learning process. We must also be cognizant of the great physical demands made of the student who is learning to play a musical instrument.

Regardless of the degree to which learning or physical problems affect the student's performance, the following guidelines summarize a general approach to teaching the handicapped. (Some of these suggestions cannot be applied to the visually impaired.)

(1) Be supportive by always encouraging the student's best efforts. Avoid all sarcastic criticism.
(2) Make certain the student is listening when instructions are given.
(3) Keep verbal and written instructions concise and to the point.
(4) Present only the information or instruction needed at the time.
(5) Immediately follow the explanation of an important point with an opportunity for the student to demonstrate understanding through performance.
(6) Present difficult concepts or skills in small steps, each of which develops logically from the preceding one.
(7) Select piano materials carefully, considering factors such as the size of the staff, rate at which new concepts are introduced, and the amount of visual distraction on the page.
(8) Print written instructions clearly and have the student read back an assignment before leaving the lesson. Rely more on verbal instructions for the student who has difficulty reading and understanding written language.
(9) Be prepared for some inconsistencies in rate of learning and

memory. If difficulties continue, alter the teaching approach, change materials, or work in a different direction for a while.
(10) Observe in what part of the lesson the student is most alert to instruction. Concentrate on new material during this period.
(11) Establish realistic expectations for the student. Standards are extremely important, and they must be individualized.
(12) Design learning experiences which build on success, not failure.

The handicapped student requires a positive teacher who, with understanding and patience, can reinforce even the smallest of achievements. The special teacher who can do this and successfully guide the student's musical development can have a profound effect on the individual's feeling of competence, enjoyment of the arts, and total educational development.

APPENDIX 1: REFERENCES ON LEARNING DISABILITIES

National Association for Children with Learning Disabilities. 5225 Grace Street, Pittsburgh, Pennsylvania 15236.
National Association for Music Therapy, Inc., Central Office, Box 610, Lawrence, Kansas 66044.

RECOMMENDED READING

Brutton, M., C. Mangel, and S. Richardson. *Something's Wrong With My Child.* New York: Harcourt Brace, 1973.
Clark, L. *Can't Read, Can't Write, Can't Talk Too Good Either.* New York: Walker and Co., 1973.
Gilles, D. and V. Kovitz. "What To Do with the Learning Disabled." *Clavier* September 1973.
Shaftel, P. "The Piano Teacher as Psychotherapist." *Clavier* April 1977.
Steele, A.L. "Learning Disabilities: A Music Therapist's Perspective." In Zollinger and Klein, ed., *Learning Disabilities: An Interdisciplinary Perspective.* Cleveland, Ohio: Case Western Reserve University, 1975.

APPENDIX 2: REFERENCES ON THE VISUALLY IMPAIRED

Braille and Large-Print Music: Music Textbooks

Library of Congress, Music Section, Division for the Blind and Physically Handicapped, Washington, D.C. 20542.
American Printing House for the Blind, 1839 Frankfort Avenue, Louisville, Kentucky 40206.
Braille Book Bank, National Braille Association, 85 Godwin Avenue, Midland Park, New Jersey 07432.
Braille Services Guild, 2140 Westwood Boulevard, Los Angeles, California 90025.
Howe Press, Perkins School for the Blind, Watertown, Massachusetts

02172.

Illinois Braille and Sight Saving School, 658 East State Street, Jacksonville, Illinois 62650.

Johanna Bureau for the Blind and Visually Handicapped, Suite 540, 22 West Madison Street, Chicago, Illinois 60602.

J. Norton, Publishers, Listening Library, Inc., Park Avenue, Old Greenwich, Connecticut 06870.

Royal National Institute for the Blind, 224 Great Portland Street, London W1N 6AA, England.

Seminar Cassettes, Ltd., 218 Sussex Gardens, London W2 3UD, England.

Volunteer Services for the Blind, Inc., 919 Walnut Street, Philadelphia, Pennsylvania 19107.

General Resources

The Musical Mainstream. Free subscription from the Library of Congress, Music Section, Division for the Blind and Physically Handicapped, Washington, D.C. 20542.

Handbook for Teachers of the Visually Handicapped. Free copies from the Instructional Materials Reference Center, American Printing House for the Blind, 1839 Frankfort Avenue, Louisville, Kentucky 40206.

RECOMMENDED READING

Coates, Eyler Robert. "Teaching the Blind Musician." *The American Music Teacher* November–December 1976.

Eisenberg, Robert A. *Orientation and Mobility.* Los Angeles, Calif.: California State College, 1970.

Knoll, Catherine D. "Guidelines for Teaching Blind Students." *The American Music Teacher* April–May 1978.

Napier, Grace D. and Mel W. Weishaha. *Handbook for Teachers of the Visually Handicapped* (2nd ed.). Louisville, Ken.: American Printing House for the Blind, 1970.

Schut, A.L. *Anatomy and Physiology of the Human Eye.* Kalamazoo, Mich.: Western Michigan University, 1974.

Recitals

HAZEL GHAZARIAN SKAGGS

Student recitals in one form or another are integral parts of music education. They are convenient, welcome mileposts in the course of study and furnish periodic goals toward which the student can strive. They can provide added motivation for practice, transforming what might otherwise be considered a routine chore into a meaningful endeavor with an easily grasped, concrete purpose. Also since piano study is very much concerned with performance, recitals provide the audiences which are necessary for the total training of the student-performer. If the recital is properly planned and prepared for, it can be a friendly, satisfying public acknowledgement of the student's efforts. In its more formal manifestations it also can be an important event for the youngster, similar to a graduation or confirmation.

Depending on the number of students involved, their overall ages, grade levels and capabilities, local circumstances and facilities, and numerous other pedagogic, social, and economic factors that teachers must carefully weigh, the recital may range from an entirely informal one in the teacher's studio to a formal event in a public place. The tendency today is toward the more informal approach: two or three semipublic performances during the school year, attended by family and friends.

PROGRAM SELECTION

Selecting the right piece may mean the difference between success and frustration. First it should be ascertained that the student likes the work. It may be a good idea to give the student the opportunity to make the final choice from among two or three selections. Furthermore, while the work should properly and appealingly represent the youngster's ability and achievement, by no means should it tax to the limit technical and musical capabilities. As the piece will be performed under some degree of tension, the teacher must make sure that the student will be able to give a creditable performance with somewhat less than 100 percent concentration. The student's age will have much to do not only with the piece's grade level and length, but also its character and title. Compositions depicting activities and emotions of the very young child ("My Dolly's Birthday" or "Lollipops on Parade") will not appeal to older students and may offend their sensibilities. Finally a recital solo does not have to be a masterpiece; it can be in a somewhat lighter vein, although never cheap or hackneyed.

Selecting pieces for a recital might be organized in such a way as to play a significant role in the student's musical training. The event may stress the music of today's composers and their different styles of expression; an all-American program may focus attention on the musical culture of the United States; and a complete program of piano ensemble may stimulate the formation of piano teams.

A teacher may add further musical interest to the program by inviting a guest singer or instrumentalist. Also, the teacher who is a concert pianist may provide the final virtuoso number.

PREPARATION

Ideally, the learning of the recital piece should take place within the daily alloted time for practicing, without additional claim on the youngster's time and attention; neither should the preparation for a recital interfere with the normal course of study. When the music is chosen, the teacher should first discuss with the student the composition as a whole, so that its style, form, phrasing, structure, and underlying mood are understood. Next, such technical matters as fingering, dynamics, and touch can be clarified. If certain technical hurdles persist and are not eliminated within a reasonably short time, the work is obviously not within the student's scope of technique and should be replaced without delay. At no time should the formality and seriousness of the event put such strain on the student and teacher that lessons become filled with tension and anxiety. Repetitive drill-like practice month after month can drive even the most musical child away from piano study.

When lessons begin, the student's sole audience is the teacher (plus other class members if there are group lessons). At home, the family comprises the audience. Later, when the recital class or recital-class party (made up of about eight to twenty students) is introduced, the immediate objective to perform before their peers stimulates the students to more careful and extended practice, and provides the first realization that playing before an audience requires not only careful preparation but experience.

The recital class generally leads to the studio recital, further stimulating the incentive to work, not because of an increase in the number of listeners, but because the audience includes parents. Depending on space, the studio recital audience may be as small as that of a recital class or as large and diversified as that of a small public recital.

The public recital, the apex of all these activities, generally includes all or some of the students of one teacher, and provides the larger audience of family, friends, and outsiders. Now the incentive to perfect skills becomes even greater. Public recitals by teachers' organizations, community groups, and music clubs create still greater audiences for the students. A gifted student capable of playing a complete recital program may be presented by the teacher either at the studio or in a public auditorium. Often several such students are invited to share a program.

RECITAL CLASS

The least formal of public performances is the recital class. It may be attended by eight to twenty students and is very much like a lesson; therefore, the music performed may still be in preparation. Often students are asked to listen critically to each other in order to offer constructive criticism. Some teachers also include such activities as sight reading, keyboard harmony, and improvisation. The teacher who gives public recitals utilizes the recital class as a rehearsal for the "big event." In this case the class might be more formal and include the practice of stage deportment. Classes may be organized according to age or grade levels. When the classes are by age, the grade levels may be mixed, since one ten-year-old may be a beginner while another ten-year-old may be intermediate. In group or class piano, such gatherings are organized by inviting two or more compatible groups.

These recital classes may meet as often as once a month. Teachers of private lessons may regularly schedule these classes in order to make available the socialization and group dynamics that are lacking in solitary study. On the other hand, group teachers offer the recital class as an extra bonus lesson that gives the children an opportunity to play for other members of the studio.

The recital class party is yet another form of the recital class, but added to it are the party features: refreshments of soda, cookies, cake, or ice cream. Often teachers schedule these at festive times, such as Halloween and Christmas. Then the theme of the holiday is carried out in the selection of repertory. Decorations and costumes may be added features. The fun aspect of recital parties helps make performance a happy as well as a worthwhile pastime.

A teacher who is seriously dedicated to giving the student a complete musical education through the piano might give a demonstration instead of a recital. A demonstration is very much like a recital class except that it may take place in a public auditorium. On such a program students may improvise, play some jazz, rock, or even their own arrangements of popular songs, take scale, transposition, or sight-reading tests, perform recital repertory, and whatever else they might be working on at the studio. The students may select those activities in which they excel. Therefore every child can shine, not just the performer. If no extra preparation is involved, the demonstration is a snapshot of the studio at work and provides essentially what the parent whose child attends is interested in seeing and hearing.

The recital class turns into a studio recital when parents and possibly others are invited. It may be as informal and instructive as the recital class or it may be similar to a demonstration or public recital.

PUBLIC RECITAL

In the past, a teacher's merit was judged by the quality and grade level of the music performed by the students in the final year-end recital, and as a result, teachers were overly anxious in the preparation and presentation of their programs. Since some teachers wanted to or were expected to transform average youngsters into junior concert pianists, pieces for the event were sometimes assigned as early as the first lesson of the season. These recitals always began with the youngest and least experienced, and progressed toward the star pupils. These star pupils played the same impressive war-horses year after year to prove that they were gifted and their teachers were competent enough to train them in virtuoso performance. Usually the programs lasted several hours.

Now that the emphasis is likely to be on enjoying music rather than on training concert pianists, the year-end recital serves a more realistic purpose. It is given not only as a showcase of what has been achieved during the season but also for the pleasure of both students and parents. Students, particularly elementary ones, enjoy recitals. A change of attitude has definitely lessened or even obliterated the trauma of public performance. The recital, although important and purposeful, is a fun event; no one is forced to participate, no one is forced to play a piece of the teacher's choice, and no one is forced to play from memory when it is inadvisable. For the pleasure of the parents, programs are kept shorter—about one hour (two one-hour recitals may be scheduled on the same evening instead of one long recital). The students play the kind of music that they and the parents enjoy, and the musical selections are kept as interesting as possible. If followed by a reception, the recital becomes a social event where parents meet each other and, in the case of group piano, their children's classmates.

The ideal recital brings a sense of achievement for the child, satisfaction for the parent, and added insight for the teacher. It may be given in the studio, a private home, public auditorium, or recital hall. When held outside the studio, it is best to have a rehearsal at the recital place a few days (or up to two weeks) before the event. Ideally, training for the public recital might begin in the recital class, followed by studio recitals. If either or both of these steps is omitted, more effort and time for the necessary recital training must be given at the lesson and the prerecital rehearsal.

Training for recitals often includes the study of stage deportment—correct behavior on stage. Generally, the performer approaches the piano from the front of the instrument, sits down with hands on lap, and doesn't begin to play until the feet are positioned over the proper pedals. When finished, the student returns hands to lap, takes a step forward from the piano, bows in acknowledgement of the applause, and finally returns backstage.

For some students, bowing is an ordeal that they refuse to endure. If correct stage deportment is to be insisted upon, the training had best begin early in the season. Then it may become a natural and easy procedure.

Instead of keeping their students backstage, some teachers prefer to have them sit on stage or in the first few rows of the auditorium. Then students may not only listen and learn from the performance of the others, but be inspired by those who play exceptionally. With this kind of seating arrangement, the recital will be less formal and the students may feel more relaxed.

SPECIAL RECITALS

Holiday programs, when carefully planned, can add another dimension to recitals. The first holiday of the season, Halloween, offers the opportunity for youngsters to come in costume. Even without costumes, spooky Halloween repertory such as "Witches' Dance," "Haunted House," a few recitations of Halloween verse, and Halloween refreshments may well lessen and even banish the usual recital tension children experience. And Halloween, which comes early in the fall, provides the impetus for a recital at a time when both student and teacher are free of the pressures that accumulate during the school year.

The Christmas recital might include carol playing and singing, pieces about Christmas presents, and appropriate poems to read. Valentine's Day, St. Patrick's Day, and Thanksgiving can all inspire unique programs. Skits or story recitals may be written about these holidays, or the students may pick serious themes such as the evolution of the piano or music around the world. The titles of the pieces, combined with the narration, tell the story. Some teachers use fairy tales; Cinderella, Jack and the Beanstalk, and many others are available with music and words. Piano arrangements of such suites as "Nutcracker" and "Peer Gynt" also make attractive story presentations for recitals.

Minirecitals—a series of short recitals, each lasting from five to twenty minutes, and performed by one student—might be considered by the teacher whose pupils have extensive repertoires. Friends and parents can be notified as to the approximate time of each recital so that no one need stay two or three hours listening to performers in which one has no interest.

Another way to reduce the length of recitals is to schedule a test recital. Students come prepared with their entire list of pieces but play only one, which is determined by chance.

Often a teacher's choice of the type and place of recital depends on the available funds. Community auditoriums, such as those in schools and libraries, may be used without charge or at a nominal rental fee or voluntary donation. With today's low-cost reproduction of typed sheets, the expenditure for programs may also be kept at a minimum, so that the total recital expense may well be below what the teacher earns in one day.

A lavish formal recital, on the other hand, with printed programs, tuning of piano or pianos, flowers, ushers, and other extras may well run the bill up to and even beyond the teacher's weekly income. If it is important to the students and teacher to have such a program, the teacher and students may sell tickets or the parents may pay a recital fee that will in turn entitle them to a fixed number of tickets.

GENERAL SUGGESTIONS

The following are suggestions for the student to observe for a successful recital performance:

- The student must realize that preparation for a successful performance begins from the moment the new music is introduced. If the preparation is adequate, tension will be at a minimum.
- The music to be performed must be tried out before family, friends, the studio class, and whoever is willing to listen in order for the student to play it confidently at the recital. It takes experience to play before an audience.
- The student had best not play the recital work just before the program. If the playing does not go well, it may create such anxiety as to mar the actual performance.
- Instead of going over recital pieces as a last minute warm-up, the student should do scales, arpeggios, exercises, or sight reading. (Chopin used to practice Bach on the day of his recitals.)
- If the student feels nervous when about to play, a deep breath or two, with a moment of waiting, may help.
- In case of an error (wrong note, faulty rhythm, etc.) the playing should proceed as if nothing had happened. Repeating, correcting, interrrupting the flow of music would just accentuate the error. In case of a memory lapse, the student should keep going, even if it means improvising, repeating, or jumping ahead.

Some suggestions for the teacher:

- When assigning a recital piece, the teacher might stress the importance of careful preparation and study. Mistakes in notes, fingering, or rhythm must be corrected immediately to avoid becoming accustomed to faulty playing.
- At the prerecital lesson, the teacher should try to be encouraging and only stress the importance of playing expressively.
- Both at the last lesson and the rehearsal, the teacher should avoid making suggestions about substantial points which are difficult to

carry out or correct in time for the performance. This would only add to the student's anxiety.

- If poor memory persists, the teacher may encourage the student to use the music copy at the recital. (Dame Myra Hess may be cited; she knew her music by memory, yet preferred it in front of her).
- The teacher's calm, confident behavior at the rehearsal and recital will help the students feel more at ease.

CONCLUSION

The advantages of a recital are many. For the teacher it provides an occasion for reassessing pedagogical skills; for the student, an incentive to practice and build a repertory; for the parent, an opportunity to observe the child's progress. Any performance before an audience develops the student's poise, confidence, and appropriate recital behavior, and (it is hoped) be an inspiration to continue musical studies with renewed interest and vigor.

RECOMMENDED READING

Baird, Peggy Flanagan. "Accent on Fun–Not Fear." *Clavier* September 1974.

Chronister, Richard. "Recitals: When Can I Play?" *Keyboard Arts* Spring 1975.

Edwards, Ruth. "Piano Party." *Clavier* November–December 1964.

Erdmann, Hazel. "Recital Games." *The Piano Teacher* March–April 1964.

Farrar, Ruth Price. "New Formats for Interest." *Clavier* May–June 1964.

Gloyne, Howard F. "Butterflies in the Stomach." *The Piano Teacher* November–December 1965.

Martin, Anna Y. "Concomitants of Stage Fright." *Music Educators Journal* January 1964.

McCloskey, Helen. "Recital Skits." *The Piano Teacher* March–April 1964.

Ottenheimer, Ruth F. "Mini-Recitals." *The Piano Quarterly* Summer 1975.

FOUR

SURVEY OF STYLES AND IDIOMS

Styles in Composition and Performance

DENES AGAY

Numerous definitions exist that try to pin down the essence of style in music. While this elusive concept can be explained, to a degree, by objective facts and data, the ultimate insight into its nature can come only through a thorough understanding of, and instinctive identification with, the music at hand. For an actor to play Hamlet convincingly it is necessary not only for him to be familiar with Shakespeare's language and with Elizabethan theater, but, in fact, to *become* Hamlet on the stage. Similarly, a pianist performing Mozart must assume a Mozartean stance, with all the mental, emotional, and physical preparations and preconditions such an attitude implies.

For the purposes of this essay—to furnish the piano teacher with a pedagogically feasible and practical starting point—we define *style* here as the collective characteristic traits of musical works in reference to a certain period or a certain composer. In this sense we may speak of baroque or romantic style, Mozart or Chopin style, and so on. The term *style* can also be applied to a manner of rendition which adheres to musicologically proven performance practices of an era, such as a stylistic Bach, Mendelssohn, or Bartók performance.

In the literature of keyboard works we usually distinguish four major periods and corresponding styles: *baroque* (from about 1600 to 1750), *classical* (about 1750 to 1820), *romantic* (from about 1820 to 1900), and *contemporary* (the twentieth century). It should be noted immediately that the division of music history into these four periods is rather tentative and flexible, entailing a great deal of chronological and idiomatic overlapping. The works of Bach's sons, for instance, may be catalogued as either late baroque or early classical. Sibelius, Rachmaninoff, and Richard Strauss are twentieth century writers with unmistakably romantic traits. Also, within the four large eras and often transcending their boundaries, there are many stylistic subdivisions, according to regional traits (German, French, Italian baroque, for instance), individual creative characteristics (late Beethoven, Chopin, Satie, Ives, etc.), or compositional techniques (polyphony, modality, impressionism, etc.).

The piano student's stylistic education is a long and continuous process. It should begin as early as possible, certainly as soon as the simplest little pieces of the masters become negotiable. A little two-voice baroque minuet or a simple German dance by Haydn can well illustrate polyphony and homophony, respectively. They can also furnish attractive examples of elementary two- and three-part song forms. Brief biographies of the composers help to put them and their works into an historical and stylistic perspective, or at least into a chronological time-frame even the very young can understand. (For instance: Mozart lived 200 years ago, was a contemporary of Washington, Jefferson, and Franklin; he began to compose and give recitals at the age of five; he played on pianos which were smaller and lighter in weight and tone than today's; his compositions usually consist of melody in the right hand and accompaniment in the left; he wrote not only piano pieces, but also symphonies, chamber music, operas, etc.) Characteristic features of various forms, textures, and compositional techniques, as well as conventions in the performance practices of various eras, should be pointed out to the student gradually, parallel with the growing capacity to play, understand, and enjoy a progressively planned curriculum from all segments of keyboard literature.

The following four sections present synopses of each period's most important style elements, to serve as a guide and checklist for imparting this information to the student.

THE BAROQUE PERIOD (An Amazing Age of Limitless Variety)

The first flowering of keyboard literature occurred during the baroque period. The astonishingly varied creative output of this era is in many respects the fertile soil from which the forms, tonal organizations, and modes of expression of subsequent periods grew. The pedagogic implications of this fact are extremely important. A piano student's musical growth and technical training are unimaginable without considerable reliance on the music of this era.

The Instruments

Baroque keyboard works were not written for the piano, but for a variety of other instruments: the harpsichord, clavichord, virginal, and organ. Every opportunity should be seized by the teacher to demonstrate these instruments (especially the first two) to the student; a description of them, including their characteristic sonorities, can be found on pages 339-41. Acquainting the student with the harpsichord and clavichord should by no means, however, implant the idea that it is wrong or unstylistic to perform baroque works on the modern piano. This pedantic notion, which had many adherents during the past few rigidly authenticity-conscious decades, is fortunately giving way to a less stilted and less narrow view. To adopt a reasonable and proper approach to this problem, one should keep in mind that baroque composers were not particularly instrument-conscious in the modern sense. Bach, especially, did not conceive a work for one specific instrument exclusively (a trait, incidentally, which was largely shared by Mozart). Consider Bach's many transcriptions from one instrument to another, or the almost complete lack of stated preference whether a piece should be performed on the harpsichord or clavichord.

The piano, properly handled, is a most appropriate vehicle for the realization of baroque ideas. Obviously its full sonorities and expressive capabilities do not have to be, and should not be, unleashed when playing this music, but neither do they have to be constrained to the point of merely imitating the baroque instruments. The best advice is "to preserve in a piano performance all the esthetic qualities of the harpsichord that we can: brilliance, sudden dramatic changes of dynamic level and color, above all its clarity. But beyond this there is no need to perpetuate its limitations, particularly its inability to shade or to produce a prolongued crescendo. (These disadvantages irked Couperin, and to assume that Bach was less musically sensitive is ridiculous.)"* The clavichord, of course, was capable of shadings within its modest range of dynamics and can serve as an inspiration, but not as a model, for today's pianists when performing eighteenth century works of gentle and subtle character.

Forms and Textures

The texture of baroque music is predominantly polyphonic and rich in imitative counterpoint. The most frequently occurring forms are the fugue, fantasy, toccata, suite (of dances), variations (chaconne, passacaglia, ground) and numerous other smaller forms such as inventions, preludes, and cappriccios (brief descriptions of these forms may be found on page 183-87).

To introduce the student to the baroque world, it is best to start with little dance pieces in slow or moderate tempo, such as the minuet, gavotte, polonaise, or sarabande, with simple two-voice textures and minimal ornamentation. The source of such pieces should not be restricted to the few well-known selections culled from Bach's *Little Notebook for Anna Magdalena Bach*, as is too often the case. Baroque masters, including some of the lesser-known ones, created many small keyboard works which are utterly melodic, simple in structure, easier than the Bach Inventions, and as such are ideally suitable preparatory

*Louis L. Crowder "The Baroque Period" (introductory article to *An Anthology of Piano Music*, Denes Agay, ed. Yorktown Music Press).

studies for polyphonic play and a delightful introduction to baroque keyboard music in general. A common mistake is to confront the student with Bach's Two-part Inventions too early. These unique little masterpieces, which demand secure technical control and quite mature musical understanding, belong in every serious student's repertory, but should be assigned only at the proper time, after adequate preparation. A progressive repertory of charming and still largely neglected preparatory materials can well be assembled from folios listed at the end of this chapter.

Harmonic concepts in prebaroque periods, especially during the Renaissance, were predominantly based on the church modes (Dorian, Phrygian, Lydian, and Mixolydian). Baroque masters developed the major and minor scales and through them a rich harmonic vocabulary which was to dominate compositional styles for at least a century and a half. The theoretical principles of this harmonic system were so clearly defined and organized (by Rameau and others) that a bass part alone, with certain appropriate figures above or beneath it, was sufficient notation from which to reconstruct and play a complete four-voice harmonic texture. This stenographic manner of keyboard notation, a continuous figured bass running throughout the composition, called *thorough bass* or *basso continuo*, was so widely used during the baroque that the era is often referred to as the "thoroughbass period." From the figured bass the player was able not only to fill in the correct harmonies in an improvisatory manner, but also to execute patterns of accompaniment which fit the composition's mood and character. This ability, rather rare today, gives evidence of the baroque performer's secure musicianship and also explains the wide interpretative leeways and freedoms enjoyed.

Performance Practices

Baroque masters did not notate their works in complete detail. Even when committing to paper all notes to be played, they left many aspects of execution, including tempo, dynamics, and phrasing, to the performer's discretion. This wide choice of options available to the seventeenth- and eighteenth-century performer is one of the essential facts to keep in mind when playing a baroque *Urtext*. It is especially important today, when the search for and insistence on stylistic authenticity in editions and performance practices has often been exaggerated to the point of obsessive rigidity, putting inhibiting pressures on teachers and performers alike. All objective data and historical facts confirm that a stifling of interpretative freedom and initiative is in sharp contrast to baroque principles and to the composer's original intent.

Before applying this privilege (and responsibility) of choices, today's performer must, of course, become familiar with the basic stylistic conventions of the period. This, however, is not such an awesome task as some overzealous purists would make it appear. One does not need a degree in musicology to grasp the more important fundamental principles of baroque performance and thereby relax and enjoy the great variety, depth, and vigor of this music. As a first step the following essential guidelines should be kept in mind:

Tempo: Generally steady, with a pronounced metric pulse. Excessive speeds should be avoided. Retards in concluding measures can be taken for granted. (See also "Tempo," p. 29).

Dynamics: The range is between ***p*** and ***f***; extreme contrasts (***pp*** – ***ff***) are unidiomatic. As a rule a dynamic level should be maintained for at least a phrase or phrase-section (terrace dynamics), although slight shadings (*cresc.*, *dim.*) within these form units are also feasible, if applied occasionally and with moderation.

Touch and Articulation: Legato, non legato, and *staccato* are all acceptable if applied knowingly within a consistent articulation scheme. Observe, for instance, the various possibilities of articulating the following excerpt:

Froberger: Canzon

Any of the following three articulation patterns is possible, if applied consistently to *all* appearances of the theme:

A. An even non legato, as notated above.

B. All eighth notes staccato, sixteenth notes slurred:

C. A somewhat refined variant of version B:

Pedal: Should be used very sparingly, mostly in "short touches," or not at all.

Ornaments: Familiarity with the proper execution of basic symbols is essential. Equally important is the realization that all tables of ornamentation, even the most authoritative ones, are only guidelines, and the final shaping of an embellishment properly belongs in the performer's domain. This means that certain liberties can be taken, which, if done with taste and moderation, will not violate baroque performance practices. Ornaments should always be performed lightly, gracefully, in a quasi-improvisatory manner; never should they sound heavy or clumsy. It is preferable to alter, simplify, or omit a certain ornament than to let it become a hurdle in the path of an otherwise smooth and pleasing performance. (See "Ornamentation," p. 123).

Expression: This is the lifeblood of musical interpretation and it applies to baroque music as well as to music of any other period. The student should learn early that a steady tempo and polyphonic textures are not incompatible with expressiveness. Romantic sentimentality is, of course, out of the question, but noble eloquence, deep feeling, and even passion are not. It can be very helpful and inspiring for the student to hear the teacher play a few simple selections illustrating the rich emotional content and vitality of baroque music. It should be conveyed to the pupil at the earliest possible stage that these works are not cold museum pieces, not dusty examples of a great but archaic art, but *living* music, as valid, inspiring, and diverting today as they were two to three centuries ago.

RECOMMENDED READING

Bodky, Erwin. *The Interpretation of Bach's Keyboard Works*. Cambridge: Harvard University Press, 1960.

Bukofzer, Manfred. *Music in the Baroque Era*. New York: W.W. Norton, 1947.

Dart, Thurston. *The Interpretation of Music*. New York: Harper & Row, 1963.

Dolmetsch, Arnold. *The Interpretation of the Music of the Seventeenth and Eighteenth Centuries*. London: Oxford University Press, 1915. (More recent paperback reprints are available in the U.S.)

Donnington, Robert. *A Performer's Guide to Baroque Music*. New York: Scribner's, 1973.

RECOMMENDED COLLECTIONS

The following list of pertinent collections can provide an ample source of appealing and, in many cases, rather rarely encountered introductory materials on the easy-to-intermediate levels:

"The Baroque Period." *An Anthology of Piano Music*, vol. I (Agay, ed.). Yorktown.
The Joy of Baroque (Agay). Yorktown.
Introduction to the Study of Bach, vol. I (Mirovitch). Schirmer.
Early Keyboard Music, vol. 2 (Ferguson). Oxford.
German Masters of the Seventeenth and Eighteenth Centuries. Kalmus.
Airs and Dances, vol. 2 (Dorolle). Boosey & Hawkes.
Anson Introduces Handel, Book 1. Willis.
First Scarlatti (Kreutzer). Boston.
Telemann: *Three Dozen Klavier Fantasias* (Seiffert). Bärenreiter.
Telemann: *Little Klavier Book* (Irmer). Schott.
Purcell: *Pieces for Klavier or Harpsichord* (Hilleman). Schott.
C.P.E. Bach: *Piano Pieces* (Luithlen-Kraus). Universal.

THE CLASSICAL PERIOD (Golden Age of the Sonata)

Within the relatively short span of hardly more than half a century (approximately between 1760 and 1820) a magnificent literature of music was produced which in simplicity, serenity, and perfect balance of form and content has remained unsurpassed. The period is also noteworthy on numerous other accounts. It is the time when the pianoforte replaced the harpsichord as the most popular keyboard instrument, an event which had far-reaching implications on successive compositional styles, sonorities, techniques of interpretation, and pedagogy. Also, this is the age of the first solo recitals, the first traveling virtuosos, the appearance of the first piano methods and teaching publications by Türk, Dussek, Hummel, and others. Most important, this is the era in which the sonata, that supreme configuration of musical architecture, was perfected by the three great protagonists of the era: Haydn, Mozart, and Beethoven.

What is the importance of the sonata in musical education? During the past two centuries an overwhelming portion of great music was written in this form, which includes not only solo sonatas, but also string quartets, trios, and symphonies, all of which are sonatas conceived for various instrumental combinations. Familiarity with this form is thus essential for all students and practitioners of music.

Of course, the study of forms should not start with the sonata, but with the component form elements: motive, phrase, sentence, and the small song forms (binary, ternary). Music of the classical period is ideally suited for all phases of form analysis, because of its compact clarity, symmetry, and uncluttered texture. On the earliest grade levels, the charming German dances, minuets, contredanses, and ecossaises of the masters, which illustrate with textbook clarity all constructional features, can be used for this purpose, preparatory to the study of sonatas.

The Sonata

The word *sonata* comes from the Italian *sonare* "to sound." Originally, during the sixteenth and seventeenth centuries it meant merely a *sound piece*, a musical thought sounded on one or more instruments. It was first applied to a keyboard solo by Kuhnau (1696). As developed and crystallized by the classical masters, the sonata, as a musical form, is the first section of a work usually consisting of three or four movements. This form, often referred to as *sonata-allegro* form or *first-movement* form, is essentially a simple ABA patterned structure (exposition–development–recapitulation) which the mind grasps easily and which, at the same time, is sturdy and elastic enough to be the repository of an infinite variety of musical inventions and manipulations. This form concept has acquired tremendous significance in the organization of musical thoughts ever since.

To create an extended work, the baroque composer had to depend on stringing together small sections of various tempos, rhythmic characters, and textures as in the dance suites, partitas, toccatas, and fantasies. The sonata form enabled composers of subsequent periods to convey ideas of larger dimensions within a thematically constructed unified scheme. The typical sonata form comprises the following elements:

EXPOSITION				DEVELOPMENT	RECAPITULATION				CODA
First Theme or Theme Group	Transition	Second Theme or Theme Group	Closing Theme (optional)	Expands or manipulates Themes or Theme fragments of the Exposition	First Theme or Theme Group	Transition	Second Theme or Theme Group	Closing Theme	Concluding section of varying lengths
KEY: Tonic	Modulatory	Dominant or Related Key		Various Keys	Tonic				Tonic

The *sonatina* "little sonata" is usually shorter and easier to perform than the sonata, and does not always contain all components of the sonata form. The closing theme of the exposition is often missing and instead of a development section there is just a brief modulatory transition leading to the recapitulation. Sonatinas were and are often written for instructional purposes. They are marked by simplicity and clarity of design and, in most cases, make rather moderate demands on technical facility. For these reasons they are excellent preparatory materials for the exploration of the sonata literature.

It should be noted that many excellent sonatas and sonatinas written before the end of the eighteenth century represent this form in a transitional stage, not fully developed in its classical sense. Many of these charming and useful works by Benda, Hassler, Cimarosa, and others, are constructed in two- or three-part song forms. To view the sonata form in its fully developed stage, but still within the early-to-intermediate levels of difficulty, the Clementi Sonatinas (opus 36) and the easiest Mozart and Beethoven Sonatas are recommended. The middle section of a three-movement sonata or sonatina is usually a melodic *andante* or *adagio*, constructed in an extended song form. Another movement, preceding or following the slow section, is usually a *minuet* or *scherzo*, both dance forms.

The sonata's last movement is, in most cases, a *rondo*. This form is of French origin, often employed by the *clavecinists* (Couperin, Rameau, and others). It has an ABACA pattern, where A represents the main theme, and B and C the episodes (couplets). A more developed classical rondo pattern is ABACABA. Here the sections are not set apart but follow in a smooth, uninterrupted sequence with the proper transitional materials between the themes. In some cases the middle episode (C) is replaced by a development section, which brings the construction quite close to the sonata form. Examine the last movements of Haydn's Sonata in D major Hob. XVI:37 (pattern ABACA) and Mozart's Sonata in C major K. 545 (pattern ABACA coda where episode C is a development section). The rondo movements of most Clementi and Kuhlau sonatinas are also ideal subjects for analyses.

Performance Practices

From about the middle of the eighteenth century composers began to notate their works in ever-increasing detail; indications of tempo, dynamics, and articulation appear with some measure of regularity. However, by no means are all particulars spelled out consistently, and so the performer is still quite often left to his or her own resources. Of course, the leeway is not as wide and the options not as numerous as in performing baroque music, but still, whatever choices are made and decisions arrived at must be based on sound musical and stylistic judgment. Toward that end the following guidelines are helpful.

Tempo: Within a section, the pace is generally uniform and steady, but without the constant, firm, and unyielding metric pulse underlying much baroque music. In the classics the natural accents of the bar are not pronounced, only hinted at; the forward momentum is airier and lighter, propelled and shaped by the component form elements (motives, phrases). Given tempo marks should be adhered to, but in some instances, slightly adjusted toward moderation at both tempo extremes; not extremely slow and not excessively fast should be the motto. A presto indication by Clementi, for instance, can safely be taken at an allegro pace. Also tempo modifications (rit., accel., a tempo) are not always marked and should be employed at the player's discretion. Just before the entrance of the second theme in a sonata, for instance, it is often natural and desirable to relax the pace slightly. Mood contrasts in a set of variations also may frequently call for minor adjustments of tempo. A delicate rubato, of the kind where the melody sings out with a certain freedom against the strictly maintained pulse of the accompaniment (*melodic rubato*), is also at the player's option.

Touches and Articulation: In the absence of other indications, the "normal" keyboard touch is *non legato* at least until Beethoven's middle period, when, probably under the influence of Clementi, the "legato as a rule" trend became predominant.

Legato slurs, *staccato*, and *tenuto* signs appear with increased frequency in the music of the classics, but cannot at all times be accepted at their face value, because of frequent inconsistencies and certain idiomatic notation habits which differ from modern usage. For instance, the three staccato marks of Haydn and Mozart—the stroke ❙ , the wedge ▼ , and the dot • —had nearly identical meanings as far as we can judge today. Certainly, the wedge was not yet the mark of a sharp staccato (*staccatissimo*) which it became during the early nineteenth century, when the dot came to be the normal staccato sign. Whatever marginal differences there may be between the true meanings of these signs as the classics used them will have to be decided by the performer on the basis of musical clues, such as tempos, articulation patterns, and dynamic contexts. Within an adagio movement, for instance, staccato should not be as short and crisp as it can be in a fast tempo. Note values will also influence the character and sharpness of a particular staccato. Obviously, the dots over the quarter notes in the following example call for a shorter sound than the ones over the half notes.

Beethoven: Sonata no. 8, op. 13
("Pathetique")

The placing of slurs is also quite strange and ambiguous in the classical literature. Only rarely does a slur cover a complete two- or four-measure phrase; rather it is drawn from bar line to bar line, as in the following excerpt:

Mozart: Sonata, K. 570

The above notation notwithstanding, a bar-to-bar articulation would be misplaced here; the phrase should be performed as if indicated by a single unbroken slur extending from the first note to the downbeat of measure four. This, indeed, is the manner in which Mozart notated the theme in several subsequent repetitions.

When slurs connecting small note groups are meant to denote a certain touch, stress, or articulation within the phrase, the indications are usually valid and should be strictly observed:

Haydn: Sonata, Hob. XVI:37

Ornamentation: In this era ornamentation is not as rich as during the baroque. Many compound ornaments disappeared or became simplified; composers increasingly wrote out trills, appoggiaturas, and turns in full notation. Certain ambiguities, however, remain and must be resolved in performance. The trill, for instance, still starts on the upper auxiliary note, in theory at least, but there are many exceptions; each case must be decided on the basis of its technical and expressive context. By the time of Schubert, trills generally began on the main note. A specific symbol often used by Haydn should also be clarified here. The sign should be performed as a turn and not as a mordent.

Expression–Pedal: Behind a disarmingly simple facade, the music of classicism offers a wealth of variety, vitality, and subtle emotions. This should be expressed through sensitive, graceful articulation, within a framework of steady but not rigid tempo. The dynamic range should not be excessive and the contrasts not overdramatic.

The use of pedal is at the performer's discretion, as Haydn and Mozart did not indicate it and Beethoven did so only erratically. To preserve the clarity of melodic lines and harmonic sequences, pedaling should be judicious and restrained at all times.

RECOMMENDED READING

Badura-Skoda, Eva and Paul. *Interpreting Mozart on the Keyboard.* New York: St. Martin's press, 1957.

Ferguson, Howard. *Keyboard Interpretation from the Fourteenth to the Nineteenth Century.* New York and London: Oxford University Press, 1975.

Newman, William. *Performance Practices in Beethoven's Piano Sonatas: An Introduction.* New York: W.W. Norton, 1971.

Rosen, Charles. *The Classical Style: Haydn, Mozart and Beethoven.* New York: Viking Press, 1971.

Rothschild, Fritz. *Musical Performance in the Times of Mozart and Beethoven.* Fair Lawn, N.J.: Oxford University Press, 1961.

THE ROMANTIC PERIOD (Century of the Piano)

Of all the musical styles and periods, romanticism is the one to become the principal source of our everyday musical diet. The bulk of concert repertories and study materials was written in the nineteenth century, and even popular music, in its best manifestations, is nourished by the melodic and harmonic ingredients of the romantic idiom. In contrast to the universality, serenity, and restraint of the classical era, the esthetic ideals of romancism extol the artistic freedom of the individual and the unrestrained expression of personal feelings. To convey these ideals, new forms, sonorities, and compositional techniques were created. The sonata, a uniquely apt vehicle for classical expression, could not by itself, suffice. A host of other smaller musical structures, mostly lyric character pieces, were conceived: *impromptus, moments musicaux, songs without words, nocturnes, intermezzi.* The modern piano, emerging in the early 1800s, provided the new sonorities and inspired composers to create an unprecedented wealth of piano music of every kind and for every degree of advancement. Although the baroque and classical eras both contributed enormously to the literature of keyboard music, by far the largest windfall came from romanticism during the nineteenth, the "century of the piano."

There is of course a great variety in style, form, intensity, and quality of expression within the romantic school itself, from the still classically oriented Schubert and Mendelssohn, through the strongly innovative expression of Schumann, Chopin, Liszt and Brahms, to the late-romantic, ethnically flavored and often preimpressionistic tendencies of Grieg, Fauré, Albéniz, Rachmaninoff, and others.

In spite of these widely variegated traits, however, certain stylistic characteristics emerge as generally valid and may be noted as helpful guidelines in the understanding, playing, and teaching of this vast repertory.

Performance Practices

Although romantic composers notated their works in great detail, their scores are by no means complete and free from ambiguities. This is due largely to the built-in imperfections of the Western notation system, which, among other things, cannot satisfactorily convey the subtle tempo fluctuations and dynamic nuances inherent in the sophisticated textures of much romantic music. In addition, the notation habits of numerous nineteenth century masters are quite idiosyncratic, requiring awareness and familiarity on the performer's part. Thus the performance of romantic music calls not only for an emotional involvement—as is, unfortunately, so often the case—but also for an intellectual stance to channel and guide these emotions within esthetically and stylistically proper conduits toward a pleasing and tasteful interpretation. The suggestions that follow are meant to promote familiarity with the main earmarks of romantic style.

Tempo: Markings in one form or another are always supplied by nineteenth century composers. Often they are quite precise, coupled with mood descriptions and metronome indications. In spite of this, one of the most difficult tasks confronting the performer of truly romantic music is the right choice of tempo, including its fluctuations. The key here is the proper and effective use of *rubato*, with all its possibilities for interpretative enhancement and all its pitfalls for tasteless exaggerations. By tempo fluctuation is meant not only *melodic rubato* in which, in Chopin's words, "the singing hand may deviate, the accompaniment must keep time," but also the *structural rubato*, in which both melody and accompaniment divert from the rigid tempo.

Thalberg, the great nineteenth-century piano virtuoso, on hearing some Chopin works performed by the master himself, wondered how such music could be committed to paper in a manner that could give a faithful indication of the many subtle tempo deviations and dynamic shadings. It is true that such nuances can only be approximated through notation, in spite of all the composer's painstaking efforts. Chopin, in his Nocturne in C-sharp minor (op. 27 no. 1) for instance, gives the following indications, in quick succession, of his intended tempo fluctuations in bars 49 to 70: sostenuto – rit. – agitato – poco a poco cresc. ed accel. – ritenuto – con anima – ten. – stretto – ten. Within a brief span of twenty-one measures there are nine instructions affecting tempo to a greater or lesser degree. This assiduously detailed notational effort is very helpful, but even its most faithful observance will result only in a cold, mechanistic, insensitive performance if the player lacks empathetic emotional involvement and firm esthetic control. This is the very essence of good romantic playing—that instinctive give-and-take in the melodic flow, rubato.

Metronome: Metronome marks appear with increased frequency in nineteenth-century music. They should always be carefully noted, but never blindly trusted. There are several reasons for this. The marks of some masters, Beethoven and Schumann included, are often incorrect and misleading to begin with and need careful examination and testing before acceptance. (After Schumann's death, his widow, Clara, altered many of his metronome marks in his editions.) A metronome mark judged reasonable can be useful in determining the basic tempo within a movement or section; but always keep in mind that certain deviations are natural and inevitable.

Textures: The romantic piano literature is almost entirely homophonic (melody and accompaniment). Momentary instances of contrapuntal writing do occur, mainly as a device to add harmonic and rhythmic color and piquancy to the forward momentum of melodic flow.

Schubert: Allegretto

Grieg: "Longing for Home," op. 57 no. 6

The characteristic texture of romantic music is a single melodic line supported by chords or other subordinate parts. In many instances this is a three-tier texture: melody, bass, and inner voices. The performer's primary task is to recognize and properly balance these three components, usually according to the familiar hierarchy of sound: the melody line predominates, closely coordinated in volume with the bass part, and both are supported, more discreetly, by the inner voices and figurations. The melody may appear, in any of the three tiers, and always receives dynamic priority. The following are typical romantic voice textures:

Single melody line in treble with solid or broken chord accompaniment:

Chopin: Nocturne, op. 55 no. 1

Top-line melody in the upper notes of harmonic intervals:

Mendelssohn: "Venetian Boat Song," op. 19 no. 6

Melody in top notes of chord sequences:

Schumann: "Important Event," op. 15 no. 6

Melody in middle voice:

Brahms: Intermezzo, op. 117 no. 1

Melody in bass:

Chopin: Prelude, op. 28 no. 6

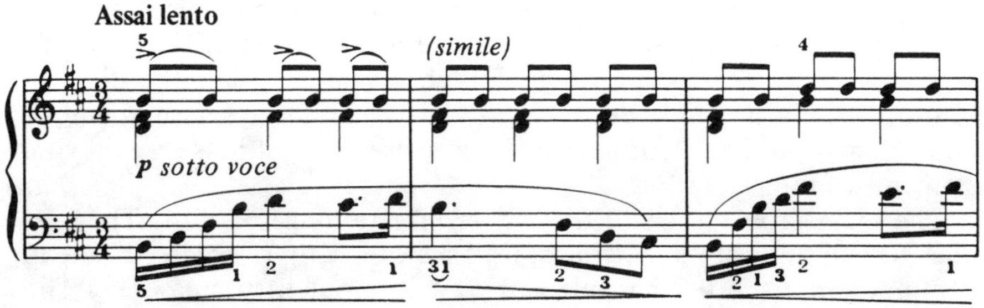

Dynamics: With the increase in the weight and power of the nineteenth-century piano, and with the many marked improvements in its player mechanism, composers had a wider dynamic scope at their disposal than ever before. Schubert, Mendelssohn, and Schumann stay pretty much within the ***pp***-to-***ff*** range, but Liszt, Brahms, and occasionally even Chopin indicate a ***ppp*** or ***fff***. But more important than absolute dynamic values is a judicious and sensitive apportioning of sound levels among the components of a given texture (melody, bass, middle voices).

Accents: There is a profusion of accent marks in the notation of romantic music; it is important that their meaning, including their relative intensity, should be clearly understood. The idiomatic and occasionally obscure usage of marks by some of the masters also needs clarification. Schumann's often-used sign <>, for instance, is obsolete and can safely be considered the equivalent of today's most often-used symbol, >. On occasion both Schubert and Schumann also use the ***f*** sign as an accent.

Schumann: Novelette, op. 99 no. 9

The ***f*** sign in the third measure is the culmination of a crescendo sequence and as such is a dynamic mark; the two ***f*** signs at the end are accent marks.

It should be remembered (and this is often overlooked by even experienced players) that an accent mark over a note does not necessarily prescribe loudness, except in those cases where the emphasis is indicated with letter-like signs involving the ***f*** mark (***sf***, ***sff***, ***fp***, ***sfp***, or simple ***f***); the other graphic symbols (> ∧ –) should be read within the prevailing dynamic level and can, within the context of a soft sequence, indicate only a delicate emphasis. (Schumann: "The Prophet Bird," op. 82 no. 7, first measure.)

Phrasing and Articulation: Sensitive, well-articulated melody playing is the single most important factor in the performance of the romantic repertory. Nineteenth-century composers usually notate the delineation of melody in ample detail, but by no means always with unambiguous clarity, so the performer's esthetic sense and instincts are still vital elements of interpretation.

The main problem is still the indeterminate usage of slurs. The long ones usually indicate a general prevalence of legato. (Chopin's Etude in F minor, op. 25 no. 2 has one slur over the first fifty measures.) The shorter ones, in addition to serving as legato signs, also outline form elements of various lengths and, in contrast to classical usage, freely cross bar lines in a structurally more realistic manner. The form segments encompassed by these slurs may be a phrase or half phrase (Schumann: Melody, op. 68 no. 1) or, as is more often the case, smaller subdivisions denoting details of articulation (Schumann: "First Loss," op. 68 no. 16).

Phrases, by virtue of their structural role in musical architecture, are usually repeated to form larger units, and the repetition often differs from the first presentation of the phrase. One of the many charms of Chopin's music is the skill and inventiveness with which he alters such recurring themes. Sometimes the changes are minimal, such as the addition of a single grace note (as in bar 4 of his Nocturne, op. 55 no. 1), or they can involve more substantial melodic and rhythmic alterations, as in measures 3 and 4 of the following example from the same work:

Chopin: Nocturne, op. 55 no. 1

Even when the notation does not indicate any variation in the repetition of phrases, the performer of romantic piano music has a clear option to provide subtle changes in the repeated section. Contemporary accounts of the performances of nineteenth-century virtuosos, including Chopin and Liszt, amply substantiate the stylistic propriety of this interpretative freedom. It goes without saying that such changes may not ever tamper with the work's basic melodic, harmonic, and rhythmic elements as notated by the composer. They may, however, involve delicate new dynamic shadings, slight tempo modifications, various metric accents, and pedal colorations.

Technique: In the romantic era the technique of piano playing reached a plateau of virtuosity which has not been surpassed since. The twentieth century, with all its innovations in sounds, textures, and colors, could add but little to the romantic arsenal of pianistic capabilities. These skills encompass the gamut of playing patterns: rapid passages of scales and figures, arpeggios, double notes, octaves, chords, wide stretches and leaps, all manners of touches from molto legato to staccatissimo, and, last but by no means least, a secure, sensitive handling of the sustaining pedal.

It is obvious from the foregoing that light and nimble finger action, which had been the mainstay of classical keyboard technique, did not by itself suffice in performing the romantic repertory, and the involvement of the larger muscles of hands, arms, and shoulders became necessary. Even the most elementary aspect of romantic playing—the production of a fine singing tone—necessitates the application of varying degrees of arm weight.

Pedaling: The sustaining pedal is an indispensable tool of romantic interpretation, and there is hardly a piece in the nineteenth-century repertory which could dispense with it. Anton Rubinstein called the pedal "the soul of the piano," and Czerny thought it as useful as if it were a "third hand," enabling the bass notes to vibrate while the two hands are engaged in playing the melody and accompaniment. The pedal, when properly used, actually does much more than sustain certain sounds; it also increases carrying power, enhances a singing tone, generates dynamic shadings, and makes possible the rendition of sophisticated textures, such as voice leading in inner parts, countermelodies, and a multitude of other nuances.

The masters' pedal notation is not always reliable and should not be followed blindly. The differences in the mechanisms and sonorities between nineteenth-century and modern pianos account for this. The prevalent, rather indefinite older notation method (*ped. . . .**), which did not always pinpoint where the pedal should be depressed and released, is another causative factor. When in doubt about the appropriateness of a given pedal mark, the player must decide on the basis of other evidence. As a rule, pedaling is guided by harmonic changes, but a variety of other factors may also have to be considered, including aspects of articulation, dynamic priorities, and technical conveniences.

Modern pedal marks in the form of brackets └──┘ └─∧─┘ are more precise as to attack and release, but even these cannot indicate fine nuances such as "half pedal," "short touches," by which the damper mechanism is lifted only partially or is manipulated in various other ways to allow some but not full vibration of the strings. These are important coloring devices of romantic interpretation and are left entirely to the performer's discretion. (See "Pedaling Technique," p. 91)

Ornaments: In the nineteenth-century repertory, ornamental symbols are fewer and the notation of embellishments more explicit than in the literature of previous eras. Often the ornaments are written out in full (Chopin: Polonaise, op. 26 no. 1, bars 39, 42, 43, etc.). The correct execution of trills still requires discernment. As a rule they begin on the main note, except in Chopin's works, where, in the absence of contrary indications, they should start on the upper auxiliary. Beginnings and termination of trills are usually written out (Chopin: Nocturne, op. 55 no. 1, bar 30). If the notation is not explicit, all alternatives, including whether the first note of an ornamental group should be played on the beat or begin before it, should be decided by the performer on the basis of musical context and technical convenience.

RECOMMENDED READING

Abraham, Gerald. *Chopin's Musical Style*. Fair Lawn, N.J.: Oxford University Press, 1960.

Einstein, Alfred. *Music in the Romantic Era*. New York: W.W. Norton, 1947.

Klaus, Kenneth B. *The Romantic Period in Music*. Boston: Allyn and Bacon, 1970.

Ferguson, Howard. *Keyboard Interpretation from the Fourteenth to the Nineteenth Century*. New York and London: Oxford University Press, 1975.

Longyear, Rey M. *Nineteenth-Century Romanticism in Music*. Englewood Cliffs, N.J.: Prentice-Hall, 1969.

THE TWENTIETH CENTURY (A Dazzling Musical Kaleidoscope)

The music of our time, a time of search, turmoil, experimentation, and discovery, is a faithful reflection of the profound changes in twentieth-century society. It does not have the relative unanimity of ideals and purpose that other periods exhibit. It is kaleidoscopic, often puzzling, and, at times, unsure of its direction. It is, however, richly imaginative and, in point of diversity at least, unparalleled since the baroque. The many significant trends of twentieth-century compositional styles—impressionism, neoclassicism, expressionism, polytonality, atonality, serialism—and combinations and variations of these styles, often spiced with jazz and folk elements, offer a profuse variety of musical fare. And if after more than a half-century Schoenberg and Bartók still perplex or affront anyone, that person may find composers writing in traditional idioms not far removed from more familiar sounds.

Because of this great variety of musical expression from conservative to avant-garde, today's listener is often confused, indeed bewildered, for lack of a secure, comfortable esthetic vantage point so readily available when listening to or playing music of earlier periods. This confronts the piano teacher with certain problems and tasks which are quite unique, and must be dealt with in an intelligent, empathetic, and constructive manner.

Why the Esthetic Insecurity

When teaching or playing the music of the eighteenth and nineteenth centuries, one has at one's disposal a carefully charted hierarchy of values, which reveals the excellence, mediocrity, or inferiority, the importance or irrelevance, of nearly all specific works and forms of musical expression. We do not have to form opinions and judgments on our own initiative. We know, because of the imprimatur of critical consensus, that Bach is greater than Telemann, Beethoven greater than

Clementi, and Stephen Heller inferior to Chopin. Although one can and does have individual preferences and may indulge in a degree of nonconformity, the main guidelines are given and by and large adhered to. No such assistance and directives are available to the listener of modern music. On hearing a new work we must employ our own esthetic yardsticks,and arrive at our own judgements. Although certain solid and durable values seem to have already crystallized (Debussy and Ravel, for instance) other trends, after having been extant for several decades (serialism, for example) are still on probation as to their viable future.

The insecure, erratic critical stance toward new works in general is due mainly to the fact that twentieth-century music, however fascinating in its numerous manifestations, is in a constant flux and as yet has been unable to evolve a solid and dependable set of artistic tenets which could serve as generally applicable critical standards. Consequently, the frame of reference in listening to modern music is still largely derived from eighteenth- and nineteenth-century sounds and patterns. This, of course, is anachronistic and unrealistic, and can be remedied only by enlarging and enriching the artistic premises by adding new concepts and devices to the old ones and accepting them as feasible, but not necessarily preferable, tools of the creative process.

A modern composition should not be spurned because of the listener's *a priori* aversion toward its mode of expression (atonality, for instance); it should be judged solely on whether or not, or to what extent it can convey a musical experience of esthetic validity and emotional import, regardless of its idiomatic label.

Guidelines for the Teacher

"There is no excellent beauty that hath not some strangeness in the proportion," said Francis Bacon, and the statement is as pertinent today as it was nearly four centuries ago. The piano teacher's task is to acquaint the student with this "strangeness," to analyze it, explain it, strip from it the aura of oddity and make it a familiar phenomenon in the glossary of musical concepts at the earliest possible stage. Children, who are known to be able to learn a foreign language within a few months, do not, as a rule, resist confrontations with novelty; being unencumbered by rigid preconceptions they readily accept and absorb new ideas and concepts. The older, more mature student may require a more cautious, systematic approach when exploring the frontiers of modern music.

In this writer's experience atonality is the most challenging hurdle in the path of such explorations. The traditional pull of gravity toward a secure tonal base, the yearning for a tonal habitat, is sometimes so strong that it may require a conscious effort and patient direction on the part of the teacher to remove the encumbrances. In such cases one should proceed gradually from the more traditional and only slightly innovative styles to the more daring, radically new ones.

As a first step it might be helpful to point out that the centuries-old reign of major and minor tonalities has never been absolute. To attain a special mood or effect, some romantic masters have allowed themselves the freedom to forego a concluding tonic cadence in favor of a different harmonic function (Schumann: "Child Falling Asleep," op. 15 no. 12; Chopin: Mazurka, op. 17 no. 4, etc.). More importantly, melodic and harmonic formations based on the church modes had been employed with increased frequency during the nineteenth century to give works a certain archaic or ethnic flavor (Mussorgsky, Grieg, and others). In impressionism and folk-oriented modern idioms, the role of modality is even more basic and becomes one of the most important stylistic earmarks. The ancient pentatonic scale is also the source of many modern works.

Impressionism, still within tonal boundaries, revolutionized the old rules of harmony with a fascinating array of new devices: whole-tone chords, chord clusters, novel harmonic sequences. Also maintaining strong ties with tonality, although often sharply dissonant, is *pandiatonicism*, which utilizes tones of a single key or mode (usually the white keys of the piano) but without any harmonic implications; each tone is independent and not a "degree" of a scale. Stravinsky was the initiator and most successful exponent of this idiom. *Bitonality* uses two keys simultaneously. In piano music the division is usually between the two hands. After having examined and savoured the foregoing idioms, all of which maintain links of varying degrees with tonality, the student should be better prepared and in a more receptive frame of mind to meet other, more radical styles.

Atonality is a compositional technique in which a definite tonality, or key center, is lacking; the twelve tones within the octave are independent, unrelated units, not components of any scale. The letter names of these tones (C, C-sharp, D, D-sharp, etc.) do not furnish an adequate nomenclature for these autonomous pitches, because the names imply a derivative relationship between C and C-sharp, D and D-sharp, etc., where, within the scheme of atonality, none exists. The lack of the accustomed key center does not necessarily mean that the listener is left adrift in an uncharted sea of sound. Other aural landmarks of pitch and rhythm are usually present to serve as guideposts of orientation and as a framework of musical construction. Furthermore, many modern works, although not tonal in the traditional sense, maintain certain tenuous ties with key centers. For instance, in Bartók's "Bear Dance" from *Ten Easy Pieces* the repeated Ds serve as a quasi-tonic foundation supporting a whole-tone construction. In Schoenberg's entirely atonal Little Piano Piece op. 19 no. 2, the oft-repeated harmonic interval G–B is the magnetic device around which all other elements coalesce.

Farthest removed from conventional tonality are pieces built on a *tone row* or *series*, a predetermined order of the twelve tones manipulated in various fashions (retrograde, inversion, transposition, etc.). But even with this technique certain rhythmic, melodic, or intervallic configurations invariably stand out, propelling a forward momentum and giving the piece an explicit constructional profile.

The leading composers of our century, while breaking new grounds, may bypass or abandon the aural and constructional premises of the past, but they do not eradicate them; rather, they transform them within the context of their aims and musical ideology. Whether or not we, the audience, can understand, adopt, and ultimately enjoy their language depends not only on the esthetic value and durability of their ideas, but also on our, the audience's attitudes. Certainly, the assimilation of modern sounds and forms requires a degree of active participation on the listener's part; perhaps hardly more than a measure of interest and alertness. The piano teacher, of all people, can especially ill afford the "luxury" of submerging exclusively in the comfortable sounds of the past. Today's youngster cannot be brought up, musically speaking, on teaching materials written solely a hundred or two hundred years ago; exposure to the music of our time is indispensable. Hence the importance of familiarity with the various contemporary idioms and the ways to convey their essential traits to the student.

Technique: The emergence and flowering of modern music, with its dazzling repertory of new sounds and its revolutionary compositional systems and procedures, is largely due to the creative exploits of the pianist composer at the keyboard. Many of the great innovators—Debussy, Ravel, Stravinsky, Bartók, to mention a few—were also pianists of high caliber. Consequently, it is no wonder that all aspects of technique, all pianistic problems extant for the past three centuries, are profusely represented in the keyboard literature of our time. Because of the diversity of idioms, no generalization can be made as to the performance of twentieth-century piano music; the details of technical execution must depend on the stylistic orientation of each work.

Impressionism demands a pliable tempo, a supple forward motion. The resulting subtle rubato is guided by pictorial considerations rather than emotional impulses (as in Chopin). A sensitive, refined touch and a most sophisticated pedal technique (including half pedal, fractional pedaling, etc.) are the brushes with which the pianist can reproduce the shapes and hues on the canvas of musical impressionism. The dynamic range is full, but never harsh or brittle, with some moderation toward the high decibels. Gradations of sound (cresc., dim., accents, etc.) involve the most delicate tolerances ever employed in the performance of music.

The neoclassicism and pandiatonicism of Stravinsky, Hindemith, and others, require the generally steady tempo of eighteenth-century music, with no rubato, or only the sparsest hint of it. Clearly drawn lines, projected with a secure, right-on-target technique and a well-controlled, variegated touch are called for here. Bartók, Prokofiev, and their school, too, need an "objective" approach to interpretation. The earmarks are well-maintained, even tempos; occasional rubatos in slow sections, in the manner of ethnic inflections, a touch which can be fiercely percussive or gently caressing; and the full dynamic range of the modern piano.

Becoming familiar with the trends of twentieth-century music is a task that the piano teacher cannot shirk. This is a process of self-education which if pursued diligently, with an open and inquisitive mind, can have its rewards every step of the way for teacher and student alike. (See "Twentieth-century Music: An Analysis and Appreciation" page 343 and its bibliography.)

RECOMMENDED READING

Larue, Jan. *Guidelines for Style Analysis.* New York: Norton, Nov. 1971

Moore, Douglas. *A Guide to Musical Styles: From Madrigal to Modern Music.* New York: Norton, Jan. 1963

The Search for Authenticity (The Lost Art of Thoroughbass Playing)

DENES AGAY

The search for authenticity in editions and performance practices, a dominant and all pervasive trait in the musical life of our time, came about as a healthy and most welcome reaction to the editorial excesses of the nineteenth century. Editors of the romantic period so thoroughly and abundantly marked, annotated, analyzed, and dissected the works of baroque and classical masters—they so overburdened the originally clear, uncluttered note picture with slurs, brackets, and a profusion of expression marks—that the composer's original conception, in essence the music itself, was nearly obliterated, and sunk under the weight of editorial overlay. Eliminating the excessive markings and getting back to the original texts (*Urtexts*) as notated by the masters themselves was like clearing a path in a jungle, or like opening a window and letting fresh air into a musty, overstuffed Victorian parlor. As a result of this trend, today's teachers, students, and performers have at their disposal a very wide choice of dependable texts in all areas of keyboard literature.

Unfortunately, this noble crusade has been somewhat marred of late by an excess of zeal and dogmatic pedantry, which, unwittingly perhaps, tends to turn the quest for reliable editions into a doctrinaire compulsion. (Recently I heard this malaise aptly diagnosed as "Urtext-itis.") Without elaborating on the various hair-splitting aspects of this trend, suffice it to say that it is one thing to search for authenticity,

---

Portions of this section are reprinted from *Clavier*, November 1975. By permission of the Instrumentalist Company.

and quite another to let it become a rigid cult, with the Urtext as the gospel, with every particle of the note picture an object of devout veneration and any manifestation of interpretive freedom an act of heresy. All this is not only terribly inhibiting for the student, teacher, and performer, but also in direct contradiction to the baroque practice of allowing the player a considerable degree of interpretative freedom.

The baroque masters' manuscripts are rather sparing, in that they present only the notes, with hardly any other marks of interpretation. It was left to the performer to select the proper tempo, dynamics, and phrasing, and to bring to life the skeletal text with warmth and imagination. The performer was not only allowed to do so, but indeed, expected to do so; this was his or her privilege and responsibility. We should hasten to add that, from all we know, performers were quite up to the task. The goal of music education during the eighteenth century was not only technical prowess, but thorough musicianship through knowledge of harmony, counterpoint, and improvisation, including the ability to fill in at sight the missing voices when a work was notated only by the melody and a figured (or sometimes unfigured) bass (*basso continuo, thoroughbass*), a very common practice during the seventeenth and eighteenth centuries.

Present-day music education does not equip the player with all these skills, and this is why the absolute insistence on textural authenticity is somewhat unreasonable from a pedagogical point of view. We proclaim the sanctity of Urtexts and pressure everyone to abide by them from the earliest grades on, but we largely fail to give the student even a fraction of the interpretative know-how the baroque performer had.

What is needed is a simple preparatory course dealing with such topics as the baroque conventions of tempo, dynamics, touch, and articulation; a description of the mechanics and the sound of the keyboard instruments the pieces were written for; the composer's notation habits, which quite often differ from modern rules and usage; and the rudiments of thoroughbass playing, or at least an awareness that a great deal of baroque music was notated in a stenographic manner which the player was expected to supplement. Many selections in Bach's *Little Notebook for Anna Magdalena Bach* and Leopold Mozart's *Notebook for Wolfgang* were meant to teach this skill and are ideally suited for that purpose even today.

WHEN AND HOW TO FILL IN VOICES

It should not be assumed that *basso continuo*—the method of improvising keyboard accompaniment from the bass notes only—was employed solely in pieces where the top line was meant to be played by a melody instrument (flute, violin, recorder, etc.) or voice. A good deal of solo keyboard music, especially during the first two-thirds of the eighteenth century, was also notated in this manner and was meant to be performed with tastefully interpolated voices, even where figures indicating harmonic functions were missing.

As many simple two-voice compositions of this type are used in early-grade piano instruction, one wonders why this notation method and the proper execution of works written this way does not generate more interest, or why, indeed, it is largely ignored. Several possible reasons come to mind. The believers in "Urtexts only on all grade levels" may be concerned that any addition of notes by the performer may establish a dangerous precedent and undermine the credo of absolute adherence to the venerated texts. Others may refrain from filling in voices because they lack the proper guidelines and simply do not know whether, in a specific case, this procedure is proper or not. Most important, today's student is not oriented and trained thoroughly enough to be able to do it. In any case, a step in the right direction is to recognize the fact that the addition of mid-voices in a certain type of two-voice baroque keyboard music is proper and stylistically correct.

What type of keyboard music is this? First, it should be remembered that these are pieces written mostly for the harpsichord or clavichord. Works written originally for the piano rarely qualify. Also excluded are all works of a contrapuntal and polyphonic nature, especially where the two voices are engaged in an imitative motivic play, as in the Bach Inventions and Partitas; neither do the Scarlatti Sonatas, the Handel Suites or the works of the French clavecinists belong in this category. On the other hand, many small dance pieces and fantasias by writers of the middle and late baroque (Handel, Telemann) and especially by the exponents of the so-called gallant style may well be amplified and enhanced by additional voices, especially when performed on the instruments they were written for, the harpsichord and clavichord. Not only would this inflict no stylistic damage, but, on the contrary, would conform to the composer's intention. To avoid any doubts and confusion, the characteristics of such a piece should be well understood and clearly remembered. All of the following traits must be present: a two-voice texture consisting of a distinct top-line melody, supported by a typical bass line in which each note implies a definite harmonic function. The two voices are usually at least an octave—more often even further—apart, without any thematic relationship or motivic interaction; the role of the bass is only to serve as harmonic underpinning for the treble.

In the following excerpts the large notes represent the composer's original notation; the small notes furnish an example of the many ways the textures may be amplified.

Telemann: Minuet

3
3
Telemann: Fantasia
Vivace
tr
Handel: Bourrée
(Allegretto)
Handel: Minuet
(Andantino)
p
mf
p

After all this has been said, it should also be emphasized that this article does not mean to encourage an indiscriminate practice of voice additions, even in those pieces where careful analysis would indicate it to be stylistically correct and musically feasible. There are several reasons for this. A two-voice texture may sound rather thin and dry on the eighteenth-century instrument for which it was written; the modern piano, however, with its superior built-in resonance, sustaining power, and expressive capability, will in many cases deliver a rounded and satisfying sound without additional tones. More importantly, thoroughbass playing is a skill which requires specialized training; the added inner voices have to be not only harmonically correct, but applied with secure knowledge and fine instinct to be consonant with the composition's style and mood. Only those capable of doing this should be tempted to enrich the texture between the treble and the bass line. As to the printed version of such bass realizations, the desirable method is to have the additional notes printed in small type, so that the performer has the option to play or not play the voice additions, or—if capable of so doing—to change them to suit individual taste.

Amplifying such two-voice textures should always be done with taste and restraint. Heavy chords, or thick layers of added notes at each harmony change, are out of place. In most cases a few interpolated sustained notes and some harmonically illuminating inner voices here and there are sufficient to give the piece a fuller sound and a more interesting profile, without impairing its simple, often fragile character.

To repeat: the notation of a great deal of simple eighteenth-century keyboard music implies some amplification on the performer's part. Whether or not today, on the modern piano, one should or should not add voices, and if so, how one should go about it, is best left to well-informed individual judgments and convictions. The search for authenticity should always be a quest for more complete esthetic fulfillment, and not an ever-narrowing road to dogmatic restrictiveness.

Not long ago, at a concert and subsequent symposium on early music, I witnessed two experts become embroiled in a shouting match and nearly come to blows over the question of whether all baroque trills should start on the upper auxiliary note. It was quite a scene—absurd and thought-provoking—all in the name of authenticity. There is clearly a great pedagogic need for more well-balanced information, more constructive dialogue, less pedantic hair-splitting, and less academic rivalry. Most important, the student should be taught gradually and systematically, from the earliest stages of study, the elements of style, the various fashions in composition and performance, and the changing attitudes toward the music of the past; he or she can then approach the urtexts fully equipped, relaxed, and able to enjoy the baroque music the way it was meant to be: with a degree of freedom, guided by the taste one develops through knowledge.

RECOMMENDED READING

Keller, Hermann (Carl Parrish, tr.). *Thoroughbass Method*. New York: W.W. Norton, 1972.

See also "Styles in Composition and Performance," p. 311.

Baroque Keyboard Instruments

DENES AGAY

The *harpsichord* is the principal stringed instrument of the baroque period. Most of the keyboard works of Bach, Handel, Couperin, Rameau, Scarlatti, and scores of other masters of the seventeenth and eighteenth centuries—including the early works of Haydn and Mozart—were written for this instrument. Although today these works are performed mostly on the modern piano, it is of utmost importance that the player become familiar with the harpsichord's tone production and sound. Not, to be sure, in an attempt to imitate it, but rather to be guided by its esthetic qualities: the crispness of sound, the clarity in reproducing polyphonic textures, the dramatic possibilities in sudden dynamic changes, all of which are essential traits of stylistic baroque interpretation.

In appearance the harpsichord resembles a slender grand piano with a compass of at least five octaves. Strings are stretched from front to back, at right angles to the keyboard. It often has two manuals, each activating a separate set of strings tuned an octave apart. The basic difference between the piano and the harpsichord is in the manner of tone production. On the piano, strings are *struck* by felt hammers; on the harpsichord, strings are *plucked* by quills or leather plectra, producing a somewhat clipped, quite brilliant pizzicato-like sound. Since the harpsichord has no sustaining pedal, gradations of dynamics (crescendo-decrescendo) are not possible and the player has little direct control over the quality and volume of sound, except through mechanical means. This involves the manipulations of various stops and registers, similar to those of the organ, through which sets of strings may be coupled or disengaged, or some other special effects attained. An accomplished player can, however, expand the expressive potential of this fascinating instrument through nuances of touch and attack, and through a sensitive application of agogic accents.

During the past two or three decades, thorough explorations of baroque music literature and performance practices have also brought about a renewed interest in the harpsichord on the part of composers, performers, and teachers.

The *clavichord* is one of the most ancient of keyboard instruments. Its origins go back to the thirteenth century and it reached the height of its popularity during the baroque era. In appearance it is a rectangular, often quite ornate, wooden box, about two-by-four feet, either placed on a table or standing on legs. Its compass is from three-and-a-half to five octaves. The strings, metal or gut, are stretched horizontally, parallel to the keyboard. When a key is depressed, it activates a metal wedge, called a *tangent*, which strikes the string from below, producing a pleasing mellow sound. Tone quality, including dynamics, can be controlled to some extent by the player's manner of touch. An especially characteristic vibrato effect can be obtained by keeping the key depressed with a rocking motion of the finger (*Bebung*).

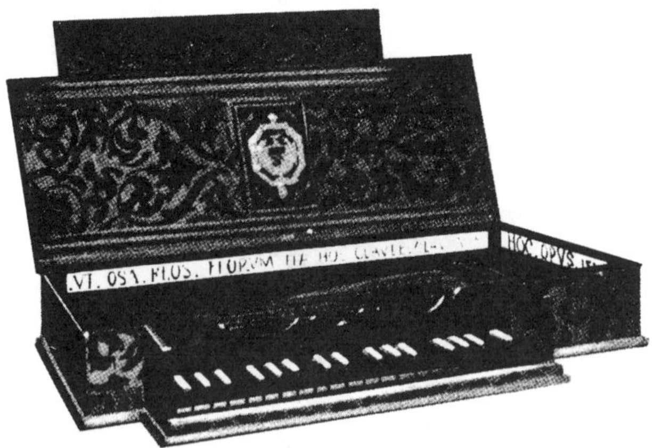

Because of its lack of volume and limited dynamic range (from ***pp*** to ***mf***), the clavichord is rarely used in a concert hall, or as an ensemble instrument. Its delicate, expressive sound makes it ideally suited for performance in an intimate atmosphere, such as a private home.

Music written expressly for the clavichord is rather rare, but there is no doubt that a large body of baroque and rococo keyboard music was, by preference, performed on this subtle, expressive instrument. It remained popular until the end of the eighteenth century.

The *virginal*, a small keyboard instrument of the harpsichord family, was very popular in sixteenth- and seventeenth-century England and the Netherlands. It has an oblong-shaped case, usually set upon a table, with a single keyboard encompassing about four octaves. The strings run parallel to the keyboard. Contrary to popular belief, the instrument was not named after Queen Elizabeth I ("the virgin queen"), who was an expert player on it. The term was in use well before her time, and probably originates from the Latin *virga*, meaning a little stick, or jack, which is part of all harpsichord-type mechanisms.

Music written for this instrument by the English masters William Byrd (1543–1623), John Bull (1563–1628), and Orlando Gibbons (1583–1625) embodies a rich and idiomatic keyboard style of composition, which had great influence on the harpsichord literature of the high baroque.

The *spinet* is a small harpsichord, usually in a wing-shaped or triangular case with one manual. The strings run at about a forty-five degree angle to the keyboard. It was a popular home instrument during the seventeenth and eighteenth centuries. The origin of the name is obscure, possibly deriving from its Italian inventor, Spinetti. Today the name is also applied to the early oblong-shaped pianoforte, or the modern miniature upright piano.

Cembalo, an abbreviation of *clavicembalo*, is the Italian and German name for the harpsichord; *clavecin* is its French name. A *claveciniste* is a harpsichord player, but it also refers to a French composer of the baroque period who wrote works for the clavecin (Couperin, Rameau, Daquin, Dandrieu, and others).

Clavier is the German generic name for stringed keyboard instruments, which include the harpsichord (virginal, spinet), clavichord, and fortepiano. Bach's Forty-eight Preludes and Fugues (*Das Wohltemperierte Clavier*), for instance, were intended for either the harpsichord or clavichord, depending on the player's preference or access. In Bach's time the term *clavier* also included the organ. In the nineteenth century the preferred German spelling became *Klavier*, and its meaning was restricted to the piano only.

The *clavicytherium* is an upright harpsichord, or vertical spinet. Today it is found only in museums.

RECOMMENDED READING

Harich-Schneider, Eta. *The Harpsichord: An Introduction to Technique, Style, and the Historical Sources*. St. Louis: Concordia, 1954.

James, Philip. *Early Keyboard Instruments from Their Beginnings to the Year 1820.* Chester Springs, Pa.: Dufour, 1930. Reprint: New York: Barnes & Noble, 1970.

Neupert, Hanns. *Harpsichord Manual: A Historical and Technical Discussion.* Kassel: Bärenreiter, 1968.

Russel, Raymond. *The Harpsichord and Clavichord*. London: Faber, 1973.

Winternitz, Emanuel. *Keyboard Instruments*. New York: Metropolitan Museum of Art, 1961.

Twentieth-Century Music: An Analysis and Appreciation

JUDITH LANG ZAIMONT

. . . in the long run the only human activities really worthwhile are the search for knowledge, and the creation of beauty. This is beyond argument; the only point of debate is which comes first.

–Arthur C. Clarke
Profiles of the Future

Is not beauty in music too often confused with something which lets the ears lie back in an easy chair?

–Charles Ives
"Postface" to *114 Songs*

THE COMPOSER

Without doubt, ours is a period of kaleidoscopic musical richness.

The spirit of scientific inquiry–an objective, general curiosity about the nature of things–characterizes our age and has prompted increasing performances of older music and a general growth of interest in music from all eras. Serious music performing groups vie with one another in directing the general listener's attention to their specific interests: the music of the Renaissance, the baroque, the classic or romantic eras, or that of our own time. As a consequence, the living composer has to struggle just to gather an audience; if his or her music then turns out to be difficult to assimilate on first hearing, he or she has only a small chance of success in communicating artistic substance, particularly if the audience's expectations have been formed mostly through exposure to music of the past.

Would we be better able to understand today's music if we weren't distracted by "historical" alternatives? Yes, if we greet the new music on its own terms, with understanding, and (to carry Coleridge's admonition beyond the realm of the theater) with a "willing suspension of disbelief." We should realize that the twentieth-century composer has been keeping pace with the tempo and temper of fluctuating times, via experiments and innovations that seem to have been, in hindsight, inevitable. It is the audiences who cling to the known in place of the new, who must be reassured that a given artwork has its place in the esthetic continuum.

What is it about the art of our time that seems to differentiate it so radically from that of the past?

Any art is best understood within its own frames of reference. The most easily distinguished factors affecting the progress of musical composition in our century are the political and social upheavals accompanying two global wars, and the growth of a constantly expanding communications network that promotes cross-fertilizations between Western music and the musics of Asia, Africa, Eastern Europe, and folk cultures throughout the world.

As a consequence of this cross-fertilization, composers have reevaluated the raw materials of their musical heritage (which might be described as a synthesis of melody, harmony, and simpler rhythmic motives) and have turned instead to exploring intricate rhythmic figures (hypnotically repeated and only slowly permuted) and melodic arabesques (of a freer, chantlike quality) borrowed from other cultures at the expense of harmony.

Sociopolitical upheavals have provoked an even more important alteration in outlook: our age has become, in Auden's phrase, "the age of anxiety," distinguished by the increased conviction on the part of most of us that the works of humankind are essentially impermanent. Never before has the creator felt so cut adrift from the art of the past; so decidedly, so overtly a composite tradition-breaker and history-maker. Indeed, since "our civilization is the first to have for its past, the past of the world, [since] our history is the first to be world history,"[1] the composer of our time has become obliged to juggle two burdens at once: to clarify his or her art as an outgrowth of the music of the past, and to sustain it as an art in evolution, responsive to the changing needs and requirements of modern times.

This is a tall order and one that most composers of the past felt no need to fill. They were much more likely to be commended by the public for demonstrating a conservative attitude than to be encouraged to innovate; the contexts of their times demanded it.

Our Western musical heritage, from the baroque through the romantic eras, may be described as a context,

> distinguished by [a] developing and characteristic kind of musical thinking [in which] every musical event has a "function" or a functional role [relating] it to what has come before and what will happen next. The basic psychological principle here is expectation; the basic musical technique is that of direction and motion. Out of this grow the characteristic ways in which musical lines will rise and fall and the ways in which simultaneous musical lines will relate to one another in harmonic patterns. The idea of expectation suggests the use of resolutions and non-resolution; of so-called dissonance and consonance; of intensity and relaxation; of cadence, accent, and articulation; of phrase and punctuation; of rhythm and dynamic; even of tempo and tone color.[2]

Historically, evolution by sudden jump was discouraged. Basic changes in raw materials, formats, and the composer's own orientation with respect to artistic materials were expected to take place gradually, over the space of several creative generations.

Not so in our century: the distinctive feature of twentieth-century music has been that change occurs at a dizzying pace. "More has happened in music in these few years than in any previous five-hundred-year period. . . . Every element of the musical language [has] had to be subjected to [deliberate] reappraisal and examination before it could be made part of the new art. . . ."[3] As a consequence, audience bewilderment has increased many times over. Being largely unaware of the separate steps that inspired most twentieth-century compositional innovations, listeners are naturally at a loss when confronting the end result.

Composers themselves have not let go of the past without a struggle. Although many alternatives to functional tonality were explored around the turn of the century, the upheavals of World War I prompted a step sideways rather than straight ahead, with a return to the materials, musical forms, and ideals of the eighteenth century (neoclassicism).

By contrast, after World War II artists consciously sought to cut their ties to a past now rendered horrific. To deny the past, through any and all means, became esthetically important, and the development of an objective, dispassionate, eminently rational music became the goal. Total conscious control of every musical element was the result: "integral" or "total" serialism, a compositional method in which composers were obliged to think objectively and rationally about every musical component, thus creating an entirely new music devoid of any vestige of tonality's "expectations" and/or the individual artist's "unconscious" inspirations.

Within the past two decades integral serialism's rationality has begun to be tempered by the reappearance of more subjective modes of expression. Complete control of musical materials is no longer the rule. Room has been made for the individual's voice to be heard again, within a more traditional context (neoromanticism); for the performer to become a partner in the creative process (aleatory music, the music of chance); to allude to music of the past or quote it directly, in either affectionate parody or pastiche (collage); to freely employ all twelve chromatic pitches in a nonrigorous manner, either in a tonal or nontonal framework; to create an expressive yet nonpersonal music using melodic and rhythmic materials (and philosophical ideal) borrowed from other countries and other cultures, including jazz or other popular music idioms of the West; to expand the sonic palette indefinitely by using electronic instruments, either alone or in conjunction with live performers; or to combine music with the other performing arts in the complex theatrical panoply termed a "mixed-media event."

Our time, then, is truly a period of kaleidoscopic musical richness: a stimulating, fertile era for composers of all persuasions.

THE LISTENER

But is it as stimulating a period for the listener? Perhaps it is not so much stimulating as bewildering.

When the listener says, fretfully, that the music of our time is too difficult, too alien, too complex to comprehend easily or all at once (or at all!), he or she is forgetting that one listens within the context of a specific acculturation. It's not just the new music of our own culture that may appear incomprehensible to the listener; music from other times and countries might seem equally impenetrable.

Although we like to think that our esthetic viewpoint is neutral and unbiased, in fact,

> contemporary musical ideas are still communicated in the context of a musical life whose structure, means, and institutions are largely derived from the late eighteenth and nineteenth centuries. . . . Some of our most fundamental ways of thinking about music and musical creations are also inheritances from the recent past. Indeed, our whole notion of "art" and artistic creation as a unique and separable human activity is a relatively modern Western idea, by no means universal in human experience. . . .[4]

Our cultural-historical framework, then, is quite specific, and operates not only as a mind-set for esthetic evaluation but also materially, in the continued conservation of musical institutions and implements which reached their full development between 1700 and 1900. These include the modern orchestra, opera, and chamber ensemble; the idea of a solo recital; the most common instruments; the bulk of the concert repertory for those instruments; the techniques for teaching music theory and performance through manipulating individual instruments; and the concept of the conservatory.

Once we understand the context from which we judge, we will no longer dismiss a piece on first hearing simply because it seems difficult or foreign. In truth it is too easy, and not strictly honest, to call a composition "beautiful" or "worthy" merely because it "lets the ears lie back in an easy chair." A surprising number of works originally damned as "monstrous" or "barbarous" *appear* to have matured over the years into distinguished masterworks.

Music, by its nature the most ephemeral and abstract of the arts, imposes its own framework for communication. In its "purest" form, music speaks to us through one sense only (hearing), unrolling steadily in time. Individual moments within a composition can never crystallize for prolonged examination (as with a painting or sculpture) but must be savored as they pass by. Without the buttress of a *visual* complement (as in ballet) or a *visual-linguistic* complement (as in film or opera), music must communicate fully through the narrow channels of sound and time alone.

Composers have long been aware of the limitations placed on them by the nature of their medium. As a result, the larger of the traditional musical forms are also the most highly redundant of all artworks. This must be. In order to sustain communication, involvement, and understanding with the listener, the music cooperates by stressing certain necessary aural landmarks via periodic repeats, variants, or echoes of previously heard material. It is no wonder, then, that at first hearing an extended through-composed piece of absolute music is the most difficult of all for even a cooperating listener to comprehend fully; if, in addition, its idiom is one which avoids the expected grammar and syntax of functional tonality, communication will be at a minimum.

Thus, it is not surprising to realize that opera, ballet, songs, choral works, and program music in general are the most popular of musical genres. With the program as a buttress, even a particularly abstruse musical configuration may be understood with relative ease. Programs may either unroll in time along with the music (as do song texts), or exist independently, in written or schematic form, for the purpose of being studied before the piece is played, as in the case of scenarios for tone poems.

These latter—the "program notes"—have changed since the last century to fit the more rational, highly constructed music of our time. Instead of merely providing a description of the series of events, works of art, or psychic struggles "depicted" in the music, the notes now usually contain information about the prescription according to which the piece has been written: its generative procedure or theoretic basis (for example, its specific tone row). The composer provides this information as an aid to listening, and the notes are a valuable, indispensible feature of concerts devoted solely to new music. Though they may occasionally seem complex and highly technical, they serve the same purpose as the scenario for *Ein Heldenleben* or the titles of Victor Hartmann's "pictures at an exhibition."

Aside from listening through a general cultural and esthetic filter, each of us hears through a personal filter established by the musical experiences of our youth. In our early years we heard and appreciated without intellectualizing; we thought that each piece was in perfect proportion, emerging whole from the composer's conscious. It may be quite different to return to these pieces in later years and view them critically. The music that once seemed so perfect may actually be flawed in detail or execution, according to a more mature understanding; yet it is difficult to consider these "old friends" as objectively as we consider music which has come to our attention more recently. Because we listen so uncritically when we're young, that is the best time for us to be introduced to newer idioms. If the new sounds can be accepted as natural then, we will be at least sympathetic to even more radical innovations as they are introduced.

However, we should remember that when we play or listen to music of the past we're dealing with works whose overall quality is remarkably high; we cut our musical teeth on Bach, Mozart, Beethoven, Chopin, and Debussy, not Buxtehude, Kalkbrenner, Türk, Moscheles, and Sinding. For music from our own century, however, the situation is different. Unless we choose to stay a strict sixty years behind the times, we must offer our ears and our cooperation equally to the music of all, at least on a first go-round. This is not just fair, but stimulating and esthetically gratifying as well.

COMPOSER AND LISTENER TOGETHER

It is true, though, that some composers don't go out of their way to make it easy for the listener. The same sophisticated technology that permits minute control over each musical element and shortens the time needed to develop and perfect every new idiom also permits the composer to operate free of technical limitation and to pursue continuous innovation as a goal in itself. Particularly in the last two-and-a-half decades, many composers have tunneled directly ahead (glancing back over their shoulders now and again at the dread specter of history catching up with them) on the premise that each new work should represent a "significant breakthrough." Rarely do these creators take the time to mine the veins of stylistic ores they have uncovered, nor do they permit their listeners time to linger over and savor the special qualities of each innovation, nor increase their understanding through repeated exposure to a particularly novel concept.

If, in truth, "the bond that connects all of twentieth-century music grows out of the fact that each composer and each piece has had to establish new and unique forms of expressive and intellectual communications"[5]; if, for example, "Stockhausen has knocked down his own house and built it up in a different way for every new work"[6]; if, in short, each composer becomes the sum total of a separate artistic movement, then listeners will have to learn to accept the situation, and draw up "scorecards" to keep track.

However, if composers recognize the inevitability of cultural lag and try to allow for it by slowing their flight to the future just a little, both listener and composer will benefit. Compromise on both sides is overdue:

> The time is past when music was written for a handful of aesthetes. Today vast crowds of people have come face to face with serious music and are waiting with eager impatience. Composers, take heed of this: if you repel these crowds they will turn away from you to. . . vulgar music. But if you can hold them you will win an audience such as the world has never before seen.[7]

This is as true for us today as it was for Prokofiev in 1937.

CHRONOLOGICAL SURVEY OF TWENTIETH-CENTURY STYLES

Before considering musical innovations in detail, it may be helpful to review briefly the various styles which have been formulated during this century. Only in the case of the first few styles will it be possible to categorize composers definitely; indeed, the trend so far has been toward eclecticism rather than compartmentalization.

For example, we might chart Stravinsky's growth in progressive terms, by style explored: juvenile works in an extended romantic vein with an infusion of impressionistic color consciousness, composed under the guidance of the great orchestrator Rimsky-Korsakov; the three ballets–*Firebird* (1910), *Petrouchka* (1911), and *Rite of Spring* (1913)–in which he added national flavorings to an impressionistic base at first, then gradually forged his personal, rhythmically vital, nonrigorous expressionism. After World War I he moved away from large canvases to works for smaller forces, written in a French-international vein incorporating a flirtation with jazz; some folk color is still present in *Les Noces* (1923), but more typical of this period is the lean, clean *l'Histoire du Soldat* (1918). Neoclassicism was the style of Stravinsky's middle years, always distinguished by his personal feeling for rhythms; a spare orchestral sound comprised of nonblending instrumental colors; astringent sonorities; and, in the area of form, a penchant for making transpositions by direct juxtaposition, without bridges. Perhaps the masterpiece of this period is the *Symphony of Psalms* (1930). In the mid-1950s Stravinsky adopted serial procedures, perhaps for their comforting frame of ordered rationality; *Agon* (1957) and *Threni* (1958) are two later works that are serial at least in part. Thus is it possible to think of Stravinsky's career as a counterpart to Picasso's, since both creators made it their business to keep abreast of every innovation in technique or esthetic philosophy, and to incorporate into their own vocabularies whatever might be of interest or relevance.

In the list below, I have attempted to place each composer in an appropriate context, based on the stylistic language he or she most commonly employed. One composer may appear in several categories. Readers may possibly disagree with certain of the categorizations, and are encouraged to do so.

(1) **Late Romanticism**: continuation of the Germanic romantic tradi-

tion. The music is often overblown, characterized by heavy emotionalism, huge orchestras, great symphonic lengths, and advances in harmony and orchestration.

Germany and Austria:	Anton Bruckner (1824–1896)
	Gustav Mahler (1860–1911)
	Hugo Wolf (1860–1903)
	Richard Strauss (1864–1949)
	Max Reger (1873–1916)
	Erich Korngold (1897–1957)
England:	Gustav Holst (1874–1934)
	Ralph Vaughan Williams (1872–1958)
Denmark:	Carl Nielsen (1865–1931)
Finland:	Jean Sibelius (1865–1957)
Russia:	Alexander Scriabin (1872–1915)
	Sergei Rachmaninoff (1873–1943)

(2) **Impressionism**: a style which attempts to capture a mood or evoke an atmosphere; the musical counterpart to symbolism in poetry and the paintings of Renoir, Monet, Pissarro, Dégas, and Cézanne. It still is a potent force today, particularly in the music of Olivier Messaien (1908–1992)) and George Crumb (1929–).

France:	Claude Debussy (1862–1918)
	Maurice Ravel (1875–1937)
	Jacques Ibert (1890–1962)
	Germaine Tailleferre (1892–1983)
	Germaine Tailleferre (1892–)
England:	Frederick Delius (1862–1934)
Italy:	Ottorino Respighi (1879–1936)
U.S.:	Charles Griffes (1884–1920)

(3) **Expressionism**: expressing the inner self, especially the subconscious. In the first part of the century this meant a jagged, uneasy music, achieved through using all twelve divisions of the octave impartially and denying a tonic in a nonrigorous fashion (atonality). After World War I, use of the twelve chromatic pitches was systematized: when placed in a prescribed order, they become the unique theme-scale (series) for each piece, which is then composed according to the contrapuntal rules governing imitative textures. Strict serial procedures may further be used to control musical materials other than pitch. In the last fifteen years rigorous control of all musical elements has been partially given up; the "new expressionism" concerns itself more with the end "sound" result than with the exact technical procedures used to generate a piece.

Atonalists

Germany and Austria: Arnold Schoenberg (1874–1951)
Alban Berg (1885–1935)
Anton Webern (1883–1945)
Ernst Křenek (1900–1991)

Stricter Serialists

France: Pierre Boulez (1925–)
Germany: Karlheinz Stockhausen (1928–)
England: Humphrey Searle (1915–1982)
Italy: Luigi Dallapiccola (1904–1975)
U.S.: Wallingford Riegger (1885–1961)
Stefan Wolpe (1902–1972)
Ben Weber (1916–1979)
George Perle (1915–)
Milton Babbitt (1916–)
Ross Lee Finney (1906–1997)
George Rochberg (1918–) (now moving toward neoromantic style)

New Expressionists

Switzerland: Frank Martin (1890–1974)
Poland: Witold Lutoslawski (1913–1994)
Krzysztof Penderecki (1933–)
U.S.: Carl Ruggles (1876–1971)
Roger Sessions (1896–1985)
Hugo Weisgall (1912–1997)
Elliott Carter (1908–)
Miriam Gideon (1906–1996)
Leon Kirchner (1919–)
Ruth Crawford Seeger (1901–1953)

(4) **Objective movements**: two rigorously nonpersonal, unsentimental approaches.

"Urban" or *"Machine" Music* (music imitating machine sounds)
Switzerland: Arthur Honegger (1892–1955)
U.S.: George Antheil (1900–1959) (early works)

"Gebrauchsmusik" ("functional music," written for special occasions or a specific purpose)
Germany: Paul Hindemith (1895–1963)
Kurt Weill (1900–1950)

(5) **Neoclassicism**: a return to the ideals of the eighteenth century; a detached, objective style. French neo-classicists added a humorous, gently satiric note.

Russia/France: Igor Stravinsky (1882–1971)
Germany: Paul Hindemith (1895–1963)
France: Erik Satie (1866–1925)
Francis Poulenc (1899–1963)
Darius Milhaud (1892–1974)
Russia: Sergei Prokofiev (1891–1953)
Dmitri Shostakovich (1906–1975)
U.S.: Walter Piston (1894–1976)
William Schuman (1910–)
Peter Mennin (1923–)
Louise Talma (1906–1996)

(6) **New Nationalism**: used scientific methods to research folk music, and stressed national color within the context of art music.

Russia: Aram Khatchaturian (1903–1978)
England: Ralph Vaughan Williams (1872–1958)
Hungary: Béla Bartók (1881–1945)
Zoltán Kodály (1882–1967)
Spain: Manuel de Falla (1876–1949)
Czechoslovakia: Leoš Janáček (1854–1928)
Bohuslav Martinu (1890–1959)
Argentina: Alberto Ginastera (1916–1983)
Brazil: Heitor Villa-Lobos (1881–1959)
Mexico: Carlos Chavez (1889–1978)
Silvestre Revueltas (1899–1940)
Cuba: Ernesto Lecuona (1896–1963)
U.S.: Charles Ives (1874–1954)
Douglas Moore (1893–1969)
Howard Hanson (1896–1981)
Roy Harris (1898–1979)
Aaron Copland (1898–1990)
Elie Siegmeister (1909–1991)

(7) **Extended Romanticism**: music which preserves and strengthens the nineteenth-century heritage of a fundamental lyric impulse by combining it with many twentieth-century chromatic, textural, and tone-color innovations. Basically tonal, avoiding trite harmonic progressions, this approach leans toward large-scale, programmatic works.

U.S.: Alan Hovhaness (1911–2000)
Samuel Barber (1910–1981)
Gian-Carlo Menotti (1911–)
Norman Dello Joio (1913–)
Leonard Bernstein (1918–1990)
Australia: Peggy Glanville-Hicks (1912–1990)
England: Benjamin Britten (1913–1976)
Switzerland: Ernst Bloch (1880–1959)

(8) **Tape Music**: electronically produced (synthesized) sounds: *musique concrète*; computer music. With the invention of the tape recorder in the late 1940s, a new means of expanding the sonic palette arrived. In 1948 Pierre Schaeffer established an electronic music studio in Paris, and in 1952 Otto Luening and Vladimir Ussachevsky began their experiments at Columbia University. This early music used pre-existing real sounds ("concrete" sounds) as raw material; they were taped and then altered by manipulating the tape in various ways or modifying it electronically.

A second kind of tape music used electronically generated tones for raw material. (Interest in electronic instruments goes back to the inventions of the Theremin [1924] and the Ondes Martinot [1928]. Both used two vacuum-tube oscillators to produce complex wave forms or "beat" notes.) In the electronic music labs of the '50s, pitches and timbres were created at the composer's discretion from sound-wave generators, and taped one by one.

In both concrete and electronic music the most violent contrasts and minute gradations of sound may be produced at the flick of a switch, resulting in an aural collage.

A significant step in the synthesis of sound occurred in 1955, when Harry Olson of RCA invented an "Electronic Music Synthesizer": an improved version of the machine was installed in the Columbia-Princeton Electronic Music Studio in the late '50s. In the RCA Synthesizer, as well as in Moog, Arp, Buchla, and other synthesizers, "every aspect of both pitched and nonpitched sound—including duration, quality of attack and decay (dying away), intensity, tone color and so forth—can be set out with precise definition, and any sound can be tested immediately and, if necessary, readjusted down to the finest possible gradations."[8] Control is usually accomplished by means of a keyboard or patchboard.

In *musique concrète*, the performer's role has been reduced to that of a "generator" of raw material; in synthesized and electronic music the performer is dispensed with entirely. Certain composers seem to be uncomfortable without human participation, and the most recent development has been an upsurge in pieces for tape and live performer. Among the most striking of these are Mario Davidovsky's *Synchronisms 1* through *6*, and the Variations for Flute and Electronic Sounds by Walter Carlos.

A further refinement in tape music has been provided by introducing the computer as a compositional tool. Now the entire musical environment can be built from scratch: not only may the timbres be constructed; not only may the sequence and juxtaposition of sounds (pitched and unpitched) be consciously controlled; but also the rules for proceeding from sound event to sound event. These must be broken down into their smallest components and fed into the computer via a detailed, comprehensive program. In addition, the aural result cannot be precisely determined until the computer's read-out is transformed into electromagnetic impulses on recording tape and played back through loudspeakers.

Thus, the computer may function either as a close approximation to a universal sound synthesizer or as a more active partner, the composer's agent. In the latter role, when properly programmed, the computer can make choices and decisions at any stage of the compositional process and to any degree desired. Interestingly enough, this leads to a kind of programming in which the machine makes similar "random" decisions to those made by a human performer in music of chance.

Nevertheless, "no matter how far-reaching the computer's participation in the composition, it remains the agent. The computer does not compose, it carries out instructions. Though its part in the process may increase significantly, the *computer as composer* must be considered a mirage."[9]

A partial list of composers active in this medium:

France:	Pierre Boulez (1926–)
Italy:	Luigi Nono (1924–1990)
	Luciano Berio (1925–)
Germany:	Karlheinz Stockhausen (1928–)
U.S.:	Edgard Varèse (1885–1965)
	Otto Luening (1900–1996)
	Vladimir Ussachevsky (1911–1990)
	Mario Davidovsky (1934–)
	Lejaren Hiller (1924–1994)

(9) **Music of Chance (Aleatory Music)**: the performer is invited to participate in the creative process by making certain decisions at the moment of performance. Chance or aleatory music (from the Latin *alea*, "game of dice") leaves the performer free to exercise his best judgment in one or more areas, such as in the choice of dynamics, register, timbre, duration, etc. The freedom may be total or selective.

Morton Feldman: "Last Pieces," no. 1

In stochastic music the performer may elect to play only certain of the notes or sonorities offered; or to play phrases or sections of a piece in his own preferred order, using either all the given material or some of it in combination.

Directions for playing "Mobile":

Begin by playing any one of the outer, lettered squares; continue with any one of the connector squares; continue by returning to another lettered square, or the original one, if you wish, followed by another connector; and so on.

The order in which the given musical materials are played is mostly up to the performer. Thus, the overall form will vary from performance to performance. Other elements left to the performer's choice are tempo, dynamics, touch, etc.

The piece ends when everything on the page has been played at least once—unless a larger piece is preferred, in which everything will be played at least twice. Obviously, no two performances will be alike.

Sample performance scheme:

> N–two–N–three–I–three–U–three–E–three–B–one–A–one–G–three–G–one–D.

Merrill Bradshaw: "Mobile"

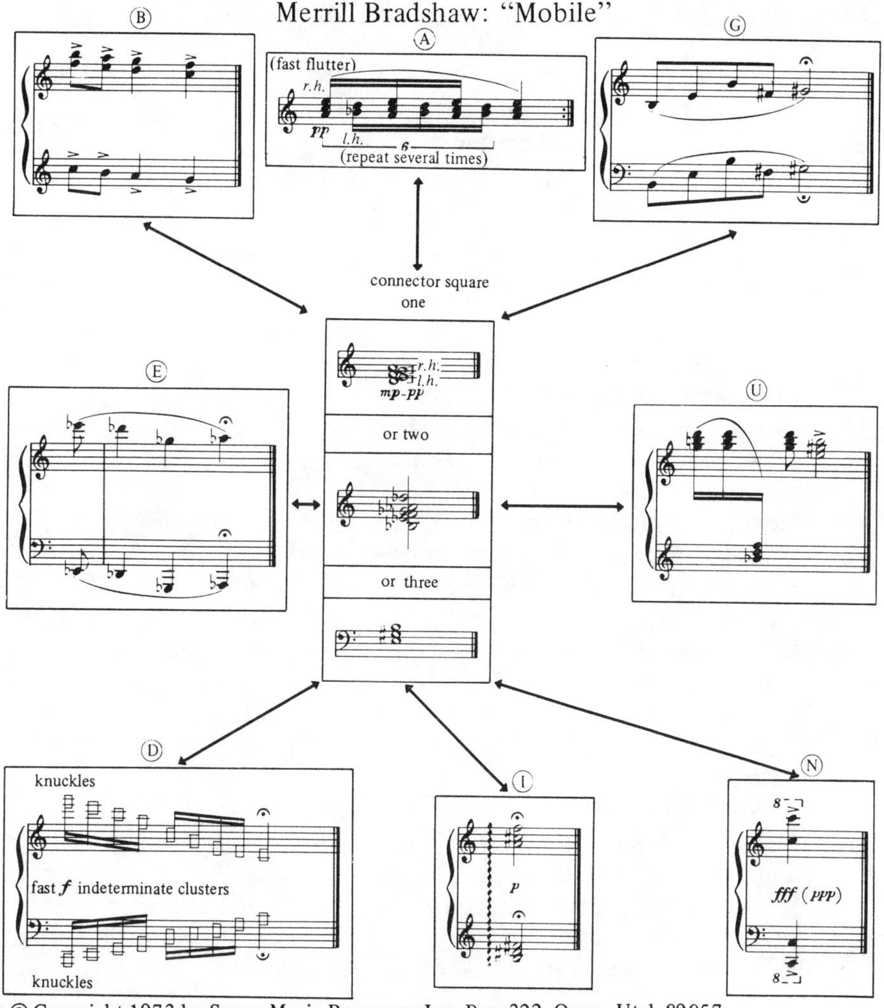

Improvisation on given materials (pitch, dynamics, articulations) may be offered by the composer. The given materials are usually boxed:

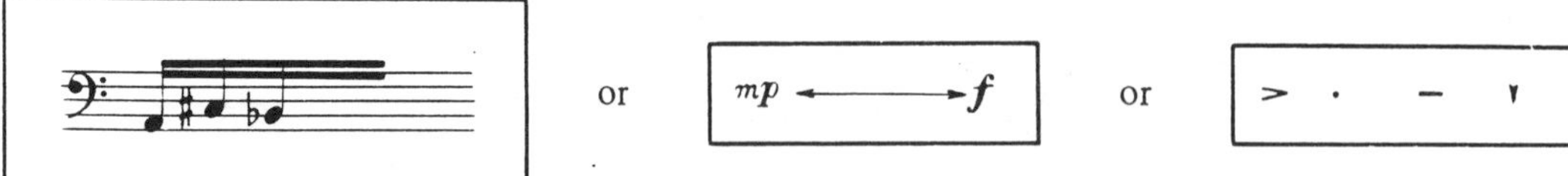

The listener may become the "performer" when composed sounds are purposefully trivial or absent. In John Cage's 4'33"(1954), a performer sits at a piano in silence (hence the title); the music comprises the random sounds which occur in the concert hall during the performance.

Indeed, all this music is linked through a common ideal: the desire to "destroy conventional musical continuity and liberate sound from the governance of memory, desire, and the rational mind."[10] To this end, the composer may choose to permit the content of the piece to be determined entirely randomly, perhaps by a roll of dice.

U.S.: Henry Cowell (1897–1965)
John Cage (1912–1992)
Lou Harrison (1917–2003)
Morton Feldman (1926–1987)

(10) **Individualists**

Harry Partch (1901–1974): investigated microtonality and built new instruments to perform his music.

Carl Orff (1895–1982): best know for stage works; the music features blocks of sound fashioned from percussive, repeated rhythms and simple diatonic harmonies.

Edgard Varèse (1885–1965): grandfather of electronic music and a man of vision. A pioneer in incorporating "noise" elements with pitch into the sonic palette.

George Gershwin (1898–1937): the American jazz-impressionist.

André Jolivet (1905–1974): noted for the subjective lyricism of his music, often built from scales of his own devising.

Olivier Messiaen (1908–1992): his is a personal, lyrical, expansive music that includes religious overtones and sounds from nature spread across vast canvases.

George Crumb (1929–): a specialist in highly programmatic music, he concocts beautiful, disturbing sound pictures from mere wisps of sound.

Steve Reich (1936–), Terry Riley (1935–), Philip Glass (1937–), Pauline Oliveros (1932–): using rhythmic and harmonic materials similar to those stressed by Carl Orff as well as an infusion of Eastern ideas on the meditative properties of music, these minimalists have contrived a hypnotic approach to music, still in its formative stages.

Steve Reich: *Piano Phase* for two pianos or two marimbas

Directions for performance of Piano Phase:

The number of repeats in each bar is not fixed, but a minimum of 16–24 per bar should be observed. The point throughout is not to count repeats but to listen to each bar until its two-voice relationship becomes clear to performer and listeners, then begin gradually to shift over to the pattern in the next bar.

The first performer starts at bar 1 and, after about six to twelve repeats, the second gradually fades in, in unison, at bar 2. After several seconds of unison the second player gradually increases the tempo very slightly and begins to move ahead of the first until he or she is one sixteenth note ahead, as shown at bar 3. The dotted lines indicate this gradual movement of the second performer and the consequent shift of phase relation between both performers. This process of gradual phase shifting and then holding the new stable relationship is continued.

NEW WAYS OF USING TRADITIONAL MUSICAL MATERIALS

When one looks into specific twentieth-century practices it soon becomes apparent that many are actually rooted in nineteenth-century developments. In the expanded timbral consciousness of Berlioz', Wagner's, and Mahler's orchestrations; in Schumann's preoccupation with syncopation; in the organic, compact and highly integrated forms devised by Brahms in his later years; and in a loosening tonal consciousness characteristic of the music of Wagner, Mussorgsky, Wolf, and Scriabin, we discover intimations of developments to come.

New ways of handling the traditional musical elements—rhythm, pitch, melody, tonality and harmony, texture or design, timbre and form—are also foreshadowed. In particular, "chromaticism; the extended and freer use of dissonance; the establishment of harmonic and melodic freedom; the use of harmonic, melodic, and structural ideas derived from folk music and early Western music; the concept of the structural interrelationships between all the parts of a musical composition; the discovery of the distant past and of non-Western music; the vast expansion of instrumental technique and color; the new freedom, complexity, and independence of rhythm, dynamics, and tone color—all these modern ideas have roots deep in the last century.[11] That composers have basically continued to explore the traditional elements, rather than turning from them, is a testament to the infinite potential inherent in these raw materials.

Two broad trends characterize the progress of music in our time: a desire to loosen the standardized supports of functional tonality and regularized rhythms to render them more plastic and more responsive, and a desire to make of music a more rational, less intuitive art by increasing the composer's conscious control over every aspect of every element.

RHYTHM

Rhythm, "the principle of organization that regulates the flow of music in time,"[12] animates and controls every aspect of a composition, placing each in correct proportion within the overall context by controlling duration.

In traditional terms, we talk of an "infinity" or "universe" of *pulses*, governed by the *rate of speed* at which they flow (tempo), and grouped according to a regularly recurring *accent pattern* (meter). Particular rhythms either reinforce the accent pattern of a meter

(e.g. $\frac{3}{4}$ 𝅗𝅥 ♩ | ♩. ♪ ♩ | ♫ ♩ ♩ ||)

or run counter to it, for refreshment. Perhaps the greatest innovations in twentieth-century music have come in the domain of rhythm, which has become free from all restraint.

Nineteenth-century rhythmic refreshments were few in number and carefully regulated. Each movement usually preceded within a single meter, subject to "interference" via a) *syncopations*; b) *hemiolas*; c) *crossrhythms*, of the two against three variety, or more rarely, d) three against four.

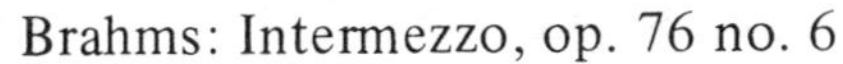

Chopin: Fantasy-Impromptu, op. 66

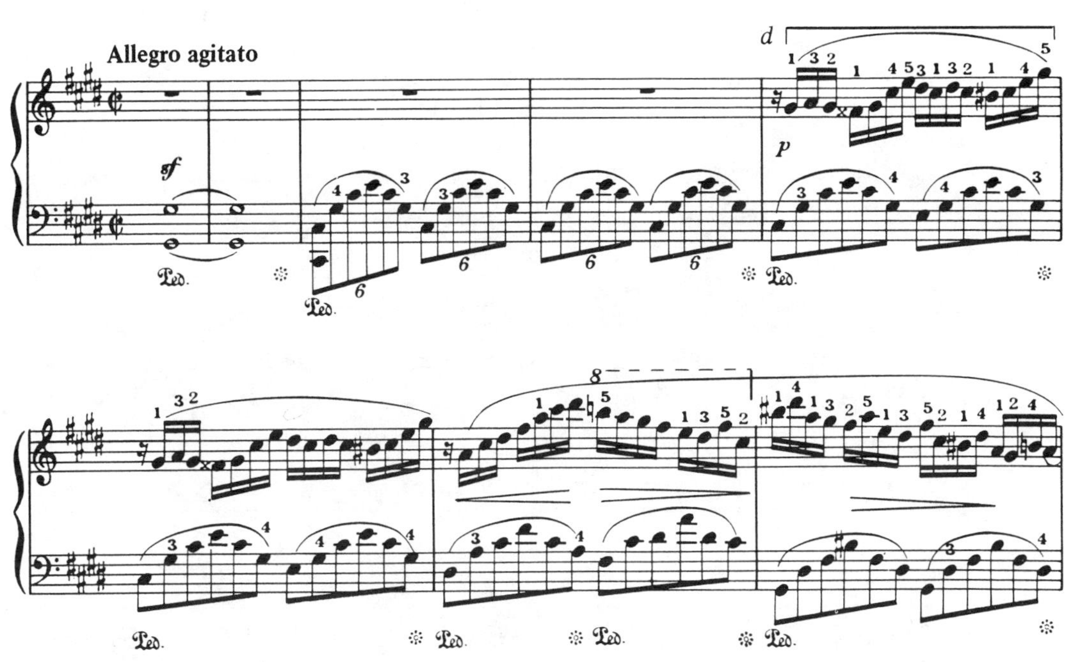

Scriabin: Sonata no. 5, op. 53

The rise of nationalist schools around the middle of the nineteenth century added the refreshment of accent patterns based on speech rhythms or national dances: Polish mazurkas and polonaises; Hungarian and Bohemian dance patterns (in the music of Liszt, Dvořák, Brahms, Smetana and others); the Norwegian influences in Grieg, etc. (Similarly in our century, much of Bartók's rhythmic verve derives from successful integration of Hungarian rhythms into a more complex rhythmic framework.) The Russians in particular loosened the straight-jacket of the inevitable downbeat by employing irregular or shifting meters.

Mussorgsky: *Pictures at an Exhibition*, "Promenade" theme

This century has extended rhythmic refreshments in two directions, both of which were explored specifically to loosen the "tyranny of the bar line."

One trend returns to the freer rhythms of prose (or Eastern musics). Lines become more supple, less regularized; the bar line evolves into a visual device for the performer's convenience only, moving away from its former function as an orientation point for both performer and listener:

Strauss: *Till Eulenspiegel's Merry Pranks*

Music may be unbarred entirely (as in Feldman's "Last Pieces") or bar lines may be used merely to indicate the extent of thought groups, in the manner of recitative:

Judith Lang Zaimont: "April"
from *Calendar Collection*

The second trend has been to intensify the pulsed aspect of music, while at the same time remaining free from the closure of a regularly anticipated downbeat. Borrowing the nervous syncopations of jazz accomplishes this very well.

Barber: Sonata, op. 26
(fourth movement)

Multimetric writing becomes common, with meters changing in virtually every bar. Bars are grouped into phrases with great flexibility; phrases appear to grow beyond the confines of the bar (see below); and meters themselves become intricate, compounded in an additive sense from smaller rhythmic nuggets: $\frac{5}{4}=\frac{2+3}{4}$ $\frac{7}{8}=\frac{2+2+3}{8}$ $\frac{10}{4}=\frac{3+3+4}{4}$

Hugo Weisgall: *Sine Nomine*

Roy Harris: "Children at Play"
from *Little Suite*

An extension of the cross-rhythm is the *polyrhythm*, in which differing rhythms are superposed for long stretches. To unify the whole, *rhythmic ostinato* comes to the fore (particularly in the music of the neoclassicists). The modern *ostinato* (the Italian for "obstinate") is most effective when it is uneven with respect to the meter, or when several ostinatos of different lengths are used in combination. (Note left-hand ostinato in the previous and following examples.)

Hindemith: Sonata, no. 2
(first movement)

Visually, one can identify certain styles, both personal and general, by their typical rhythmic configurations alone. Expressionist music—particularly totally controlled music—may be rapturous or spasmodic, but either way it tends to splinter the visual "beat" (usually a quarter note) into many tiny fragments of irregular length.

Milton Babbitt: "Partitions"

*The durational values on this line are intended solely to facilitate reading of the rhythmic aspects of the music by indicating those simpler subdivisions of the measure within the scope of which the less usual subdivisions occur.

By contrast, neoclassic music usually builds its more intricate rhythms by "writing large" and increasing the tempo:

Peter Mennin: Toccata,
from *Five Easy Pieces*

PITCH

One way of viewing the increasing sophistication of pitch materials through the course of musical history is to consider the evolution of music in terms of a "progress" up the harmonic series.

*not in tune with tempered scale

This illustrates a *fundamental* pitch (𝅝) and its family of *overtones* or *harmonics* (●). Each component of the series is called a *partial*; partials are numbered according to their place in the series, with the fundamental as 1.

In ancient and primitive musics, pitch materials were consistent with partials 1, 2, 3, and 4, displayed in a monophonic context; this includes medieval organum. As the major and minor third became increasingly accepted (for example, in *fauxbourdon*), the triad (partials 4, 5, 6) emerged as a mainstay in the musical fabric. From the baroque through the early part of the romantic eras, the dominant seventh (partials 4, 5, 6, 7) was the prime chord of harmonic tension, containing as it does the strongest contrapuntal puller, the tritone, within the larger frame of a diminished triad (partials 5, 6, 7). The late nineteenth century saw the expansion of the dominant seventh to a dominant ninth chord (partials 4, 5, 6, 7, 9). Twentieth-century composers have gone beyond these lower partials to emphasize pitch materials drawn from the series' upper reaches.

Western music usually accepts the semitone as the smallest possible interval and divides the octave into twelve chromatic half steps. In our century, an infusion of Eastern music—which features many, more minute divisions of the octave—has given rise to a variety of artificially constructed musical systems devoted to *microtonality* (microtonal pitch materials lie beyond the seventeenth partial in the harmonic series):

> Theorists and composers argued that there were no important reasons why the octave could not be divided into smaller divisions than the semitone. Joseph Yasser, for instance, offered a nineteen-note scale consisting of twelve primary pitches (the tones of the chromatic scale) and seven microtonal auxiliaries; Busoni suggested a thirty-six note scale, with some pitches no more than a sixth of a tone apart; Harry Partch developed a forty-three tone scale; Alois Hába introduced new notational symbols for the quarter-tone scale.[13]

The Mexican composer Julian Carillo constructed a "chromatic harp" which uses 100 equidistant divisions of the octave. Many composers have followed Bartók's lead in his writing for strings, which routinely employs the quarter-tone as a heightened inflection. With the development of electronic instruments in the past thirty years, pitch discriminations of minute exactness are now possible and available for immediate use, obviating the need for specially constructed microtonal instruments.

Even when keeping strictly to the traditional twelve chromatic pitches, composers have aimed for a new flexibility in their ordering. We commonly think of a *scale* or *mode* as a succession of tones, usually separated by half or whole steps, arranged in ascending or descending order. Actually, it is the successive *pattern of intervals* that truly defines a scale, by specifying its pattern for construction. For example, the major mode,

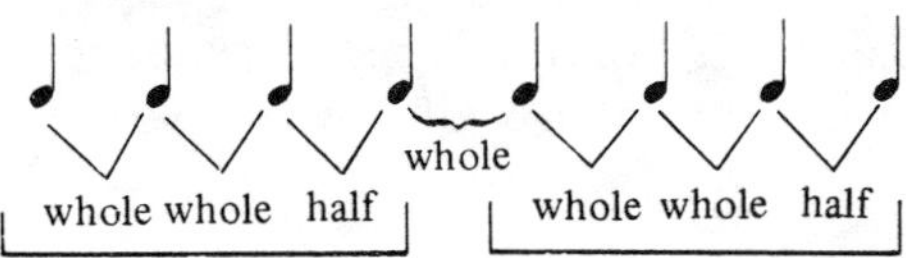

which may be considered as two identical *tetrachords* linked by a whole step. (The Dorian and Phrygian modes are also based on two identical tetrachords.)

In the twentieth century new scales or modes—both of the tetrachordal pattern and "through-composed"—have been consciously constructed.

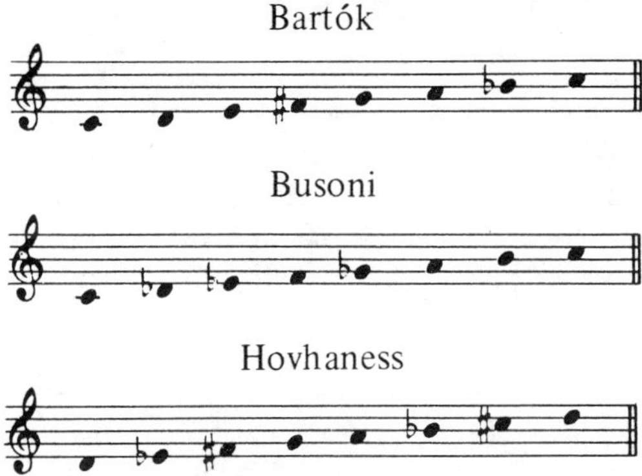

A scale need not contain seven pitches. The *pentatonic* (five-note) scale, a favorite of the impressionists, is found in Chinese, African, and Polynesian music, as well as in the music of American Indians, Celts, and Scots. In *La fille aux cheveux de lin* ("Girl with the Flaxen Hair"), Debussy uses a pentatonic scale to conjure a Scottish atmosphere, since this prelude was inspired by a poem by Robert Burns.

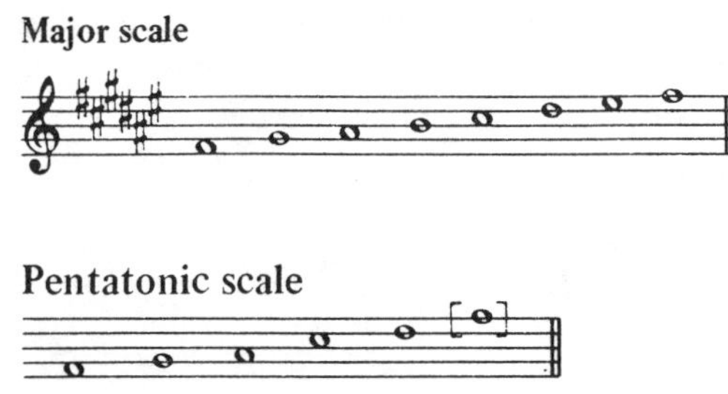

Debussy: *Nuages*

An interesting feature of the pentatonic scale is its "skeletal" nature: it lacks a leading tone. When spread over several octaves, it is seen to contain many potential tonic-dominant relations, each implying its own discrete scalar environment and equally persuasive:

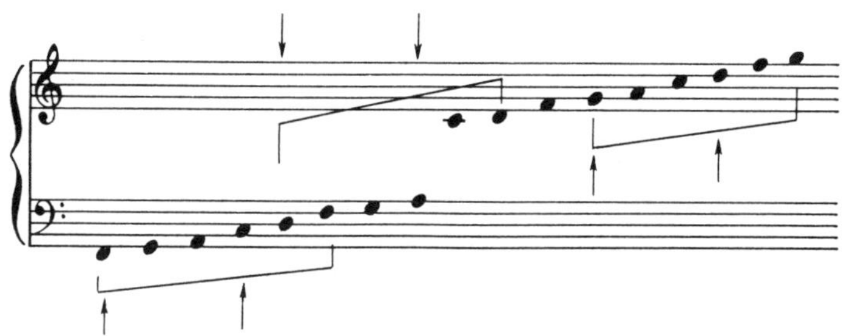

The *chromatic* scale is not really a scale, but rather a glossary of all possible pitches. When these are subdivided equally (according to a pattern implicit in the ordering of partials 7, 8, 9, 10, 11, of the harmonic series), two whole-tone scales result, each radically different from traditional scales because the "sol-do" relation is no longer present:

(The chromatic "collection" separated into the two whole-tone scales.)

The swimming, amorphous quality of whole-tone writing was much enjoyed by the impressionists and became a characteristic feature of their music. In *Voiles* ("Sails") from the first book of Preludes, Debussy uses a whole-tone environment almost exclusively. In addition, he often interpolates whole-tone passages within other pieces which are basically well-seated in major or minor, in order to maximize the contrast between the modes and highlight the suspended effect of the whole-tone sections:

Debussy: "Reflections in the Water,"
from *Images pour piano*, Book 1

Only two possible whole-tone scales exist. Within each, the sense of a particular tonic pitch can be achieved only by reiterating or otherwise highlighting a specific note; however, a vague dominant sensation may be produced through contrasting one whole-tone collection (in the role of dissonance) with the other (consonance).

MELODY

When we compare it to the vocally inspired melody of the nineteenth century, contemporary melody seems to have changed its character drastically. In shape, length, and construction it has become infinitely less rigid and less regularized, being now conceived instrumentally rather than vocally. It is true that in a few instances contemporary melody may be entirely athematic and unpredictable. Usually, however, the reasons for atypical configurations can be traced to strong influences from other musical elements on the melodic design:

(1) Melody may grow from a rhythmic impulse:

Bartók: *Mikrokosmos*, vol. 5 no. 122

(2) Melody may come from some implication inherent in the pitch materials of the piece, such as a nontraditional scale, an ethnic influence, or a consciously controlled pitch environment, such as the ordering of the row in twelve-tone writing.

Ross Lee Finney: "Tired," *24 Piano Inventions*, no. 7

(3) Symmetry and exact repetition are avoided. There is less of a build-up or traditional arch in the contour. Repetitions, when they occur, are likely to be compressed variants of the original material; composers prefer to state a thing once rather than two or three times.

Jane Young: "I Won't Go,
Oh Yes You Will"

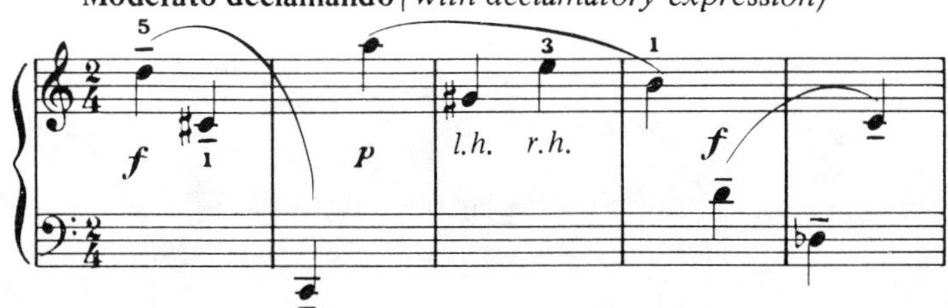

(4) Traditional punctuations are sidestepped: cadences are slurred over and the standard four-bar phrase is avoided, thus emphasizing the melody's asymmetric design (see Mennin's Toccata above).

(5) The melody may not grow from a harmonic framework at all, nor be supported by a background of regular rhythms and traditional harmonic progressions. "Individual tones are [liberated] from their former functions of upper neighbor, passing tone, appoggiatura, chord tones, etc."[14] This is absolutely the case in atonal expressionist music. The melody itself tends not to proceed in traditional scalewise motion or triadic leap, but instead moves disjunctly. One commonly encounters successive wide leaps in opposing directions, usually by an expressive or tensed interval: tritone, minor second, major seventh, major or minor ninth, etc.

(6) In length, the melodies may be either *discursive*—unfolding in long, convoluted arabesques of tones as in Samuel Barber's Adagio for Strings—or *epigrammatic*—either made from several short, self-contained convulsive bursts, or composed by continuously varying a single motivic cell. (This last is the very essence of Stravinsky's characteristic, additive melody: "the reiteration of similar melodic material in constant variation within a highly confined pitch field. One hears the same notes in ever new situations, the alternations being defined primarily by very subtle. . . rhythmic manipulations."[15])

Stravinsky: Allegro,
from "The Five Fingers"

The jagged look of twentieth-century melody derives from a technique called *octave displacement.* The following might conceivably be a melody of our time.

Actually, it is the theme from the second Kyrie of Bach's B-minor Mass subjected to octave displacement:

Bach: Kyrie, Mass in B minor

The procedure involves shifting selected tones (starred in the example) an octave above or below the register occupied by the body of the melody. The resultant contour is rich in expressive leaps and determinedly antivocal.

In the next example we can easily trace the steps by which Stravinsky constructed the lovely instrumental fugue subject in the second movement of *Symphony of Psalms,* which gains much of its expressive power from extensive use of octave displacement.

Raw material in rhythm:

As a single line, in one register:

Final version, with octave displacements:

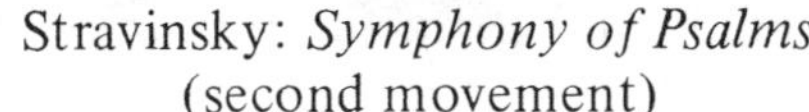

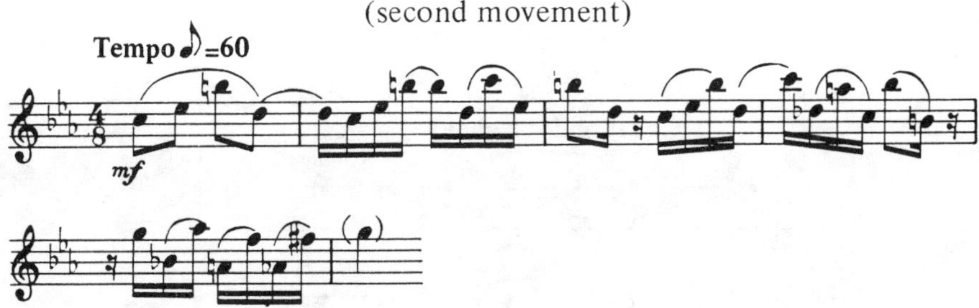

Notice that voice leading in the first of these operates in traditional fashion; it is only in the final version that loose ends appear to be left dangling, due to octave displacement of selected pitches. At the same time, note that the final version is by far more striking and effective than either of the two intermediate ones.

The idea of doubling the melodic contour with a subsidiary line a fixed interval away goes back to the very beginning of Western polyphony. Parallel organum, used in the early middle ages, is an example of consonant melodic doubling.

In the twentieth century, consonant doubling is no longer the rule and melodies may be freely doubled at any dissonant interval:

Doubling at the interval of a seventh:

Stravinsky: *Rite of Spring*

Indeed, organumlike sonorities or complete chords may be used in parallel with the melodic contour, as in Debussy's *La Cathédrale engloutie* ("The Sunken Cathedral") or in the following excerpts from *Pour le piano*:

Debussy: Sarabande
from *Pour le piano*

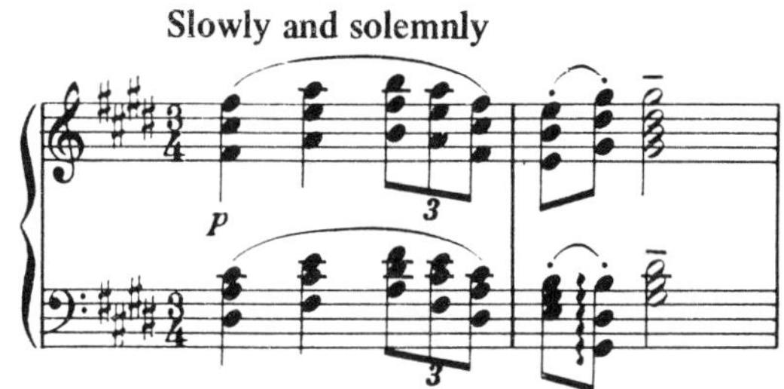

Debussy: Sarabande

Stravinsky: *Rite of Spring*

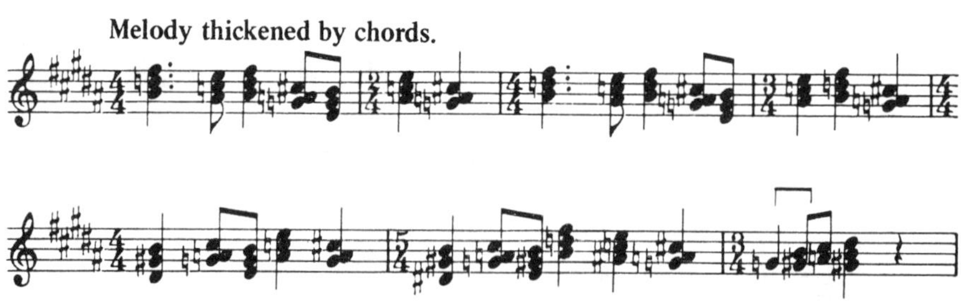

In fact, the musical contour—the overall shape and direction of the melodic line—has now assumed paramount importance, being accorded a significance greater than that warranted by merely summing up the totality of pitch content in a given passage. A precedent for the pre-eminence of contour over specific pitch content may be found in the venerable *glissando*, a gesture defined solely in terms of its precise extent and overall shape.

TONALITY AND HARMONY

Tonality, "the sense of relatedness to a central tone,"[18] —provides a center (the tonic) from which to judge relative consonance and dissonance. "Dissonance is the element that supplies dynamic tension, the forward impulsion that extends itself and comes to rest in consonance."[19] However, defining the active principle—dissonance—*absolutely* is virtually impossible.

From music's beginnings, our ears have progressed toward a greater and greater tolerance. For twentieth-century listeners, the distinction between what is consonant and what is dissonant has almost disappeared: we now term a sonority consonant simply because it seems less dissonant than its surroundings. The degree of a listener's musical sophistication directly influences perception in this matter. Other influences have to do with the sonority itself, with respect to the register in which it is placed, its duration, assigned dynamic level and articulation, timbre, and tempo.

Consider what happens to the perfect fourth (considered a definite dissonance in strict Palestrinian two-voice counterpoint) in the following two excerpts.[20]

In the first, the fourths are perceived as dissonant because the surrounding intervals (sixths) seem more stable. By contrast, in the second, the perfect fourths appear to be the only points of relative stability, since the rest of the intervals appear more tensed.

In *The Craft of Musical Composition*, Paul Hindemith systematized his perceptions of relative consonance and dissonance. The following table of intervals[21] illustrates his conclusions, arranged in order of increasing consonance.

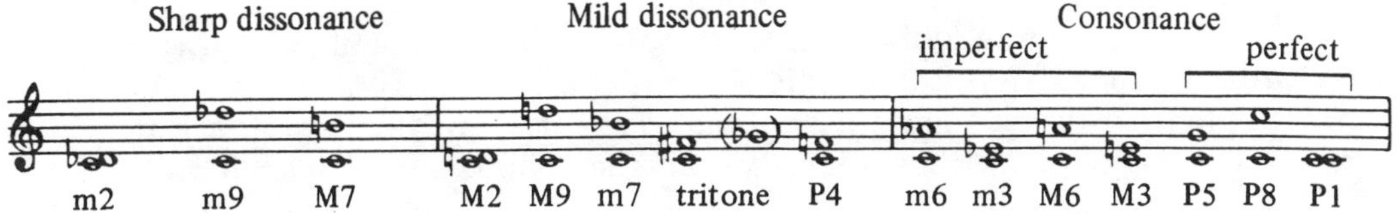

It is useful to compare this table with one's own perceptions. Although most of us will agree with the contents of the categories of sharp dissonance and consonance, the ordering of the middle group, mild dissonances, is open to question, particularly with regard to the tritone.

Once our perception has progressed to the point where at least certain of the mild dissonances are accepted as relatively stable, we must look beyond the pulling power of the traditional chords of tension—VII^{07}, V^7, V^9, etc.—for fresher, more compelling alternatives. For many, the solution lies in displacing traditional dominant pivots with chords drawn from far afield, foreign to the chromatic domain of the home key. Prokofiev's hallmark is just this kind of displacement, using unexpected chords to replace chords of dominant function or in place of the VI as resolution of a truly *deceptive* cadence.

Prokofiev: *Peter and the Wolf*

Once composers took the first step of replacing the mainstays of traditional tonality with harmonic alternatives, the natural next step was to grant all twelve tones the freedom to circulate equally in orbit about a tonic pitch (or tonic sonority). In the following example, Bartók clearly establishes B–F-sharp as the locus around which all other pitches travel. The idea of major or minor no longer matters, and a key signature would only call for extra labor on the composer's part, since he would be obliged to cancel many of its accidentals in every measure. (Note how the idea of a *gesture* or *configuration* becomes paramount in measures 8 to 15; here, the shape and direction of the line matter more than individual pitches).

Bartók: Bagatelle, op. 6 no. 6

As an intermediate step between displaced harmonies a la Prokofiev and free chromaticism around a tonal center, *pandiatonic* harmony was introduced (around 1920) by the neoclassicists, notably Stravinsky. In reaction to the profligate chromaticism of both whole-tone and atonal idioms, the neoclassicists voluntarily restricted themselves to using only the pitches of a single key or mode—but according to *no* specific harmonic rules. Thus, triadic harmonies could be scrapped, if desired, without losing the sense of a single tonality governing over all.

Stravinsky: Andantino,
from "The Five Fingers"

American neoclassicism is distinguished by its penchant for pandiatonic and/or bitonal writing. (This is not surprising, in view of the fact that many of these composers studied with Nadia Boulanger of France, where they imbibed a Gallic sense of nicety in detail and overall proportion, as well as a predilection for "neat" sounds—all of which result in "civilized" scores.) Pandiatonic writing is not precisely equivalent to white-key music; the latter is a subcategory of the former, although a large one, since many composers purposefully chose C as tonic to emphasize their antichromatic stand.

In a parallel development, the triad was subjected to distortion by "fattening" it to a monstrous thickness. Third was piled upon third until "skyscraper" *polychords* were formed, essentially perceived as organumlike thickenings of the melodic line.

Stravinsky: *Petrouchka*

Coupling the idea of harmonic thickening with displaced harmony led to music which moved in broad, independent planes of sound:

William Schuman: *A Three-Score Set*
(second movement)

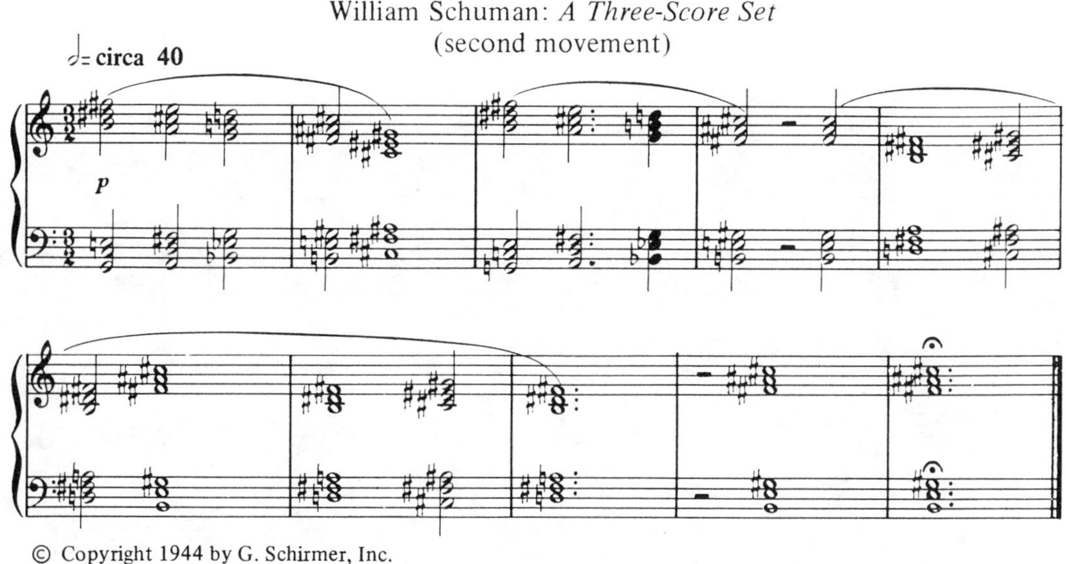

Pandiatonicism and polychords deal essentially with "disguised" triads. A more radical innovation was the decision to scrap the triad altogether and build sonorities based on intervals other than the third. Thus, we find the emergence of harmonic systems built on:

- the fifth (quintal harmony)

Gerhard Wuensch: "La Danse à Quinte"
from *Twelve Glimpses into Twentieth Century Idioms*

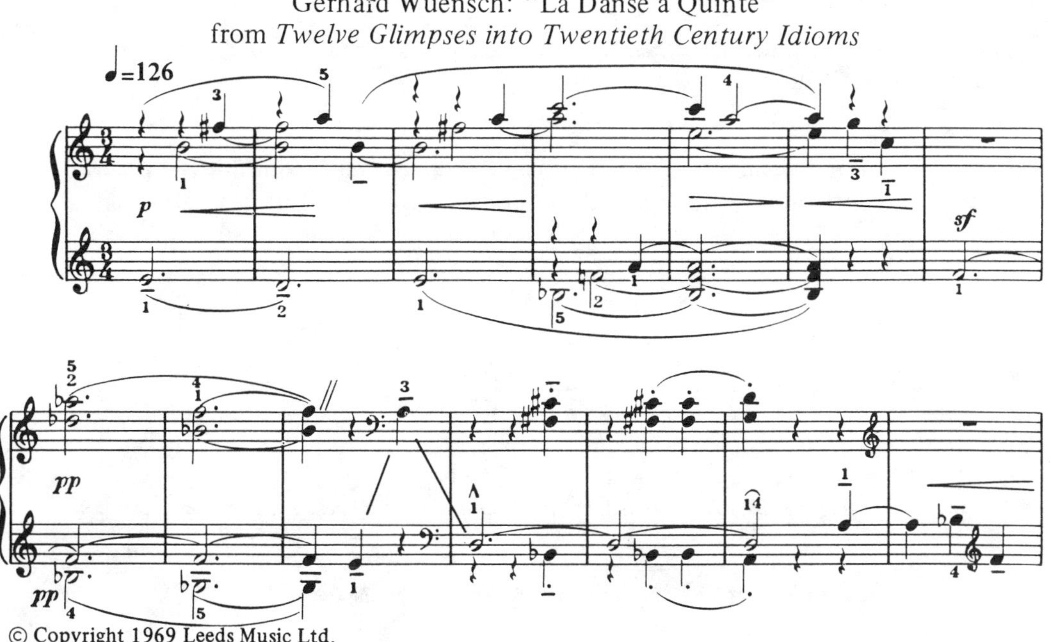

- the fourth (quartal harmony)

Gerhard Wuensch: "Four Square"
from *Twelve Glimpses into Twentieth Century Idioms*

The striking beauty of Paul Hindemith's personal idiom derives from his use of quintal and quartal harmonies within a contrapuntal, tonal frame:

Hindemith: "A Swan"
from *Six Chansons*

- Seconds may be added to fourths, fifths, or triads, or in *clusters*. Clusters may be either relatively mild (as in the Bartók) or abrasively dissonant (as in the Doris Hays):

Bartók: *Mikrokosmos*, vol. 4 no. 107

Bartók: *Mikrokosmos*, vol. 6 no. 144

Doris Hays: "Sunday Nights"

TEXTURES, DESIGNS, AND PROCEDURES

In this century *linear* thinking has come to the fore, with its focus on the horizontal rather than the vertical plane.

An emphasis on line has led to the abandonment of a single key or a single central tone as a unifying factor over the course of an entire movement or piece. Now, two or more keys may be used simultaneously (in piano music, one for each hand) in a bitonal or polytonal design that derives its bite from clashing semitones:

Stravinsky: *Petrouchka*

Prokofiev: *Sarcasms*, no. 3

Bitonal or polytonal writing may or may not feature contrasting key signatures. Often in bitonal piano music, white keys are assigned to one hand and pitted against black keys in the other.

Each line in a texture need not be assigned an individual harmonic plane in order to achieve independence: the overall design may be merely a free, *dissonant counterpoint* (so called because the dissonances occur when the sharply directed lines coincide to "energize the movement and add to the propulsive power of the line"[22]). Hindemith's procedures are usually termed dissonant counterpoint, but the phrase may be equally descriptive of individual works by other composers:

Bartók: *Mikrokosmos*, vol. 3 no. 91

The idioms in which linear thinking is paramount are atonality and dodecaphonic (twelve-tone) writing.

A development of Arnold Schoenberg, atonality represents the next step beyond free chromaticism: all twelve chromatic pitches are defined as precisely equal, and any hint of a tonic is avoided by strictly forbidding any single tone to predominate. Naturally, all references of a traditional nature (any kind of chordal building-block, scale, etc.) are discarded along with the sense of tonality. Schoenberg's first true atonal composition is *Three Piano Pieces*, op. 11 of 1908.

Schoenberg: Three Piano Pieces, op. 11 no. 1

In truth, atonality is not in any sense a compositional method but rather a philosophic guide to the act of composing. Because new principles of organizing materials had to be developed for virtually every piece, each composer's atonal works are apt to be quite individualized.

Around 1915 Schoenberg began to feel that atonal music needed a definite organizing principle and compositional technique of its own, and he developed the concept of a *series*. A series or *tone row* is a particularized arrangement of pitches (usually all twelve chromatic ones) that becomes the theme-scale for a piece. The order in which the pitches are stated becomes all-important: by using the pitches in strict serial order only, any sense of a predominant tonic pitch is lost, and the *intervallic pattern* established by the original row (functioning as a template, in the manner of a traditional scale-pattern) enables the composer to transpose the series at will, by beginning it on any other of the remaining eleven pitches.

An entire composition mav be constructed from the row in its original configuration (Webern's *"Kinderstück"*, op. post.) either in the "home key" or with transpositions; or the row may be subjected to contrapuntal manipulations similar to those of traditional counterpoint. Pitch materials for *Twelve Easy Pieces* by Ernst Křenek:

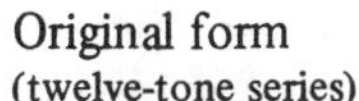
Original form
(twelve-tone series)

Inverted form of the original
(obtained by changing ascending intervals to equivalent descending ones, and vice versa)

Retrograde form of the original
(obtained by proceeding from the last tone to the first)

Inverted form of the retrograde
(obtained by reading the inverted form backward)

The *original* form of the row may be stated in reverse order (*retrograde*); *inverted* intervallically (note the symmetrical contours of the row and its inversion); and in *retrograde inversion*. The entire composition will thus consist of restatements of the series in any of its numerous guises, predetermining the entire pitch content of the piece—vertical as well as horizontal.
(Using only the retrograde and inverted forms of the row.)

Křenek: "Glass Figures,"
from *12 Short Piano Pieces*

Andante ben tenuto ♩=63

Later, strict serial procedures were adapted by the integral serialists to control all other musical parameters, as well as pitch: dynamics, articulation, registral placement, rhythm, and timbre.

It is interesting to note that the system of ordering devised by those composers who rigorously sought to deny tonality is now being used to compose tonal music as well. Series of fewer than twelve pitches are often used; and one might construct a series of seven diatonic pitches (though not in scalar order), or something like the following, with strong tonal implications:

E C	A F	D A-flat B	G
I	IV⁶	VII°⁷	"V"

TIMBRE AND FORM

"Form in new music can be examined from two points of view: first, there is *outer form*, which results from the sectional arrangement of musical idea, and second, there is *inner form*, which results from thematic and motivic connections." [23] Both outer and inner forms still rely on the basic architectural principles of repetition and contrast, but *compression, variation,* and *disguise* serve to veil structural outlines to such an extent that now we often perceive a single movement as an organic whole, and not as something composed of separate sections.

In particular, the twentieth-century sonata has been altered. It is frequently cast as a single movement whose outer design bears but a distant kinship to the classical architectural design of exposition–development–recapitulation (see Berg's Sonata, op. 1.).

The search for overall unification has produced an increasing number of both large and small works cast in *arch* or *mirror* form. In these, composers "permit the piece to unfold until the middle section has been reached, and then. . . have it reverse itself to the end: *i.e.*, ABCBA, ABACABA, etc." [24] Arch forms offer an excellent compromise between through-composition and the symmetrically balanced forms originally derived from various dances. Among the works using arch forms are Berg's *Lyric Suite*, Webern's *Six Pieces for Orchestra*, op. 6, Boulez' Piano Sonata no. 3, and Gregg Smith's *Magnificat*.

> The central formal problem facing the composer today, however, is not one of being able to create new outer arrangements, but rather either ways of achieving inner thematic unity, or even deciding whether inner thematic unity is any longer relevant in the music of today. In other words, it is a matter of how much control, and what specific types of control, the composer may justifiably use in creating a piece. [25]

Composers who favor maximally controlled music feel that deriving every element of the piece from relationships set forth in this initial series assures that the composition will be formally convincing–and consequently, they deny the role of intuition. On the other hand, composers of chance music feel that intuition–if it is "of the moment" and "all of a piece"–can go far toward eliminating the need to spell out structural relations in detail, in advance.

In both controlled and noncontrolled music, timbre has become an important form-building element. Instruments are being pushed to their registral and technical limits in the course of efforts to enlarge the sonic palette; at the same time, the "klang," or overall sound event of the moment, is fast becoming the new-music equivalent of the traditional theme or motive. In such diverse works as "The Game of Pairs" from Bartók's Concerto for Orchestra, Varèse's *Ionisation*, and Penderecki's *Threnody for the Victims of Hiroshima*, timbral contrasts largely determine sectional divisions, and are considerable factors in insuring the integrity and logical unity of the form overall.

INNOVATIONS IN PIANO TECHNIQUE AND NOTATION

In the last 125 years the role of composer has gradually grown distinct and separate from that of conductor, instrumentalist, singer, musicologist, acoustician, or any other music specialist. Such intense specialization within the field of a single performing art has proven to be a rather mixed blessing, mainly because of the increasing separation between the creator and re-creator, or performer.

However, isolating the role of "composer-specialist" has produced some remarkable advances and innovations in technique, because it has given the composer the luxury of enough time in which to examine the medium scientifically, detail by detail. Thus, every musical element can be broken down into its smallest component–its "molecule"–and subjected to experiment in order to determine the resultant sound effect of any change in its nature, however small. As a consequence, terms such as *pitch*, *duration*, and *loudness* became inexact for descriptive purposes when discussing an individual tone. A tone may now be specifically identified through noting its *frequency* (cycles per second, including any variations from the basic pitch produced by vibrato, tremolo, or microtonal inflection) and the length and dynamic character of each minute component: initial *attack*; main segment (*sustain*); tail (*decay*); and *cutoff*.

Naturally, such precise control over every aspect of every note meant that scores in traditional notation would grow increasingly detailed; and that one could look forward to the invention of new notational symbols to represent new effects.

Until the early 1950s, innovations in piano technique focused mainly on enlarging the instrument's timbral resources while increasing the independence of the hands at the keyboard. (Bitonality, for instance, may be considered an outgrowth of permitting each hand maximum autonomy by allotting each its own harmonic domain.)

In the rhythmic area we find the following techniques increasingly prevalent: an emphasis on intricate rhythms (Babbitt: "Partitions," p. 364, and Bartók: *zmiktokodmod*, p. 370; noncoordinating ostinatos; multimetric writing (Mennin: Prelude, p. 390) and Bartók: Bagatelle, p. 391); irregular meters (Mennin: Prelude, p. 390); greater use of polyrhythms (Babbit: "Partitions," p. 364); nonsymmetric phrase structures (Bartók: Bagatelle, p. 377); and frequent temp changes (Bartók: Bagatelle, p. 391).

Bartók: *Mikrokosmos*, vol. 5 no. 133

Allegro, ♩=152

Mennin: Prelude,
from *Five Piano Pieces*

Allegro brillante (♪ + ♪ = 144)

p *cresc.*

dim.

pp

Bartók: Bagatelle, op. 6 no. 12

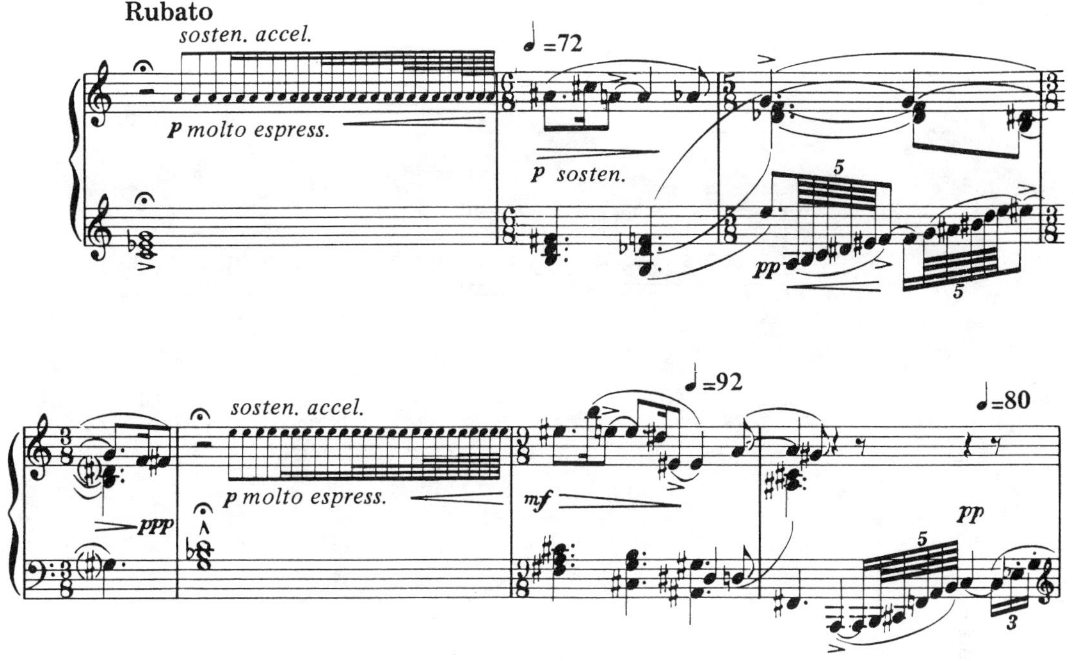

A single musical figure may be dispersed throughout the keyboard, and disparate textures succeed one another with great rapidity (Riley: *Five Little Movements*, p. 392). The hands no longer remain relatively stable in the center of the keyboard, but are often widely separated (Barber: Sonata, p. 393).

Dennis Riley: *Five Little Movements*, no. 2

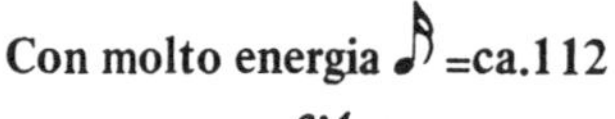

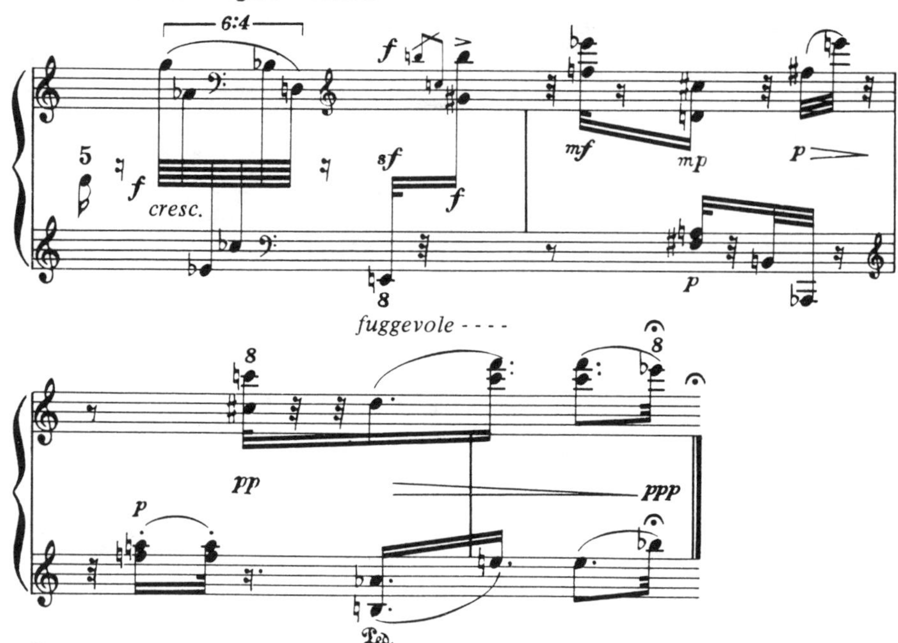

Webern: Piano piece, op. posth.

Barber: Sonata, op. 26
(fourth movement)

Doublings may be called for at unusual intervals. Chord spacings often lie outside traditional harmonic patterns and may be of the cluster type.

Schoenberg: *Six Little Piano Pieces*, op. 19 no. 6

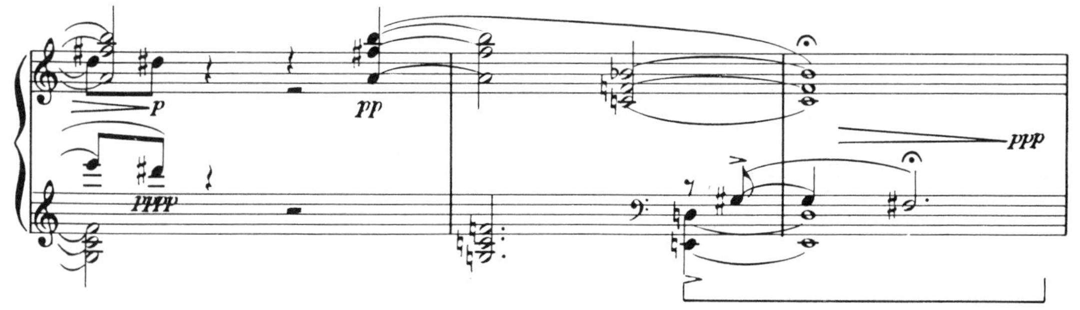

The whole musical fabric is likely to be discontinuous, demanding extreme agility on the performer's part in the negotiation of sudden registral shifts, awkward across-the-body cross-hand maneuvers and single-note exchanges, as well as expert control over a wide spectrum of variegated attacks and dynamics.

Webern: *Variations for Piano*, op. 27
(second movement)

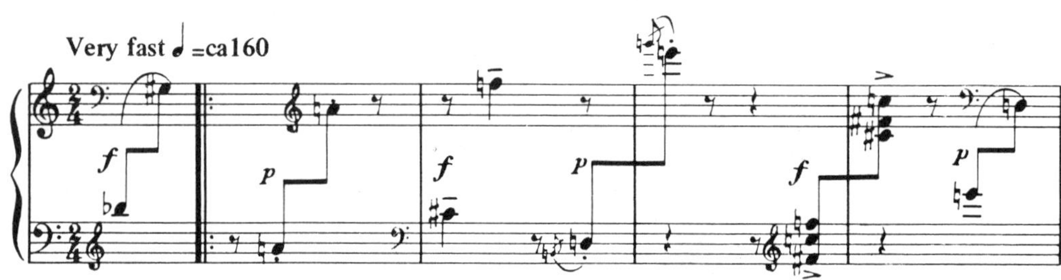

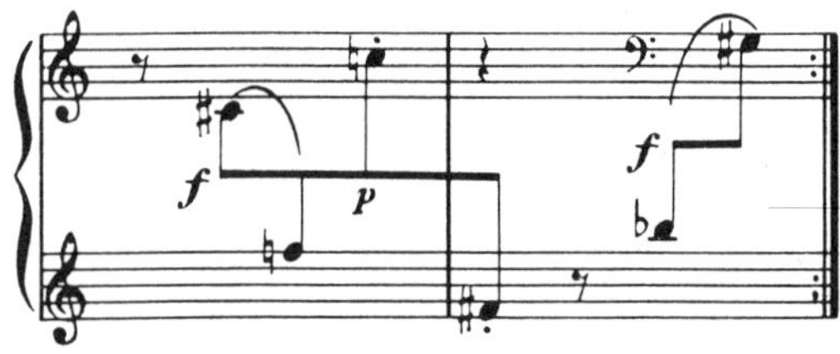

Attributes emphasized in nineteenth-century literature—seamless legato, singing tone, and expressive playing—are no longer of importance when tackling music written expressly for an instrument "with hammers." The percussive approach is stressed in the music of Cowell, Prokofiev, and Bartók. "Independent action of the fingers is often replaced by hammerlike strokes of the whole hand, molded into a specific pattern, often with the scope of an octave or more . . . . One hand will sometimes be called upon to play six- or seven-note chords, often percussively repeated. Octave passages and thirds do not glide, but are hammered out. . . . The peculiar technique is vital to the expression of the music, even in places where it is not vital simply to hitting the right notes." [26]

Prokofiev: Toccata, op. 11

Another common percussive device is the repeated pitch, "beaten out . . . with emphatic accent on each note, to set up a steady hammering sound." [27] Tone clusters, first used and named by Henry Cowell, add bite and vehemence.

Another innovation we owe to Cowell is that of playing directly on the piano strings, using the fingers or the whole hand to make them vibrate by plucking, stroking, strumming, or slapping. Cowell's "Aeolian Harp" is an excellent piece illustrating many of these performance techniques.

INNOVATIONS IN NOTATION

Most of the innovations in technique discovered or exploited since World War II have centered on expanding the timbral palette even further. Both totally controlled music and music of chance required the invention of new notational symbols and perfection of the old so that (1) every one of the composer's instructions could be indicated with minute exactness or that (2) it be made quite clear to the performer exactly which components were previously defined by the composer, and which left to the performer's discretion to improvise at the moment of performance.

Many composers insterested in total control turned to tape music. Here, since the taped result is at once the piece itself and the definitive performance, a score becomes superfluous, at least in its function as an instrument of communication to a performer. However, as more and more composers begin to write music for tape and live performers (which once again required a score), they were obliged to invent symbolic equivalents for electronic music sound events. Ironically, many of these notation symbols turned out to be strikingly similar to graphic notations already devised by composers of chance music.

Tone clusters became prominent features of the new music. Henry Cowell first used the term to mean a strongly dissonant group of neighboring pitches, which could be entirely chromatic (G–G-sharp–A–A-sharp–B); diatonic (F–G–A–B–C, D-flat–E-flat–G-flat–A-flat–B-flat, or A–B–C-sharp–D–E); or a mixture of both (C–D–E-flat–F-sharp–G–A-flat). In any case, they were precise clusters of a more or less narrow compass, meant to be played with the fingers, and perfectly capable of being notated in traditional fashion.

Clusters soon evolved beyond a narrow compass, becoming approximate rather than precise in pitch content, and began to be played with fists, flat of the hand, or forearm. A symbolic notation was developed for these clusters of wider compass, which has recently been refined:

(1) Precise clusters notated symbolically, in which the thick vertical line connecting a harmonic interval indicates that all chromatic tones within the interval are to be played:

all black keys

(2) Approximate clusters notated symbolically (all illustrations are eighth notes):

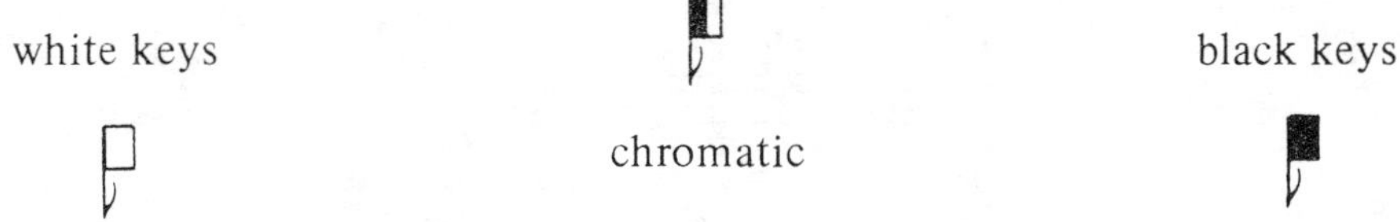

Either precise or approximate clusters may, in addition, be notated *proportionally*, that is, in a system where "all durations must be noted in spatial proportion to each other."[28] This is accomplished by precisely equating a note's horizontal placement on the page with the relative duration of its sound:

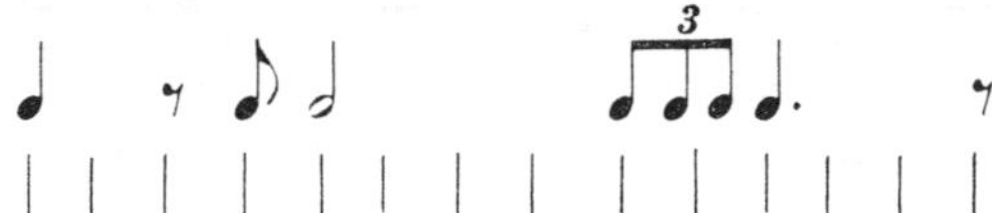

> If the durations are taken care of by horizontal distances, then there is no further need for durational symbols, such as the distinction in traditional notation between black and white noteheads, or flags, beams, dots, triplet numerals, and so on. All that are needed in proportionate notation are noteheads to indicate pitches and a single beam to show how long the pitches are to sound (beam=sound; no beam=silence)." [29]

Thus, precise clusters notated proportionally:

and approximate clusters notated proportionally:

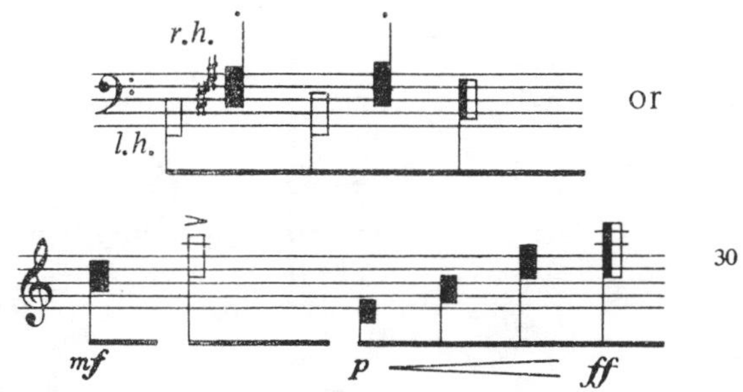

Also explored was the phenomenon of *sympathetic vibration*, in which keys are depressed silently (thus lifting the dampers), permitting the strings to vibrate in sympathy with overtones from other pitches actually sounded. Schoenberg adopted the diamond-shaped note head, usually used for string harmonics, for this effect.

The damper pedal has been brought to the fore as a timbral device. It may be used traditionally, in full and half pedals; to build several clusters into huge reverberant blocks of sound; to enhance attack effects:

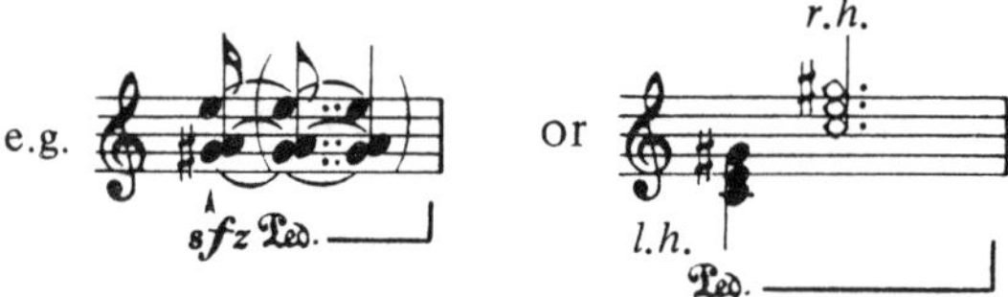

or all by itself, as a sound:

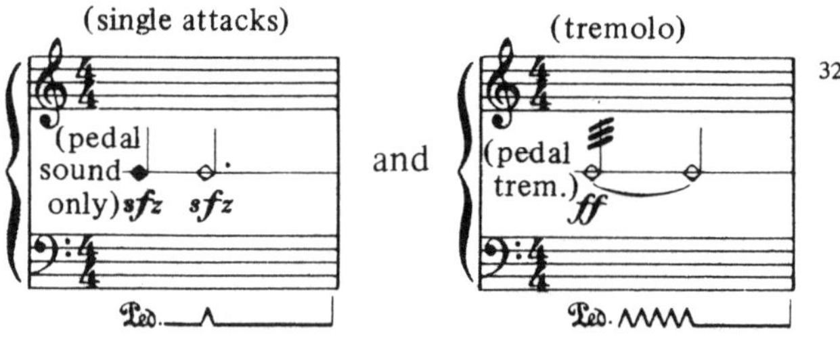

Huge expansion of the sonic palette became possible when composers began to consider *noise* as a sound component.

> John Cage's early experiments with the "prepared piano" paved the way for a wide range of unconventional usages. . . . Rubber threaded through the strings at harmonic nodes will give sounds of quiet, pale harmonic quality. Bolts or screws left free to move will produce buzzing tones, while those fixed firmly will make for dull, thudding percussive sounds with little or no "piano" tone. . . . Wire-wrapped bass strings can be scraped with knife blades. . . [or] the tone can be modified by pressing strips of plasticine over the strings and then playing the keyboard. . . . If metal rules are laid over the strings a percussive, clanging effect is obtained. With the sustaining pedal depressed, one can obtain magnificent cluster sounds by rapid glissandos over the strings or by striking several strings at once. . . . The use of a microphone inside the piano will greatly enhance these sound potentialities. [33]

"Nor is the pianist limited to the keyboard. He may be called upon to slam the lid down, strum the strings inside, even screech the piano stool across the floor ever so delicately; no noise possibilities are excluded if they can produce the desired effect." [34] These include slapping one's hands or fists on the music desk, the keyboard cover, or other parts of the instrument; and non-piano-involved participations by the performer, such as speaking, humming, shouting, singing, whistling, grunting, or other vocalizations.

Much use has been made of the piano's interior in both prepared and traditional setups. Indeed, individual strings are so often called for that the suggestion has been made to urge piano manufacturers to color the dampers black and white in the same pattern as the keyboard, to facilitate locating any given string. [35]

The strings may be excited to vibrate either by means of a plectrum or beater (such as a steel needle, a soft tympani stick, etc.), or directly by the player. Strumming and plucking—with the finger tip, nail, or knuckle—are commonly called for. In addition, when playing entirely inside the piano, the free hand may be called on to muffle or "stop" the string while the other hand actually sounds the pitch. As expected, extreme agility is required whenever it becomes necessary to maneuver from keyboard to strings and back again.

It is interesting to note that the new notation symbols, although originally devised to aid in the communication of specific effects, have themselves become the inspiration for further innovations.

Especially for music in which perceptible control over particular features is left to the performer, graphic rather than symbolic notation may prove a more perfect means of communicating the composer's intent. Picturing the intended result rather than giving detailed instructions on how to achieve that result may be the best and most economic way to communicate in certain idioms, particularly in situations calling for a sweeping but imprecise gesture.

Ross Lee Finney: *32 Piano Games*, no. 22

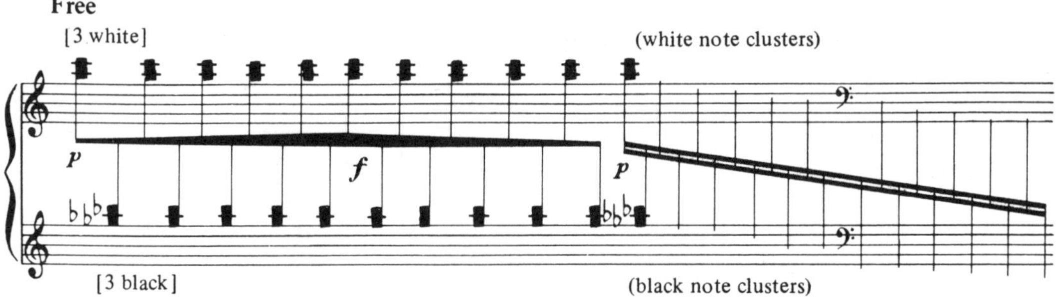

Ross Lee Finney: *32 Piano Games*, no. 28

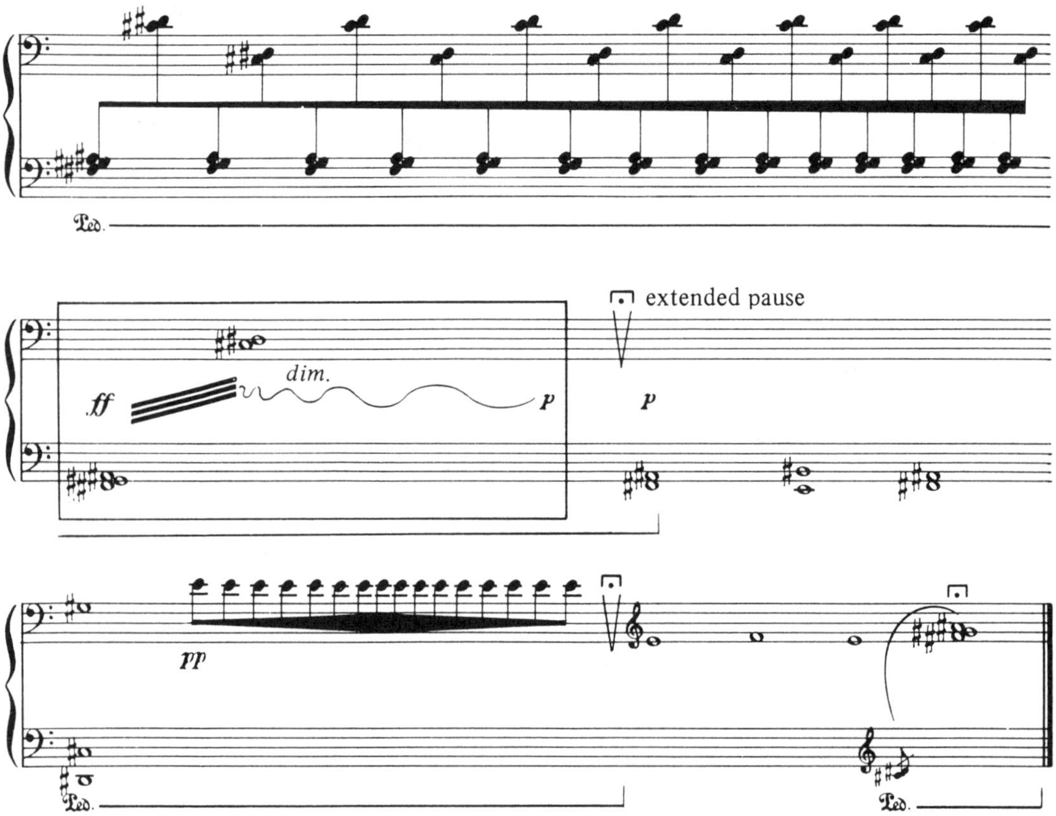

During the last seventy-five years we have seen music slowly evolve into dynamic sonic sculpture, taxing the composer's creative ingenuity and resourcefulness every step of the way. With the guidance of concerned and sympathetic teachers from this point on, we can look forward to a new generation of performers and listeners, equally sympathetic and resourceful, who will consider the new music in no way other than as a perfectly natural and congenial means of expression.

NOTES

1. Johann Huizinga, "A Definition of the Concept of History." In Raymond Klebansky and H.J. Paton, eds.: *Philosophy and History*. New York: Harper Torchbooks, 1963, 8.
2. Eric Salzman, *Twentieth-Century Music*, 4.
3. Reginald Smith Brindle, *The New Music*, 186; 6.
4. Salzman, op. cit., 2.
5. Ibid., 6.
6. Brindle, op. cit., 133.
7. Sergei Prokofiev, *Notebooks* (1937).
8. Salzman, op. cit., 156.
9. Gerald Strang, "Ethics and Esthetics of Computer Composition." In Harry B. Lincoln, ed., *The Computer and Music*. Ithaca: Cornell University Press, 1970, 41.
10. Brindle, op. cit., 126.
11. Salzman, op. cit., 3.
12. Joseph Machlis, *Introduction to Contemporary Music*, 40.
13. Donald Chittum, "Music Here and Now," Part 2: "The Pitch Materials of New Music," 30.
14. Alice Canaday, *Contemporary Music and the Pianist*, 10.
15. Robert P. Morgan, "Towards a More Inclusive Musical Literacy," Part I, 11.
16. Cited in Marion Bauer, *Twentieth-Century Music*, 191.
17. Ibid.
18. Machlis, op. cit., 32.
19. Machlis, op. cit., 23.
20. Cited in Welton Marquis, *Twentieth-Century Music Idioms*, 48.
21. Adapted from Marquis, op. cit., 49.
22. Machlis, op. cit., 52.
23. Chittum, op.cit., Part 1: "Gesture and Organization in New Music," 23.
24. Ibid., 23, 46.
25. Ibid., 46.
26. Susan Calvin, "Modern Revolution in Piano Writing," 42.
27. Ibid., 41.
28. Kurt Stone, "New Notation for New Music," Part 2, 56.
29. Ibid.
30. Cited in ibid., 58.
31. Quoted from "International Conference on New Music Notation Report," 96.
32. Quoted from ibid., 94–95.
33. Brindle, op. cit., 160–61.
34. Calvin, op. cit., 42.
35. "International Conference on New Musical Notation Report," 96–97.

BIBLIOGRAPHY

Bauer, Marion. *Twentieth-Century Music: How It Developed, How to Listen to It* (rev. ed.). New York: G.P. Putnam's Sons, 1947.

Brindle, Reginald Smith. *The New Music: The Avant-Garde Since 1945*. London: Oxford University Press, 1975.

Cage, John (compiler and arranger). *Notations*. New York: Something Else Press, 1969.

Calvin, Susan. "The Modern Revolution in Piano Writing." *The American Music Teacher*. April-May 1969.

Canaday, Alice. *Contemporary Music and the Pianist: A Guidebook of Resources and Materials*. Alfred Publishing Co., Inc. 1974.

Chittum, Donald. "Music Here and Now." *The American Music Teacher*. Part 1: "Gesture and Organization," September-October 1971, 23, 46; Part 2: "The Pitch Materials of New Music," January 1972, 30, 35; Part 3: "Improvisation, Chance, Indeterminacy," February-March 1972, 30, 37, 40; Part 4: "Serial Music and Total Organization," April-May 1972, 34–35; Part 5: "Tape Music and Multimedia," June-July 1972, 28–29.

Contemporary Music and Audiences. Canadian Music Council, 1969.

Copland, Aaron. *The New Music 1900–1960* (rev. ed.). New York: W.W. Norton, 1968.

Crowder, Louis L. "Piano Music of the Twentieth Century." *An Anthology of Piano Music:* Volume 4: "The Twentieth Century," Denes Agay, ed. New York: Yorktown Music Press, 1971.

Hindemith, Paul. *A Composer's World: Horizons and Limitations* (Charles Eliot Norton Lectures 1949–1950). Garden City: Anchor Books/Doubleday, 1961.

——. *The Craft of Musical Composition*, rev. ed. New York: Associated Music Publishers, 1945.

"International Conference on New Musical Notation Report." *Interface: Journal of New Music Research*, November 1975.

Lincoln, Harry B., ed. *The Computer and Music*. Ithaca: Cornell University Press, 1970.

Machlis, Joseph. *Introduction to Contemporary Music*. New York: W.W. Norton, 1961.

Marquis, Welton. *Twentieth Century Music Idioms*. Englewood Cliffs, New Jersey: Prentice-Hall, 1964.

Morgan, Robert P. "Towards a More Inclusive Musical Literacy: Notes on Easy Twentieth Century Piano Music" (Parts 1 and 2). *Musical Newsletter*, January 1971; April 1971.

Myers, Rollo H. *Twentieth-Century Music* (2nd ed.). London: Calder and Boyars, 1968.

Peyser, Joan. *The New Music: The Sense Behind the Sound*. New York: Delacorte Press, 1971.

Read, Gardner. *Music Notation: A Manual of Modern Practice*. Boston: Allyn and Bacon, 1964.

Salzman, Eric. *Twentieth-Century Music: An Introduction*. Englewood Cliffs, New Jersey: Prentice-Hall, 1967.

Stone, Kurt. "New Notation for New Music" (Parts 1 and 2). *Music Educators Journal*, October 1976; November 1976.

Wilder, Robert D. *Twentieth-Century Music*. Wm. C. Brown Company, 1969.

What Is Jazz?

STUART ISACOFF

When Bartolommeo Cristofori invented the pianoforte in 1709, the event ushered in a new musical and social era. Earlier, musical performances were often buried in the inner sanctums of aristocratic parlors, or restricted and controlled by High Church decree. In 1449, for instance, the king of Scotland declared that minstrels were to live "decently" or leave the country: any minstrel found performing would have his ears cut off; if caught a second time, he would be hanged. Of course, official attitudes were not always so severe, but it was not until the mass production of pianofortes in the late eighteenth century that instrumental music became the commoner's plaything.

The distinction between popular (frivolous) and classical (important) music remains even today, however. "Serious musicians" are usually thought to be free from contagion by popular tastes, despite a growing recognition that such categories are silly and artificial. A case in point is the early attitude toward jazz, a kind of music which, according to John Philip Sousa, "makes you want to bite your grandmother." But the spontaneity and drive which characterize jazz are as much the experience of Bach, Beethoven, and Mozart as that of Thelonious Monk, Bud Powell, and Duke Ellington. Throughout history the greatest masters have also been consummate improvisors, and many gems of our musical repertoire are simply notated versions of superb improvisations. Although jazz, as a synthesis of African, American, and European traditions, falls within certain distinctive stylistic boundaries, its basic elements are the same as those which form the backbone of all musical craft.

Thus, the teacher may use jazz materials to instruct the student in all of the traditional concepts–harmony, rhythm, voice leading, dynamics–while employing a format which is appealingly contemporary, and which holds great interest for most students. There is a rich and varied repertory of jazz materials written with intelligence, wit, and feeling. It is, therefore, well worthwhile for piano teachers to investigate the characteristics of jazz style. The task is not a difficult one. From its primitive beginnings to contemporary sophisticated works there are common threads which bind and clarify this art and make it accessible.

JAZZ RHYTHM

The heart of jazz is its distinctive rhythm, a combination of African and European elements, reflecting two different musical approaches. In both idioms notes and note groups are accented through such common, orthodox devices as:

However, the differences between the African and European concepts of rhythm are more pronounced than the similarities.

European rhythmic elements are organized to reinforce a strong metrical scheme, a repeating pattern of accents that usually appear in groups of two, three, or four beats. Hence, the music flows out of a constant tension and relaxation effected against a metrical background. This feature strongly characterizes and dominates the musical life of the West; as C.P.E. Bach wrote, "each meter carries a kind of compulsion within itself."

African rhythm, on the other hand, is additive: one rhythm added to another, no bar lines, and no sense of meter. This is derived from the rhythm and stress of tribal language; it evolved and developed through the use of "talking drums," a tool of communication. The three elements of speech in West African languages–rhythm, intonation (or pitch inflection) and accent–become translated to percussion music, and African melody clearly reflects African spoken languages.

SYNCOPATION

Since African rhythm is free of metrical boundaries, one of the most noted features of early jazz, syncopation, finds its origins not in an African contribution to jazz music, but in European composition and performance practice since the fifteenth century. How did syncopation develop as a major expressive and stylistic device among early ragtime and jazz musicians? By tracing the strands of European and African influences (and the social context in which they merged), a clear answer presents itself, one which sheds light on the whole history of jazz.

The earliest writings on syncopation are by the fourteenth-century theorists Philippe de Vitry and Johannes de Muris. The original concept was one of breaking up a series of rhythmic values by changing the placement of a large-value note to situate it between two shorter ones. Thus, the figure,

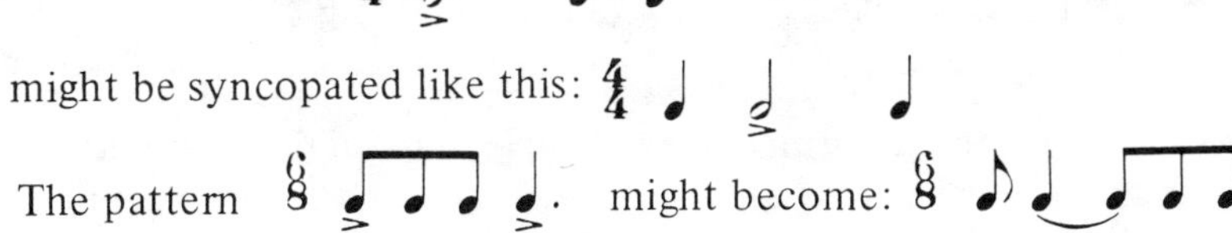

In the classical period, syncopation was used extensively to create rhythmic and melodic tension. A conflict is created between the accents implied by the bar line and those found in the melody: a sort of war over where the strong beat belongs.

accents implied by bar line:

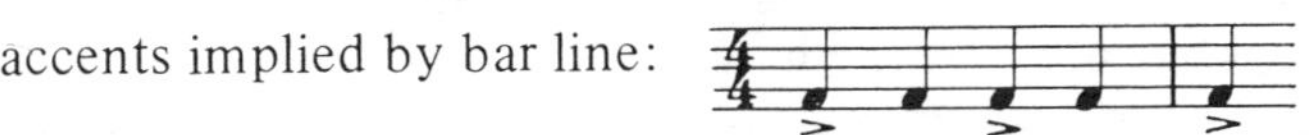

accents of syncopated phrase:

This tension, however, is short-term, and finds release quickly in a reestablishment of the expected order.

Beethoven: Bagatelle, op. 126

Syncopation in African music is actually not syncopation at all, according to its Western theoretical meaning. Of course there is a good deal of rhythmic polyphony, with overlapping downbeats giving Western ears an impression of shifting meters and syncopated patterns. For the African musician, however, each line is a musical entity in itself, not an off-beat complement to the line being played with it. Observe, for instance, the overall effect brought into play by the concurrent rendition of these three independent rhythmic patterns:

This music is simply an exciting, instinctively constructed pastiche of numerous individual repetitive ideas performed simultaneously, much like the collective improvisation of a Dixieland band.

African slaves brought this musical conception to the United States in their work songs, dances, and rituals. Music played an important social role; it was used in healing, marriage, hunting, and other occasions. In some African cultures, litigants in civil suits sang their cases before the chief and village. These songs of complaint may very well have been the wellsprings of the blues.

In America, the dominant culture of European immigrants had a tremendous influence on the shape of black music. The Africans' rhythmic polyphony became molded within metrical boundaries. Independent lines took on the appearance of syncopated phrases, with one difference: the repetitive aspect of African musical lines was retained. Whereas European syncopation was used to create momentary suspensions of normal pulse and displacement of metric accents, African lines became "ragging" patterns, "boogie" basses, etc., constant and ever-present.

These repetitive bass patterns were employed by jazz pioneers like Jimmy Yancy:

The Europeans had other musical devices which lent themselves to this synthesis of traditions called jazz. The "jazz feel," for example, in which note values are spontaneously lengthened and shortened during performance, has its equivalent in the baroque convention known as *notes inégales* (literally "unequal notes"), the altering of the relative time values of certain pairs of notes, especially those moving in stepwise progression. The exact degree of unequalness was at the performer's discretion and eludes precise notation. An approximate illustration could be given by the following options:

played (any of the following versions):

In modern jazz, eighth notes and dotted eighths followed by a sixteenth are played with a triplet feeling: or =

The character of early jazz, especially ragtime, also relies heavily on certain time-honored patterns of Western rhythm known as the *scotch snap* and the *hornpipe* ,

which the slaves must have heard in the white man's fiddle music and folk songs. The works of baroque and classical masters also abound with these formulas.

Mozart: Serenade no. 6, K. 239
(*Serenata Notturna*)

Handel: *Water Music*

Beethoven's Piano Sonata, op. 111, contains some surprisingly syncopated variations on the hornpipe pattern:

(simplified notation)

Beethoven: Sonata, op. 111

The right-hand syncopation Beethoven uses in the second measure is very close to the augmented hornpipe rhythm—Charleston syncopation—used in jazz as a left-hand accompanying device:

Ragtime is a natural habitat for both the hornpipe and the scotch snap.

Turpin: "A Ragtime Nightmare"

Lamb: "Ragtime Nightingale"

The hornpipe is also evident in the boogie-woogie figures shown earlier as well as in the blues "shuffle":

in the "easy" swing style of the '30s and early '40s:

Butterfield: "Salt Butter"

in the relaxed and detached "cool jazz" approach of Dave Brubeck and others in the '50s:

Isacoff: "One for Dave"

and even jazz-rock musicians have used the hornpipe by simply placing it, in augmented form, after the downbeat of a measure:

Of course, in actual performance, none of these examples will reflect the precise hornpipe rhythm. The easygoing, loose quality of true jazz defies exact notation; there is always a harking back to the African influence, to that fluid rhythmic freedom unhampered by meter and bar line. In the course of a performance (which in jazz is nearly synonymous with improvisation) the jazz musician is likely to vary the degree of syncopation from measure to measure, causing something like rhythmic vertigo or *notes inégales* gone wild. He may, for example, vary figures from 3 to

play quintuplets; set up a disparity, a kind of metrical divergence between the left and right hands, such as

Isacoff: "Out-of-Phase"

This technique also has a European classical equivalent, although a milder one: the *melodic rubato*, which C.P.E. Bach described as follows:

> When the execution is such that one hand seems to play against the bar and the other strictly with it, it may be said that the performer is doing everything that can be required of him. It is only rarely that all parts are struck simultaneously. As soon as the upper part begins slavishly to follow the bar, the essence of the rubato is lost, for then all other parts must be played in time.

One might say that some aspects of jazz rhythm are a cubist version of classical rubato.

Recent developments in jazz involve other manipulations of accent and meter. These include:

Accent shifts:

Meter changes:

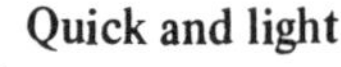

Conversion of meters (most frequently from three beat units to four, or vice versa). Observe, for instance, how the following repetitive rhythm pattern in $\frac{3}{4}$ acquires an excitingly new profile through its placement into $\frac{4}{4}$:

All the foregoing rhythmic devices can be traced to a combination of African and European roots.

JAZZ MELODY

In all but the most recent phases of jazz style, melody is based on the chordal structure which underlies the original tune used for improvisation. Even in so-called jazz tunes, there is always a clear connection between the melody and the harmonies which support it, so that the melody appears to spring from the harmonies rather than the other way around. Several approaches are used to create these melodies, including scales and modes, chordal and passing tones, upper and lower neighbors, sequences, and embellishments.

The so-called blue notes, those notes which add a bluesy sound to jazz melodies, are non-European in origin.

One might speculate that, just as the Afro-Americans created rhythmic formulas which consistently resided outside the normal metrical pulse, so might they have created a melodic counterpart which suspends the distinctions between major and minor tonalities, between perfect and diminished intervals. In practice, the effects of these blue notes are achieved by contrasting them with the ordinary major scale. Just as the rhythmic fluctuations and syncopations found in jazz playing must periodically return to a metric home base, so must the blue notes be used with discrimination: when used too often in a short span of time, they become monotonous and boring.

How were these blue notes selected? Gunther Schuller suspects that they result from two tetrachords:

These tone sequences are found in abundance in African music. Here is one song excerpt in which major and minor thirds, as well as perfect and diminished fifths, are interchanged:

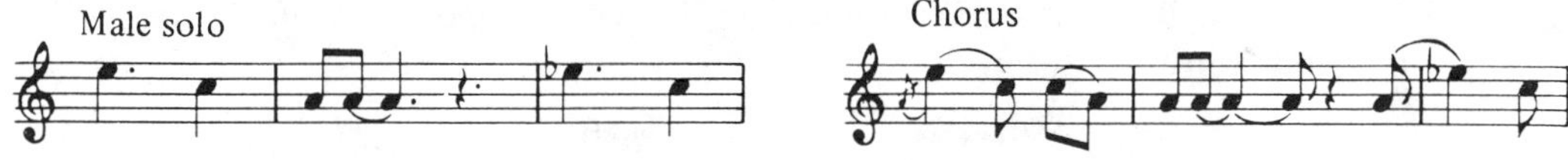

The form in which the "blues scale" is often presented,

is actually a pentatonic scale in inversion:

The one factor which, more than any other, accounts for the ambiguity in the quality of the intervals used in jazz melody, is clearly the indifference the Afro-American musician must have felt toward the rigid major scale. The languages from which Africans derived their musical concepts often have as many as nine different pitch levels affecting the semantic and grammatic structures of their sentences. After years of living with these subtle pitch distinctions, it could not have been easy or desirable for Africans to remold their musical world into a European diatonic framework.

Traditional: "Amazing Grace"

European version

Afro-American version slide

Somewhat related to blue notes in effect, but traditionally European, is the device of embellishment, an important melodic factor in jazz playing. This can take the form of a simple grace note (a half step below the main note), or melodic variations on certain note sequences, as in the following example:

In the 1950s, jazz melody gained added sophistication through the gifted practitioners of the bebop trend (Charlie Parker, Dizzie Gillespie, and others). Chord tones and blue notes were integrated with such elements of European musical tradition as passing tones, upper and lower neighbors, and the rich chromaticism of late nineteenth- and early twentieth-century music.

Powell: "Strictly Confidential"

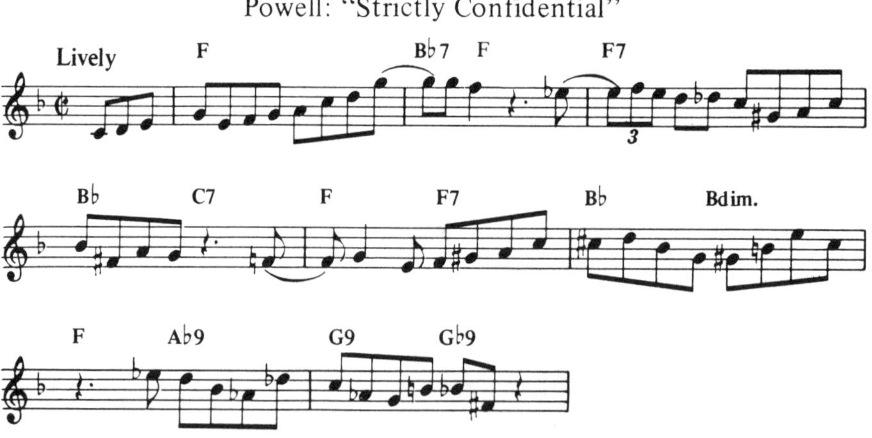

Contemporary jazz figurations sometimes employ *real sequence* which often creates a polytonal flavor.

JAZZ HARMONY

Harmonization in jazz is based heavily on the sound of the dominant seventh chord and often employs a good deal of parallel motion:

In fact, the progression V-I is often accomplished by a simple half-step descent in the upper voices, making use of the harmonically ambiguous augmented fourth or diminished fifth (tritone), with its dominant sound:

A combination of nonscale tones such as blue notes and the influence of modern European harmonies of Debussy and others have produced a jazz chord vocabulary which includes ninths, elevenths, and thirteenths in their unaltered, augmented, and diminished forms; as well as quartal harmonies and other dense chords of almost tone-cluster quality.

Gerald Martin: "Patterns"

Note that the C13 becomes a G♭7 (♯9) when a G-flat is placed in the bass, and a G♭13 becomes a C7 (♯9) when a C is placed in the bass.

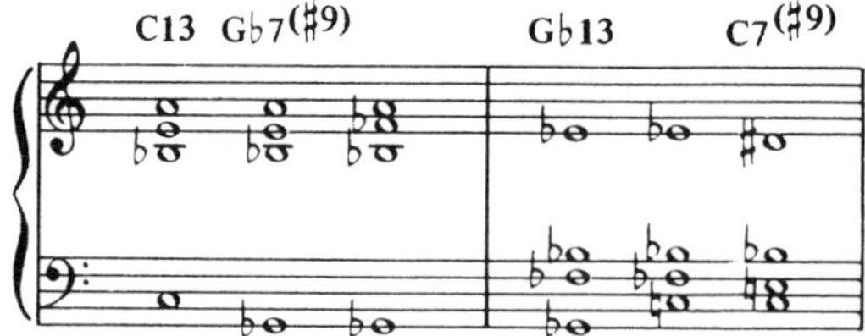

Because of this tritone relationship, any circle-of-fifths progression may be executed as a series of parallel, chromatically descending voices as in the example below.

Chords in jazz are often used in unexpected ways. Sometimes, for example, a dominant chord may be freely exchanged with one whose root is a tritone away (as in the previous example). At other times a chord will be played in which the root tone is left out; these voicings sometimes make use of the sound created by placing notes a minor second away from each other. In fact, the minor second is one of the most important intervals in modern jazz harmony.

chords with root missing (note minor seconds):

Isacoff: "Justice"

other chords with minor seconds:

Monk: "Off Minor"

Em7(♯11) A7
D7(♯11)
G+7 D7(♭5)

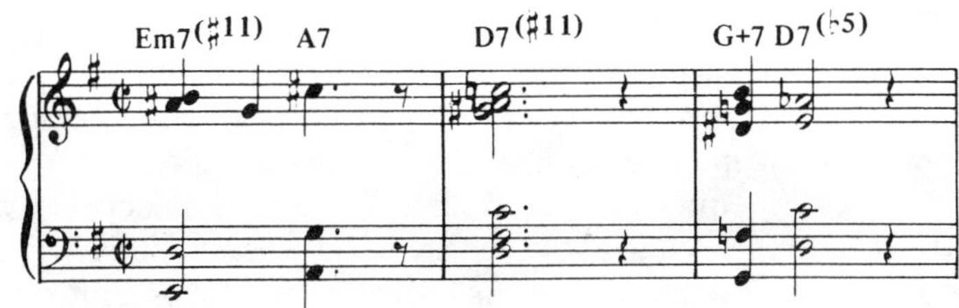

Whenever possible, successive chord tones (whether altered or not) should follow the voice-leading rules of classical European harmony. A mark of good jazz writing and playing is the smooth and logical manipulation of voices from one chord to the next.

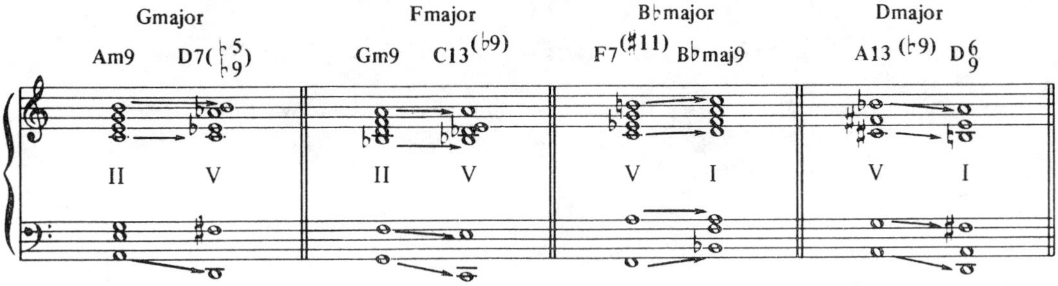

Gmajor
Am9 D7(♭5 ♭9)
II V
Fmajor
Gm9 C13(♭9)
II V
B♭major
F7(♯11) B♭maj9
V I
Dmajor
A13 (♭9) D6/9
V I

These qualities of harmonization, integrated with attractive spontaneity of melody and rhythm, are well illustrated by the following excerpt:

Powell: "I'll Keep Loving You"

Slowly

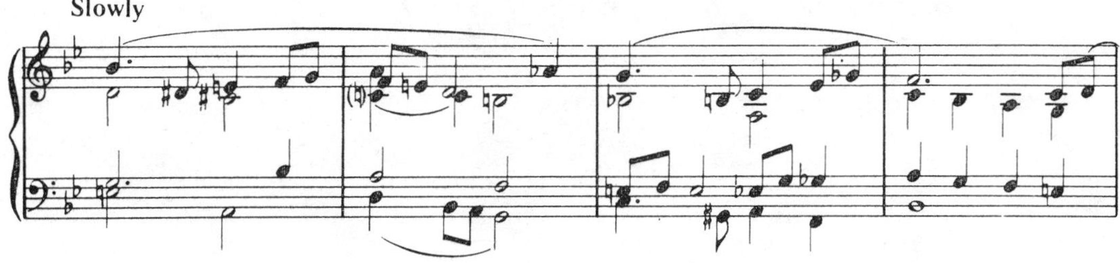

Jazz is a genuinely American musical expression deeply influenced by African folk traditions and European classical elements. Its various forms and stylistic manifestations—including ragtime, blues, swing, bebop, modern jazz—are a fertile ground on which rhythmic flair, technical dexterity, and improvisational skill can grow. Playing jazz can offer the student an opportunity, rare in the traditional teaching process, to alter the concept of a piece with each performance. In summary, one might answer the question posed in the title of this section by paraphrasing the famous saying about chess: "As a game it is science, as science it is a game." What is jazz? As entertainment it is a musical education, as musical education it is entertainment, which has intrigued and delighted people of the twentieth century the world over.

RECOMMENDED READING

Brandel, Rose. *The Music of Central Africa.* The Hague: Martinus Nijhoff, 1961.

Dankworth, Avril. *Jazz: An Introduction to its Musical Basis.* London: Oxford University Press, 1968.

Schuller, Gunther. *Early Jazz: Its Roots and Musical Development.* New York: Oxford University Press, 1968.

Southern, Eileen. *The Music of Black Americans.* New York: W.W. Norton, 1971.

Stearns, Marshall. *The Story of Jazz.* New York: New American Library, 1958.

Tirro, Frank. *Jazz—A History.* New York: W.W. Norton, 1977.

Jazz and the Piano Teacher

DENES AGAY

Introducing the piano student to the pleasures of jazz requires, first of all, a degree of sympathy and identification with the idiom on the teacher's part. To teach jazz and to impart the joy and vitality of this American musical expression to the student, one should be familiar with its musical essence (see "What Is Jazz," p. 403) and, most important, should not harbor any esthetic or pedagogic reservations about it. Once these preconditions are present, the teacher is well advised to outline a plan of preparatory steps whereby the characteristic elements of jazz can be introduced gradually and, as much as possible, on the simplest levels.

One must keep in mind that good jazz playing is not just the result of assiduous study; rather, it depends on an instinctive, improvisatory application of certain creative impulses in the fields of rhythm, melody, and harmony, projected with the right kind of digital facility. Its ultimate refinement and excellence cannot be taught. However, those students (and there are many of them) who like jazz and want to study it can be given the proper start and be guided, at least part of the way, to a point where their individual capabilities and motivations can take over.

The heart of jazz is improvisation, an extemporaneous molding and shaping of the underlying musical elements. Its idiomatic profile is given not so much by what is played but by how it is played. In the mainstream of music literature, styles—classic, romantic, impressionist, etc.—were created by the master composers of various periods and embodied in their works. In jazz, styles have been established by outstanding individual performers. Jazz, however, does have certain traits which are common to all its variants. The introduction of these common characteristics should be the first step in any teaching plan.

One such basic trait is a steady, strong metric pulse, a pronounced beat underlying and supporting the entire structure of musical manipulations. This pulse should be felt and implied even under long-held notes and chords. In the beginning, and even later on, light tapping of the beat units with the right foot (heel on the floor) will help to maintain and emphasize the metric momentum. There is a wide choice of suitable appealing materials among the many well-known folk songs, play tunes, children's songs, and spirituals. The following tentative plan may furnish some ideas as to how these traditional melodies can lead the early grade student on a progressive exploration of the jazz idiom. It should be remembered that each of the following examples illustrates only one sample of many possible variants. At every step of the way the student should be encouraged to make up individual versions of the same tune. Naturally, only those patterns and variants should be used which are consistent with the student's grade level and native skill.

- Select a well-known melody. Play it "straight" at first with a pronounced beat. Tap the beat units with your foot, or with the left hand on the piano.

"London Bridge"

- Provide the melody with a simple bass. There are several kinds of bass patterns which will fit a melody. Play this one, at first without the melody, with a good beat, then add the tune in the right hand.

• Arrange the melody notes into a syncopated pattern. Play it at first with the right hand only (tapping the beat), then add the bass (which is the same as in the preceding examples).

• Try this more interesting variant of the melody, with some changes in the bass, too. The hornpipe pattern (♩. ♪) occurs very often in jazz.

• Melody in thirds with a "walking bass":

• Another version, with the simplest ostinato boogie pattern in the bass:

• For a more modern harmonization of the melody, try this step-by-step sequence of diatonic seventh chords:

• Keeping the same chord progression in the left hand, the melody may be varied in many ways. Play this version and also invent one or two others.

• From ragtime to modern jazz, a commonly used accompaniment pattern is the familiar "oom-pah" formula, variously called "swing bass" or "stride bass." (The middle voice in the right hand is optional.)

• The innumerable variation possibilities inherent in a good tune can take the jazz player as far afield as imagination and ingenuity allows. The following "ballad" version varies all elements of the theme and retains only the form (phrasing) structure. (Slight alterations of the melody's rhythm pattern are possible:

At this point teacher and student should select a few other simple tunes which lend themselves to these treatments. Make at least one or two jazz versions on each song. The many suitable ones include "Aunt Rhody," "Merrily We Roll Along," "When the Saints Come Marchin' In," "Three Blind Mice," "This Old Man," "Jingle Bells," "Turkey in the Straw," "Row, Row Your Boat," "The Drunken Sailor," "Ol' Time Religion," "Skip to My Lou," "Li'l Liza Jane," "Frère Jacques," etc.

In an imaginative jazz arrangement the repetitions of the main theme usually occur in varied forms:

Quite often variety is provided by the addition of *breaks* (*riffs*), improvisatory fillers on phrase-ending long notes:

"There's No Hidin' Place"

Fats Waller: "Sneakin' Home"

A

Slowly

B

Interesting melodic variety can be achieved by the addition of grace notes, blue notes, and various other embellishments:

Although purists may disagree, Dixieland, ragtime, blues, boogie, swing, bebop, and rock can all be considered jazz styles, as far as the piano student is concerned. All these popular genres emerged on the American musical scene one by one from about the turn of the century to the present. For the purposes of early-grade jazz study, blues and boogie are especially suitable idioms because of their easily identifiable elements and their appealingly full sound even at the simplest grade levels.

The prototype of blues is a harmonic sequence of twelve measures, divided into three phrases, with a freely improvised, expressive melody line:

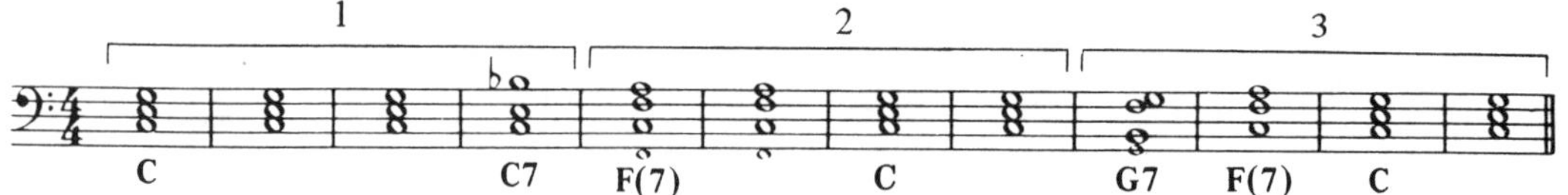

This sequence is not rigid, of course; harmonic shifts and chord enrichments (seventh chords instead of triads, for instance) occur very often:

Boogie-woogie, as developed in the '20s and '30s, was originally built on the harmonic scheme of the blues. Its mood and tempo, however, became quite different: more joyful and more propulsive. The essence of boogie is an ever-recurring bass pattern, a usually lively "basso ostinato" providing a solid rhythmic background for a strongly punctuated right-hand melody. The following two excerpts illustrate combinations of blues harmonies and boogie bass patterns:

"The Lonesome Road"

Gerald Martin: "Good Night Boogie"

Below is a progressive listing of other bass figures in the boogie vein. Each pattern should be practiced in a I-IV-V-I (tonic-subdominant-dominant-tonic) chord sequence, repeating once each measure. Also, each sequence should be transposed to one or two other suitable keys, in which the shifting patterns lie easily under the hands. (All patterns can also be played .)

a
5 2
b
5 1
c
d
e
f
g
h
i
j
3
3
k
2 1
l
m

As the student's technical and musical capabilities progress, other, somewhat more demanding styles can be introduced to further stimulate creative thinking and introduce more recent and current idioms. Bebop was formulated in the 1940s by solo improvisations of a few outstanding instrumentalists (Dizzie Gillespie, Charlie Parker, and others). Its characteristics are a lively beat, complex rhythms, and a driving, restless melody line, often sung to nonsense syllables. For instance:

Given the proper preparations and having acquired a measure of improvisatory skill and bravado, the student may want to undertake converting some well-known tunes into bebop and modern jazz vignettes. Using the familiar "London Bridge" as a melodic springboard, this version jumps quite a distance:

Rock and roll has been dominating the field of popular music since the mid-1950s. Pianists should be aware that this is not as keyboard oriented a genre as most other jazz styles. Its most conspicuous traits are the placing of accents on the second and fourth beats of a measure, instead of the normally accented first and third beats, and a pronounced eight-to-the-bar pulse. Also characteristic is the frequently modal flavor of melodies and harmonies. Some of the simplest rock-bass patterns are these:

The following example is a rock version of "London Bridge." Try other bass patterns and select other tunes appropriate for such treatment.

Good jazz playing requires a considerable degree of creative contribution from the player. Even a most meticulously notated jazz piece or arrangement will sound stiff, artificial, and anemic if played note by note as written, without an imaginative input from the performer. Delivery must be easygoing, relaxed, and individualized at all times. The advancing student should increasingly be left to his or her own devices in jazz explorations. The selection of tunes to be arranged, the style and treatment the theme should receive, and the details of execution should gradually become the student's creative domain, under the teacher's guidance and constructive supervision. There are now many fine publications available which furnish interesting and instructive jazz repertories; some of them also supply varying amounts of theoretical and pedagogical information. Jazz can be a pleasurable and useful phase of piano education and it certainly merits the teacher's earnest and sympathetic attention.

RECOMMENDED SELECTIONS

JAZZ SOLOS, JAZZ DUETS (Recital Notebooks Nos. 9 and 10) Agay (Yorktown)
THE JOY OF JAZZ, THE JOY OF BOOGIE AND BLUES, THE JOY OF RAGTIME Agay (Yorktown)
S. SCHWARTZ JAZZ LIBRARY (11 vols.) (Hansen)
JAZZ FOR PIANO Konowitz and others (Lee Roberts-Schirmer)
JAZZ, BLUES, RAGTIME PIANO STYLES Matt Dennis (Mel Bay)
ROCK WITH JAZZ, 5 vols. Stecher, Horowitz, Gordon (Schirmer)
JAZZ AND BLUES, 6 vols. Kraehenbuehl (Summy-Birchard)
HOW TO PLAY BLUES PIANO Kriss (Acorn)
MORE REAL COOL PIANO Agay (Presser)
ROCK ME EASY Olson (Carl Fischer)
AN ADVENTURE IN JAZZ Noona-Glover; AN ADVENTURE IN RAGTIME Hinson-Glover (Belwin)
BLUES FOR FUN Sheftel (Douglas)
JAZZ—AND ALL THAT 2 vols. Clarke (Myklas)
FROM RAG TO JAZZ Isacoff (Consolidated)
JUNIOR JAZZ Gordon; FACES OF JAZZ Smith (Marks)
JAZZETTES Berkowitz (Frank)
FOUR DANCE IMPRESSIONS Agay (Presser)
REFLECTIONS IN MODERN JAZZ Waldron (Fox)
JAZZ SAMPLER McPartland, Brubeck and others (Marks)
RHYTHM FACTORY 135 rhythmic patterns Metis (Marks)
ROCK MODES AND MOODS Metis (Marks)
POP/ROCK SKETCHES One piano, four hands Metic (Marks)
THE RAGTIME CURRENT Bolcom, Morath and others (Marks)
THE JAZZ PIANIST (3 books) Mehegan (Fox)
STYLES FOR THE JAZZ PIANIST (3 books) Mehegan (Fox)
POPULAR AND JAZZ PIANO COURSE (3 vols.) Stormen (Progress)

The Piano Teacher and Popular Music

DENES AGAY

The pedagogic challenge inherent in the title of this section has been present since the dawn of piano instruction. This writer's first involvement with the problem occurred at the age of five—not as a teacher, of course, but as a student. Being a musically precocious child, by that age I could play by ear the melodies and pieces I heard and liked: folk songs, popular tunes, and pleasing fragments from the piano-teaching repertory to which I had been exposed through my older brother's practicing. When shortly after my fifth birthday it was decided that I should begin formal piano lessons, my mother took me to our small town's only teacher, Aunt Kornelia; and after proper introductions, my proud mother coaxed me to perform for the dear old lady. Without hesitation, I plunged into *The Merry Widow* waltz. After my closing chord the teacher drew my mother into a corner of the studio for a whispered conference, then came over to me, put a benign hand on my shoulder and said, "This is nice, son, but we'll have to stop this kind of playing now that you will begin to learn how to really play the piano."

Although I have not forgotten the scene and the statement, it has never been entirely clear for me whether the somewhat cryptic condemnation referred to the type of music I played or to the way I played it. Probably it referred to both and, needless to say, it considerably dampened whatever enthusiasm I may have had for piano tutoring. I did attend my lessons, practicing the given curriculum dutifully, if somewhat reluctantly, but the fun of playing the tunes I liked, in my own way, was largely gone.

In fact, the little pieces and exercises Aunt Kornelia assigned were the well-known, musically dull staples so popular in the piano primers of that day, which—while they did fit it into a somewhat staid and anemic pedagogical scheme—were, as pure music, hardly superior to *The Merry Widow* waltz. All this I discovered, of course, only much later in life, after having had the opportunity to analyze and draw conclusions for myself.

THE IMPORTANCE OF A WIDE-SPECTRUM REPERTORY

Piano study should not alienate and abruptly tear the young student away from everyday musical experiences and diversions. It should not lift the child into a kind of pedagogical ivory tower where only carefully prescribed, pedigreed music is played and heard, and where the prevailing sounds of the world around us are all but filtered out. On the contrary, the repertory of piano study should present the widest possible musical spectrum, incorporating not only the literature of piano, past and present, but also well chosen samplers of other appealing, lighter musical idioms the student is exposed to in everyday life, provided that these selections are esthetically acceptable and can be made to serve a useful purpose within the teaching plan.

The question of whether popular music has a place in the student's repertory is answered affirmatively here—but with some important qualifications. This is a personal view, of course, but it can be supported by historical precedent, pedagogical consideration, and sound psychological reasons. Certain popular dance forms have always been a part of the teaching repertory. In the eighteenth century the minuet, gavotte and polonaise, in the nineteenth century the waltz, polka, and mazurka, to mention a few, were standard teaching fare; so there could hardly be a valid reason, in principle at least, why the dance forms and rhythms of our time should be excluded.

Important teaching books of the past, going back as far as two centuries and more, can well illustrate the imaginative and uninhibited manner in which the student's needs for a well rounded, up-to-date repertory were met. For instance, the *Little Notebook for Anna Magdalena Bach*, which dates from 1725, contains, in addition to Bach's two partitas, many light, melodic keyboard dances by unknown writers and also numerous vocal pieces of both religious and secular nature. One of these, in the latter category, praises the pleasures of pipe-smoking.

An even better example is the delightful and meticulously organized *Little Music Book* Leopold Mozart gave his son, Wolfgang, on the boy's seventh birthday (1763). There are more than one hundred pieces in this collection, grouped into twenty-five suites. A great variety of selections here—dances, songs, and character pieces—are all in a light, popular vein, in the so-called gallant style. Telemann is represented by numerous little dances, but most of the other selections are either anonymous or were written by composers who are all but forgotten today. One of these obscure writers merits special attention within the context of this discourse. He is Sperontes, pseudonym for J.S. Scholze, a gifted and enterprising German musician who collected about one hundred popular keyboard pieces of his time, commissioned a poet (what we would call a lyricist) to set words to them, and published the result in two volumes of Odes. These collections became phenomenally popular, inspiring many imitators throughout the eighteenth century. There are numerous vocal selections, written in the manner of Sperontes, in the Mozart *Notebook*. The collection is strictly "contemporary"; none of the pieces included was more than thirty years old at the time of compilation. It is also interesting to note that the period's almost insatiable demand for minuets was well catered to by the inclusion of thirty-two such dance pieces. We can easily guess the motive for this: Leopold Mozart, an erudite musician and educator, knew that Wolfgang was not only a prodigy and a genius, but also a normal seven-year-old student, whose attention and interest had to be held and stimulated with astutely assembled popular teaching pieces; hence the dozens of minuets and the overall light vein of the collection.

THE CLASSICS' USE OF POPULAR THEMES

There was another route by which the popular melodies of the eighteenth and nineteenth centuries found their way into the literature of piano study: the variation form. Nearly all keyboard composers of those periods, including the great masters, utilized popular tunes, arias, and little dance pieces as themes of such works. It is true that the real value of these variations lies in the craft and ingenuity with which simple ditties are transformed into larger, many-faceted, often imposing musical structures. The fact remains, however, that the source of inspiration was a popular melody, which was chosen by the composer not only because it contained the germ of possible development into a larger form, but also because it was popular; the people wanted to play it and to hear it. It almost automatically held a promise of wide appeal for the entire work.

The great pedagogues of the past, beginning with Clementi, Hummel, Dussek, Czerny and continuing with a long succession of important nineteenth-century teacher-composers, made frequent use of musical materials with wide popular appeal. Their piano methods and teaching books contain a profusion of study pieces based on folk songs, operatic themes, and other popular melodies of varied description. All this is not meant to imply that such selections had unquestioned musical value or pedagogic validity in every instance, but only to point out that these notable musicians and teachers had no esthetic qualms about arranging, transcribing, or paraphrasing popular melodies of their time whenever they felt that these themes could be put to good didactic use.

"SALON" REPERTORY

The purists of today are inclined to view this with a condescending smile and ascribe it to a naive aberration of taste, which, they feel, left its stamp on a considerable body of nineteenth-century piano music of the so-called "salon" variety. There was, to be sure, a prodigious amount of music written for the pianist of those days, and for a good reason. The piano in the parlor being the only medium of home entertainment (there was no radio, television, or phonograph a hundred years ago), the demand for all kinds of piano music was great and unceasing. Inevitably the quality of the output was uneven, a good portion of it mediocre or worse. However, it should be remembered that this vast repertory of piano music contained—had to contain—everything the musical public wanted to hear and play. In the absence of mechanical or electronic reproduction media, most musical enjoyment and entertainment originated through live performance at the piano. As a result, nearly all music, weighty and light, was available in keyboard versions. Solo or duet arrangements of symphonies, string quartets, orchestral overtures, and operatic excerpts, intermingled with a prodigious conglomeration of piano solos from Chopin, Mendelssohn, and Schumann to "The Maiden's Prayer," "The Dying Poet," and "The Ben-Hur Chariot Race," were staple items of the Victorian piano bench. Under these circumstances the piano student's craving for light popular fare was not too difficult to satisfy. Clearly, the piano teacher did not run a great risk of being censured by assigning a student a "Home Sweet Home," *La Donna è Mobile*, or "Oh! Susannah" if these strains could often be heard in august concert halls—if in more pretentious versions—played by the great virtuosos of the day.

"SERIOUS" VS. "POPULAR"

This cozy nineteenth-century coexistence of serious and popular music in the study repertory was not too long-lived. In a few decades, certainly by the 1920s, the dichotomy of the two categories became increasingly more pronounced, and the concommitant problems for the teacher more acute. The reasons for this were numerous: the advent of phonograph, radio, and later, television, made the piano in the parlor nearly obsolete as the focal point of family entertainment. The pushing of a button or turn of a knob instantly produced music. Through these media, songs could become popular overnight, fizzle out in a few months and be replaced constantly by new ones. The life cycle of popular music became accelerated, in sharp contrast to the solid durability of the classical repertory.

Other important shifts took place within music and pedagogy itself: changing attitudes toward musical styles and idioms, including an especially critical stance toward the peripheral output of the romantic era; increased emphasis on stylistic authenticity in performance and editions and a trend, continuing to the present, to teach only from the original text (*Urtext*) and to limit the course of study to pieces written expressly for the piano. From this evolved a curriculum of sturdier musical content, but also one which, we are beginning to realize, had tendencies to become overly restrictive and pedantic. Teaching pieces based on familiar themes became questionable not only because they were popular music, but also because they were "arrangements," not originally written for the keyboard.

It would take more space than is available here to list all the sound arguments as to why arrangements, per se, should not, and indeed, cannot, be entirely excluded from the repertory, especially during the early years of instruction. Suffice it to say that a rigid attitude of banning all keyboard adaptations is not only lacking in valid esthetic and pedagogic justifications, but also would deprive the student of many valuable, appealing, and useful teaching pieces at a time (in the early grades) when the original keyboard literature does not offer an adequate variety and certainly not an abundance of materials. (see "Arrangements: To Teach or Not To Teach Them," p. 441)

POPULAR MUSIC AS STUDY MATERIAL

To what extent and in what manner may popular music arranged for piano serve the purposes of study? Many important considerations should be kept in mind. First, we must realize that popular and dance music is much more youth-oriented today than it ever was in the past. Until the years following World War I, young people in their late teens and twenties were the pacesetters and taste-makers. In the 1930s, the midteen "bobbysoxers" were the dominant group to be catered to, and two or three decades later the screaming fans surrounding Elvis Presley and the Beatles were to a large extent even younger. This gradual lowering of the age bracket has had a substantial influence on the style and character of popular music.

In the past it was the melody–easy to grasp, ingratiating–that was the essential element. Today, especially in rock and roll, a strong, steady, visceral beat is the dominant factor and a melody, more often than not, is only a utilitarian chant through which the message of the lyrics is communicated. These lyrics, incidentally, now often go beyond the customary variations on the "I love you" theme: they express many other adolescent sentiments, aspirations, social comments, and a rebellious impatience with the growing-up process. In other words, the pop tunes of today are not only musical entertainment, but also a social phenomenon, which makes the task of integrating them into the piano student's course of study a difficult and delicate one.

Another purely musical problem is that rock and roll, by and large, is not pianistic. Its essence and main attraction, that infectious rhythmic vitality, is best conveyed by various instrumental groups (guitar, bass, brass, synthesizer, etc.) but is all but lost, or at least considerably paled, in a solo keyboard version. Numerous other popular idioms are eminently pianistic: ragtime and boogie are *par excellence* piano music, and folk songs naturally lend themselves to a well-sounding pianistic treatment even on the earliest grade levels. These categories offer a potentially large reservoir of materials, which, with a properly constructive and sympathetic attitude on the teacher's part, may go a long way toward satisfying the student's thirst for up-to-date music. In addition, there is an ever-increasing literature of attractive, pedagogically sound contemporary pieces written in popular styles specifically for study purposes.

All this will help but cannot solve all the problems. The world of popular music is in a constant state of flux, with trends, fashions, and styles appearing and disappearing, with new melodies reaching the top of the popularity charts and others fading away in rapid succession. It can be anticipated that a good portion of the student body will always be fascinated by this steady parade of hits and will express a desire to play and to learn whatever is the newest and latest.

TEACHERS' ATTITUDES

Reactions to such requests should be guided by the student's age, ability, and background; inevitably, the teacher's taste, preferences, and pedagogic principles will also play a decisive role. On one end of the spectrum we have the teacher who refuses to have anything to do with the "popular stuff" and will say, in effect, "I have a good method, an interesting curriculum, and the student who wants to play something else can find another teacher." A highly principled attitude, perhaps, but also, I believe, a narrow, dogmatic one which may scare off a potentially good student, without an effort having been made to guide him or her on to broader musical understanding. The other extreme is the teacher who, to prevent a possible dropout or, for a variety of other reasons, uncritically yields to all requests, thereby diluting the repertory with an assortment of inferior and useless popular items.

Between these two widely divergent attitudes are numerous middle-ground stands. One involves occasionally yielding to the student's request to add a pop tune or two to the regular study materials, mainly to appease, perhaps to help the student over a certain adolescent phase, in the hope that the student eventually will come through this stage of rag, boogie, and rock and return to the fold, to the study of classics, to "good" music. Some teachers will include popular music only after the study and practice of other materials. Still another widely held view is that popular songs should not be assigned as part of the lesson, but a student who wants to play them should be encouraged to do so independently, as a kind of off-the-record social activity. Playing these tunes by ear and improvising on them may also be approved, but only on the student's own time and not under a structured teaching plan.

These approaches, while displaying a degree of understanding and flexibility in handling the problem, also share an unmistakably aloof, negative stance toward popular music. It is placed in a distinct, separate category, apart from the "regular" teaching fare, and marked, at least by implication, as something automatically inferior and lacking in educational substance. A growing number of educators feel, as does this writer, that a more constructive plan is desirable and possible, without sacrificing sound musical and teaching principles.

It is of primary importance that a teacher not be entirely isolated from the popular music scene. An open mind and an inquisitive ear are recommended if one is to be aware of what is going on along the Tin Pan Alley marketplace. Periodic surveys can be made to ascertain what, if any, items show enough quality, or at least enough redeeming features, for inclusion in the regular repertory. True, a large portion of the pop field is a musical wasteland, but a sufficiently patient and sympathetic scrutiny will often reveal gratifying melodic and harmonic surprises. Songs, pieces of sufficient interest which will not degrade the study course and will please the student, can serve a useful teaching purpose: promote technique, make the study of theory (harmony, form) more palatable, and inspire creativity through improvisation, arranging and composition.

In general terms, the most important factor is the teacher's attitude; he or she should be alert as to the availability of suitable melodies and pieces, and inventive enough to adopt such materials, if necessary, to the individual student's needs, so that the pieces correspond to the grade level of other lesson assignments. It is imperative that the playing of such popular pieces not mean the abandonment of the sound principles of technique; the correct position of hands, fingers, wrist, and arm applies here too, and any relaxation of these standards may lead to sloppy and harmful playing habits.

ADAPTATIONS FOR STUDY

If the regular piano-vocal edition of a song is not the right version for a student, as often happens, the desired changes may be marked on the copy by the teacher. Should substantial alterations seem necessary, a new, neatly notated copy can be prepared. (All popular songs, with the exception of genuine folk tunes, are protected by copyright; multiplication and sale are prohibited by law.) Songs on the top of popularity charts are often available in simplified versions, and these too can be modified to suit specific needs. Gradually, with the proper direction, the student should be able to make these changes and prepare the copies. On the earliest grade levels a melody may be divided between the hands, with an occasional harmonic interval providing accompaniment in the left hand; or the teacher may want to participate by playing a few supportive notes in the bass. Some tunes lend themselves to being played on all-black keys ("Amazing Grace" and "Old Mac Donald," for instance) and can then be shifted a half step higher to practice transposition.

Some songs, especially the folk-based ones, may often be harmonized just by the tonic, subdominant, and dominant chords ("Love Somebody," "Michael, Row the Boat Ashore," "When the Saints Come Marching In," and others):

I IV V7 I

The same chords in proper sequence will also furnish the harmonic underpinning for the classic twelve-bar blues pattern. (See "Jazz and the Piano Teacher," p. 417).

These chord sequences should always be practiced in various keys, with constant encouragement for playing by ear and improvisation. In songs presenting a more extended harmonic vocabulary, chords may be similarly simplified so they lie easily under the hands, without wide jumps and constant lateral motion. The harmonic functions and chord names should at all times be clear to the pupil.

TEACHING THEORY AND TECHNIQUE

Since the texture of popular music is predominantly homophonic (melody with accompaniment), it is eminently suitable for the study of harmony, or more specifically, for developing familiarity with chord functions and sequences through keyboard experience. This can equip the student for preparing arrangements; that is, for providing melodies with fitting harmonies in suitable patterns of pianistic accompaniment. In this area, as in the field of ear training and improvisation, popular music offers built-in educational opportunities. The classical or "serious" repertory must be performed always as written, without deviation from the printed note picture. No such restriction inhibits the playing of popular songs; on the contrary, a good tune, whether played from notes or by ear, can be the springboard for the player's creative manipulations: improvisation, variation, arranging, all of which should be encouraged by the teacher.

The basic form elements of music, especially the phrase, can be well illustrated with popular songs, because of their melodic simplicity. Analysis of their phrasing patterns can further lead to the understanding of binary and ternary forms, which are indeed the most common frameworks in which popular songs are written.

A dance tune usually must be played in strict time and with rhythmic precision. These are disciplines which, once learned, can serve the student in the performance of the entire repertory. On the other hand, the typical romantic rubato, a freely flowing melody in the treble, against the regular beat of the bass, is also the heart of a nice, soulful blues improvisation.

The various aspects of technique and formulas of execution embodied in the teaching literature of the eighteenth and nineteenth centuries also apply to the performance of popular music. Cantabile touch is the right one to project the melody of a love theme or ballad; forearm rotation and relaxed wrist action are necessary to play the steadily moving, fluent bass patterns of boogie and blues; solid chords, repeated and broken chords—usually in triplets—provide the harmonic and rhythmic support of rock music; firm finger action will achieve rhythmic precision; the conventional ragtime accompaniment, octave basses leaping to middle-range chords, can make a fine placement study; and good jazz playing requires technical competence in all its phases and aspects.

"I often include popular music in the lessons, but I have no specific, separate formula for teaching it: I don't treat it as something different," a respected teacher wrote to me recently. This statement goes to the heart of the matter. Properly selected favorite songs of the day, with a little interest and imagination on the teacher's part, can be integrated into the standard teaching repertory and may well serve specific teaching needs. The key element in this endeavor is the teacher's attitude, the way he or she views, evaluates, selects, and utilizes this material. To that end the following suggestions might be considered:

- Listen to, rather than ignore, the teenager's music.
- Make the student aware that you are interested in his world of entertainment; establish a warm rapport in discussing frankly, openly, and on a mature level, new songs, new recordings, new trends; whether you agree or disagree, you will gain esteem and affection.
- Evaluate and select teaching pieces with an open mind; discard the inhibiting notion that music is divided into two distinct, separate categories: serious and popular. Judge all music as being good, bad, or mediocre, regardless of whether it is played in a concert hall or on the hit parade. Have an understanding of all idioms and a love for all kinds of good music, from baroque to jazz and rock.
- Through a continuing process of discussing and analyzing popular music, guide the student, gently and systematically, toward more discriminating levels of musical perception and taste. With this attitude, music educators ultimately may even influence and improve the quality of songs mass-produced to please the adolescent generation.

RECOMMENDED SELECTIONS

See also "Jazz and the Piano Teacher," p. 417)

Broadway Classics, vols. A-B-C, arr. Agay (Warner).
Broadway Classics as Duets, vols. A-B-C, arr. Agay (Warner).
Broadway Showcase of Famous Melodies, vols. A-B-C, arr. Agay (Warner).
Lots of Pops–and Technic Too, 3 vols., Glover, (Belwin).
Something Light, 3 vols., Olson (Carl Fischer).
Sixty-two Easy Popular Piano Pieces, arr. Brimhall (Hansen).
Popular Choice: 53 Pieces, (MCA).
Sounds of Today, 3 vols., (Warner).
Hundred Giant Hits, arr. Lane (Big 3).
The Wonderful World of Richard Rodgers arr. Glover (Chappell).
Guidelines to Improvisation–Quick Steps to Pop Piano 3 vols., Kahn (Warner).

Arrangements: To Teach or Not to Teach Them

DENES AGAY

The piano teacher can hardly avoid being confronted with this problem, for which, it may be stated at the outset, there is no simple, unequivocal answer. There certainly is no dearth of views and utterances, pro and con, on the subject, some of them valid, others too opinionated and biased. On the one hand our age of authenticity, with its insistence on textural and interpretative purity, either outrightly condemns the didactic use of arrangements, or views it with utmost suspicion. Opposing this stance are those who, in the name of practical considerations and plain musical common sense, urge a more relaxed and tolerant attitude. How should a teacher decide? What should be the guiding principles?

Perhaps it is best first to clarify the terms involved. *Arrangement* is usually defined as an adaptation of a piece of music for a medium other than the one for which it was originally written, without any alterations in its musical substance (a piano arrangement of a vocal or string composition, for instance). *Transcription* is considered by most as synonymous with arrangement, with perhaps just a hint of more adaptive leeway. A *paraphrase* is a free adaptation of a piece, usually for a solo instrument, in which the musical ideas of the original serve as a springboard for the adapter's inventive manipulations and elaborations, and as such is quite close to the *variation* form. (Liszt's paraphrases of operatic arias, for instance).

The dichotomy between *arrangement* and *original composition* as two distinct categories of music was not always as pronounced as it is today. We tend to forget or overlook the long and venerable history of arrangements and arrangers, beginning with the profusion of anonymous lute adaptations of vocal pieces in the sixteenth century and continuing with Bach, Mozart, Beethoven, Brahms, Liszt, and an illustrious succession of other masters who frequently, and without esthetic qualms, arranged, rearranged, transcribed, and paraphrased their own and other composers' themes and pieces. Obviously, the reorganization or translation of certain musical ideas into new media did satisfy their artistic credo, regardless of whether the basic material they adapted was of their own or someone else's invention.

When and for what reasons did these attitudes change? Why did arranging, for centuries a respected creative activity, become an esthetically suspect act of musical rethinking? The proliferation of clumsy, inept, and tasteless adaptations certainly contributed to the change of climate, but by far the strongest factor has been the prevailing and often obsessive present-day concern for authenticity in texts and performing manners. A violin piece arranged for piano, or vice versa, becomes automatically condemned on the grounds that it distorts the composer's original intentions, the well-known arranging practices of Bach, Mozart, et al. notwithstanding.

A few years ago, in an article written for the *Musical Times* of London, Hans Keller, noted British critic, diagnosed quite admirably the reasons for this stiff antiarrangement attitude: "We do indeed show an overriding need for authenticity, so much, so unthinkingly so that it looks a little like a collective compulsion, an obsessional neurosis. I recently played some old records of Bronislav Huberman to a composer friend, an ex-violinist whom I knew to be interested in unconventional, unstreamlined interpretations. He was delighted as long as he heard original violin pieces. But when I proposed to play him one of Huberman's Chopin arrangements (in which, to my mind, he shows more understanding of Chopin's structures than many a Chopin specialist at the keyboard), he was horrified. . . . He was unwilling to give Huberman the benefit of that minimum of *a priori* confidence which is a great artist's due. . . . Strictly speaking, our authenticity cult is really a midcentury affair: even in the late '30s when Huberman might play these Chopin arrangements as encores, nobody, even musicologists, noticed anything amiss. It is, I think, the progressive artistic insecurity of our age that has gradually turned our search for authenticity into a compulsion: the less you know instinctively what's good, both in creation and in interpretation, the more frantically you depend on extraneous, historical, scientific evidence."

THE IMPORTANCE OF UNBIASED JUDGMENT

The above analysis is sound and clear, and worth remembering. We can resist extraneous pedantic pressures and can avoid being influenced by rigid, preconceived attitudes only if we are able and confident to judge on our own what is good and what is inferior in music, regardless of the music's origin. The question of whether or not, or to what extent, arranged materials should be used can then be decided the way it should be: with an open mind, guided by taste and the student's individual needs.

What the student needs is a teaching repertory of quality and variety. Unquestionably, original pieces by masters of all periods must form the core of such repertory; and the more advanced the student becomes, the more restricted he or she should be to the original keyboard repertory. This, however, does not mean that arrangements, especially during the early years of instruction, should, or indeed can, be entirely excluded. The literature of elementary, original keyboard pieces is rather sparse and the use of adaptations during the first year or two of instruction is nearly inevitable. But even on the intermediate levels, the total exclusion of arrangements could hardly be justified by any sound esthetic or pedagogic standards. Such an inflexible attitude would deprive the student of numerous categories of attractive, enjoyable, and useful pieces at a time—during the early years of study—when the original keyboard literature does not furnish an abundance of materials.

An intelligently maintained middle-road attitude seems to be the soundest approach to this problem. Both extremes should be avoided. It is wrong to dilute and degrade the student's repertory with indiscriminately selected, inferior arrangements, but equally wrong is a stiff, unyielding exclusion of all adaptations.

At a national convention of piano teachers a couple of years ago, I was expounding my views on these matters at a seminar, and was challenged with a strong dissenting opinion by one teacher in the audience. "I teach only original piano music," she declared; "there is plenty of it and I would not touch an arrangement with a ten-foot pole." To prove her point she immediately produced a handsome printed program of her last student recital. Even a cursory examination of this program yielded some interesting clues to the basic weakness and vulnerability of such an unyielding doctrine. To begin with, there were at least three items on the program, which, strictly speaking, could not be classified as original piano music: a German dance by Haydn, often anthologized, which is a piano version of a minuet movement from one of his symphonies; a rondo from one of Mozart's Viennese Sonatinas, which the master originally wrote for three wind instruments, and a contradanse in E-flat by Beethoven, originally conceived for orchestra and later also used in a more elaborate piano version as part of an extended variation. I pointed out these facts to the teacher, but had no opportunity to pursue the matter further. It would have been most interesting to find out whether or not the revelation about the original status of these works caused their banishment from her repertory. More important, the same program contained numerous pieces of notorious mediocrity, which proved conclusively that the lofty banner of "original piano music only" was just a convenient camouflage for questionable taste and insecurity of judgment. One can draw an obvious conclusion from this episode. The fact that a piece was originally composed for the keyboard does by no means guarantee its quality and didactic usefulness. Similarly, howver, the concept of "arrangement" should not get an automatic imprimatur unless and until it has been examined, to quote Hans Keller again, to ascertain "what has been arranged, what the purpose of the recreative act is, and how the job has been done."

WHAT, WHY AND HOW TO ARRANGE

Let us deal with these criteria one by one. What type of music, adapted for the piano, merits inclusion in the student's repertory? Generally speaking, any kind of appealing material—vocal or instrumental, old or new—which has some inherent musical quality. If someone finds *musical quality* hard to define, perhaps we can construe the requirement simply as music which has something pleasing and interesting to say; music which conveys its composer's inventiveness and skill. In any case, it should be of the type, in style and texture, which lends itself to a well-sounding pianistic treatment in the adapter's chosen grade level, from the earliest to the most advanced. The wonderful world of folk music admirably meets these requirements on all counts, but there is a profusion of suitable materials in other areas too: music written for the voice, for other instruments, for orchestra, the theater, and carefully chosen items from the constantly changing catalog of popular music. There is one category of arrangements which should be approached with extra scrutiny: the simplified versions of works originally written for the piano. It does not make much sense, pedagogically or otherwise, to assign to the student a simplified arrangement of a piece which, in the not too distant future, he or she may be able to play as originally written. On the other hand, if an unpromising, early-grade student expresses an irresistible urge to play Chopin's "Military Polonaise" or Liszt's *Liebestraum*, (to mention only two typical examples of very popular but technically very demanding works), which most likely will never be accessible to him in the original, the teacher may decide in favor of letting him play a competent adaptation. Each case should be decided according to its specific circumstances: the work in question; the student's grade, caliber, and overall potential; and numerous other possible considerations of personality and background.

The purpose of arranging music for piano is, or should be, to infuse variety and diversity into the teaching repertory, especially on the early grade levels, and to give the student an opportunity to reproduce on the piano frequently heard music to which he is attracted. In brief, the role of arrangements is to supplement the repertory of original keyboard music, not to replace it.

After examining the criteria of what is proper and suitable material for piano adaptations, and what the purpose of such arrangements should be, there remains the most important aspect of scrutiny: the evaluation of the arrangement itself, the critical appraisal of how the job of adaptation has been done. Here a piano teacher cannot compromise, but must apply the highest standards. Only a good arrangement is acceptable, regardless of the merit of the underlying musical idea.

An arrangement is good if in a pianistic setting it preserves and possibly enhances the musical substance of the original. The mood and character must remain intact. Melody, basic harmonic functions, and rhythmic patterns should not be altered, but rather "translated" to the language of the piano, with only the smallest, musically negligible changes, made inevitable by the anatomy of the hands and the topography of the keyboard. At its best, the arrangement should reflect not only the adapter's high professional competence, taste, and pianistic instincts, but also a creative involvement and gift of invention. With all these attributes present, an arrangement can approach, indeed attain, the status of an original creation. Bartók's piano adaptations of Hungarian, Slovakian, and Rumanian folk tunes are outstanding examples in this category. Of course, we cannot expect or insist on such creative excellence in every instance, but we can regard these miniatures as ideal models to guide our standards of judgment. (See "The Piano Teacher and Popular Music," p. 431).

CHART OF FREQUENTLY-USED CHORDS

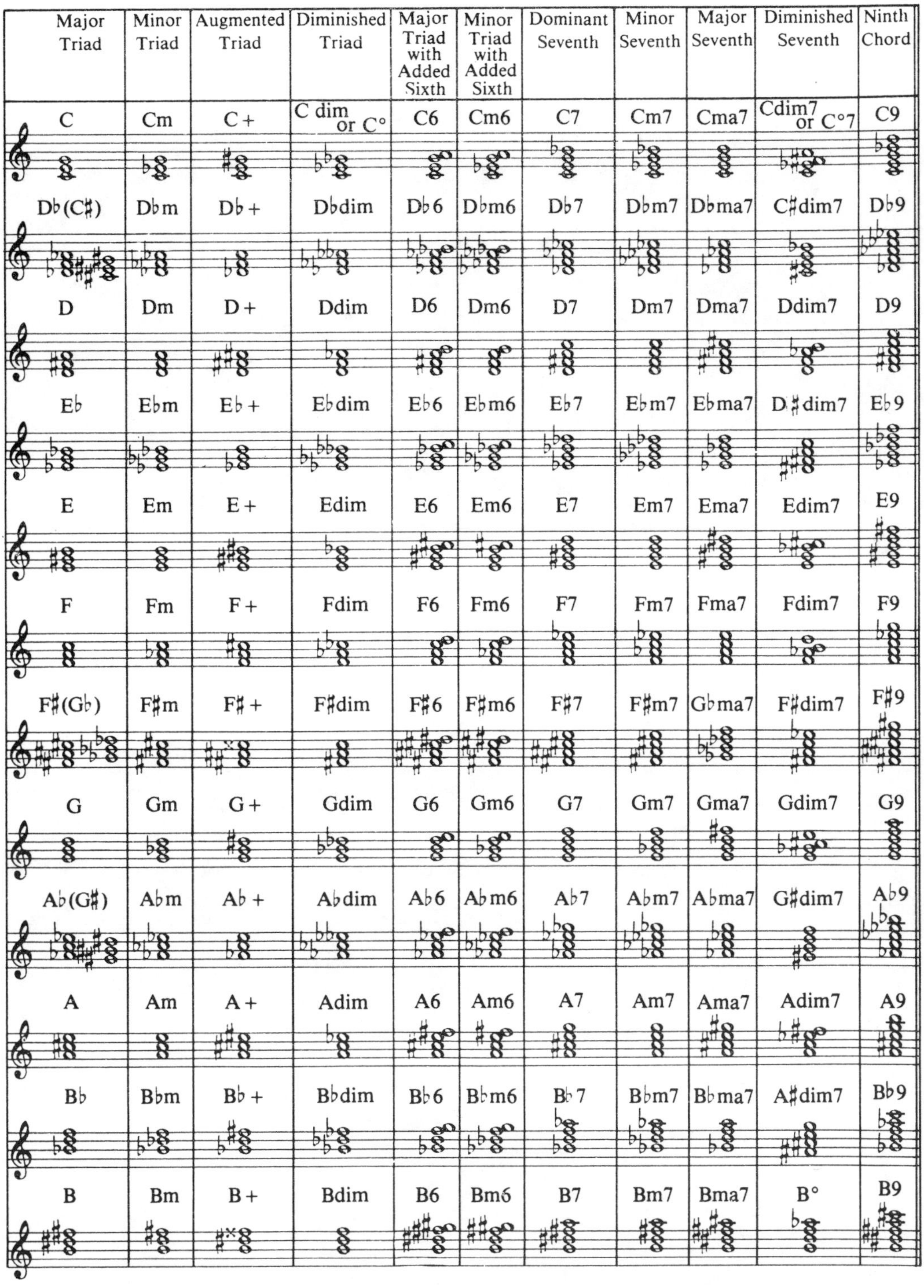

Major Triad	Minor Triad	Augmented Triad	Diminished Triad	Major Triad with Added Sixth	Minor Triad with Added Sixth	Dominant Seventh	Minor Seventh	Major Seventh	Diminished Seventh	Ninth Chord
C	Cm	C+	C dim or C°	C6	Cm6	C7	Cm7	Cma7	Cdim7 or C°7	C9
D♭(C♯)	D♭m	D♭+	D♭dim	D♭6	D♭m6	D♭7	D♭m7	D♭ma7	C♯dim7	D♭9
D	Dm	D+	Ddim	D6	Dm6	D7	Dm7	Dma7	Ddim7	D9
E♭	E♭m	E♭+	E♭dim	E♭6	E♭m6	E♭7	E♭m7	E♭ma7	D♯dim7	E♭9
E	Em	E+	Edim	E6	Em6	E7	Em7	Ema7	Edim7	E9
F	Fm	F+	Fdim	F6	Fm6	F7	Fm7	Fma7	Fdim7	F9
F♯(G♭)	F♯m	F♯+	F♯dim	F♯6	F♯m6	F♯7	F♯m7	G♭ma7	F♯dim7	F♯9
G	Gm	G+	Gdim	G6	Gm6	G7	Gm7	Gma7	Gdim7	G9
A♭(G♯)	A♭m	A♭+	A♭dim	A♭6	A♭m6	A♭7	A♭m7	A♭ma7	G♯dim7	A♭9
A	Am	A+	Adim	A6	Am6	A7	Am7	Ama7	Adim7	A9
B♭	B♭m	B♭+	B♭dim	B♭6	B♭m6	B♭7	B♭m7	B♭ma7	A♯dim7	B♭9
B	Bm	B+	Bdim	B6	Bm6	B7	Bm7	Bma7	B°	B9

FIVE

ASPECTS OF PEDAGOGY

The Training of the Piano Teacher

HAZEL GHAZARIAN SKAGGS

In general, the training of a teacher should provide a thorough knowledge of music, competence as a pianist, and the skills and personality necessary for teaching.

COURSES OF STUDY

A survey of catalogs shows that colleges, including universities and music schools, attempt to fulfill the above criteria through three or four categories:

- Performance
  - Applied music (private piano study, generally two half-hour lessons a week)
  - Recital class
  - Recital in the senior year
  - The requirement of such courses as sight reading, ensemble, or piano accompaniment
  - Public performance in ensemble groups may also be required
- General Musicianship
  - Sight singing
  - Ear training
  - Harmony
  - Keyboard harmony
  - Counterpoint
  - Theory—form and analysis
  - Composition

History of music
Literature of the piano

- General Education
  - English
  - Humanities
  - Physical, biological, social, and behavioral sciences (psychology)
  - Language
- Pedagogy (not available at all colleges)

  Pedagogy–generally from two to four credits during the entire four-year program–includes methods of piano teaching with a survey of materials, possibly teaching demonstrations, and in some instances the opportunity to teach a few students every week.

  Psychology courses, such as general psychology, child development, and adolescent psychology may be considered here as well as under general education.

Upon completion of a four-year program with course work from all three categories, and possibly two to four required credits in pedagogy, one qualifies for the bachelor of music degree. Advanced degrees concentrate on such specialized fields as education, performance, and composition.

If the undergraduate program offers no pedagogy courses, it is advisable to enroll in one of the many summer workshops offered to teachers. Many of these provide college credit and may be of additional value even if one's college does have a good pedagogy program.

SELECTING A SCHOOL

In selecting a college or conservatory, the chief concern should be the study program offered and the caliber of teachers on the faculty. The schools' catalogs provide the most pertinent information. Some schools, particularly universities, demand more academic studies than others. A diploma program, on the other hand, will include the least number of liberal arts courses.

If the student plans to live away from home, he or she should make sure there will be adequate practicing facilities; financial aid and placement opportunities may also be important considerations, and a visit to the school's campus ought to be included in the final decision-making.

MUSIC COLLEGE ADMISSION REQUIREMENTS

The student applying for admission into a music degree program must not only be a high school graduate but must also show sufficient talent and promise in his or her chosen area of study; in some instances the student may be accepted on a tentative basis. Those students majoring in piano usually must pass a proficiency test similar to the following example, to be performed from memory:

- All major and minor scales and arpeggios
- A composition by Bach, possibly as easy as a two-part invention or as difficult as a prelude and fugue from the *Well-Tempered Clavier*
- A difficult sonata (or sonata movement) by Haydn, Mozart, or Beethoven
- A nineteenth-century composition and/or a twentieth-century one

CHOOSING PRIVATE OR COLLEGE STUDY

Some students may prefer to study privately rather than enroll at a school; the advantage is that the student can select his or her own teachers, own time, and own pace of advancement. Furthermore, practicing will not be jeopardized by a rigid schedule of classes and examinations.

No specific training is mandatory for the private piano teacher, as opposed to preparing for a career in school music education. If several busy, successful teachers in the same area were interviewed, it would certainly develop that all had vastly different backgrounds. One teacher might have been trained privately; another partly privately but including courses at a conservatory; another may have a diploma from a first-rate music school plus advanced private study; and another may have earned both a bachelor's and a master's degree in music. With such diversity of background among successful teachers, the young pianist may find it difficult to decide how to prepare for his career as teacher. However, since a college degree has become essential in qualifying for many career positions today, it is probably advisable to choose accredited college training rather than private study. Perhaps a combination of the two—four years in college, followed by several years of private study—may provide the best of two possible worlds. The three-year diploma course offered by some conservatories may also allow more freedom in practicing and curriculum choice.

The pianist who wants to teach on a school faculty, however, no longer has the freedom to study only privately. He *must* go to college, for a bachelor's degree is required, and eventually a master's and a doctorate are usually expected. On a school faculty one of his commitments may well be to perform periodically for the faculty and student body on campus, so his or her training as a performing pianist will have to be rigorous and complete. (This does not mean that a private teacher need not or does not have equally superior qualifications as a pianist.)

CONTINUING STUDIES

For the established teacher continuing his studies either to maintain or improve skills, there are many options. More and more colleges and master teachers are offering pedagogy workshops during the summer vacation. *Clavier* magazine (1418 Lake Street, Evanston, Illinois 60204) publishes an annual directory of summer workshops in its March issue, followed by a supplement in a later issue. These workshops may be on such topics as pedagogy and materials, group piano, class piano, group teaching for the very young, or principles of the Maier technique. They may last only a few days or several weeks. The teacher may select one for both study and relaxation on a campus where one can also have comfortable living accommodations.

Those teachers who continue practicing and performing often arrange for private study with a master teacher on a semimonthly or even less frequent basis. Some teachers continue to work toward advanced degrees. Others rely solely on teachers' magazines, conventions, and meeting programs for new materials, methods, and ideas.

PERSONAL QUALIFICATIONS

In addition to having the necessary credentials to teach, it is important that teachers cultivate desirable personality traits and conduct their business in a stable and ethical way. Whether or not piano teachers must be concert pianists as well as teachers is a matter of personal preference. Average full-time teachers with a myriad of adult responsibilities are unlikely to have the time and energy for their own practicing. Essentially, they need not necessarily be up to concert performance, but they should be able to sight-read well enough to hold the respect of their students.

SCHOOL CATALOGS

The following school catalogs were used in the preparation of this section:

(1) Brandon University, Brandon, Manitoba, Canada 1976–1977
(2) Elizabethtown College, Elizabethtown, Pennsylvania 17022, 1973–1975
(3) Fredonia State University College, Fredonia, New York 14063, 1975–1977
(4) Indiana University, Bloomington, Indiana 47401, 1976–1977
(5) Kansas State University, Manhattan, Kansas 66506, 1976
(6) Madison University, Harrisonburg, Virginia 22801, 1976–1977
(7) Manhattan School of Music, New York, New York 10027, 1976
(8) Peabody Conservatory of Music, Baltimore, Maryland 21202, 1976–1977
(9) Sherwood Music School, Chicago, Illinois 60605, 1975–1977
(10) Stanford University, Stanford, California 94305, 1975–1976

RECOMMENDED READING

Egbert, Marion S. *Career Opportunities in Music*. Chicago: American Music Conference, 1966.

Laster, Harold M. "You Too Should be an Admission Counselor." *The American Music Teacher* May–June 1978.

Ward, John Owen. *Careers in Music*. New York: H.Z. Walck, 1968.

Four-Way Piano Teaching: Criticism, Demonstration, Analysis, Inspiration

WALTER ROBERT

CRITICISM

The usual piano lesson consists of a more or less finished performance of a prepared piece "executed" by the pupil, and by more or less detailed criticism of the performance by the teacher. This may range from a vague (I call it low-frequency) comment, "Very nice, but practice it some more, it could be still better," to the ultrasensory "Already too loud!" pronounced by the hypersensitive maestro right after, if not before, the first chord is struck by the student.

Very often, the student's performance is a fractured rendition, punctuated by the student with pithy remarks such as "oops" and "wait" and concluded, not with a bang, but with the whimper, "At home I played it perfect." If the teacher allows these lecture recitals and spoken program notes to become established performance practices, the pupil may never be able to perform without stoppages.

Frequently, however, it is not the student who stops the piece midway, but the teacher who breaks in with a criticism. I do not mean to say that the teacher must listen in mute suffering until the last blow has been struck against the composer, but that he or she should not interrupt a student every other measure to make corrections. If the first few measures show that a working session is in order, then phrases, harmonies, and even notes should be scrutinized thoroughly. On the other hand, if the performance is reasonably adequate, then I believe the

Reprinted from *Clavier*, January 1971. Used by permission of the Instrumentalist Company.

teacher should listen and make specific recommendations later.

While the student should be told both the good and the bad features of the lesson, the teacher should not indulge in generalities such as "pretty good, but still a little rough in places." Remarks like "It does not have enough profile," "Your playing lacks depth," "It should sound more brilliant" do not help the student, unless the teacher also makes it clear that the *siciliano* rhythm that did not have "profile" was played not, as it should be, like "Amsterdam, Rotterdam," but more like "Liverpool, Manchester," that "depth" requires arm weight, emphasis on the bass, and richer pedal, while brilliance cannot be achieved with the pulse-feeling in $\frac{4}{4}$ instead of $\frac{2}{4}$.

General criticism might be noted by the teacher in writing, at the head of the composition, in addition to the oral discussion. For detailed criticism, a system of symbols understood by the student is the neatest and clearest method for marking up a page of music. The marks should be carefully written and placed, not scrawled across a page. Circle the wrong note or notes; indicate pedals by one of the prevailing methods; use breath marks or carefully drawn slurs for phrasing. Abbreviations can be used: *Rh* for rhythm, *T* for technique, *fing.* for fingering, *art.* for articulation, ∽ for *rubato*, ⟶ for *accelerando*, ⟵ for *ritardando*, and others you and your students agree upon. An *X* at the area in question and the proper symbol or abbreviation placed in the margin makes the exact meaning clear.

The teacher must bear in mind that sooner or later it is time to stop criticizing. There are almost always psychological reasons and other considerations that force the teacher to be satisfied, at least temporarily, with the plateau that the student has reached at a given point.

Teaching by criticism was developed almost to a ritual by the violin pedagogue Carl Flesch. His students played from an unmarked copy while he sat at a distance and marked up a second copy. This copy was used for detailed discussion with musical illustrations. The markings were erased for the next lesson.

A successful teacher of my acquaintance writes her criticisms into the student's notebook while the pupil plays. This saves time and gives the student a ready reference manual for the week's practice. It is a sure stopper for "You did not tell me this" or "Last time you said. . . ." It also is a great help to the parent.

Another useful tool is the tape recorder. I use it to record my criticisms, illustrations, and the student's attempts at imitation. Occasionally I will put the entire lesson on tape although usually I do not turn the machine on until after the initial play-through. The student marks up the score while listening to the tape at home.

A student's progress can be measured through periodic tapings of lessons, and I sometimes keep these tapes for my own records, but I do not allow the student to retain the tape longer than a few days.

DEMONSTRATION

Teaching by example probably is the approach with the longest tradition. According to available sources, the *bel canto* singing teachers of the eighteenth century taught exclusively by demonstration, and much of the piano teaching of the nineteenth century was done in this way.

In those days, the teacher was often the only model available. Our ancestors were lucky if they could hear two different interpretations of Beethoven's "Appassionata" Sonata in a decade. We can hear recorded and live versions almost at will.

The most effective way of teaching by demonstration is, of course, repeated performance of sections of a composition to set up a model for the student to follow; the purpose may be to show a more musical and expressive interpretation of a phrase, or to illustrate the motions required for the desired effect.

Many teachers use artists' recordings for demonstrating. Most advanced students strive to hear a recording of a piece they have just been assigned.

In either case there are drawbacks. If incapable of performance of that piece, the teacher may not have the aural acuity to perceive the salient features of the recording to point them out to the student. And it is doubtful that the student really hears what is recorded; also, it has been my experience that students often hear what they want to hear. A student will give a pedal concert with keyboard accompaniment because "that's how Rubinstein plays it."

For these reasons the type of teaching that was commonly practiced in the nineteenth century, especially the authoritarian infallibility of the master who demonstrated and expected the student to imitate unquestioningly, is not for our time.

For the beginner, the teacher will play almost everything assigned. As the student advances and becomes more self-sufficient, it will not be necessary for the teacher to perform everything concert fashion. But the teacher must have the potential to perform the work decently if given the proper time to learn it.

No piece of music should be assigned that the teacher has not played at least slowly, without pedal, note by note, preferably also single hand and with conscious attention to rhythm, harmony (accidentals!), and fingering.

There are many "standard" mistakes that I get at every extended examination period or contest:

> C instead of C-sharp in Bach's first Invention, measure 11, last eighth note.
>
> D instead of D-sharp in Haydn's Sonata in D major, first movement, fourth measure of the development section, last eighth note.

Eighth-note motion instead of sixteenths at the opening of the middle section of Beethoven's "*Für Elise*."

D instead of D-flat in Beethoven's Sonata, op. 2 no. 1, in the thirteenth, eleventh, and ninth measures before the end of the first movement.

In Brahms' Intermezzo, op. 117 no. 2, E-flat instead of E-double flat on the third beat of measure 35.

The octave C-C instead of A-A in Brahms' G-minor Rhapsody, measure 2, last beat.

A wide selection of wrong notes in Mozart's D-minor Fantasy, starting with G instead of G-sharp on the last sixteenth note of measure 23.

When I witness this type of involuntary note-slaughter, I am sure that it is seldom accidental, and that it is the teacher, not the student, who is guilty.

ANALYSIS

Students very often are unable to distinguish between melody and accompaniment, especially in compositions of the romantic period, where the melody is often embedded in the accompaniment texture. First point of analysis: isolate the melody. Second point of analysis: establish the direction and shape of the melody; in other words, its underlying dynamic curve. The accompaniment may include neighbor notes, passing tones, grace notes, or what not, which can be sources of misreading and note mistakes.

Students should know in what key they are playing, not just at the beginning, but in the middle of a piece. Merely pointing out a wrong note does not help a student know why he or she misread the score. To insure insight and transfer of learning, you must analyze the harmonic content and explain to the student why the wrong note was wrong.

Some rhythms need to be broken down (analyzed) by counting out loud each of their component shortest values, or better, by making sure that the student "feels" the flow of the music.

Analyze the technical difficulties of a passage by

(1) subdividing the passage into its recurrent component parts, thereby explicating its harmonic basis;
(2) establishing a fingering principle;
(3) analyzing the most appropriate motions to achieve the desired result.

Especially in this last phase, analysis is sorely needed and rarely forthcoming. How often do we not find a student coming in after a week of conscientious practice, hitting a wrong note time and again, not because it was misread, but because of an awkward manual approach, perhaps combined with a poor fingering.

All this analyzing, I believe, should be done in a manner that avoids theorizing, academese, and five-syllable terms. In fact, scarcely any talking is necessary. The melody should be played without accompaniment; then the accompaniment without the melody; wherever possible the accompaniment may be blocked, nonharmonic tones omitted; this will lead to insight into the chord progressions, resolutions, and cadences. This is truly a case where learning by doing is the exciting thing. Rhythms must be felt, not mathematically calculated; counting aloud, clapping, finding words that fit the note values are much more efficacious than lectures on iambic, anapestic, or asymmetrical groupings of notes. The same practical approach should be used for the breaking down of passages into components, finding fingerings and purposeful motions. Terminology is the business of the theory teacher. Just as orchestras hate talkative conductors, piano pupils resent lecturing piano teachers. The student and the teacher should interact making music, not talking about it.

INSPIRATION

The fourth method of teaching is by inspiration. By this I mean that the piano teacher assumes the role of the orchestra conductor and treats the student as a one-person symphony. This is achieved by counting aloud, singing or playing along with the student, leading on by gestures or by whatever means, on the spur of the moment.

This method is more exciting for teacher and student than any other. It presupposes certain conditions *sine qua non*. First of all, the student must be able to play the piece correctly up to tempo and with enough ease to be able to follow the teacher's signals; he or she must be responsive and willing to respond. The teacher must have imagination, inner hearing, and the reasonable assurance of a right vision of the composer's intentions to be Pygmalion and breathe life into his Galatea. He or she must be enough of an extrovert and possess enough personal magnetism to make signals unmistakably clear and convincing, even coercive.

Moderation and restraint in the use of this method are necessary to preserve the teacher's voice as well as to prevent the student from turning into an automaton executing the orders of a once-a-week Frankenstein.

SUMMARY

An experienced teacher will immediately and almost instinctively feel which approach—criticism, demonstration, analysis, or inspiration—is the most appropriate in working with a student, and have the empathy to use one or the other, or a combination, in a given learning situation. He or she will plan lessons so that different approaches are used within the lesson and in the sequence of contacts with the student.

All four ways should be used—none is the only valid one—and all have their limitations. The teacher must beware of narrowing the teaching approach to only one of the four. Personality will probably make a teacher more effective in one or two, rather than equally in all four. We should all reexamine our teaching routines and not permit ourselves to fall into the rut of teaching only by criticism, or only by demonstration, or only by analysis, or only by inspiration.

What Are the Elements of a Good Piano Lesson?

MAY L. ETTS

The answer to this question will depend on a number of factors. Who is taking the lesson? A seven-year-old, an adult beginner, or a teen-ager who has studied for four or five years? Is the lesson private or group? A half-hour or an hour? In any case one must realize that a good lesson plan should cover not only a single session, but the whole term, for each student.

First of all, the teacher must establish a warm rapport with, and gain the confidence of, the pupil, whether a beginner or a transfer student. Psychologists have found that a student who apparently had no aptitude for a given subject when studying with one teacher suddenly took an interest in that subject when transferred to another instructor.

The time that the student spends with the teacher is very short, whether a half-hour for a beginner or an hour for a more advanced student, whether in a group or alone. To reap the most from every precious moment, the teacher should prepare the lesson in advance, know what each pupil has accomplished and what is to be taught, and be ready for the difficulties in playing each piece, study or technical drill, rather than coming upon them unexpectedly.

It is important that the pupil learn how to practice. From the new assignment, take a difficult measure or passage. Have the student play it slowly, each hand alone, to the first beat of the next measure. (This is to avoid a pause at the end of the measure, or accenting the last note of the measure.) Practice to avoid faults that occur frequently in stu-

Reprinted from *Keyboard Consultant*, Spring 1973. Used by permission.

dent performances: are the rhythmic values correct? Is the pupil able to clap the rhythm and count the values? Are the notes correct? What about fingering? After playing hands alone slowly and correctly, play faster. Next, play hands together, slowly, then faster. Whatever the problem–rhythmic, technical, accuracy, reading for self-study, or sight reading–it should be worked out at the lesson, as it is expected to be practiced at home. This helps establish good study habits.

Pieces for self-study, easy enough for the student to be able to play well within one week without help from the teacher, are very important. Later, several pages may be assigned, but only one heard at the lesson. Unless a student is able to play self-study material easily, sight reading will be a problem. Sight reading, of course, is a most important part of the lesson. The material assigned must be easy and contain only those elements with which the student is familiar. One can "sight read" a daily newspaper in a familiar language, but not in an unknown foreign language.

Technique, touch, and tone studies should be presented. The hand position usually requires much attention, and technique, touch, and tone suffer when the hand falls on a collapsed fifth finger, when the thumb hangs, or when joints "break." Simple "tickling" of the keys with the fingertips is a helpful first step. Some pertinent technical drills may be played at the beginning of each lesson as warmups and then integrated with problems in the studies and pieces. This procedure, while very valuable, actually requires little time.

Theory, ear training, and keyboard harmony, as well as some creative work, are other important elements of a good lesson, and should not be omitted. Decide what the student should cover during the season and assign something for each lesson, possibly varying from week to week, including assignments of written work. Analysis is helpful. Students may identify or write scales, chords, intervals, phrases, and cadences which are contained in their pieces or study material.

Review is also very important. Through review the student develops ease, style, and finesse. Only through thoughtful repetition may a well-prepared piece be brought to exhibit fine polish, greater musical contrasts, more musically shaped phrases, cleaner pedaling, more secure memorization.

Repertory must not be forgotten; not only memorization of new pieces, but maintaining a group of pieces in a state of readiness to play at any time. It is a mistake for a student to feel that once a piece is memorized it is "finished," dropped forever and forgotten. How can a teacher hear memorized pieces in the short period of a lesson? Some weeks hear a complete piece or two, other weeks hear sections. Ask to hear the last page or even the last line, the section after the double bar, or the beginning of the G-major section, and so on. This keeps the student prepared. Repertory classes and studio recitals are valuable, save time, provide great incentives, and give the necessary experience of playing for an audience. At such classes, having students constructively criticize each other fosters alert observation. Students should be encouraged to play at church, school, community events, and at home.

Ensemble playing is one of the greatest aids for developing rhythm, precision, fluent reading, and enhancing musical pleasure. It has tremendous value in developing coordination, cooperation, and listening, and it helps to eliminate self-centered attitudes. The student may learn a part alone, and when ready to play together, a partner may come in at the end of the lesson, or vice versa. If a duet is being learned, the students may practice at each other's homes; for two-piano works, special rehearsal periods may be assigned. Whatever the problems may be, the interest, enthusiasm, and resultant stimulation of work in general make any effort more than worthwhile.

Rote Playing and Rote Teaching

DENES AGAY

Learning by rote means learning by imitation and retention. It enables the student to memorize and reproduce certain aural impressions and kinetic keyboard patterns without having to read or in any way refer to a written score. The teacher demonstrates; the student repeats by imitating the specific motions to produce the desired sound. A good many pianistic dexterities, especially in the fields of technique and sight reading, are attained by this method of learning, often without the player's being aware of it. Rote learning aids in mastering scales, chords, arpeggios, harmonic progressions, and cadences; it also helps tone production and keyboard touches (legato, staccato, portamento, etc.). Fluent sight reading is also promoted by the instinctive application of motion patterns assimilated by a repetitive (rote) practice.

Despite its many practical applications, rote playing and teaching is considered a somewhat controversial subject in some pedagogical circles. Those opposed to it feel that rote playing on the elementary level may inhibit and hinder learning to play by reading notes, and gives the student an artificial sense of accomplishment. This simply is not so, if the teacher knows when and how rote teaching should take place. True, if rote playing is overdone or indiscriminitely taught, the student's mechanical keyboard experiences may get ahead of the theoretical capacity to read and understand music. In other words, what the student can play by rote may overshadow in sound and overall effectiveness the material he or she can play by reading notes. This should not be allowed to happen and, indeed, does not happen if rote teaching is carefully planned to proceed parallel to and in preparation for the teaching of pertinent theoretical concepts.

Playing carefully selected rote pieces holds important advantages for the student, whether young or adult, during elementary studies. Playing without the printed score focuses all mental attention and physical responses on the tactile problems at hand, without the necessity for eye involvement to follow the score and without the analytical-mental process of interpreting printed notes and translating them into kinetic responses. Another advantage of rote teaching is that it can be tailored to the individual student's needs and capacities. Emphasis can be given to strengthening weaknesses while at the same time giving the student confidence. There is now a wide choice of attractive rote pieces available in print. These pieces can be learned without much effort as they lend themselves to imitative learning and to easy aural and tactile retention. Rote teaching has sound pedagogical justification. It can materially contribute to the general advancement and learning pleasure of students, especially those, regardless of age, who for various reasons progress at a slower than average pace, and who may need more time and special considerations in acquiring necessary skills.

THE FIRST KEYBOARD CONTACTS

This section is meant to give teachers some ideas and furnish concrete examples whereby the beginning student can be introduced to the piano and be guided in the first keyboard explorations through little pieces and exercises learned by rote.

Even the very first lesson presents opportunities for taking advantage of the usefulness of rote procedures. The topography of the keyboard, the arrangement of black-key groups, the location and direction of high and low notes, can easily be taught through the first little pieces the student can play by rote. It is important that these first playing experiences involve a wide range up and down the keyboard so that the student can immediately gather aural and tactile impressions of the entire instrument.

In the beginning the student does not have to know the letter names of the keys or the notes on the staff. Rote playing is based on imitation and memorization. The pupil is shown, by logical steps, what to do, and repeats what is shown. Nor does the student have to count. The short phrases, especially when supplied with words, strongly indicate meter and rhythm. Even when counting is introduced, it is advisable that at first, the student chant the words while playing, then turn to counting.

Here are some examples for initial keyboard explorations. Many others can be created by the imaginative teacher to suit individual needs.

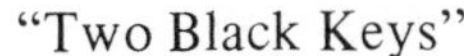

"Two Black Keys"

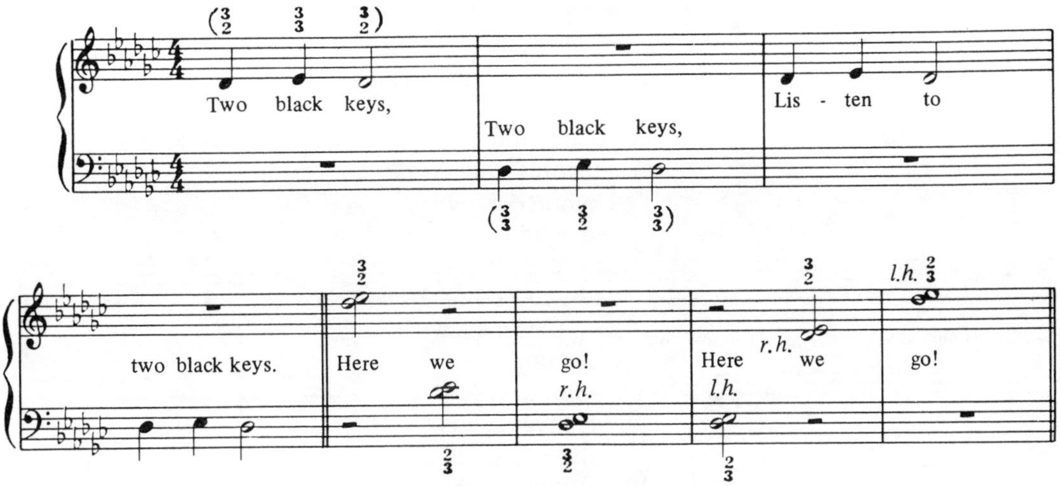

Two black keys, Two black keys, Listen to two black keys.
Here we go! Here we go!

"Three Black Keys"

Three black keys, Three black keys, Listen to three black keys.
Here we go! Here we go!

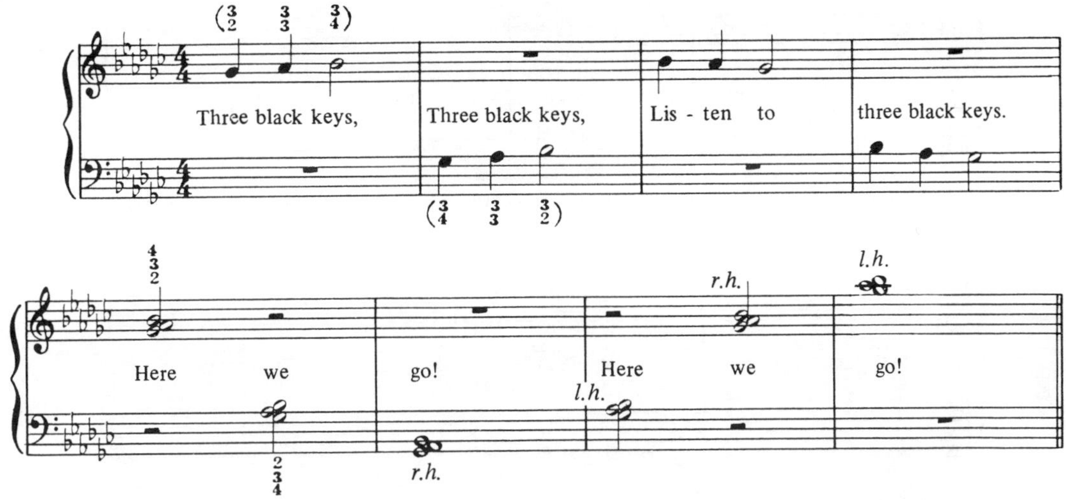

"Bells Are Ringing"

Bells are ringing ting-a-ling, Bells are ringing ding-dong.

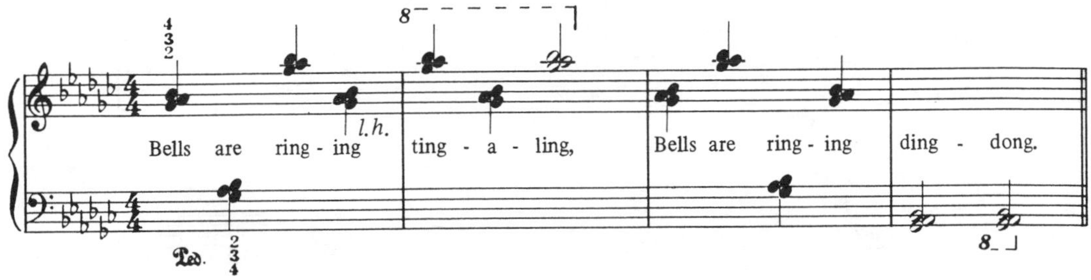

"Up and Down"
r.h.
l.h.
This way up, This way down. This way down, This way up.
"High and Low"
High, low, high; Low, high, low, High, high, low.
"Mountain Climb"
Climb - ing up moun - tains we're climb - ing up high.
Com - ing down to the ground and say good - bye.
"Black Key Frolic"
r.h.
l.h.
r.h.
l.h.
r.h.
l.h.
r.h.
l.h.

"Black and White"

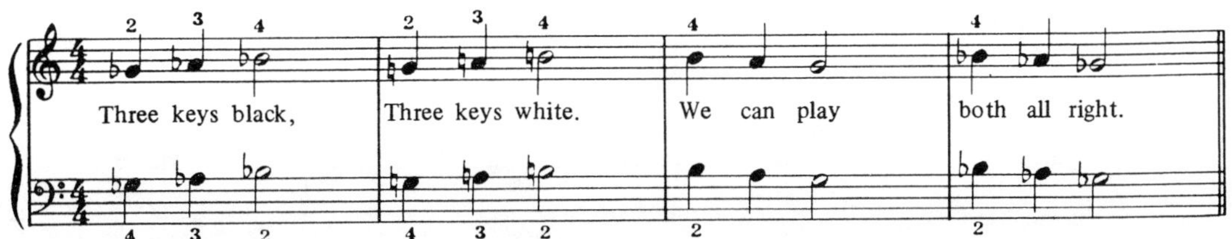

Playing *legato* is a rather difficult discipline for beginning pianists, and usually requires time and practice. The weight of the hand or arm, securely supported by the fingertips, must be transferred gradually from one key to another for a smooth continuity of sound. At first this is best accomplished by the three middle fingers because of their approximately equal length and anatomical structure. The following example should be played both in G-flat and in G, at first by each hand separately, then by both together.

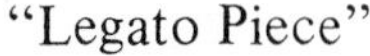
"Legato Piece"

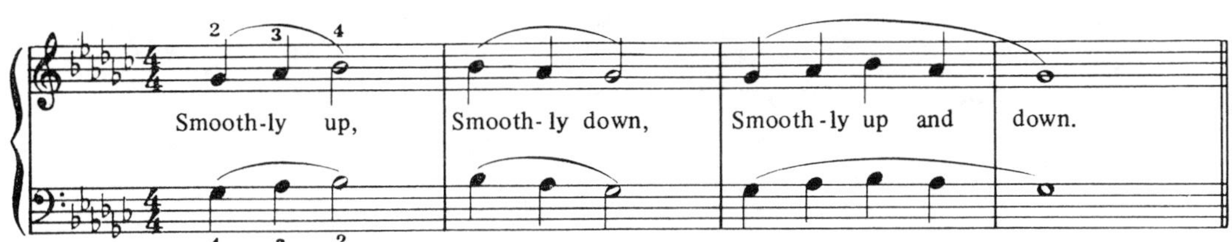

At this point "Mountain Climb" may be repeated so that the three-note groups are played strictly legato.

"Staccato Piece"

"Little Scherzo"

Pieces involving all five fingers should be introduced early.

"What a Day!"

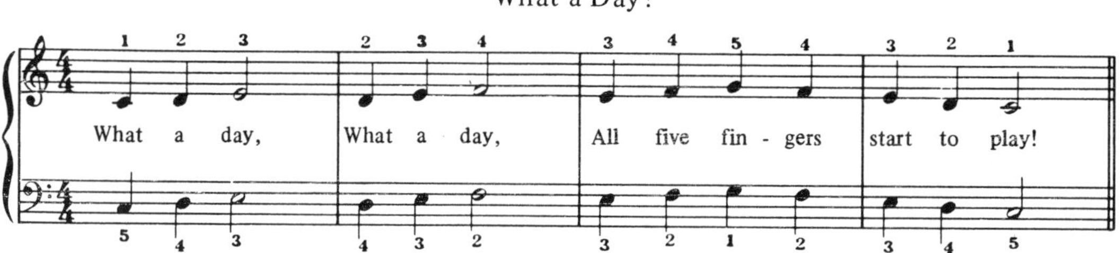

The above piece can also be taught by playing all quarter notes *staccato*. Transpose into several other keys. The next piece—"Play Tune"—is in a shifting five-finger position.

The three-measure phrases should be played legato. The piece can also serve as a staccato étude: quarter notes played *staccato*, half notes *tenuto*. Transposition into G major may also be useful.

Agay: "Play Tune"

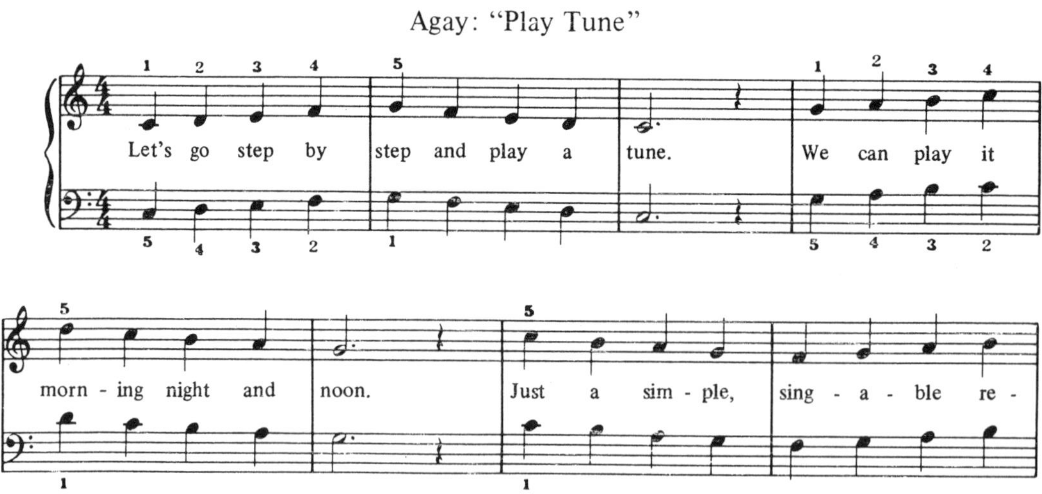

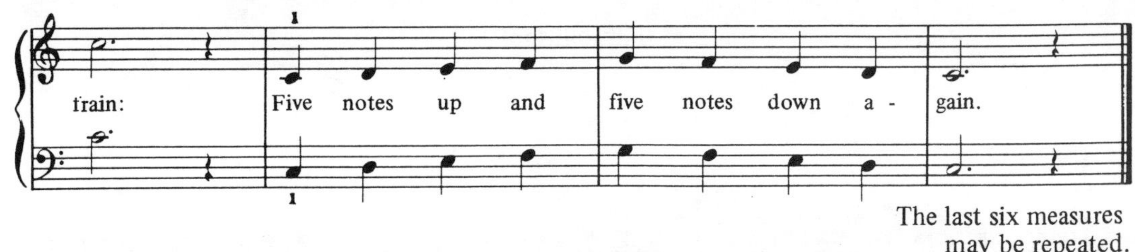

The last six measures may be repeated.

When learning the notes' letter names, the student's first task can be playing and naming all white keys successively from the bottom of the keyboard (A) to the top, using the third finger first with the right hand, then with the left.

Three "A-B-C Songs"

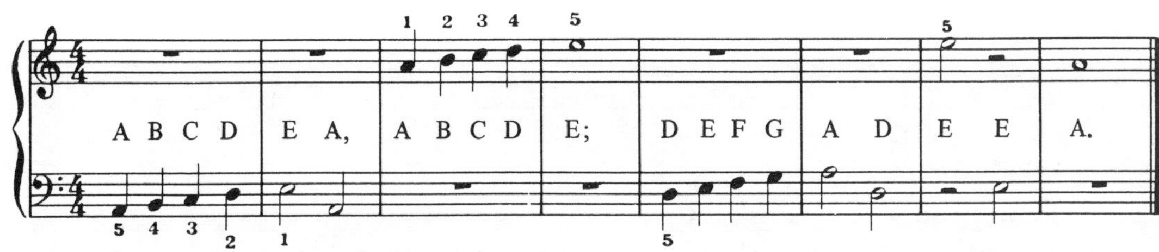

Arpeggios and *arpeggio*-like figures are especially suitable and showy vehicles for over-the-keyboard travels. The following piece is built on the twelve-bar harmonic sequence of the blues: I-IV-I-V-I. The legato arches should be played smoothly.

"The Glider"

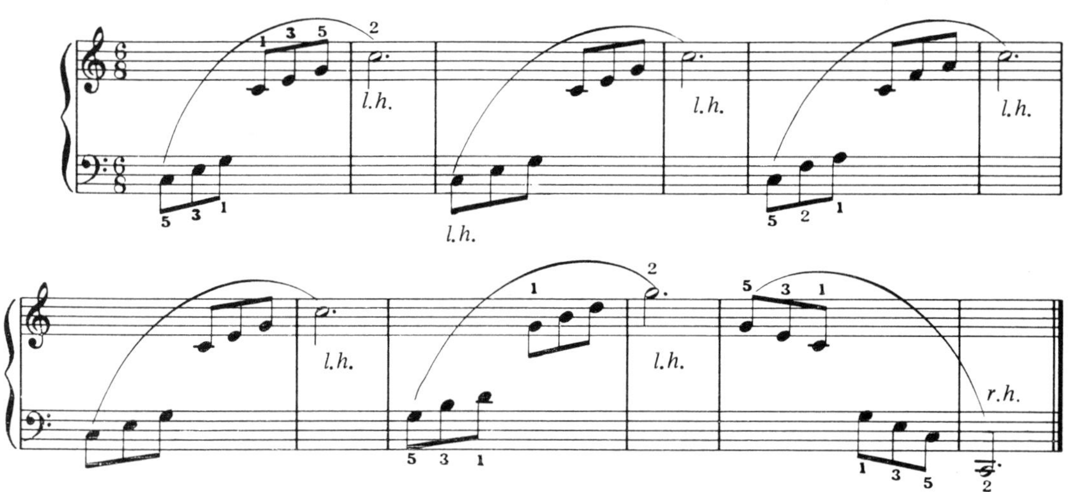

By playing the next piece and singing the words, the student can get an idea of how the black keys derive from the white ones, and gain familiarity with the half-step interval. (At first, play one hand at a time.)

"Sharps and Flats"

The following two pieces offer an opportunity for playing on various dynamic levels, as well as double notes and chords.

"The First Serenade"
Moderato
p
mf
"From Olden Times"
Andante
f (repeat p)
f
p rit.
"Scale Melody"
r.h.
l.h.

All the pieces presented so far were meant only to provide guidelines and examples of how technical and theoretical concepts can be introduced and learned through rote playing. The teacher's files should contain an ample number of appropriate selections, a varied repertory of attractive rote pieces, illustrating practically all aspects of elementary keyboard skills and theoretical matters, ready to be given to the student progressively from the very beginning. In addition, the teacher must be alert and creative enough to adapt materials or compose new ones to fit the student's individual needs. It is extremely important that the selected rote materials should be interesting, well written, and suitable for the intended teaching purpose. Also, they must be constructed in a manner that features *repetitive patterns* of melody, rhythm, and harmony so that they can be easily imitated and memorized. It often helps if the piece has a descriptive title, which promotes understanding, identification with the music, and more effective performance.

Ostinato bass patterns of all sorts are especially suitable features of rote pieces. The repeated patterns in the left hand are very easy to remember, so all attention can be focused on the right-hand part.

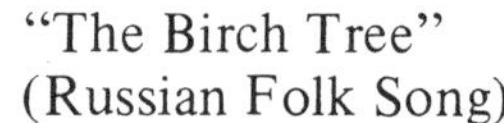

"Moody Dance"

"Skip to My Lou" Boogie

The following steps in teaching rote material are suggested:

- The teacher plays the piece through from beginning to end, to give the pupil an idea of what it is and how it should sound.
- The teacher plays the piece again, slower this time, breaking it down into sections and pointing out repetitive or other important features. Questions can be asked to make sure that the student has a grasp of the particulars. (Can you hum the melody? Is it repeated? Where? Is it repeated exactly or is there any change? Can you clap this rhythm? How many times does this rhythm appear?)
- The pupil begins to play the piece, imitating the teacher's demonstration phrase by phrase, section by section. Once individual sections are memorized, they are gradually connected.

The next two selections (which can also serve as little recital pieces) contain many of the constructional elements and keyboard features which were dealt with individually in previous examples. They can also furnish the teacher an opportunity to analyze and test the step-by-step teaching procedure outlined above.

"Keyboard Frolic"

Allegretto

Agay: "Moonlit Pagoda"

Moderately; gently moving
p
pp
l.h.
Ped.

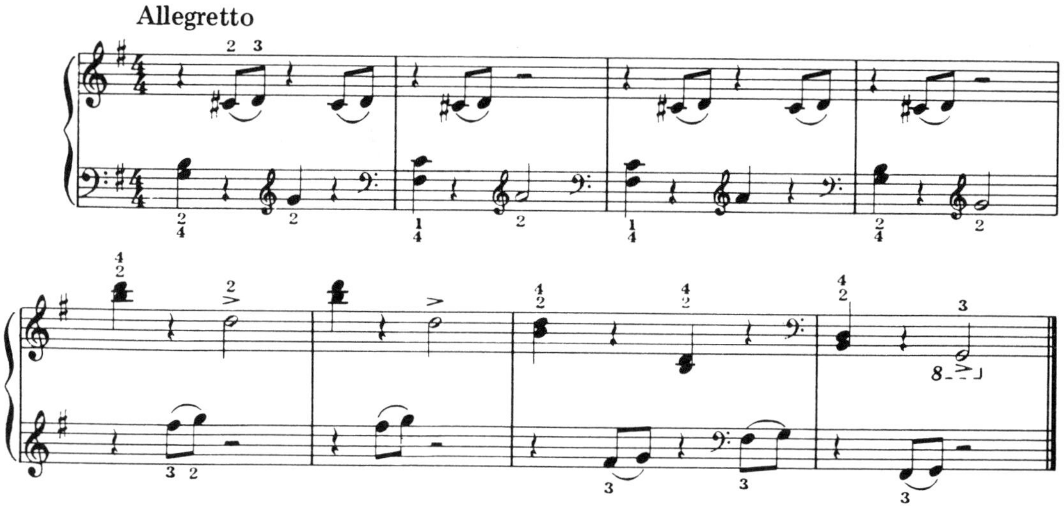

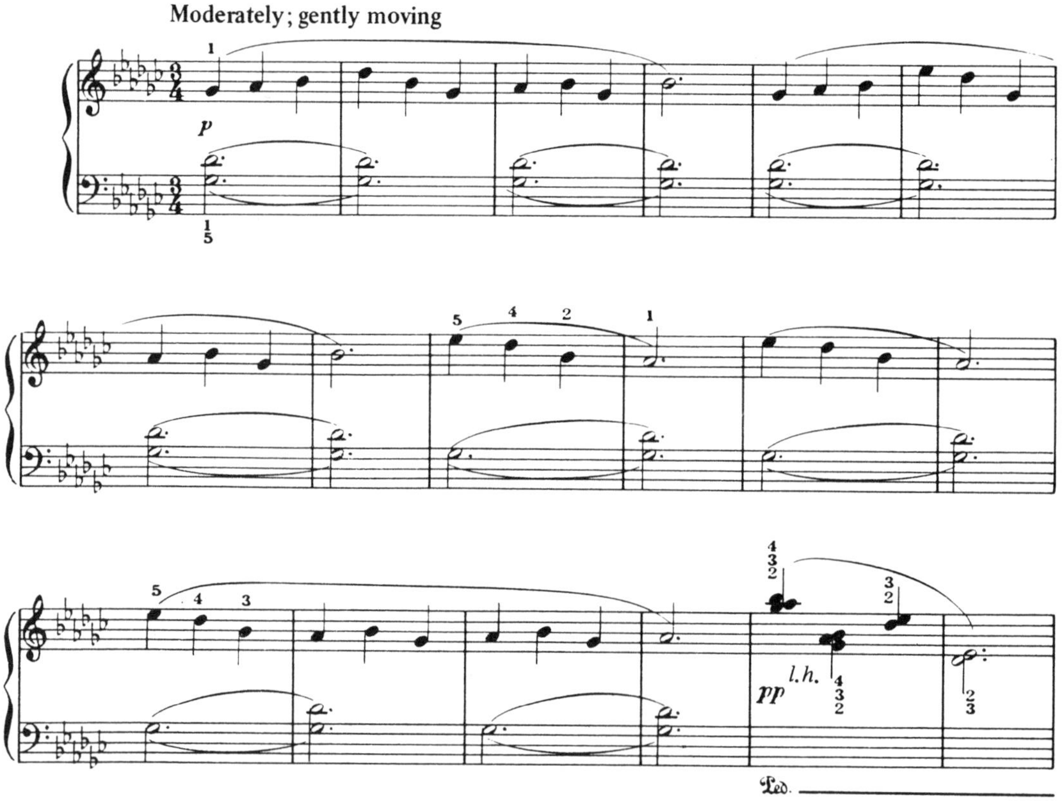

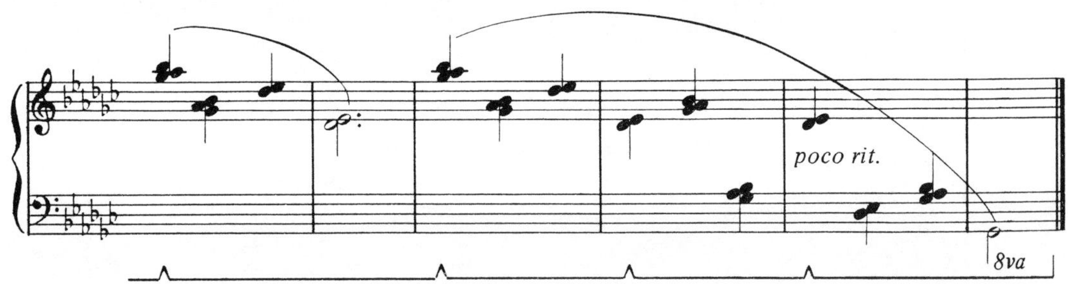

In summary it should be emphasized that rote playing can be an important pedagogical tool in teaching many keyboard skills and musical concepts. If guided properly and with judicious restraint, it can also be an unfailing confidence booster and a source of incentive for all budding pianists.

RECOMMENDED READING

Agay, Denes. *The Joy of First-Year Piano*. New York: Yorktown Music Press, 1972.

Cornfield, Edith. "Teaching by Rote." *Clavier* September 1969.

Diller, Angela. *Rote Teaching–What It Is and How To Do It*. New York: G. Schirmer, 1953.

Last, Joan. *Keyboard Games for the Very Young Pianist*. London: Oxford University Press, 1972.

Maier, Guy and Helen Corzilius. *Playing the Piano: A Course of Rote Training for Beginners*. New York: J. Fischer and Bro., 1929.

The Tape Recorder: An Indispensable Teaching Aid

YLDA NOVIK

Only a few years ago, tape recorders were rarely found in the studio of the private piano teacher. He or she would enviously eye the university or conservatory colleague who could schedule access to a machine for recording students' performances. Now that inexpensive tape recorders are available, many private teachers consider them as necessary a part of their teaching equipment as pianos and blackboards.

I confess that initially the sole use of my first tape recorder was to record the annual student recital and then play each child's performance back so he or she could listen in awe and wonderment. Also, what greater joy for the proud parents than to resavor little Vladimir's performance for yet another time? That limited use resulted from my absolute terror of operating all things electrical, from vacuum cleaners to televisions, until they had been in our house for weeks, by which time I was certain that they were thoroughly domesticated and would not bite when touched. My scientist husband coped with the beast for me at recitals.

At last, when he bought a new model for me, which he said "anyone could operate," it was placed next to the piano for daily teaching purposes. And how the uses seemed to increase as time went on!

USE AT REPERTORY CLASSES

My students became very performance oriented as a result of partici-

---

Revised by the author from an article originally published in *The American Music Teacher*, June–July 1968. Used by permission.

pation in my repertory classes. Fortunately, they have outlets for performance via the large number of recitals sponsored by local music teachers' organizations. Therefore, the first and most obvious use for our tape recorder was in preparation for these performances. As we all know, it is invaluable to hear ourselves as a means of discovering obvious mistakes and rough spots. Furthermore, the tape preserves the playing so that colleagues and coaches can comment on errors that our subjectivity might blur or gloss over. Also the psychological factor of knowing the "ear" was listening makes the taped performance one in which student's play with greater concentration than if they were only playing for their good friend, the teacher.

Once the piece is taped, we work in one or a combination of several possible ways. Sometimes we play back the entire piece without commentary, then discuss it as a whole after it is concluded. At other times, the student is asked to stop the tape when something is displeasing, and rework it, there and then. Still another approach is for me to stop the tape and make the comments. Often we tape a small stubborn fragment, in order to polish phrasing, dynamics, or technical evenness, playing it over numerous times until we are both pleased. Then the entire composition is taped once more, with the two versions played back in succession, so the pupil can hear the improvement.

Occasionally, an argumentative student will dispute having played out of time, or having hit a wrong note. He or she has to play for "the truth machine" and then must accept what he or she hears. "Hearing is believing" is our motto.

PREPARATION FOR CONCERTS

Then there is the student who comes to a series of lessons unprepared or misprepared. I say, "We're going to play back your performance of this piece right now so that you will have to listen to it and suffer as I do every week." This never fails to put an end to a slump, and progress resumes. The adage of being one's own best critic most certainly applies to all musicians, as well as piano pupils—if they are given an opportunity for self-criticism.

In addition to being performance oriented, my students are also "contest happy," and participate in two large national student-level competitions which utilized taped performances. The Baldwin keyboard achievement awards are judged from reel tapes, sent in to state, then divisional, and finally national levels. It is open to students in grades 7 through 9, or roughly twelve through fourteen years of age. I have been very much impressed by watching my contenders taping and retaping and polishing their pieces to the utmost level of their abilities. The growth in each and every participant continues into a vastly improved quality of work thereafter, regardless of what stage of the contest has been reached.

The Young Chopin Competition held in Buffalo for students under seventeen has its preliminary round submitted on reel tape and serves as a good example. The finalists are selected from their tapes, then compete in person. Again, as in the Baldwin, it has been thrilling to see my students strive for that almost unattainable level of absolute perfection. I turn my piano and tape recorder over to these contestants on weekend hours when no lessons are scheduled and they work entirely on their own at the tapes. Generally, I am at my desk in another part of the house, marveling at their maturity, determination, and endless patience, as they spend hours on any given piece.

TAPED LESSONS

And now, the most important use of the tape recorder: taping every lesson. With the advent of the inexpensive, easy-to-use cassette recorder (even the really cheap ones are adequate), all of my students are required to have their own affordable versions of these remarkably convenient machines. The student comes in for a lesson with a cassette tape, puts it in my cassette recorder, and the entire lesson is recorded from start to finish. (This is also a convenient half-hour timekeeper.) This tape, needless to say, played once or twice at home during the ensuing week, serves to remind students of all the things which were said and done at the lesson. They say that it is like taking me home with them for an extra lesson or two each week. I should add that this does not create an overdependent situation because there comes a time when we stop taping. This is only when I am certain that practice habits are well established, and in all cases there is no decline in the quality of lesson preparation.

Since not every student can afford to buy recordings of the pieces being learned—and many of the easy ones are not recorded—students borrow another cassette on which I record for them the music they are studying so they may become familiar with it. Of course, there are two definite schools of thought about listening to music on which one is working. Since I believe in utilizing every possible means to familiarize oneself with the compositions—such as thematic and harmonic analysis—I am ardently in the buy-the-records-and-learn camp. But I say with great emphasis, "Do not copy the performer's style. Use the record only as a means of becoming better acquainted with the music. Remain objective."

Another fallout of the taped lesson occurs when a student comes for a lesson but has forgotten to bring the music. Once upon a time this meant that the student might use my music for the lesson, but had no satisfactory way of annotating the lesson comments because I preferred not to have markings on my copies. Now I can lend a cassette, and tape the lesson as usual.

Occasionally, I have students who live so far away that they are able to study only once a month. Midway between lessons they mail me a tape of their playing so that I may comment on their progress and make any corrections. This process is not as impossible as it appears to be, since I now own not one, but several tape recorders of each type (reel and cassette). I make my remarks into a second tape recorder, phrase by phrase, as the lesson tape is being played on the first tape recorder and simultaneously being recorded on the second. Both tapes are mailed back to the long-distance student, giving essentially all the benefits of an in-person lesson. Twin tape recorders are also put to use for making copies of any contest or recital tapes which students want duplicated. It is really a good idea to have multiple copies of precious tapes as a form of insurance should anything happen to the originals.

Take-home tapes are also an excellent means of drilling the student in ear training. For example: I make up simple four- or eight-measure tunes which are to be played at home by ear, first in the original key and then transposed to all twelve keys. For the next step, the students add chords and improvise different styles of accompaniments.

Each new student who comes to me is given instructions to tape each piece he learned, when we both feel it is polished. Actually I don't check on this consistently, but I try to impress upon the student the fact that he or she can have a life-long music diary, something to chuckle about years later while listening again to those fruits of the early years of study.

Yet another facet of the tape recorder's versatility is in concerto and two-piano work. In each case I tape the other piano part so that the student can use it at home to become familiar with the ensemble. Such a short-cut and time-saver on rehearsals! I must confess that, as half of a two-piano team, I have inveigled my partner into taping his part. Thus in our busy lives we require a minimum of rehearsals, inasmuch as he was only the flick of a switch away.

There are undoubtedly many other uses of the tape recorder for teaching and playing music that have not occurred to me but are obvious to my colleagues. As I utilize this indispensable teaching aid more and more, I can only regret the years that I did not use it to full advantage.

The Teacher-Student Relationship: Some Common-Sense Suggestions

HAZEL GHAZARIAN SKAGGS

To insure the best possible learning climate and relationship between themselves and their students, piano teachers may be guided by the following common-sense rules:

(1) Show your students that you care about them. The teacher is a friend to each student, but not a pal. Gatherings such as rehearsals, recital parties, and concerts may provide further opportunities to affirm your interest in the student as a person.
(2) It is best to establish your authority at the first meeting and retain it at all times so that your students respond with friendly respect.
(3) Recognize individual differences. For instance, challenging material may motivate one child but frustrate another. A recital may be exciting for an outgoing child and devastating to a shy one.
(4) Reinforce good behavior. Inappropriate behavior, unheeded, may disappear. The child who constantly cries and receives comfort because of it will be encouraged to continue crying. Also, clowning will continue with an appreciative audience, but usually will disappear when unobserved.
(5) Encourage students; don't be negative. Rather than say "You forgot to make the crescendo here," comment: "This section is well done, and when you make the crescendo here, it will be even better." A sense of achievement, not failure, provides motivation for continued learning.
(6) Work toward improving the student's self-esteem. There is,

however, the danger that overpraise may lead to the student's considering an artistic career when his or her talents are not solid and broad enough to meet the demands of a life goal.

(7) In working with groups, do not resort to anger to maintain discipline. A display of anger is a waste of time and energy; it is debilitating and it diminishes your dignity and authority.

(8) In helping students, use common sense rather than psychoanalytical methods. Unless trained as a psychologist, the teacher can do more damage than good. If, in your opinion, a student's behavior is highly inappropriate, it is best to relate your observations, *not* your conclusions, to the student's parents.

(9) Furnish the studio so that it is a pleasant and cheerful place, reflecting your outlook, taste, and personality.

(10) Remember, the lesson time is for the student. Do not overdo talking or demonstrating at the piano.

Parental Involvement

DENES AGAY

The ideal parents, from the teacher's point of view, are those who display a constructive interest in the child's study and progress without being overzealous or meddlesome about it. Some degree of parental involvement, then, is entirely normal, even desirable. Parents who are totally indifferent or disinterested will not help the child's progress; on the contrary, they will create a musically dull and sterile home atmosphere, which may stifle the child's initiative. It is extremely important for the teacher to realize this and not to regard every parental inquiry and request as unreasonable or unnecessary interference.

It may happen, of course, that parental attention becomes exaggerated and disruptive. To cope with this is often a delicate problem requiring not only professional competence but a great deal of tact and diplomacy. Obviously it would be impossible to suggest remedies that would apply in every situation, except one ancient common-sense rule: head off trouble before it starts. The teacher should realize that most problems can be avoided and friction averted by certain preventive measures taken at the very beginning of the instruction.

The first and most important step is to establish and maintain a relationship with the parents which is open, friendly and relaxed— a relationship which is based on cooperation and mutual understanding. The parent's goodwill and willingness to cooperate, however, may not be enough; it helps more if they know *how* to cooperate, how to handle certain problems which are likely to occur between lessons, and, in general, how to maintain and stimulate the child's interest.

For this reason it is advisable to have an informative talk with the parents when lessons begin. During this talk the teacher may outline methods and planned curriculum and discuss the solutions to certain problems with which the parents may easily become involved: the age-old problem of practicing, for instance.

How much is the child supposed to practice? What time of day is the best? Should an unwilling child be coaxed to practice? These and numerous other related questions should be discussed so that the parents are equipped to form a sound opinion about them from the beginning. This will prevent later complications and misunderstandings.

It should be pointed out to the parents that children usually make very good progress under a set routine, and there is nothing wrong in keeping them in line and reminding them of their daily duties, whatever these may be: homework, taking a bath, or practicing the piano. At the same time it should be remembered that the practice period should not interfere with the youngster's rightful recreational activities. Furthermore, practicing should never be imposed as a matter of punishment. Parents should express pleasure and not be stingy with praise for work well done; also an occasional request to play a certain piece will no doubt be appreciated and act as a booster. In general, the rule should be motivation and incentive, not coercion.

In another area, parents should be urged to be flexible and understanding in their attitude toward different musical styles. For instance, if the child enjoys playing contemporary music, parents should not be critical, even if they happen not to be attracted toward the modern sound. Popular songs should not be frowned upon, either; they may provide the student with the necessary "shot in the arm" to maintain interest or overcome certain lags in the daily practice habit, so that eventually the student can proceed to study material of a higher caliber.

These, of course, are just a small sampling of the topics which may be discussed. The teacher can prepare a long list of other pertinent items and, naturally, the parents, too, should be encouraged to ask questions and express thoughts about the entire subject area. It is important to remember that the proper spirit of the meeting is not one of teacher's lecturing parents but of a friendly discussion during which ideas are exchanged. The teacher may prefer to have the meeting with a group of parents instead of just one or two. These meetings may be held at regular intervals, such as at the beginning and the end of the school year, or as the need arises.

Despite all careful preliminary briefings, complications may still arise. Some parents may turn out to be "difficult," all precautionary measures notwithstanding. For these cases we would like to offer the teacher the following suggestions:

- Be cool and calm; do not, under any cirsumstances, lose your temper.
- Examine, as carefully and as objectively as you can, the child's entire curriculum and review the progress made.

- If you feel that there is no objective reason for any complaint or dissatisfaction, bring this (as tactfully as you can) to the parents' attention. This does not mean that you have to be stiff and unyielding in every respect. Slight adjustments and harmless excursions can be made within the student's repertory to please parents.
- Should parental attitude become hopelessly unreasonable so that you have no choice but to discontinue the child's instruction, bow out with dignity and, if possible, without traces of ill-feeling.

We earnestly feel, though, that the giving up of a student because of parental difficulties should be an extremely rare occurrence. In most cases it can be avoided by know-how, patience, and tact. It should be kept constantly in mind that music lessons are a three-way effort by teacher, student, and parents. If the parents are made aware that their attitude and cooperation play an essential part in this joint effort, their involvement will rarely be the kind which could lead to serious complications.

RECOMMENDED READING

Wills, Vera G. and Ande Manners. *A Parent's Guide to Music Lessons*. New York: Harper & Row, 1967.

Appendix I: The Master Teachers and Their Pupils

DENES AGAY

	pupil of:	*teacher of:*
Eugène d'Albert (1864–1932)	Franz Liszt	Wilhelm Backhaus
C.P.E. Bach (1714–1788)	Johann Sebastian Bach	J.C. Bach Jan Dussek
Ludwig van Beethoven (1770–1827)	Christian Neefe	Karl Czerny Ferdinand Ries
Felix Blumenfeld (1863–1931)	Nikolai Rimsky-Korsakov Anton Rubinstein	Vladimir Horowitz
Ferruccio Busoni (1866–1924)	Wilhelm Mayer	Rudolf Ganz Percy Grainger Joseph Lhevinne Selim Palmgren Egon Petri
Teresa Carreno (1858–1917)	Louis Gottschalk Anton Rubinstein	Edward MacDowell Egon Petri
Frédéric Chopin (1810–1849)	Friedrich Kalkbrenner	Karl Mikuli
Muzio Clementi (1752–1832)	Carpani Santarelli	Johann Cramer John Field Johann Hummel Friedrich Kalkbrenner Ignaz Moscheles

	pupil of:	*teacher of:*
Alfred Cortot (1877–1962)	Louis Diemer	Gina Bachauer
Karl Czerny (1791–1857)	Ludwig van Beethoven	Joseph Dachs Theodor Kullak Theodor Leschetizky
Joseph Dachs (1825–1896)	Karl Czerny	Vladimir de Pach-mann
Edward Dannreuther (1844–1905)	Ignaz Moscheles	James Friskin
Louis Diemer (1843–1919)	Antoine Marmontel	Alfredo Casella Alfred Cortot Robert Casadesus Emil Frey
Anna Essipoff (1851–1914)	Theodor Leschetizky	Alexander Borovsky Sergei Prokofiev
John Field (1782–1837)	Muzio Clementi	Maria Szymanowska Alexander Villoing
Leopold Godowsky (1870–1938)	Camille Saint-Saëns	Clarence Adler David Guion Harold Henry Mana-Zucca Walter Rummel
Louis Gottschalk (1829–1907)	Camille Saint-Saëns	Teresa Carreno
Vladimir Horowitz (1904–1989)	Felix Blumenfeld	Byron Janis Ivan Davis
Johann Hummel (1778–1837)	Muzio Clementi Joseph Haydn W.A. Mozart	Adolph Henselt Ferdinand Hiller Sigismond Thalberg
Friedrich Kalkbrenner (1785–1849)	Muzio Clementi	Frédéric Chopin George Mathias Camille Saint-Saëns Sigismond Thalberg
Wanda Landowska (1877–1959)	Moritz Moszkowski	Alice Ehlers Ralph Kirkpatrick
Theodor Leschetizky (1830–1915)	Karl Czerny	Fanny Bloomfield Alexander Brailovsky Anna Essipoff Ignaz Friedman Ossip Gabrilovitch Mark Hambourg Ignace Paderewski Wassily Safonov Artur Schnabel Isabella Vengerova Arthur Schnabel

	pupil of:	*teacher of:*
Rosina Lhevinne (1880–1976)	Wassily Safonov	John Browning Van Cliburn Mischa Dichter
Franz Liszt (1811–1886)	Karl Czerny Antonio Salieri	Eugène d'Albert Hans von Bülow Moritz Moszkowski Moriz Rosenthal Emil Sauer Alexander Siloti Constantin von Sternberg Carl Tausig Stephan Thoman
Guy Maier (1892–1956)	Artur Schnabel	Leonard Pennario
Antoine Marmontel (1816–1896)	Pierre Zimmermann	Charles V. Alkan Isaac Albeniz Georges Bizet Claude Debussy Louis Diemer Vincent d'Indy Marguerite Long Edward MacDowell
Georges Mathias (1826–1910)	Friedrich Kalkbrenner	Isidor Philipp Stepane Pugno
Tobias Matthay (1858–1945)	George Alexander Macfarren	Clifford Curzon Myra Hess Ray Lev Irene Scharrer
Karl Mikuli (1821–1897)	Frédéric Chopin	Moriz Rosenthal
Ignaz Moscheles (1794–1870)	Muzio Clementi	Edward Dannreuther Edvard Grieg Rafael Joseffy William Mason Felix Mendelssohn
Moritz Moszkowski (1854–1925)	Theodor Kullak	Gustave Becker Josef Hofmann Wanda Landowska Joaquin Turina
Ignace Paderewski (1860–1941)	Theodor Leschetizky	Harold Bauer Ernest Schelling Sigismond Stojowski

	pupil of:	*teacher of:*
Isidor Philipp (1863–1958)	Georges Mathias Camille Saint-Saëns	Maurice Dumesnil Guiomar Novaes Beveridge Webster
Sergei Rachmaninoff (1873–1943)	Nicolai Zverev	Gina Bachauer
Moriz Rosenthal (1862–1946)	Franz Liszt Karl Mikuli	Robert Goldsand
Anton Rubinstein (1829–1884)	Alexander Villoing	Felix Blumenfeld Teresa Carreno Arthur Friedheim Ossip Gabrilovitch Josef Hofmann Alberto Jonas
Nicholas Rubinstein (1835–1881)	Alexander Villoing	Emil Sauer Alexander Siloti
Wassily Safonov (1852–1918)	Theodor Leschetizky	Wictor Labunski Joseph Lhevinne Rosina Lhevinne Nicolas Medtner Alexander Scriabin
Camille Saint-Saëns (1835–1921)	Friedrich Kalkbrenner	Louis Gottschalk Isidor Philipp Leopold Godowsky
Olga Samaroff (1882–1948)	Ernest Hutcheson Constantin Sternberg	William Kapell Eugene List Rosalyn Tureck
Artur Schnabel (1882–1951)	Theodor Leschetizky	Victor Babin Clifford Curzon Leonard Fleisher Boris Goldovsky Guy Maier
Clara Schumann (1819–1896)	Friedrich Wieck	Natalie Janotha Mathilde Verne
Alexander Siloti (1863–1945)	Franz Liszt	Serge Rachmaninoff
Sigismond Stojowski (1869–1946)	Ignace Paderewski	Oscar Levant Mischa Levitzki Arthur Loesser Guiomar Novaes
Carl Tausig (1841–1871)	Franz Liszt	Rafael Joseffy

Stephan Thomán (1862–1940)	Franz Liszt	Béla Bartók Ernö Dohnányi Fritz Reiner
Isabella Vengerova (1877–1956)	Theodor Leschetizky	Samuel Barber Leonard Bernstein Lucas Foss
Mathilde Verne (1865–1936)	Clara Schumann	Harold Samuel (Cutner) Solomon

Appendix II: The Keyboard Composers: A Selected Chronological List

DENES AGAY

Byrd, William – English (1543–1623)
Gabrieli, Giovanni – Italian (1557–1612)
Sweelinck, Jan Pieterszoon – Dutch (1562–1621)
Gibbons, Orlando – English (1583–1625)
Frescobaldi, Girolamo – Italian (1583–1643)
Chambonnières, Jacques Champion – French (1602–1672)
Froberger, Johann Jakob – German (1616–1667)
d'Anglebert, Jean Henri – French (1628–1691)
Lully, Jean-Baptiste – French (1632–1687)
Buxtehude, Dietrich – Danish-German (1637–1707)
Blow, John – English (1649–1708)
Pachelbel, Johann – German (1653–1706)
Purcell, Henry – English (1659–1695)
Kuhnau, Johann – German (1660–1732)
Fischer, Johann Kaspar Ferdinand – German (1665–1746)
Couperin, François – French (1668–1733)
Telemann, Georg Philipp – German (1681–1767)
Dandrieu, Jean François – French (1682–1738)
Rameau, Jean Philippe – French (1683–1764)
Handel, George Frideric – German (1685–1759)
Bach, Johann Sebastian – German (1685–1750)
Scarlatti, Domenico – Italian (1685–1757)
Zipoli, Domenico – Italian (1688–1726)
Muffat, Gottlieb – German (1690–1770)
Daquin, Louis-Claude – French (1694–1772)

Seixas, Carlos de – Portuguese (1704–1742)
Martini, Giovanni Battista – Italian (1706–1784)
Pergolesi, Giovanni – Italian (1710-1736)
Bach, Wilhelm Friedemann – German (1710-1784)
Bach, Carl Philipp Emanuel – German (1714–1788)
Benda, Jiri Antonin – Czech (1722–1795)
Soler, Antonio – Spanish (1729–1783)
Haydn, Franz Joseph – Austrian (1732–1809)
Bach, Johann Christian – German (1735–1782)
Hässler, Johann Wilhelm – German (1747–1822)
Cimarosa, Domenico – Italian (1749–1801)
Clementi, Muzio – Italian (1752–1832)
Mozart, Wolfgang Amadeus – Austrian (1756–1791)
Türk, Daniel Gottlob – German (1756–1813)
Dussek, Jan Ladislav – Czech (1760–1812)
Beethoven, Ludwig van – German (1770–1827)
Cramer, Johann Baptist – German (1771–1858)
Hummel, Johann Nepomuk – German (1778–1837)
Diabelli, Antonio – Italian-Austrian (1781–1858)
Field, John – Irish (1782–1837)
Weber, Carl Maria von – German (1786–1826)
Kuhlau, Friedrich – German-Scandinavian (1786–1832)
Czerny, Karl – Austrian (1791–1857)
Schubert, Franz – Austrian (1797–1828)
Glinka, Mikhail Ivanovich – Russian (1804–1857)
Burgmüller, Friedrich – German (1806–1874)
Mendelssohn, Felix – German (1809–1847)
Chopin, Frédéric – Polish (1810–1849)
Schumann, Robert – German (1810–1856)
Liszt, Franz – Hungarian (1811–1886)
Alkan, Charles-Henri – French (1813–1888)
Henselt, Adolph von – German (1814–1889)
Volkmann, Robert – German (1815–1883)
Gade, Niels Vilhelm – Danish (1817–1890)
Kullak, Theodor – German (1818–1882)
Köhler, Louis – German (1820–1886)
Gurlitt, Cornelius – German (1820–1901)
Raff, Joachim – German (1822–1882)
Franck, César – French (1822–1890)
Smetana, Bedřich – Czech (1824–1884)
Reinecke, Carl – German (1824–1910)
Gottschalk, Louis Moreau –American (1829–1869)
Brahms, Johannes – German (1833–1897)
Saint-Saëns, Camille – French (1835–1921)
Mussorgsky, Modest Petrovich – Russian (1839–1881)
Tchaikovsky, Peter Ilyich –Russian (1840–1893)
Dvořák, Antonin – Czech (1841–1904)
Grieg, Edvard – Norwegian (1843–1907)

Fauré, Gabriel – French (1845–1924)
Moszkowsky, Moritz – Polish-German (1854–1925)
Sinding, Christian – Norwegian (1856–1941)
Albéniz, Isaac – Spanish (1860–1909)
Arensky, Anton – Russian (1861–1906)
MacDowell, Edward – American (1861–1908)
Debussy, Claude – French (1862–1918)
Gretchaninoff, Alexander – Russian (1864–1956)
Nielsen, Carl – Danish (1865–1931)
Sibelius, Jean – Finnish (1865-1957)
Busoni, Ferruccio – Italian-German (1866–1924)
Rebikoff, Vladimir Ivanovich – Russian (1866–1920)
Satie, Erik – French (1866–1925)
Granados, Enrique – Spanish (1867–1916)
Novak, Vitezslav – Czech (1870–1949)
Scriabin, Alexander – Russian (1872–1915)
Reger, Max – German (1873–1916)
Rachmaninoff, Sergei – Russian (1873–1943)
Ives, Charles – American (1874–1954)
Schoenberg, Arnold – Austrian (1874–1951)
Ravel, Maurice – French (1875–1937)
Falla, Manuel de – Spanish (1876–1946)
Dohnányi, Ernö – Hungarian (1877–1960)
Palmgren, Selim – Finnish (1878–1951)
Scott, Cyril – English (1879–1970)
Bartók, Béla – Hungarian (1881–1945)
Szymanowsky, Karol – Polish (1882–1937)
Turina, Joaquin – Spanish (1882–1949)
Stravinsky, Igor – Russian (1882–1971)
Kodály, Zoltán – Hungarian (1882–1967)
Webern, Anton – Austrian (1883–1945)
Casella, Alfredo – Italian (1883–1947)
Villa-Lobos, Heitor – Brazilian (1887–1959)
Toch, Ernst – Austrian (1887–1964)
Ibert, Jacques – French (1890–1962)
Martin, Frank – Swiss (1890–1974)
Prokofiev, Sergei – Russian (1891–1953)
Milhaud, Darius – French (1892–1974)
Piston, Walter – American (1894–1976)
Hindemith, Paul – German (1895–1963)
Cowell, Henry – American (1897–1965)
Tansman, Alexandre—Polish-French (1897–1986)
Gershwin, George—American (1898–1937)
Harris, Roy—American (1898–1979)
Pouenc, Francis—French (1899–1963)
Tcherepnin, Alexander—Russian (1899–1977)
Antheil, George—American (1900–1959)
Copland, Aaron—American (1900–1990)

Křenek, Ernst—Austrian (1900–1991)
Khatchaturian, Aram—Russian (1903–1978)
Kabalevsky, Dmitri—Russian (1904–1987)
Shostakovich, Dmitri—Russian (1906–1975)
Creston, Paul—American (1906–)
Barber, Samuel—American (1910–1981)
Lutoslawski, Witold—Polish (1913–1994)
Dello Joio, Norman—American (1913–)
Ginastera, Alberto—Argentine (1916–1983)

General Bibliography

GENERAL HISTORY, STYLE, PERFORMANCE PRACTICES

Apel, Willi. *Masters of the Keyboard: A Brief Survey of Pianoforte Music*. Cambridge, Mass.: Harvard University Press, 1947.

Bie, Oscar. *A History of the Pianoforte and Pianoforte Players* (1899). New York: Da Capo Press, 1966.

Dart, Thurston. *The Interpretation of Music*. New York: Hutchinson University Library, 1954; New York: Harper and Row, 1963 (paperback).

Dorian, Frederick. *The History of Music in Performance*. New York: W.W. Norton, 1943.

Gillespie, John. *Five Centuries of Keyboard Music*. Belmont, Calif.: Wadsworth Publishing Co., Inc., 1965. New York: Dover, 1972 (paperback).

Kirby, Frank E. *A Short History of Keyboard Music*. New York: Free Press, 1966.

Lang, Paul H. *Music in Western Civilization*. New York: W.W. Norton, 1941.

Newman, William S. *The Sonata in the Baroque Era* (rev. ed.). (*History of the Sonata Idea*, vol. I). Chapel Hill: University of North Carolina Press, 1966. New York: W.W. Norton, 1972 (paperback).

——. *The Sonata in the Classic Era*. (*History of the Sonata Idea*, vol. II). Chapel Hill: University of North Carolina Press, 1963. New York: W.W. Norton, 1972 (paperback).

——. *The Sonata Since Beethoven*. (*History of the Sonata Idea*, vol. III). Chapel Hill: University of North Carolina Press, 1969. New York: W.W. Norton, 1972 (paperback).

Schoenberg, Harold C. *The Lives of the Great Composers*. New York: W.W. Norton, 1970.

Ulrich, Homer, and Paul Pisk. *A History of Music and Musical Style*. New York: Harcourt, Brace, Jovanovich, 1963.

PIANISTS

Chasins, Abram. *Speaking of Pianists*. New York: Knopf, 1962.
Loesser, Arthur. *Men, Women, and Pianos*. New York: Simon and Schuster, 1954.
Schoenberg, Harold C. *The Great Pianists*. New York: Simon and Schuster, 1963.

PIANO PEDAGOGY

Bastien, James. *How To Teach Piano Successfully*. Park Ridge, Ill.: General Words and Music Co., 1973.
Benner, Lora M. *The Blue Book: A Practical Manual of Piano Teaching*. Schenectady, N.Y.: Benner Publishers, 1969.
——. *The Gold Book: Piano Materials and Teaching Methods*. Schenectady, N.Y.: Benner Publishers, 1970.
Bolton, Hetty. *On Teaching the Piano*. London: Novello, 1954.
Ching, James. *Piano Playing: A Practical Method*. London: Bosworth, 1946.
Diller, Angela. *The Splendor of Music*. New York: G. Schirmer, 1957.
Edwards, Ruth. *The Compleat Music Teacher*. Los Altos, Calif.: Geron-X, Inc.1970.
Everhart, Powell. *The Pianist's Art: A Comprehensive Manual on Piano Playing for the Student and Teacher*. Atlanta, Ga.: Author, 1958.
Gát, József. *The Technique of Piano Playing*. London: Collet's Holdings, Ltd., 1965.
Kochevitsky, George A. *The Art of Piano Playing: A Scientific Approach*. Evanston, Ill.: Summy-Birchard Co., 1967.
Last, Joan. *The Young Pianist*. London: Oxford University Press, 1954.
Newman, William S. *The Pianist's Problems* (3rd ed.). New York: Harper & Row, 1974.
Seroff, Victor. *Common Sense in Piano Study*. New York: Funk & Wagnalls, 1970.
Slenczynska, Ruth. *Music at Your Fingertips* (rev. ed.). New York: Cornerstone Library, 1968.
Whiteside, Abbey. *Indispensibles of Piano Playing* (2nd. ed.). New York: Scribner, 1961.

MUSIC FOR THE KEYBOARD

Butler, Stanley. *Guide to the Best in Contemporary Piano Music: An Annotated List of Graded Solo Piano Music Published Since 1950*. Metuchen, N.J.: Scarecrow Press, 1973.
Chang, Frederic Ming, and Albert Faurot. *Team Piano Repertoire: Manual of Music for Multiple Players and One or More Pianos*. Metuchen, N.J.: Scarecrow Press, 1976.
Hinson, Maurice. *Guide to the Pianist's Repertoire*. Bloomington, Ind.: Indiana University Press, 1973.
Hodges, Sister Mabelle L. *Representative Teaching Materials for Piano Since 1900*. Chicago: De Paul University Press, 1970.
Hutcheson, Ernest, and Rudolph Ganz. *The Literature of the Piano*. New York: Knopf, 1964.
Kern, Alice, and Helen Titus. *The Teacher's Guidebook to Piano Literature*. Ann Arbor, Mich.: J.W. Edwards Publisher, Inc., 1964.
Lubin, Ernest. *The Piano Duet*. New York: Grossman Publishers, 1970.

HARMONY

Frackenpohl, Arthur. *Harmonization at the Piano* (3rd ed.). Dubuque, Iowa: William C. Brown, Co., 1977.

Goetschius, Percy. *The Materials Used in Musical Composition: A System of Harmony*. New York: G. Schirmer, 1913.

Harder, Paul O. *Harmonic Materials in Tonal Music* (2 vols.). Boston: Allyn and Bacon, Inc., 1968.

Lloyd, Ruth and Norman. *Creative Keyboard Musicianship: Fundamentals of Music and Keyboard Harmony Through Improvisation*. New York: Dodd, Mead, 1975.

Ottman, Robert. *Elementary Harmony* (2nd ed.). Englewood Cliffs, N.J.: Prentice-Hall, Inc. 1970.

Piston, Walter. *Harmony* (3rd ed.). New York: W.W. Norton, 1962.

FORM AND STRUCTURE

Benjamin, Thomas, Michael Horvit, and Robert Nelson. *Music for Analysis*. Boston: Houghton Mifflin, 1978.

Fontaine, Paul. *Basic Formal Structures in Music*. New York: Appleton-Century-Crofts, 1967.

Lemacher, Heinrich and Hermann Schroeder. *Musical Form*. English edition revised and translated by Robert Kolben. Cologne: Musikverlage Hans Gerig (MCA Music), 1967.

Schoenberg, Arnold. *Models for Beginners in Composition*. New York: G. Schirmer, 1943.

Stein, Leon. *Structure and Style*. Evanston, Ill.: Summy-Birchard Co., 1962.

COUNTERPOINT

Jeppesen, Knud. *Counterpoint*. Englewood Cliffs, N.J.: Prentice-Hall, Inc., 1960.

Piston, Walter. *Counterpoint: Eighteenth- and Nineteenth-Century Styles*. New York: W.W. Norton, 1947.

Salzer, Felix, and Carl Schacter. *Counterpoint in Composition: The Study of Voice Leading*. New York: McGraw-Hill, 1969.

Searle, Humphrey. *Twentieth-Century Counterpoint*. London: Ernest Benn, Ltd., 1954.

EAR TRAINING

Horacek, Leo, and Gerald Lefkoff. *Programmed Ear Training* (4 vols.). New York: Harcourt, Brace, Jovanovich, 1970.

Lawton, Annie. *Foundations of Practical Ear Training* (2 vols.). London: Oxford University Press, 1933.

Thomson, William Ennis, and Richard P. Delone. *Introduction to Ear Training*. Belmont, Calif.: Wadsworth Publishing Co., 1967.

ORCHESTRATION AND CONDUCTING

Kennan, Kent. *The Technique of Orchestration* (2nd ed.). Englewood Cliffs, N.J.: Prentice-Hall, 1970.

Piston, Walter. *Orchestration*. New York: W.W. Norton, 1955.

Rudolf, Max. *The Grammar of Conducting*. New York: G. Schirmer, 1950.

UNDERSTANDING AND ENJOYING MUSIC

Bernstein, Leonard. *The Joy of Music*. New York: Simon and Schuster, 1959.

Brofsky, Howard and Jeanne Shapiro Bamberger. *The Art of Listening: Developing*

Musical Perception. New York: Harper & Row, 1969.
Copland, Aaron. *What to Listen for in Music* (rev. ed.). New York: McGraw-Hill, 1957.
Einstein, Alfred. *Greatness in Music.* New York: Oxford University Press, 1941.
Hoffer, Charles R. *The Understanding of Music.* Belmont, Calif.: Wadsworth Publishing Company, Inc., 1967.
Machlis, Joseph. *The Enjoyment of Music* (3rd ed.). New York: W.W. Norton, 1970.
Newman, William S. *Understanding Music* (2nd ed.). New York: Harper & Row, 1961.
Wink, Richard and Lois G. Williams. *Invitation to Listening: An Introduction to Music.* Boston: Houghton Mifflin, 1972.

AMERICAN MUSIC

Agay, Denes. *Best Loved Songs of the American People.* Garden City, N.Y.: Doubleday, 1975.
Chase, Gilbert. *America's Music* (rev. 2nd ed.). New York: McGraw-Hill, 1966.
Hitchcock, H. Wiley. *Music in the United States: A Historical Introduction.* Englewood Cliffs, N.J.: Prentice-Hall, 1969.
Lomax, John A., and Alan Lomax. *Folk Song U.S.A.* New York: Duell, Sloan and Pearce, 1947.
Machlis, Joseph. *American Composers of Our Time.* New York: Thomas Y. Crowell, 1963.
Southern, Eileen. *The Music of Black Americans.* New York: W.W. Norton, 1971.

MUSIC DICTIONARIES AND ENCYCLOPEDIAS

Apel, Willi, and Ralph T. Daniel. *The Harvard Brief Dictionary of Music.* Cambridge, Mass.: Harvard University Press, 1960.
Baker's Biographical Dictionary of Musicians (5th ed., revised by Nicolas Slonimsky). New York: G. Schirmer, 1958. 1965 Supplement by Nicolas Slonimsky.
Barlow, Harold, and Sam Morgenstern. *A Dictionary of Musical Themes.* New York: Crown, 1948.
Grove's Dictionary of Music and Musicians, 10 vols. (5th ed., edited by Eric Blom). New York: St. Martin's Press, 1960.
Thompson, Oscar, ed. *The International Cyclopedia of Music and Musicians* (9th ed., edited by Robert Sabin). New York: Dodd, Mead, 1964.
Westrup, J.A., and F.L. Harrison. *The New College Encyclopedia of Music.* New York: W.W. Norton, 1960.

MAGAZINES AND PERIODICALS

Clavier: A Magazine for Pianists and Organists. 1418 Lake Street, Evanston, Illinois 60204.
Keyboard Arts. National Keyboard Arts Associates, 741 Alexander Road, Princeton, New Jersey 08540.
Piano Guild Notes. Official Publication of the National Guild of Piano Teachers. P.O. Box 1807, Austin, Texas 78767.
The American Music Teacher. Official Journal of the Music Teachers National Association. 408 Carew Tower, Cincinnati, Ohio 45202.
The Piano Quarterly. Box 815, Wilmington, Vermont 05363.
The Robert Dumm Piano Review. 144 Fleetwood Terrace, Silver Springs, Maryland 20910.

Contributors' Bylines

Joseph Banowetz, pianist, pedagogue, and writer, has been performing extensively in the United States, Europe, the Soviet Union, Mexico, and Canada. An authority on the music of Liszt, he has edited and recorded numerous works of the romantic master. A professor of piano at North Texas State University, his articles appear regularly in leading periodicals.

May L. Etts, teacher and lecturer on pedagogy, was a pupil and assistant of Guy Maier. She is president of the Brooklyn Music Teachers Guild; past president of the Piano Teachers Congress of New York and the Associated Music Teachers League; an examiner adjudicator of numerous teachers' organizations; editor of highly regarded teaching publications.

Rosetta Goodkind is presently on the faculty of the Manhattan School of Music and New York University. She was on the faculty of the precollege division at the Juilliard School from 1941 to 1969. A recipient of the Mason and Hamlin Teacher Award (1969), she is a frequent jury panelist and adjudicator at piano competitions and auditions. Presently co-chairman of the New York State Music Teachers Association, District I.

Stuart Isacoff, teacher, editor, and arranger, holds an M.A. in composition from Brooklyn College, where he received a Rockefeller Foundation Grant for research in American music. He is the author-editor of numerous piano textbooks and collections. Currently he is on the jazz faculty of William Paterson State College in Wayne, New Jersey.

Ylda Novik, a highly successful and inspired teacher, died at the height of her career in early 1976. She was contributing critic of the *Washington Star*, piano editor of *The American Music Teacher* (1968–1972), author of many magazine articles, and a faculty member of George Washington University and Montgomery College in Maryland.

Sylvia Rabinof, a pupil of Simon Barere and Rudolf Serkin, has concertized extensively all over the world, frequently with her violinist husband, the late Benno Rabinof. She is on the faculty of the Juilliard School and Brevard Music Center in North Carolina. She is the author of the textbook *Musicianship Through Improvisation*.

Walter Robert, pedagogue and author, was born in Italy and studied in Vienna, where he received the Bösendorfer prize as the best graduate of the State Academy of Music (1931). An acclaimed teacher, clinician, and adjudicator, he recently retired as professor of piano at the Indiana University School of Music. He is on the board of advisors of *Clavier* magazine.

Hadassah Sahr is currently on the teaching staff of Teachers College (Columbia University) and the Manhattan School of Music Summer School. She has presented lectures, recitals, and master classes in many sections of the country and is a contributor to *The Piano Quarterly*.

Hazel Ghazarian Skaggs, group piano specialist, composer, psychologist, and author, is a graduate of the New England Conservatory of Music. She holds a B.A. and M.A. in psychology from Fairleigh Dickinson University. She is national chairperson and judge for the National Composition Test (NGPT), president of The Piano Teachers Congress of New York, member of the editorial board of *Leisure Today*, and director of Music Counseling Services.

Anita Louise Steele is currently head of the music therapy program at The Cleveland Music School Settlement. She is on the executive committee of the National Association for Music Therapy and an associate editor of the *Journal of Music Therapy*. She is the author of numerous articles on behavioral research and on teaching the handicapped.

Judith Lang Zaimont, a recipient of twenty-six awards for her compositions, studied at Columbia University, Queens College, and Juilliard. She is a Woodrow Wilson fellow, a MacDowell Colony fellow, and a Debussy fellow of the Alliance Française. Active as composer and performer, she has taught at Adelphi University, Queens College, and New York City Community College.

Index